The Way of Tea

by RAND CASTILE

with a foreword by
Sen no Soshitsu

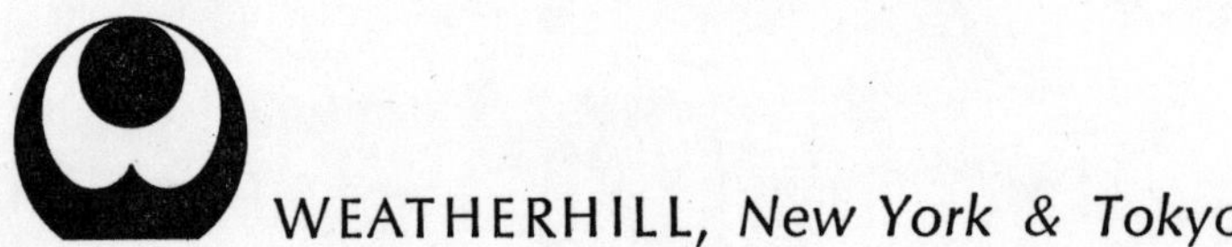

WEATHERHILL, *New York & Tokyo*

THE

WAY OF  TEA

First edition, 1971

Published by John Weatherhill, Inc.
149 Madison Avenue, New York, N.Y. 10016
with editorial offices at
7-6-13 Roppongi, Minato-ku, Tokyo, Japan

Printed in Japan

LCC Card No. 70-157271
ISBN 0-8348-0059-4

Table of Contents

PART TWO

THE TEA SETTING

PART THREE

TEA UTENSILS

PART FOUR

THE PRACTICE OF TEA

List of Illustrations

Foreword

It is good news indeed that Rand Castile's book on the Japanese tea ceremony, on which he has been working so long, is now ready for publication. Mr. Castile is one of the few Westerners who really understand *chado,* "the way of tea," and its vital relationship to Japanese history, art, aesthetics, philosophy, and life. He studied Japanese culture through the tea ceremony in Kyoto for over a year, applying himself earnestly and brilliantly to his studies with Urasenke, the school of tea I have the honor to head. And for a number of years he has been an active member of our New York chapter. Realizing how scant, or even mistaken, is the West's knowledge of tea ceremony and its important place in Japanese life, he has dedicated much time and effort to the preparation of this book. Thus much correct and new information on the subject is at last readily available to Western readers.

In Japan, Urasenke has been preserving and developing the chado tradition for almost four hundred years, and for the past twenty I myself have been trying to explain to the West the important role tea has played and is still playing here. At the same time I have been trying to suggest the possibility that tea can also have a real meaning in Western life, that it can add a new dimension to the joy of living. If Zen is important, then tea is. If Japanese art is important, tea has played a big part in its development and appreciation. If the cultivation of peace and quiet in this turbulent world is more necessary than ever, tea offers a proven way to this end. This I believe, and I am delighted to have such an eloquent ally, for this is what Mr. Castile is telling us in this excellent book.

I am happy that the West is becoming increasingly aware of the deep meaning of chado, and happy too that this book is now available to feed that awareness.

It is not enough, however, simply to understand Mr. Castile's and my common purpose. It will only be when tea has proven itself widely throughout the world as a comradely way to contemplation and peace of mind, to quiet pleasure and goodwill and understanding and beauty, that our labors will be justified.

SEN NO SOSHITSU

Kyoto, Fall, 1971

Author's Preface

Tea ceremony, like Indian ragas and jazz, is ninety percent improvisation and ten percent technique when conducted by a master. In the case of the novice, however, the percentages are likely to be reversed. As this book is intended for the student of tea—and for the general reader who wishes to learn about one of the fundamental shaping forces of Japanese culture—it is concerned primarily with the ten percent of tea that is technique, as revealed in the history and practices of the art.

Though volumes too numerous to mention have appeared in the Japanese language, no major work on the subject of tea ceremony has been written in English in thirty-five years. A. L. Sadler's *Cha-no-yu* is an important work containing a generous sampling of anecdotes about tea masters. More popular, and older, is Kakuzo Okakura's *The Book of Tea,* which is brief, but well treats the philosophical underpinnings of tea. Neither of these deals comprehensively with the subject. Though no single volume could ever cover in depth the enormously varied subjects which are the concerns of tea, it is the purpose of this book to outline the world of tea ceremony in as brief a form as practicable.

Within the scope of a one-volume treatment there is little room for exposition of the details which constitute the differences between various schools of tea. No esoteric study in the hands of a few Japanese, tea is an enormously popular art form in today's Japan, with a long history of important contributions to the people and culture of the nation. There are a number of active schools of tea, with branches scattered throughout Japan and with representation abroad. It should be made clear that, unless otherwise noted, all specific practices herein elucidated are based on my studies of tea ceremony at the Kyoto headquarters of the Urasenke school of tea. However, the matters of interpreting the contributions of tea masters, preferred styles of architecture and utensils, and the evaluation of historical records and data have been considered in light of the works of recognized Japanese scholars, through personal interviews, conversations, and my own observations. The bibliography, though a partial listing, attests to the representation of diverse points of view on the history of tea ceremony.

At this writing I have spent some three years in the active study and practice of tea. The Urasenke school was chosen for personal instruction for these reasons: it represents a tradition directly inherited from the great tea master Rikyu; it is by far the largest; it is the school of tea most active abroad, having branches in New York, London, Rome, São Paulo, and elsewhere; it has the most extensive facilities for detailed study of tea ceremony; and the size of its teaching staff and membership allows for great variety in instruction and exposure to different ceremonies.

In the course of studying tea I had the privilege of being accepted as a *kenshusei* at the Urasenke headquarters. Kenshusei are in-depth students of tea ceremony who reside at the school headquarters and are exposed to every facet of this ancient and complicated art. The students meet six days a week in the course of a regular "academic" year, for three years. I remained as a kenshusei for one year, joining their number as a regular class member. My classmates have since been graduated from the course and are now tea professionals. During my year as a kenshusei I was able to participate in several hundred tea ceremonies at the headquarters, some as host, some as guest. In addition I traveled with the classes to dozens of tea ceremonies at temples, shrines, public institutions, and private homes. No other experience in my study has been as valuable to this work. My instructors gave unstintingly of their free hours to review material and techniques with me. My classmates did more than anyone could expect to encourage my study, often meeting with me outside classes to clarify details of the ceremonies I happened to be practicing.

Most of the important tea huts of Japan are found in the Kyoto vicinity. I was able to visit almost all of these, many several times.

I met, talked, and had tea with Japanese tea men, professional and lay, from all walks of life. Priests, scholars, craftsmen, and artists were especially kind in giving of their time to answer my questions. The number of these helpful people is too large to allow personal thanks here, but I would like to acknowledge my debt and offer special thanks to the following persons: Soshitsu Sen, fifteenth-generation grand master of Urasenke, who placed the very considerable resources of his institution at my disposal, and who opened the doors of so many tea huts and treasuries for my use or examination; members of the Urasenke staff, Messrs. Kobayashi, Hayasaki, and Yamada, and Misses Akanuma and Miyahara; Yuichiro Kojiro, distinguished critic and professor; Yasuo Inoue, formerly of Kokusai Bunka Shinko-kai, and the members and directors of that staff; Messrs. Sugihara and Matsushita of the National Commission for the Protection of Cultural Properties; President Naya of Tankosha Publishing Company; Messrs. Douglas W. Overton and James L. Stewart, past executive directors of the Japan Society, Inc., of New York.

More difficult to thank is Hiroaki Sato, whose extraordinary ability in both the Japanese and English languages, whose patience and sensitivity through months of work, and whose dedication in assisting this writing has added immeasurably to what worth this book has.

To my wife Sondra, who endured so very much that this might be accomplished and who shares in every aspect of my own interests in Japan, I can only add this note of public gratitude, for without her help and encouragement this would not have been begun, could not have been finished.

I am grateful to the staff of John Weatherhill, Inc., publishers of this work, but I would especially like to thank Mr. Meredith Weatherby, whose interest and advice during all stages of my research and writing was most encouraging, and Miss Audie Bock, whose patient editing of the final manuscript was of tremendous assistance to me.

I have tried to unburden the reader of this text by omitting numerous and extensive footnotes that one might commonly find in a work of this kind. I would, however, like to thank Lindley Williams Hubbell for permission to quote his poem on page 21, and I would like to acknowledge translations from the Japanese that are not original with this text. They are: the quotation from the priest Myoe, which appears on page 22, from *Urasenke,* Kyoto, 1932; the quotation from the priest Eisai, which appears on page 23, and the quotation from the priest Dogen, which appears on page 30, from *Sources of Japanese Tradition,* edited by William Theodore de Bary, 1958; and the quotation from Karasu Mitsuhiro, which appears on page 73, from *Cha-no-yu,* by A. L. Sadler, Rutland, 1962, first published in 1933.

For errors, misjudgments, omissions, and failures, the fault is entirely mine. It is my hope that this work may contribute to the understanding of the art of tea ceremony, and in this small way serve to enhance the level of understanding between Japan and the West.

Note on Japanese Names

There are more than ten names a Japanese gentleman might use in the course of a lifetime. These include: family name, given name, baby name, coming-of-age name, artistic name, Buddhist name, pseudonym, posthumous name, and—in many cases—adopted family name. To this we should add historical titles and position names. In this field tea masters have been especially acquisitive.

The tea master we know as Rikyu was variously known in his age as Sen Yashiro, Sen no Soeki, Sen no Rikyu, and Hosensai. None of Rikyu's names derived from his father, known as Tanaka Yohei or Naya. Rikyu's grandfather used the name Senami at the court of Ashikaga Yoshimasa, and Rikyu took part of this name as his own.

The important Momoyama-period leader Hideyoshi had his name changed as his fortunes advanced. Depending upon the age of the text, Hideyoshi, who lived from 1536 to 1598, is listed as Kinoshita Tokichi, Hashiba Chikushu, or Toyotomi Hideyoshi. He is sometimes referred to by title, Kampaku or Taiko, and by various poetic names as well.

Prominent Japanese families continue the practice of using various names today. A family that has no son commonly adopts a young man who takes the name of his new family. The three sons of the fifteenth generation of the Sen family, which heads the Urasenke school of tea, each had a different family name: Sen, Naya, and Otani. The present grand master of the school was known as Soko Sen until 1965, when he inherited his father's title. Since then he has been known as Soshitsu Sen, which was his father's name. His father has now been given the posthumous name Tantansai.

In the interest of easy reading, this text regularly uses only the most commonly known name for an individual. Diacritical marks, too, have been dispensed with, as have ideographs. Where disputes occur in the pronunciation of certain Japanese names, that most popularly used by tea masters is given in this text. For the names of Japanese who lived before the Meiji Restoration of 1868, family name precedes given name; post-Meiji proper names are given in Western style. Japanese pronunciation of Chinese names is not used here, except in those cases such as "Temmoku" and "Zen," where Japanese readings are popularly known abroad.

Introduction

1. *Chado,* the Way of Tea

THE POET SAYS that a bird does not intend to cast its reflection, that a lake does not intend to receive it. This is the natural state of things, that they give and receive without intention. Tea has no mind, no intention, yet across its bright green surface virtually the whole of Japan can be seen. Tea is such a particular beverage in Japan that the drinking of it came to be a way of life. This is *chado,* the Way of Tea. Embodied in the Way is a complete art form, *cha-no-yu,* commonly translated as "tea ceremony."

Foremost practitioners of the art earnestly caution the beginner that tea requires a lifetime of devotion. They mean that the Way of Tea is more than achieving a respectable level of performance of tea ceremony, which most of us could attain after a few years' study. We are told by tea masters that the spirit of tea should be in evidence everywhere in our lives, not only in the tearoom.

In the process of studying tea there is much that can be understood with the mind, but tea is not a scientific pursuit. It is not a measurable experience. Writing about tea is dealing with the subject by description alone and cannot compare with direct experience. To study tea in earnest one must drink it. In short, he must go to the thing itself; he must practice tea ceremony.

The requirements of tea ceremony are formidable. One is called upon to exercise uncommon degrees of patience, physical skill, and sincerity. One is expected to engage in prolonged and often difficult contemplation and in an unusual amount of hard scholarship. Millions of people participate in tea, few attain mastery of the Way.

Basically, drinking tea is an ordinary experience, but in tea ceremony the experience is so concentrated that one finds himself encouraged to look within, to discover not a new self but the natural self so often covered up by successive layers of civilization. Unlike the archeologists who dig to uncover, however, the tea man uncovers by opening himself like a flower. As observers of flowers know, this kind of process involves a great deal of waiting. The tea man follows the natural course of things, alternating periods of thought and action. He studies and he serves tea. Over a period of time this alternation frees his mind and body. This is the Way of Tea.

Rikyu (1521–91) is regarded as the most outstanding tea master in Japanese history. Born when Michelangelo was in his mid-forties, and just after the death of Leonardo da Vinci, Rikyu—like them—enormously influenced his countrymen in all matters of art. Rikyu, too, had disciples from the highest councils of state. Most notable among them was Toyotomi Hideyoshi, unifier of all Japan.

The two met often. Once when Hideyoshi asked to inspect the tea master's extensive morning-glory garden, Rikyu begged off, suggesting a later date. This was arranged. When the time came for the viewing, Hideyoshi discovered that all the morning-glories had been removed from the garden. Imperiously Hideyoshi went to find Rikyu in the tea hut, where he knew the tea master would be waiting. He slid back the small door of the hut. Entering the room, he saw that Rikyu had placed a single morning-glory in the alcove. It was the essence of morning-glories.

Hideyoshi had sought the beautiful in the magnificent. Rikyu had offered beauty in a most severe form, a single blossom. For all its severity, this was not abbreviation but concentration. A flower can suggest enlightenment, or evanescence of life, or expanding universe. The qualities epitomized by a flower are not only in the mind and eye, they are inherent within the flower itself. We do not separate eye from flower. These things meet in moments, they are all part of the same ongoing universe of time and things. Tea is rooted is this kind of thought: awareness infinitely expands moments, our momentary encounters. With all the resources of his life, the tea man cultivates awareness.

Like a flower, a cup of tea is a short-lived thing. It is a wonder that anything so ephemeral, so ordinary, should have come to be the concern of such a large number of sophisticated Japanese. The British drink tea, and while they do make much of silver tea service, it would be ridiculous to say that their tea drinking constitutes the living embodiment of traditional British arts. In the case of Japan, however, we can agree with the late Langdon Warner, who wrote in *The Enduring Art of Japan*: "What can be said about the force exerted by tea ceremony on so many facets of Japanese culture since the fifteenth century is far short of the truth."

In the West there is no force, with the possible exception of Christianity, that is so persuasive, so pervasive, in our artistic life as is tea ceremony in Japan. It was not a passing fad that enjoyed brief popularity; it remained a force through many centuries and still survives today in notably healthy form.

Comparing British tea with Japan's we find three major points of difference. First, the teas are different. British tea is blackish and leafy when ready to be served. Japanese cha-no-yu tea is a pistachio-green powder. This tea is grassy-tasting and slightly bitter. The aroma is distinct and unfortified. For the most part, this kind of tea is used only in tea ceremony.

A second difference is the environments in which the teas are drunk. The British tea environment is the flat of an M.P., the parlor of a row house, the offices of a bureaucrat. In any of these we find a certain cluttering of goods, reflecting the lives of the occupants. The cha-no-yu environment, too, reflects the lives of tea men. The setting includes a tea hut, garden, and utensils. Moreover, the conversation, manners, and dress of the tea men are considered part of cha-no-yu. The Japanese setting is all-inclusive, but every detail is important and receives consideration. All of the accouterments are considered by tea men to be manifestations of a host's tea spirit.

> Americans can see a Mondrian
> But Japanese can live in one.
> That is why they do not care at all
> To put one on their wall.

This poem, by Lindley Williams Hubbell, neatly states the contrast between our own environment and that of the Japanese. Everyday life in Japan prepares one for tea. The setting is spare but carefully considered.

The tea hut and the Japanese-style house are of the same scale. They are made of common materials, with common techniques. Japanese who have lived in traditionally styled houses move easily from the one to the other. When we enter a tea hut and sit upon the mats our doubled legs make us quickly aware that the setting is not what we are accustomed to.

The third difference between Japanese and British teas is in the manner of their service. The British do take their tea seriously, but as a rule they do not engage their guests in conversation on the history of their tea etiquette, nor on the many other aspects of tea that form a major part of cha-no-yu meetings. For the Britisher, tea drinking is a pleasant habit in an orderly life. Tea for him is neither informal nor formal, neither challenge nor trivia. He expects to drink tea every day but does not expect of the occasion that it be profound.

The manner of serving cha-no-yu is another matter, and it is of great significance. Cha-no-yu had its formal beginnings in the Buddhist temples of the Zen sect and, like everything associated with religious institutions, came to be systematized. The simplicity of the ritual reflects the monastic life of priests. In the temples there are rules governing nearly every movement of the initiate's life, just as the host's movements are governed in tea. But the rules are not arbitrary, they prescribe a manner of service that is the quintessence of efficiency. Each movement has been considered over the centuries by some of Japan's finest minds. Nothing is wasted, there is no exaggerated motion. Things are done in cha-no-yu with a directness that would impress a time and motion expert.

As tea ceremony is highly structured, some critics have doubted that it could be a creative act. The orchestra conductor, the dancer, the author of a sonnet are not lacking in creativity because they operate in artistic media that are carefully structured, nor is the artist in tea. The unimaginative mind is not made free by the absence of rules, any more than the imaginative one is enslaved by them. The conductor without a score in mind, if not in front of him, cannot conduct. The dancer without choreography cannot dance.

We have a tendency to judge anything that is highly formal as pompous, insincere, or affected. The formality of the Zen monastery is none of these. The monk's life, his walking, eating, drinking, and sleeping—even his sweeping—are performed according to strict standards. His every moment is to be a manifestation of Buddha-spirit. His everyday actions are to be ways to enlightenment. Tea masters have taught that every action is a potential action of enlightenment.

From these teachings we realize that no distinction should be made between the rules of the art and the art itself; they are one and the same Way. Chado is no cult, there is no inner truth outwardly manifested; the form is not inferior to the content, it *is* the content.

Before tea was a practice of Zen it was influenced in China by both Taoism and Confucianism. We can read something of both in the inscription left by the twelfth-century Japanese priest Myoe on his favorite kettle. He outlined the ten virtues of tea in these words:

> [Tea] has the blessings of all the deities,
> promotes filial piety,
> drives away the devil,
> banishes drowsiness,
> keeps the five viscera in harmony,
> wards off disease,
> strengthens friendships,
> disciplines body and mind,
> destroys the passions,
> gives peaceful death.

The priest Eisai, a friend of Myoe's, had been in China and there learned of tea drinking. He shared an enthusiasm for it that matched his friend's. He wrote what is the earliest Japanese treatise on tea, the

Kissa Yojoki, which reads like advertisement copy for Lipton's. He considered tea in terms of medicinal value and sought its wide propagation. He is generally credited with having established tea on a national basis in Japan. He used tea in presenting the then-new ideas of the Rinzai branch of Zen. A few of his statements: "Tea is the most wonderful medicine for nourishing one's health; it is the secret of long life. . . . The basis of preserving life is the cultivation of health, and the secret of health lies in the well-being of the five organs. Among these five the heart is sovereign, and to build up the heart the drinking of tea is the finest method. . . . Our country is full of sickly-looking, skinny persons and this is simply because we do not drink tea. Whenever one is in poor spirits, one should drink tea. Drink lots of tea, and one's energy and spirits will be restored to full strength."

There is very little that could be added to the statement of either priest.

Attention has been paid to the possible relationship of tea to Christianity. Some writers have gone so far as to suggest that tea was in fact a secret expression of Christian belief after Christianity was forced underground in the 1630's. They have pointed out that there is a remarkable similarity in the priest's handling of the Eucharist and in a tea man's celebration of tea. However, the records of tea nowhere indicate that tea was an outgrowth of Japanese Christianity or that it was altered or affected by Christianity. However, some tea masters have been Christians.

Cha-no-yu was an established practice well before St. Francis Xavier came to Japan in 1549. The foremost master of tea, Rikyu, had been practicing tea for more than ten years by that time, and his teachers were nationally known and celebrated for their art. These men were not Christian, nor were they influenced by its ritual, belief, or art.

The speculation about tea and Christianity probably comes from the fact that a number of men in tea did become Christian converts. We further note, however, that cha-no-yu continued to flourish during and after the persecutions of Christians by Hideyoshi and his successors. That a few utensils for tea can be found that have a cross or other Western designs inscribed on their surface means no more than the craftsmen's interest in the exotic. Zen priests presided at the birth of cha-no-yu, and in their hands it developed as an art. When tea ceremony became independent of Zen institutions it did not embrace another religion but grew in its own sufficiency.

Zen made important contributions to tea. The strong feeling of harmony and the simplicity of the occasion are importantly affected by Zen. There is unity in the selection of utensils and the manner of their handling. This does not mean that there are utensil sets, per se. Each item is individually crafted.

The usual matching of color and design, so common in Western service ware, is not applicable to tea service in cha-no-yu. A perfectly harmonious grouping of utensils mixes many glazes, materials, forms, and ages. This harmony derives in part from tea men whose guide is Zen. The Zen aesthetic has taught the tea man always to be simple in his service, to avoid the complex and the excessive wherever possible. It has encouraged him to go beyond reason in his selection of utensils, to intuit the most satisfying combination of materials. And in the final analysis, the unity of a host's utensils is his own; it is the man who orders the disparate elements.

Tea masters long ago concluded that there is a profound agreement among the unlike. The flower lends its light to the painted screen, the screen to the flower. So it is with host and guest: each illuminates the other. This is natural harmony, the very issue of simultaneous existence. The tea men of Japan continue to juxtapose elements objectively dissimilar. The results have often been meaningful, leading to heights of awareness. The spontaneity of tea is nowhere as evident as in these instances. It has come through the boldness of masters such as Rikyu bringing together diverse and seemingly opposing forms.

What is frequently required of a tea man is that he not only bring his imagination to bear in selecting new and different materials to use but that he strike out and use things never tried before. Rikyu again comes to mind. He was once faced with unexpected guests for tea and discovered that he had no container for a flower. He went to a nearby grove of bamboo and cut a section to serve his purpose. It was the first occasion that bamboo had been used for cha-no-yu flower arrangement, and to this day it remains the perfect utensil. Rikyu made this and many other contributions by applying a keen intelligence and a boldly experimental attitude to his tea.

Rikyu used four concepts to express his way of tea: *wa, kei, sei,* and *jaku*. Wa is the complete harmony of all elements; its definition includes sincerity. Kei gives a sense of profound reverence toward all things, and is used by tea men to identify characteristics of humility and respect. Sei contains the thought of orderliness in life, cleanliness, and purity. Jaku means tranquillity, calm. These four are essential to tea. Perhaps in the whole history of tea Rikyu alone achieved the harmony, reverence, orderliness, and tranquillity of perfect naturalness. We cannot know, but his praises have been sung by Japanese and foreigners since the time of Shakespeare.

Townsend Harris, who arrived in Japan in 1856, witnessed a tea presented for his benefit, and described the event as interesting, the taste of the tea as pleasant. He called the tea gruel, and commented that the Japanese considered it a delicacy and had formed a cult for imbibing it.

At later times, Westerners participated more

fully. Edward S. Morse, who arrived in 1877, reports he actually studied tea ceremony under a master, and that he came to be proficient at it. John LaFarge and Henry Adams visited Japan at the time Morse and Ernest Fenollosa, who had come as a professor of philosophy, were there. They, too, came in contact with tea utensils and doubtless drank the green liquid. Van Wyck Brooks's *Fenollosa and His Circle* relates a number of amusing accounts about the two Americans. Sturgis Bigelow was a third member of the party. Morse, Fenollosa, and Bigelow became famous for their work in the field of Japanese art. Adams and LaFarge apparently suffered under the pressures of their forced education in things Japanese, and Adams describes Fenollosa as "a kind of St. Dominic and holds himself responsible for the dissemination of useless knowledge by others. . . . He has joined a Buddhist sect. I was myself a Buddhist when I left America, but he has converted me to Calvinism with leanings towards the Methodists."

Others were more receptive to the work of Fenollosa, including the poets W. B. Yeats and Ezra Pound. Fenollosa's studies on No drama led both men to do research and writing in the field, though Pound has never acknowledged the influence of Fenollosa in his writing. Ulysses S. Grant had conversations with Fenollosa while visiting Japan in 1879. He was shown No drama and was apparently much taken with it—he is said to have encouraged the preservation of the No by his comments to a group of distinguished Japanese, who then took it upon themselves to organize patrons for the theatre.

Sturgis Bigelow was an important financial backer to some of the early scholars of Japanese art, and he himself collected Japanese art enthusiastically. Brooks reports through conversations with the Frederick Winslows that Bigelow admired Buddhism. He was especially fond of chanting done in temples of the Tendai sect. Bigelow felt that Protestant churches in the West had erred in establishing informal prayers. He said that the Buddhist chants came to be fixed in the mind, allowing understanding to come naturally, from within. This is also used as an argument for strict rules in tea.

Lafcadio Hearn, who did much to popularize Japanese folklore, did not arrive in Japan until 1890. He and Fenollosa got on well. They shared a sense of disgust with Japan's wholesale Westernization. Hearn, Fenollosa, and Bernard Berenson were among the first to defend Japanese art against the criticisms leveled by the "anti-Japanese art" critics William Morris and Norton. Fenollosa also influenced Mrs. Jack Gardner, as did his friend Kakuzo Okakura, whose *The Book of Tea* was first read in Mrs. Gardner's Boston house as a series of lectures. Morse went on to become the first great American collector of Japanese pottery, of which his knowledge was first-rate. The works he assembled form the basis of the collection of Japanese pottery at the Boston Museum of Fine Arts.

The architect Frank Lloyd Wright spent considerable time in Japan, in the course of which he attended numerous tea ceremonies. He writes that he enjoyed it from the start, but eventually grew tired of the sheer exquisiteness of the occasions and stopped going. His analysis of some parts of tea ceremony is perceptive and interesting.

After World War II the occupation led thousands of Americans to Japan. Some of these found their way to tea, either as audience for a demonstration, or as someone's guest. The tourists who followed added still another measure of our exposure to tea.

On attending a tea ceremony in Japan, the first encounter with the setting is a garden gate, its structure being indicative of what is to follow. It is unpainted, weathering, but attractive. It stands slightly ajar, a sign that the host is expecting you. The other guests will probably arrive about the same time and be known to one another. There is no rule that says the guests must be acquainted but it is sure that all are friends of the host. As a rule a host does not invite people he does not know to a tea ceremony. He wants to share something with his friends, in an intimate and quiet setting.

When you have passed through the outer gate you enter a small garden. It is a garden without spectacular views and effects. Indeed, tea gardens are the smallest, most simple in Japan. The gardens are designed as paths from the gate to the tea hut, but along their ways you do not find waterfalls, large stones, twisted pines, or any of the other scenic devices tourists are told to look for. They do not even include flowering shrubs, aromatic plantings, or streams. The function of the garden is to lead guests to the tea hut, and along the way to allow them a moment or two to prepare for the tea. The best garden for tea has only a few local trees, common grasses, and moss laid out in no apparent pattern along the path of stepping-stones. Though it is the product of years of sensitive work by the host and his gardener, it seems to us to be nothing unusual. This in fact is the most striking quality of the tea garden, and the very quality that tea men strive for. In such a garden the guests relax and free their minds from the world's hubbub.

After a short wait the guests move along the stepping-stones toward the tea hut. The design has nothing about it that we might call striking. It is a plain hut with cream-colored walls and weathered uprights. The roof may be thatched, shingled, or tiled; none of these is unusual in Japan. The tiny edifice is barely large enough to hold the host and his guests.

There is a look of temporariness to the hut; it is evidently not a bunker that can seal its occupants from the world. Inside, the same feelings are maintained. The room is about ten feet square. The first guest enters alone and moves to the art alcove where he inspects the scroll hung in honor of the occasion. This scroll is most often a piece of calligraphy composed by a tea master or priest. What it says helps establish the mood of the tea planned by the host that day. Nearby is a single flower in a container. These two objects are the only decorations in the room.

When all the guests have entered, they take their places on straw mats. The mats are clean and crisp against the rough mud texture of the walls. Conversation stops for a moment and the guests take time to consider the room itself. There are several windows, covered with papered frames or bamboo shades; the light is subdued. The bamboo ceiling, scarcely six feet above the mats, is in shadow. Like the garden around the hut, the tearoom reveals itself only slowly. It is conducive to contemplation, and has already begun to do its work when the kettle begins to emit the sound of boiling water.

Before a guest takes his place he will have looked at the kettle, which has been set over a small charcoal fire. The kettle used in tea ceremony is beautifully crafted, the overall form and designs on the sides being subtle reflections of the season. The fire has been laid in a bed of white ashes raked in an attractive and efficiently burning manner.

The host enters from a smaller preparation room and bows to the guests. He brings the utensils into the tearoom and places them by the kettle. If this is a simple tea ceremony he will have a water jar, tea bowl, whisk, tea scoop, caddy, ladle, waste-water jar, and lid rest. None of these objects need be expensive, though Japanese have been known to invest fortunes in them. Placed in a Western show window they would attract little attention, but not so in Japan. A seventeenth-century priest from Spain commented in his diary that tea utensils were considered the crown jewels of Japan. Certainly this was true. Even today, utensils used by famous tea masters or adjudged by them to be especially good are treated with great admiration. Expensive utensils, however, are not the key to serving good tea. Even if the utensils are incomparable and the technique perfect, overlooking the basic concern of serving the guests will make the tea ceremony empty, pompous, and meaningless.

Though the host has cleaned the utensils before bringing them into the tearoom, his first act before the guests is to clean the bowl, whisk, caddy, and scoop. The caddy and scoop are cleaned with a silk napkin taken from the *obi,* the long kimono sash. He pours water into the tea bowl and examines the bamboo whisk to see that no tine is chipped or broken. He then rinses the bowl and wipes it with a small linen cloth.

The cleaning process is a demonstration of concern for the guests and respect for the utensils. It shows the host's willingness to serve. Cleaning and handling the utensils at this time in the ceremony also helps the host to steady himself, to establish a rhythm for his hands.

A small amount of powdered tea is placed in the bowl, already warmed by the water used in cleaning. The whisk is used to whip the tea to a brilliant, light froth. As the bowl is placed in front of the first guest the aroma of the tea fills the room. In thin-tea service, each guest empties the contents of a bowl individually. The tea is savored, sipped taste by taste. The host goes on making tea for each guest in turn. His movement is clean and graceful, with no interference between his thoughts and actions. There is no faltering or hesitation; whatever happens the host sustains the motion until the tea is concluded.

When the last guest has drunk his tea the utensils are prepared so that they can be examined by the guests. The host takes some of the utensils into the preparation room while the guests examine the tea scoop and caddy. He returns to discuss these with the guests. Who carved the scoop? What style is it? Where does the lacquer caddy come from? After these things are talked over, the host removes the utensils to the preparation-room door, where he turns and bows. The guests examine the scroll and flower once more before leaving through the garden.

Nothing dramatic has happened. The lives of the guests have probably not been significantly altered. They have neither witnessed miracles nor performed them. But something has happened to the senses and the mind of each participant. For a few minutes he has allowed his senses full reign, been part of an experience that unified sight, sound, smell, taste, and touch.

The simple properties of tea are worth considering in this respect. It has heat to warm the hands on a cold day, a distinctive taste that satisfies thirst, an aroma that pleases, an appearance that delights. These are small things, gentle but wonderful things. They are enjoyed as much by host as by guests. Everyone in the tea works together as both creature and creator.

Mies van der Rohe's maxim "Less is more" fits the tea spirit perfectly. Even so, the impersonality of the works of the great architect disturbs Japan's tea men, who have used that spirit for over three centuries. The most honored tea huts are hardly larger than log cabins, but they contain no fixture that has not been artfully made.

A debate still going on in tea circles in Japan is the precise influence of Japanese home architecture on tea, and tea on home architecture. Whatever the eventual decision, tea architecture has contributed significantly to the Japanese home. Its stress on the unification of garden and house, and the extension of the standardization already present in Japanese architecture are most important in this respect. The tendency to be concerned with the whole property, setting and structure, is evident in the work of many contemporary Japanese architects. Outstanding among them are Sutemi Horiguchi, Yoshiro Taniguchi, Junzo Yoshimura, and others. These men have applied the lessons of tea in scaling contemporary dwellings. Horiguchi and Taniguchi have a special relationship with tea, having studied and practiced it throughout their lives. The former is a noted scholar on cha-no-yu. His *Rikyu no Chashitsu,* on Rikyu's tea huts, is a classic.

The Japanese interior has many elements derived from tea. The number and placement of mats in a room, the prominence of the art alcove, the predominance of natural woods, papers, and certain designs are products of a tea-conscious architecture. The influence of Western forms in interior decoration has done much to clutter Japanese houses since the late nineteenth century. But the recent recognition in Japan of an international style that leans toward simplicity has helped to restore the traditional Japanese interior. A recent scholar points out that the three elements of cha-no-yu, garden, hut, and ceremony, correspond to the three characteristics of Buddhist teaching: the evanescence of all things, the selflessness of the elements, the bliss of Nirvana. The rather quiet, small, and dark setting of tea unquestionably has its place in contemporary Japan, with the world's largest city, most congested traffic, and most numbing level of noise.

While some Japanese have managed to continue to live in a traditional manner, many—most of the younger generation of married couples—have gone on to other life-styles, especially those of the West. The old way of living requires a trained, energetic overseer in the household willing to spend the time necessary to make sure things are maintained. And it requires capital. For the busy young couples living in small Tokyo or Osaka apartments it is just not possible to live as their parents did. Their incomes and free time are not sufficient to maintain the elegant, contemplative life of tea, even if they so desired.

Despite all these factors tea is still an influence in the life of the Japanese. Aside from a revival of a national Japanese style—sometimes in the guise of neo-nationalism—which seems to be prepared to incorporate the traditional arts and customs, much is going on in contemporary Japanese design that bears a direct relationship to cha-no-yu. The well-educated designers of posters, packaging, furniture, clothing, and everyday articles for consumers draw constantly on the works of past tea masters. Frequently, without their knowing it, the consumers in Japan buy and use products that can be described as tea-inspired. Tea still strongly influences the household utensils used by a Japanese housewife, for example. The plates and dishes she selects are most often those made originally for the formal meal sometimes served with the tea ceremony. This influence is also strengthened by Japanese restaurants, where the tea-ceremony meal is the standard by which one judges good food. The emphasis in the tea meal on beauty of service ware and arrangement of foods has served to educate the Japanese wife. In her choice of fabrics and patterns, too, tea standards are felt.

Thus, as more and more of the designs of tea are incorporated into the main market of the economy, tea itself is influenced in turn. This is a healthy state. Tea has always profited from changes that kept it in pace with contemporary life. If the art of tea had ever remained rigidly fixed, tied to a single man, idea, or era, it would have died.

It used to be that old men would give up their family houses and retire to a spare tea hut or temple where they could live out their days in peaceful surroundings. Few take this direction in retirement today, but men who have experienced a hectic life do often devote more of their time to tea. Alan Watts once said that tea ceremony encouraged thought so unobtrusively that it left the mind free to "roam at unusual depths in unaccustomed places." This is a good description of tea, which may not occupy the center position in the lives of millions of our contemporaries, yet nevertheless serves to release a great many from the strictures imposed by the lives they lead.

It would be misleading to think of tea as a tranquilizer for modern man. It is not an instrument used to achieve a certain end. Cha-no-yu isn't a hobby to occupy an old man's time. When a host invites his guests into the tearoom he does not attempt to make the occasion "something." The host intends nothing beyond serving tea and sharing a few moments with his friends. He doesn't try to embellish the ceremony with his sincerity, brilliant service, or fine utensils. If the tea is served and the guests enjoy it, that is enough. If things are perfectly harmonious, the moment will open like a flower, naturally. Imagine a flower "trying" to blossom, "trying" to be fragrant!

There is no sudden enlightenment in a tea ceremony. What happens simply makes life "more." Dogen (1200–1253), Zen master and founder of the Soto sect, wrote a testimony to the kind of enlightenment with which tea has been associated: "Our attainment of enlightenment is something like the reflection of the moon in water. The moon does not get wet, nor is the water cleft apart. Though the light of the moon is vast and immense, it finds a home in water only a foot long and an inch wide. The whole moon and the whole sky find room enough in a single dewdrop, a single drop of water. And just as the moon does not cleave the water apart, so enlightenment does not tear man apart. Just as a dewdrop or drop of water offers no resistance to the moon in heaven, so man offers no obstacle to the full penetration of enlightenment." This sensitive reflection on enlightenment, the most sensitive I have ever heard, may also refer to the tea ceremony.

Susanne K. Langer has written of man's ability to "feel" through art. Man, she writes, can articulate an idea, a reflection of the state of things, through artistic means. Tea is a reflection of the state of man, his situation, environment, imperfection, and sociability. Whatever absurdities and beauties the Japanese have achieved in the pursuit of a bowl of tea, it is perhaps best seen as a passion for the act of living.

PART ONE

The History of Tea Ceremony

2. The Early Years

Chinese Influence and Medicinal Tea

It could have been any beverage—examine the relationship of coffee to Islam, wine to Christianity—but it was tea that came to be most closely associated with Buddhism. Both were introduced into Japan from China, but we have no precise knowledge of the date of either import. Tradition places the advent of Buddhism in Japan at about mid-sixth century, but as China and Japan had maintained some sort of relationship before that time, it is likely that the religion was known in the latter country before this. Tea followed Buddhism to Japan a short time later, but it was not until the eighth century that records mention the beverage. It is possible that wild tea was discovered by Japanese at an earlier date, as was the case with some of the island civilizations of Southeast Asia. The eighth-century import from China was most probably an easily portable brick tea, though the records do not specify the kind. This type was popular in China from the sixth through the ninth century.

Early T'ang documents state that the Chinese had known of tea cultivation from the fourth century and that by the sixth century the practice was widespread. The same sources describe the drinking of tea and list some utensils employed in its preparation and serving—the first detailed records on the subject. Legend from China has it that Bodhidharma, annoyed by falling asleep during periods of meditation, cut off his eyelids, which, on falling to the ground, sprang up as the first tea shrubs. If the legend is correct in associating Bodhidharma with tea, it means tea existed in Chinese temples during the sixth century. Whatever we believe about its origins, tea drinking is an ancient practice among Asians, and tea was one of the many goods introduced to Japan from the older Chinese civilization.

T'ang China, ca. 600–900, was vastly superior to the struggling state across the sea, and just as Korea was overwhelmed by Chinese glory, so was Japan enthralled by and subjected to Chinese influences. Ch'ang-an, the T'ang capital, rivaled any city in the world of that time, probably surpassing all in terms of organization, splendor, and wealth. The few Japanese who went to T'ang China were determined that their own nation should be modeled after Chinese material and religious accomplishments. When Buddhism was introduced into Japan, a faction formed to encourage its propagation. This group became an important force at court, a pro-Chinese nucleus that sought to instill reforms of Japanese officials, government, arts, and the like—based on what they learned in visits to China. The pro-Chinese group was immediately in conflict with the more conservative Japanese, but the former won complete victory for their cause during the regency of Prince Shotoku (573–621), and as a result a number of missions were sent to China. Though the missions were supposed to encourage trade between the two nations, it was the scholars sent to study T'ang culture who were to have greatest effect on struggling Japan.

Much of what we recognize as purely Japanese dates from this period—more particularly from the work of these early scholars. As Professor Reischauer points out in *Japan Past and Present,* it is remarkable that a weak and emerging government had the wisdom to place among its envoys a number of young men who, by their training, could intelligently research the wealth of Chinese learning, returning to their country with some of the knowledge of their sophisticated neighbor. The scholars performed their missions with zeal and most became prominent in their respective disciplines or professions. Many of them remained in China only for the completion of the mission to which they were attached, but some stayed for years, even decades. Upon returning to Japan, they taught of China's arts, religions, sciences, and practices in law and government. These teachings were eagerly received and often adapted for Japanese use.

The audacity of the young scholars who had been to China is matched only by their successes in seeing their teachings implemented in Japanese society. Under their tutelage the island nation took on the forms of China with great speed. Japan did not become a perfect copy of T'ang, but the influence was nonetheless deeper than the mere physical alteration of existing forms. Japanese architecture and city planning did undergo transformation according to principles learned from T'ang—a notable example is the city of Nara, which was copied from the Chinese capital of Ch'ang-an—but all the other arts of the period show development along Chinese lines as well.

For nearly two hundred years the missions continued in an unbroken stream until the Japanese finally came to be disenchanted with the decay that took place in late T'ang. During this time the Japanese matured; they were no longer so eager to accept everything Chinese as worth imitating. Japan slowly returned to her former posture and former arguments of self-sufficiency. The ideas brought so carefully from China took on new form in the hands of extremely energetic and able Japanese—so much so that a classical Chinese gentleman would probably agree that the "borrowings" became purely Japanese.

At the time of the missions, tea was served at auspicious gatherings such as one recorded during the reign of Emperor Shomu (701–56), when one hundred priests were served tea at Todai-ji, Nara. A slightly earlier mention of tea is found in the *fudoki,* some of the oldest Japanese historical-geographical records. It was not until the capital was moved from Nara to more northerly Kyoto that the movement was born which was eventually to characterize Japan as a "tea culture."

Kyoto was founded in 794. Ninth-century Kyoto reflects much of the elegance of China, with great palaces, gardens, and temples abounding. As the men and women of China took their tea in graceful pavilions by the waterside, so their Kyoto counterparts are pictured by ponds in the same pursuit. Japanese literature of the era is replete with references to the famous ponds Osawa no Ike and Shinsen-en and to the forgatherings of the poetic nobility. Poems of the *Ryounshu* anthology of 814 depict the precious scenes with frequent reference to the tea and music which entertained the aristocrats. According to the poems, the experience of tea was far from the Way but rather was part of a more leisurely preoccupation with willows, moon, and court romances. However, a few poets of the time speak differently, and in their work we sense the beginnings of the "tea spirit."

> In the old cave Spring comes
> And I am looking at the azure bay,
> While steam rises from the boiling tea,
> The evening deepens, and the air is a
> quiet cloud.

Before Lady Murasaki had written *The Tale of Genji* (ca. 1010) the emperors Saga (r. 809–23), Uda (r. 887–97), and Daigo (r. 897–930), were enlisted among the growing numbers of tea drinkers, and compilations were begun of inventories of various utensils used in serving the Chinese beverage. We can imagine that when the emperors drank, the service was the considerable ceremony learned from Chinese sources. By the eleventh century tea was a habit of the establishment, with priests and laymen following the lead of the nobility. The records of Kyoto's Ansho-ji include mention of a number of vessels for tea, and chairs for tea service. The extensive tea records of Ninna-ji and To-ji, also Kyoto temples, include mention of such diverse ware as a silver caddy, celadon bowls, a lacquered stand for bowls, and various pieces of white porcelain. The amounts listed indicate that the practice of tea had become widespread and that, at least in palaces and temples, just about everyone was making tea. But in the rush for the beverage one priest, who must have had his reasons, strictly forbade his charges to taste the concoction, for in his words, "The ones who drink tea become boisterous and disorderly."

It is difficult to decide which attracted the emperors, priests, and people of Japan to tea, its taste or its medicinal reputation. No mention of tea is made in the dedication of sixty kinds of medicine to the Great Buddha of Nara. Twenty-five chests of articles were dedicated on that occasion. None of the twenty-one remaining today contains tea. However, the early records of two very influential priests, Ennin (794–864) and Kuya (903–72), stress the importance of tea as medicine. When Eisai (1141–1215) returned from China in 1191 to plant "original" Japanese tea at Fukuoka, it is apparent that the medicinal values appealed to him more than the taste of the drink. He wrote a treatise called *Kissa Yojoki,* cited above, page 23, extolling the benefits of tea for one's health, and copied it in 1214 as a gift for the shogun, a man given to alcohol. The association of Eisai with tea is so great in Japan that he is considered the "father of tea," the individual most responsible for its wide propagation. Eisai gave tea seeds to his friend and colleague Myokei, who planted them at Kozan-ji, a temple set on a steep hill northwest of Kyoto. The tea served at Kozan-ji is considered "original" Japanese tea because it comes from plants cultivated in Myokei's small garden. (Original or not, the tea is excellent and the view of nearby hillsides is worth the one-hour ride it takes to get there.) Eisai is further credited with having introduced Rinzai Zen to Japan and therefore is doubly important to chado.

Tea and Zen

The idea that "there is not much to say about Zen" extends so deep into the history of the movement that the very origins of the sect are obscure. Tradition associates the beginnings with the lidless Indian priest we know as Bodhidharma and tells us that he arrived in China about the year 520. What distinguishes Zen from other Buddhist sects is a reliance on direct perception of truth. Zen is a tradition of action and self-reliance which has never placed much faith in writing. There are no holy texts upon which belief is based, but adherents rather rely on personal insights passed by word-of-mouth from generation to generation, from masters to students. As Zen monasteries grew in China, a system was developed for judging the soundness of personal insight, and this was carried over into Japanese practice after Eisai introduced Rinzai Zen in the twelfth century. The system teaches that all men are children of Buddha, therefore every man is Buddha. One does not try to be man any more than he tries to be Buddha; he *is* man, he *is* Buddha. The rigorous training of Zen's direct method is aimed at freeing the initiate from his "trying." It involves a series of questions and answers exchanged in sessions between master and student. When correct insight is demonstrated by a student's response, a certain level of certification is attained. The process may take years before the student sets himself free by his own insight.

Eisai was followed by another important Zen priest, Dogen, who returned to Japan from China in 1227. Though Dogen never sought to associate himself with institutions, he is considered to be the founder of Soto Zen in Japan, and his great temple is Eihei-ji, one of the headquarters of the sect. Dogen took with him to China a craftsman, Toshiro, who studied the ceramics of the Sung dynasty (960–1280). When he returned to Japan he made his way to Seto, in what is now Aichi Prefecture, where he established the thriving pottery works still centered in that city. As a burial urn for Dogen, Toshiro made a fine pot that is believed to be the oldest extant product of the Seto kilns. Dogen also brought back a Chinese ceramic vessel which came to be used as a tea caddy, the "Koga kata-tsuki"; this remains one of Japan's great treasures and is a model for tea caddies used in thick-tea ceremony. A report by Dogen makes frequent mention of tea, tea manners, and tea service, all learned during his stay in China.

The great Zen priests Eisai and Dogen firmly established tea as a part of the Zen tradition in Japan, and after them every priest who ventured to make the long and difficult voyage across the sea returned with tea utensils for his own temple. The early utensils were, for the most part, inclined to be simple in glaze and form; celadon was especially favored, as was the exquisite Sung Temmoku ware. Lacquer trays of black or red and small tables used by the Chinese for the display of tea utensils are found in the inventories of various Kyoto temples dating from the time. There was as yet no large-scale Japanese pottery works turning out the vessels which are particularly associated with tea. Emperors, priests, nobles, and prominent citizens eagerly sought Chinese ware; edicts from the court of the time encourage the giving of Sung bowls and the medicine bottles that Japanese used as caddies.

From 1239 the priest Eison went about the countryside preaching Zen and offering the "cure" of tea. The work of this priest contributed significantly to the popularization of tea as well as Zen. Actually the use of medicines by priests was not new to Japan, for in earlier times the "medicine king" idea was prevalent, and Eison's teaching probably appeared as an extension of that concept. The Kamakura period (1185–1333), in which he worked, was a prosperous one for Zen, for as Eisai had succeeded in establishing Zen at court, where it was later to become the most important force among Buddhists, Eison prepared the way for widespread acceptance of the austere sect through his popular tours. In 1261 Eison traveled across Japan to the Kanto area (site of present Tokyo) and along the way stopped in scores of inns to serve tea and teach the Way. He is said to have served tea even to the outcasts and meaner elements he encountered on his trip, thus bringing tea in the thirteenth century full circle in Japanese society—the emperor and the outcast met through Zen in the common experience of tea.

One story of the time tells of Eison approaching a shepherd with an offering of tea. The shepherd inquired as to the nature of the beverage, and Eison assured him that it contained the very gift of enlightenment, for it prevented sleep and destroyed the passions. The shepherd gently refused the priest's tea, for, he said, "In my job I must work very hard—therefore I need my sleep and as I have nothing else for pleasure I cannot refuse my passions. If tea rids me of both, then I shall have none of it." Whether Eison toned down his message or met with a less harassed public we do not know, but after Eison tea became a habit for Japanese. Eison's use of tea was exuberant, and on several occasions he held "big" teas at important temples, encouraging all the Zen initiates to drink generously of his brew. He claimed that after seven bowls all sleepiness was lost, and that after nine lust itself slipped from the mind. We have no reason to doubt his authority in the matter concerning sleep, for even *chajin* (tea men) are reluctant to take tea in the late evening.

The Muromachi Flowering

In the fourteenth century Eisai's seeds began to germinate. From this time forward the records of tea are very extensive, covering every aspect of ware, service, architecture, and garden, as well as the personalities of tea drinkers. Fourteenth-century records vividly depict tea tournaments in which as many as ten kinds of tea were exhibited and drunk, with costly prizes being awarded to those who could correctly distinguish "original" from other strains of tea. The tea tournaments are comparable to the popular game of *ko-awase,* incense comparing. Both contribute a share of the rules of ceremony later to be incorporated in cha-no-yu. The tournaments were boisterous affairs consistent with the observation of the above-mentioned priest who had forbidden tea to the inmates of his temple on the grounds that drinking it made one disorderly. The situation became grave when, in 1336, a law was passed aimed at controlling the citizens who spent their time and fortunes in the luxury of the tournaments. Orders were posted on bridges and at busy intersections condemning the practice. Tea had fallen on bad days. A little earlier it had been proven that a plot against the government had actually been hatched in the setting of a tearoom. *Cha yori-ai,* tea meetings, and *renga yori-ai,* meetings at which renga verses are composed, were pretty wild affairs, and illustrations show lords lolling about in disarrayed splendor. It was the time of popular tea jokes, with cha yori-ai becoming the subject of numerous Kyogen, the humorous plays presented as interludes for No.

Tea parties were not the only sources of outrageous behavior in the fourteenth and fifteenth centuries, for the time was one of chaos, shifting loyalties, revolt and counterrevolt. The Kamakura period had been an era of unified rule, but after the Mongol invasions in 1274 and 1281, the unity became superficial. When Emperor Godaigo attempted to reestablish the imperial family as rulers-in-fact of Japan, the decay of Kamakura began in earnest. The Kamakura court sent out one general to crush the rebellion, and he switched sides against the court. A second general was given an army to crush the rebel, but that general turned on the court itself and destroyed Kamakura, bringing the period to a somewhat inglorious end. The clashes continued for some time and for a brief period Japan had two pretenders to power, but stability was restored with the assumption of rule by the rebellious family of the first general, Ashikaga Takauji.

The Muromachi period (1336–1568), in which the Ashikaga shoguns ruled, was a period of such strife and hardship that even late in the nineteenth century people could pay five *sen,* the equivalent of a few cents, at the Toji-in in Kyoto to beat statues of the Ashikaga family. Thousands of citizens died in the senseless Onin Civil War (1467–77) or from plague, famine, and catastrophes of various kinds. In Kyoto today there is scarcely a pre-Onin temple that contains a single building that survived the war intact. The opposing leaders in the Onin War died in 1473, ending the conflict, which had had no reasonable origin.

But if fire and war constitute the political history of the era, there is abundant evidence that the arts progressed at a greater rate than at any other time in Japan's history. Perhaps because of the firm pursuit of aesthetics by the Ashikagas or because of the overwhelming force of Zen Buddhism among the leaders of the time, art in all its forms was born anew. It was in the Muromachi period that tea came to be a fully realized art form in the hands of the priests. Zen priests were the force that made monasteries the centers for art and learning as well as the treasure houses for much of the fine art work that was produced.

The power and influence of Zen priests during the Ashikaga rule cannot be understated, for they were closest to the Chinese sources that preoccupied the minds of the Ashikaga shoguns. One shogun is even described as going about his palace in Chinese ceremonial robes, drinking Chinese tea and corresponding with the Chinese emperor. The priests served as valuable advisers on matters of trade, art, and religion—an early mixing of roles which was to survive long in Zen circles. As the early Ashikagas were generally without funds for extravagance, they found a natural home in the austerities of Zen. After the wars were over the hold on the court by Zen was sufficient to weather the good times.

The remarkable growth of landscape, palace, and temple architecture under the Zenists can be seen in a host of fine works dating from the period; Ryoan-ji garden in Kyoto remains the most famous of the austere Zen-inspired sand and rock constructions, but others are equally vital if not as severe. The palaces of Yoshimitsu (1358–1408) and Yoshimasa (1435–90), third and eighth Ashikaga shoguns respectively, are extremely sensitive reminders of the abilities of fifteenth-century artists interested in Zen. The rise of No drama and its perfection under master Zeami occurred at the time Shubun and Sesshu were painting: around the turn of the fourteenth century. Not surprisingly, Yoshimitsu and Zeami were strict followers of Zen, and Sesshu and Shubun were priests of the sect.

In much Muromachi art we can see how thoroughly Japanized Zen had become, for though Shubun and Sesshu, to mention but two painters, were working on Chinese landscapes in Sung styles, the work of both is somehow new, direct, and boldly Japanese. The paintings are inexplicably "Zen"—there is enormous discipline in brushing, an impatience with excess detail, an unfathomable depth in spaces, and a brilliant disposition of subjects, but words fail to express the immediate sensation of astoundingly direct perception of life that is the very quality of this painting.

The critical abstractions of highly literate priests gave little comfort to the Muromachi laymen who found themselves very much caught up in the Zen movement. Even the writings of Zen laymen were unfailingly difficult to divine. Zeami's epoch-making tome, *Kadensho,* is filled with references to *yugen,* a concept basic to No and extremely difficult even for the most agile minds, and which is symbolized as a "white bird with a flower in its beak." Though Zeami's works on No were not available to the general public, little else that could be called Zen literature was written aside from the poems in *waka* and *haiku* forms.

No was employed in the beginning as an instrument of Buddhism, and it might have become the teaching instrument of Zen, with which it was closely associated through Zeami, had circumstances been different. One problem was that No texts (with few exceptions) express a Buddhism that is more primitive and common than Zen, and the other was that No became an aristocratic pastime not popular with the masses. But the Muromachi public was a creative one, interested in participating. For these reasons, and because a form which synthesizes the arts of an era always seems to appear, tea ceremony was formalized. Although at a later time tea broke its formal associations with Zen institutions, it had become a potent expression of Zen among the people, and was especially popular among the military.

In the tea ceremonies of early Muromachi there was little of the profundity of chado. The presence of colorful figures such as Sasaki Doyo assured that tea remained sport and fun. Sasaki held vast tea tournaments and extravagant parties at which the beverage was served, and according to a contemporary chronicler his teas were as wild as his impetuous life. But it was due to such great interest in tea as entertainment that the arts particularly associated with it flourished; ceramics, ironwork, lacquerwork, architecture, and gardening attained new heights. Because of the demand for tea utensils, specialists developed in various wares; important examples are the artists who made Ashiya and Temmyo ware kettles from the mid-fifteenth century. Had it not been for the Sasakis of early Muromachi there would not have been the later Rikyus.

The Beginning of the Way: Ikkyu and Shuko

A prince turned priest began the process which brought tea to a close expression of Zen and away from riotous spirit. His name was Ikkyu (1394–1481), and he was a famous abbot of Kyoto's Daitoku-ji. As a son of the emperor he enjoyed many privileges as a youth and was often taken to temples by his mother, a student of Zen. At her encouragement he became a priest. He was a clever young man, as illustrated by the incident of his breaking a cherished tea bowl by accident. It had been a special favorite of his master. When the master returned, Ikkyu, hiding the wreck behind him, asked, "Why do people have to die?" The master consoled the boy by pointing out that everything has to die and that death is a natural process. Ikkyu laid the pieces of the bowl before the master; "It was time for your bowl to die," he said.

Ikkyu knew something of the so-called Chinese tea ceremony through his own studies, and he encouraged his prize pupil to take up Zen training by this means. The pupil, Shuko (1422–1502), accepted the challenge, and in his hands tea ceremony became a Japanese art, for his genius succeeded in adapting it for his countrymen. His style of tea was strongly influenced by his great teacher, and in this sense was unlike later, simpler tea. He had a decided preference for calligraphy in cha-no-yu decoration, certainly due to what he had seen of Ikkyu's own beautiful calligraphy, and to Ikkyu's observation that the contemplation of the writings of fine men leads to enlightenment. Ikkyu himself did not contribute much to the direct formalization of tea, but his brilliance is reflected in the style of Shuko as taught to the Ashikagas.

Shuko found the stand and utensils, including kettle and kettle-stand, which had been brought from China by the priest Nampo Shomei in 1267 and stored at Shinju-an, Daitoku-ji. Shuko used the utensils in his own development of the ceremony, and his tea was elaborate, even gorgeous.

There is, however, a debate that centers on the originality and initiative of Shuko. The question is whether he rediscovered long-neglected utensils and created new and different uses for them within the framework of his own tea service, or whether he was simply following common practice of the time. The particular object that occasions the debate is the *daisu,* or stand for implements, and the assertion is that Shuko may not have been the first to use it. Apparently Muso Kokushi, an earlier and great Zen priest, had used the same stand, and some scholars believe that the military class interested in tea took it upon themselves to imitate him. If this is true, then Shuko's teaching with the stand represents no departure from precedent, and his tea service differs less from that of his contemporaries than might be expected.

In any case, Shuko is of critical importance to the development of tea, for in his attitudes we witness the awakening of a spirit which sought to go beyond mere entertainment and consolation of guests in tea. If Shuko did not put his theories into practice he did, nevertheless, influence Shogun Yoshimasa to the extent that the latter wrote: "If someone asks of me / tell him I am leading a wabi life / in the mountains." While we cannot imagine this shogun living in a grass hut, we can at least appreciate that he thought sufficiently of the idea, as an idea, to express it in his poetry. Of course, he was living in the incomparable Ginkaku-ji (Silver Pavilion) in Kyoto at the time, and had virtually forsaken the nation for pursuits of an artistic kind, collecting superb utensils for tea and a host of marvelous Chinese paintings in the very best black-and-white Zen style. At the time of the Onin slaughter he was pacing his quiet and exquisite scene wrapped in a world of graces unknown to his countrymen, conceiving an aesthetic which was to become a rich heritage for Japan.

Shuko gained admission to the shogun's world through Noami (1397–1471), Yoshimasa's tea master. He held tea for the shogun with the help of Noami, Geiami (1431–86), and Soami (1472–1523), all accomplished artists in their own rights. During their lifetimes, Shuko and his son Soshu came to dominate the world of tea and influence Yoshimasa's attitudes greatly. The Togu-do at Ginkaku-ji contains Yoshimasa's tearoom, designed by Shuko and supposed to have been the first four-and-a-half-mat tearoom (one mat is about three feet wide and six feet long), the standard tearoom size.

Shuko is unique in tea history in that he inherited two traditions, one the "fun and games" of tea tournaments, the other a more serious attitude learned from Ikkyu, which he developed into his idea of *wabi*. Shuko had in fact been expelled from his former temple for gambling in tea tournaments, and had traveled as a judge for these contests. But when he associated with Ikkyu, he began to see tea as more than a mere gambling opportunity, and he developed the wabi idea that was to influence Yoshimasa. Shuko's most famous remark about wabi is: "It is a good thing to see a fine steed tied to a thatched hut." His idea was a wabi that existed to point up the incongruity in life and the value of recognizing contrasts. Yet he must have been a kind of underground wabi tea man, because we can hardly imagine that anything performed at the Shogun's residence was of a very simple nature.

Shuko's words express a spirit not unlike that of later masters of chado. A favorite expression of his, "I do not like the moon in a cloudless sky," fits perfectly with the *haboku* (splash ink) paintings of Japanese Zen masters, with the suggestions of No and with the "imperfect" designs of tea gardens and houses. Shuko's preference for the imperfect, incomplete, and asymmetrical anticipates chado by at least a hundred years; he stressed harmony, respect, and cleanliness. It was Shuko who designed the three basic styles of tea: *shin, gyo,* and *so,* that is, formal, semiformal, and informal, terms that derive from calligraphic art.

Whatever influences Shuko felt from Chinese sources, it is evident that tea was made Japanese by his hands. He still paid the traditional tribute to the Chinese idea, but the gesture was lip service in his tea. The climate, materials, and the increasing insularity of the Japanese encouraged artists like Shuko to become independent of the manners of classical China. Shuko reached beyond Chinese ideas and used his own Japanese sense of appropriate practice in teaching both shogun and commoner.

Further Along the Way: Jo-o and Rikyu

Taking tea further along the Japanese Way was master Takeno Jo-o (1504–55). Jo-o was born into a family that had suffered loss of fortune through the infamous Onin War and made their way to Sakai, a prosperous center of commerce outside Osaka. The fact that Jo-o was born in a city that was a center of international trade was to have great effect on the history of tea. The merchants of Sakai are famous in Japanese history for their wealth, influence in government, and pursuit of tea. Scores of visitors to Sakai have chronicled their impressions of Sakai affluence by duly noting the vast numbers of superb works for tea in the merchants' collections. Their enthusiasm in collecting somewhat parallels that of later Americans: they were eager, and had the money and the mind to buy. It is fashionable to criticize such collecting, in both cases, but if we examine closely the works that were bought, it is easy to see that funds alone did not dictate the choices made—the selections were superb and reflected a highly refined aesthetic.

Like all Japanese the merchants enjoyed their baths, but being men of leisure they developed the habit beyond the ordinary. In the first place they used sea water, which was supposed to be particularly salutary. Second, as prelude they drank tea, and then followed the bathing with sakè. The affair never became a formidable occasion but it was a meeting for the pleasure of drink, bath, and conversation—something like the popular hot-spring-resort socializing of today's Japan. Tea was frequently the conversation of the occasion, for the people of Sakai took to the developing art with sincere interest and ability. The conversations and meetings of the merchants contributed importantly to the art, and from their midst Jo-o took the lead as the most able student of tea.

Some historians dispute the assertion that Jo-o came from a rich family, saying that he came from an outcast family, but his early education in so many fields of Japanese art and thought dispels the assertion. He studied waka and Zen in Kyoto, hardly activities of a fifteenth-century outcast. Naturally he took to tea, as any man of his position would have, but he brought to his study a strong reaction against the aristocratic traditions of service, transforming it into a style more suited to his taste, acquired through Zen.

Jo-o stayed in Kyoto for some time before returning to his native Sakai, where he began teaching the art. He had learned the tradition of the daisu as handed down by Shuko and went on to develop the intentions of Shuko's tea. He liked the spirit of tea which included all classes of people, all kinds of utensils, but was served in the simplest enclosure, the grass hut. He was a man of considerable wealth, being able to purchase the extraordinary "Shonasu," a famous red clay medicine-bottle tea caddy, at a price equivalent to the annual yield of a very considerable tract of land. Nevertheless, he shunned any display of riches and preferred to have tea without a pretentious setting. While he was alive no one matched his authority in matters of the art, not even his more famous pupil, Sen no Rikyu (1521–91).

Jo-o met Rikyu and took him in as a pupil when he was eighteen. Accounts of various Sakai chajin point out that the young man was already accomplished in the art at the age of sixteen or seventeen—one of his ceremonies at the age of sixteen is recorded. As Jo-o, by far the greatest master of his generation, thought well enough of the boy to begin instructing him, we have no reason to doubt the report. Following the death of his master, Rikyu dominated tea with such creative force and superior taste that today chado is considered the "art of Rikyu." His position in tea is so important that the following chapter is devoted entirely to him. But first we must consider a movement contemporaneous with his training which strongly influenced both his teacher and himself.

Jo-o and Rikyu revolted against the prevailing spirit of tea and sought to establish a simple style based on their own personal distaste for the ostentatious and the superfluous. The revolt was part of the general attitude of Sakai merchants, held in spite of their wealth. The Sakai people took to using farmhouse settings for tea, to emphasize the relevance of their art to commoners. The Naya-shu, literally barn or warehouse school, represented something of a departure from the earlier tea schools which had suggested the use of plain huts for the environment of tea. The idea of a plain hut was taken from Vimalakirti's ten-foot-square shack for retirement: a place for a recluse seeking to break the conventional bonds of society. The farm buildings which the Naya-shu adherents suggested were not for those who quit the world, but were places to which active men could retreat for a while. Jo-o and Rikyu were part of the Sakai movement, and the importance of the background they had in common with the merchants cannot be overemphasized. Rikyu especially sought to make his art a socially related one through which followers could better meet the requirements of living.

As early as the rule of Yoshimitsu, the military class had come to study tea. During the time of Jo-o and Rikyu, the samurai gained rank as chajin equal to that of priests. The great generals who ruled Japan following the fall of the tired, effete Ashikagas were concerned only a little less with tea than with affairs of state. The extent to which this was true is underlined by the story of a general's aide who became so depressed at the amount of time his leader spent with Rikyu that he made plans to murder the master. He visited Rikyu on the pretext of learning tea himself, but the Zen-trained master quickly saw the real intent of the visitor. Rikyu invited the aide to his tearoom but entreated him to leave his sword outside. The man refused, saying he was a warrior and his sword always accompanied him, whatever the situation. Rikyu demurred, but when the two were seated in the stark room he turned over the kettle of water into the charcoal fire. In a second steam and ashes covered the room and the aide scurried in fright. Rikyu followed him outside with profuse apologies, commenting, "I have your sword here covered with ashes. Allow me to clean it and return it to you." Under the circumstances the aide could hardly carry out his plot and gave up the idea.

Rikyu understood the warrior class. He appreciated their directness and simplicity, and he had a strong bond with them in Zen. We may think it strange that Zen Buddhism is closely associated with the samurai, but actually it provides the very essentials of fighting. Zen teaches that once we have made up our minds we should go forward resolutely without looking backward. It does not encourage us to take up a murderous profession but is a strong support for anyone electing a dangerous way. The samurai of the sixteenth century were sustained in a changing, hazardous life by the tenets of Zen and many "realized" the Way by embracing the practice of tea. *Zen and Japanese Culture* contains a fine section on samurai in which Dr. Suzuki shows that Zen is a religion of the will which upholds intuition against intellection. He points out that the mind of the fighter is comparatively simple and not given to philosophizing. Strong emphasis is placed on overcoming the idea of death. The spirit which regards death without fear and is totally involved in the present moment of action is the Way of the Warrior, and the Way of Tea. Zen training awakens the same feelings in the man of tea and the man of war: vigorous alertness, unhesitating decision, complete preparedness.

The spirit of the "realized" Way teaches the tea master to see with his hands, feel with his eyes, taste with his mind. The totally prepared man opens all the possibilities of his being. Rikyu is said to have parried a sword thrust with his tea scoop while serving tea out-of-doors to samurai—apocryphal or not, this story serves to emphasize preparedness. He understood the samurai, and even as the son of a Sakai merchant, he brought to bear on his tea the same enlightened qualities they used in battle.

3. The Formative Years

The Flavor Changes

Today, anyone who speaks of cha-no-yu is referring to the tradition of Rikyu and those who followed him. Some historians state flatly that before Rikyu there was nothing that could be called tea ceremony. This is an overstatement, for in China, the *Pai-chang Ch'ing Kuei* (Monastery Regulations of Pai-chang) indicates the existence of some kind of organized tea service, at least by the eighth century (Pai-chang lived from 720 to 814). The regulations laid down in this work supposedly date from his lifetime, but the oldest surviving edition of the writing is dated 1335. Even if we do not accept a date earlier than 1335, we must admit the existence of some kind of tea ceremony in China during the latter part of the Yuan dynasty (1260–1368). This document would likely support the contention that some Japanese priests of late Kamakura did know of formal ceremonies relating to tea. However, tea ceremony as we know it today was radically changed by Japanese of a later period, and the later tea is known as cha-no-yu.

There is some evidence to support the assertion that Japanese tea was already being served ceremonially in the Muromachi period, and that regulations for the service were known to the court and government in Kyoto. One proof is the Dojin-sai tearoom of the Togu-do at Ginkaku-ji.

The other proof is a list of tea utensils, called *Kundaikan Sochoki,* drawn up by Noami, artist and teacher at the court of Yoshimasa and an expert tea man, and completed by his grandson Soami, who also served at the Ashikaga court. It is a complete record of what was done in tea during Noami's time—how utensils were displayed and used, how rooms were decorated, and so on. Today's tea service has many elements in common with that during the Muromachi period, evidence that later tea men have conducted ceremonies based on the works of Shuko, Noami, and others, and used these as the basis for further developments of the art. The list is so comprehensive that virtually every piece included in it is found in later texts, and it is a valuable source for tea students who wish to know the kind of tea served before Rikyu and his style came to be definitive in cha-no-yu. In their devotion to Rikyu, many contemporary chajin go out of their way to dismiss anything before their master's time. However, few if any scholars consider Rikyu less important than any earlier or later master in the history of tea. The importance of such men as Noami, whose thorough documentation shows that tea had gone a long way toward formalization by the end of the fifteenth century, must not be neglected.

It was the emphasis on display, the reliance on Chinese wares, and the exclusiveness of the tea meetings that distinguished tea under the Ashikagas from that which followed it. Ashikaga tea was elegant in the extreme, richly appointed with refined architecture set in splendid gardens. Guests for tea, dressed in decorated silks, proceeded to the meeting with finely costumed entourages. Costliness and splendor in everything was called for by the Ashikagas and their masters of tea. It did not seem to bother the hosts that the world outside the palaces was crumbling from lack of care and leadership. Popular discontent rose threateningly in the face of widespread war, famine, fire, and disease, but tea was served, and the palace gates shut out the horror. The shogun was a spiritual exile in his own land; the chaos did not reach to the Chinese gardens in which he took his tea.

The Young Rikyu

It is Sen no Rikyu who must be given credit for establishing simplicity as an element of paramount importance in tea. Whatever simplicity there was in tea before Rikyu was always qualified by insistence on costly wares, elaborate settings, and restriction of guest lists by aristocratic birth or education. Rikyu changed this, defied the tradition, though his own family was born to position. Senami, Rikyu's grandfather, served as an artistic adviser to the Ashikagas, retiring at the time of the Onin Civil War to a commercial city a little distance from Kyoto. Rikyu's family name was Tanaka, though he rarely used it. Born Tanaka Yoshiro, he preferred the name Sen, from his grandfather, and is known in most records as Sen no Soeki or Sen no Rikyu. No doubt he took his grandfather's name because it reflected his own interest in art, as opposed to commerce.

It is worth reiterating the importance of the fact that he became a prize pupil of the great chajin Takeno Jo-o at the age of eighteen, about 1540. Jo-o accepted Rikyu after the young man had studied for a while under master Dochin (1504–62). Jo-o saw in this young man an unusual talent, but Dochin too had recognized that this pupil was unusually gifted. Dochin's tea was of the elegant Ashikaga style and differed from Jo-o's, but they were nevertheless friends. Famed in their time, Dochin and Jo-o are most frequently mentioned today only as teachers of the great Rikyu. Dochin taught Rikyu to appreciate Chinese wares and a luxurious and graceful life. Jo-o taught him refinement, pride in the face of poverty, and something of a democratic spirit. In the young Rikyu, these varied qualities mixed to produce an all-embracing tea spirit which knew equally well the values of handling rough or refined ware. Rikyu became the first chajin in Japan to include in his own teachings a synthesis of values derived from the present as well as from the past. In this sense, Rikyu transcended the limitations of tradition and the limitations of reliance on innovation. In doing this he founded the complete art.

Rikyu's early tea meetings, beginning when he was fifteen or sixteen, are recorded. One account mentions that Rikyu used a special Chinese tea bowl and other fine wares in serving an assembly of distinguished guests. In 1537 he was still under the tutelage of Dochin, and his tea on this occasion reminds us of the luxurious character of his teacher. He provided a small meal which is also detailed. His accomplishment in hosting distinguished guests at a very early age should not be underestimated.

Rikyu trained at Daitoku-ji, famed training ground for Zen priests and men of tea. We read of another significant tea which Rikyu gave in 1544, and on this occasion he is supposed to have used one of Shuko's famous tea bowls—again no task for a neophyte. The tea of that year marked Rikyu's emergence as something more than a gifted chajin. He had become an important man in the world of tea. The following year, according to the *Matsuya Kaiki* (Records of Matsuya), has him serving tea to master Jo-o, and states that the performance was vigorous and appreciated by all present. Rikyu was still young at this time—his confidence was born of sound training and encouragement from his teachers. Being accepted by the foremost chajin of his time must also have given him a confident manner. Jo-o is recorded as having at this time praised his student's efforts and looked upon Rikyu as his successor. Apparently Jo-o did not look askance at the innovations Rikyu made in the service; he seems rather to have encouraged them. If he had not favored Rikyu's changes, he would have chastised the young man, and Rikyu would have either accepted the advice or left the master; neither was the case, so we can assume that Jo-o approved.

Jo-o has been regarded by many as something of an innovator himself. He is thought to have stressed the use of a simple grass hut, *so-an,* for cha-no-yu. This style of tea architecture became most popular under Rikyu's later urging, but Jo-o is believed to have introduced Rikyu to the possibilities of using this humble structure which contrasted with the earlier styles of tea and attitudes toward tea. During the Muromachi period, just before Rikyu's emergence in 1540, tea was in an elaborate style. Formal reception rooms, *shoin,* were used in this tea, and only valuable, imported utensils were used. Rooms were ten mats or larger, a setting reminiscent of the tea tournaments of earlier times. Aside from the four-and-a-half-mat room of Shuko, there was nothing restrained or quiet in the tea service of the Ashikagas. Other rooms used in conjunction with the actual tearoom were for receiving guests. The dignity and elaborateness of the preparations appealed to the nobility of Muromachi and were later revived by the nobles of Edo. (A good example of elaborate, reception-room tea architecture [*shoin-zukuri*] is to be seen in the Katsura Detached Palace tearoom, Shokin-tei. It is different from that preferred by Rikyu, but reflects some of the spirit Rikyu taught.)

Rikyu's Innovations

In addition to the *Matsuya Kaiki,* references to early Rikyu teas are found in Imai Sokyu's *Cha-no-yu Nikki* (Tea Ceremony Diary), a two-volume record written between 1589 and 1614. From it we learn of the kinds of utensils used by Rikyu, the guests he invited, and hints of his style of performance. The boldness of this creative man appears early in accounts of his tea; even in some of the earliest instances, it is obvious that Rikyu leaned strongly toward the less pretentious, simpler, more masculine forms. He began to use roughly made wares—many made by his contemporaries—while his fellow chajin continued to rely on exquisitely fashioned Chinese imports. Rikyu went so far as to employ common countryside ware in teas to which persons of exalted rank were invited—something no one else attempted at the time. He felt strongly that one should use that which was handy, if it seemed to fit the mood and style of service for the occasion. Rikyu did not hesitate, however, to spend a fortune for an outstanding object (he had the income) if the piece in question struck him as especially fine and appropriate to the ceremony. Most often, however, he looked about for something among the indigenous crafts; he even used the cheapest everyday Japanese objects. This sense of the appropriate is a beautiful aspect of the man. He did not feel he had to rely only on those things which had already proved successful in tea ceremony; he was both practical and innovative.

In his ability to improvise, to use anything handy, Rikyu compares with the American composer Charles Ives. As Rikyu might select an old bucket for a flower container, and match it with an exquisite Chinese tea bowl of the Sung dynasty, so Ives freely mixed casual melody with heavily structured composition. In doing so, he gave a special vitality to his symphonies. A sense of immediacy, of realness, pervades this kind of music that has room for footfalls, taxi horns, and Central Park birds. The naturalness of Ives's music is perhaps its most striking quality, and it is this same quality in the work of Rikyu that first strikes a student of tea. Neither man relied solely on tradition or accepted values, but preferred to add new dimensions to that which had gone before him in his discipline. As Ives's music was rare for its time, so Rikyu's tea was rare. The art of both men is pragmatic, practical, highly innovative. Both fit well the creative concept of the haiku poet Basho, who said: "Do not seek to emulate the old masters, / Seek what they sought."

Rikyu's innovations were not limited to the introduction of common wares, although this may be looked upon as a manifestation of the democratic spirit that moved him. He made many other daring changes that served to level the social distinctions in tea.

Before Rikyu's time there were two entrances to the tearoom. The *kinin-guchi,* a door slightly smaller than ordinary size, was for the nobility, who entered the room from a standing position in accordance with their rank. But retainers entered from a second door, the *nijiri-guchi,* a bare two and a half feet square. To enter through this small door one must double up his trunk and crawl through. Rikyu, demonstrating his capacity for leveling society in tea, insisted that everyone use the nijiri-guchi. The effect was to place all participants on an equal footing. In his tea he allowed no nobility, no commoner, to be distinguished in the manner of service.

Strange as it may seem, before Rikyu distinctions existed in the arrangements for toilet facilities. Nobles were permitted the use of a special affair that was very elegant, judging from the ones still seen among old teahouses. A less pretentious one was reserved for the less noble. Rikyu ordered one for all—the simplest kind and simplest arrangement.

A third important alteration in manner was Rikyu's requirement that the wash basin, an important element of the tea garden, be changed to one style, set low on the ground. The *chozubachi,* a high basin carved from stone, had been popular. The one Rikyu used exclusively was a much simpler *tsukubai,* crouching stone, style. It is interesting how he always sought to bring man closer to the nature which surrounds him and encouraged humility under all circumstances. Other masters, other times, insisted on physically elevating man, whereas Rikyu would have man spiritually transcend his situation.

Momoyama Japan and Rikyu

Rikyu is perhaps the perfect characterization of the Momoyama period (listed as extending either from 1568 or 1573 to 1600 or 1615). Rikyu spanned the better part of this era, a short period often seen as one of transition. It was a time of war, but one in which forces were generated for a unification of Japan. What makes the period especially interesting is that the Japanese during the time were relatively free of the inertia of the immediately preceding and immediately following periods; it was a time of unusual freedom of mind. As Toyotaka Komiya says in "Cha: Watashi no Mikata" (Tea: My Own Viewpoint), it is a period during which the closeness of death and destruction did not prevent one's experiencing the joy of life. Rikyu is a perfect representative of Momoyama in that he was fully aware of both the possibility of imminent destruction and of the joy of life, and was able to transcend them.

Rikyu lived in a dangerous era. Wars raged, men's lives were subject to the whim of their leaders. He was thrown into the heart of this world by his association with cha-no-yu and Zen. The leaders of the era were, almost without exception, devoted to tea and to the study of Zen. Priests and tea masters vied for prominence, position, wealth; and the court was rife with the intrigues of ambitious men. Rikyu achieved a place among the highest men of the land. He achieved this through personal will and intelligence. He dared to challenge his patrons and their lackeys when he felt they transgressed his authority in art—this in a time when there was no due process.

That he gained and held the supreme position in his chosen field, flexible in the face of the caprice of those whom he served, is sufficient evidence of his ability and stamina. His qualities of mind must have been very unusual, and his discipline, control, and creativity were recognized even by his rivals. He fought against the political uses of tea and exercised his authority against those who sought to bring gorgeousness into tea. He moved with precision through the labyrinths of power for many years, but he was finally put to death by the very man who had so long allowed his authority to go unchallenged. Yet even his death was a controlled exercise, much as serving tea might be, and it was his final triumph in the face of authority.

In the West, we have had few such men—men so complete in their authority that their tastes dominated an entire nation, affecting the lives of vast numbers of their contemporaries. We have had our towering figures: Michelangelo, a man of superabundant talent in architecture, sculpture, and painting. But even this Renaissance figure did not have authority that was complete in all matters of art. Rikyu, however, emerged as a man without peer in his time and one who served as arbiter of Japanese taste for the greater part of his lifetime. We tend to separate artists from the common functions of society, to regard them as special representatives of peripheral activities. Rarely do artists engage in government in our society, yet in Momoyama Japan they were frequently central figures, essential advisers to government. Rikyu served in this capacity on many occasions and was a trusted member of the ruling elite. Aside from his artistic authority, he had significant political power. He continued to hold the imagination of the nation and played a recognizable role in the shaping of Japan into a unified country.

Rikyu and Oda Nobunaga

Rikyu's first important political affiliation was with the cunning Oda Nobunaga (1534–82). With the fall of the Ashikagas, Nobunaga emerged as the strongest of many powers that rushed to fill the gap created by the absence of any central government. He was an impetuous and arbitrary ruler, often compared with Cesare Borgia (whose efforts to unify Italy under his hand took place some thirty years before Nobunaga's birth). Both men, though they were sometimes vicious, were possessed of a national vision and had the superior intelligence to enable them at least to come close to achieving their ends. That they both died in the struggle makes them interesting characters today.

Nobunaga also had a sensitive side, revealed time and again in accounts of his actions under stress. On the occasion of the battle of Okehazama (1560), Nobunaga was outnumbered in force, seriously disadvantaged by a powerful enemy, Imagawa Yoshimoto. Yet he found time to entertain his men with a dance from No that tells of the transitory nature of life and probably served to relieve tension and to steel the men for the coming battle. On other important occasions he is known to have served tea to his generals and to have taken a more than common interest in the ceremonies.

It seems natural to assume that Nobunaga used tea for political purposes, but it would be unwise to believe that he used it for that purpose alone. His enthusiastic pursuit of the Way of Tea is likely the result of his father's influence and that of Zen priests, who always seemed to be around the centers of power in sixteenth-century Japan. Oda Nobuhide, his father, was a daimyo and bore a family name related to the Taira clan (an illustrious and powerful family of the eleventh and twelfth centuries, also known as the

Heike). He died when Nobunaga was fifteen, but left his son a considerable treasury, land, and retainers. Nobuhide had many excellent tea utensils and apparently counseled his son to use them as gifts to retainers who distinguished themselves in the service of the family, and Nobunaga followed his father's advice.

We know that Nobunaga received numerous outstanding utensils from his friends and followers; many are listed in records as having been used by Nobunaga after having been presented to him. Splendid caddies, flower containers, paintings, and tea bowls are among those mentioned. He also built excellent tea huts. The Sarumen no Chaseki on the grounds of Nagoya Castle is the best known of his huts and ranks with four or five others as the finest of the era. For his master in tea Nobunaga selected Sen no Rikyu who, like himself, was young, strong-willed, and highly accomplished in difficult arts. Rikyu prepared and supervised the opening of Nobunaga's simple tea hut, modeled after a roadside stand.

Earlier, a letter from Toyotomi Hideyoshi, then on Nobunaga's staff, to one Lord Soeki of Sakai seems to indicate that Nobunaga had at that time promoted Rikyu to the position of *sado,* grand master of tea. Rikyu at the age of fifty-three was without peer in matters of tea. Jo-o had died before this, leaving Rikyu to dominate tea in Sakai and Kyoto. Rikyu was accustomed to being visited by the famous, the wealthy, and the talented, and it was Nobunaga who sought the tea master—not the reverse. The power which accrued to Rikyu from 1575 on seems more to have been thrust upon him by generals and artistic leaders who recognized his superior abilities than to have been the result of his own striving.

The relationship of Nobunaga and Rikyu must go back to before 1575—at least to 1570. The earlier date represents a visit of Nobunaga to the imperial treasure repository at Nara, the Shoso-in. On the occasion of the visit Nobunaga is known to have taken, with imperial permission, a length of the famous incense log Ranshaji. A lord's taking a piece of a priceless treasure, or anything from the treasure house, would be comparable to an American cardinal's invading the Vatican to secure for his private use some papal vestment. The importance of the event to those who witnessed it cannot be overstressed. From the eighth century the Shoso-in was a near-sacred place wherein were kept the emperor's own collection of foreign and domestic goods.

When Nobunaga visited the Shoso-in, he held a tea meeting to commemorate the occasion. His serving of tea to a small gathering of chajin is noted in several records of the times. Present then were Rikyu and Imai Sokyu, another chajin who had served Nobunaga in various capacities including that of grand master of tea. His diary has been mentioned above. Nobunaga took a fan and, placing pieces of the incense upon it, passed the rare gifts to his friends. As a gesture to chajin, the event was without precedent, without parallel in the history of tea. This was the esteem of Nobunaga for Rikyu. If one needed to mark the eminence of Rikyu from a date, the honors at the Shoso-in in 1570 would do. A few years later Rikyu's influence supplanted that of any other master close to Nobunaga. This time was the beginning of the triumph of Rikyu's Way.

The Momoyama period was the time of Rikyu's ascendancy in tea. Rikyu brought a strong taste for the austere into the world of tea which contrasted with the showy qualities usually ascribed to the era. He insisted on restraint and simplicity, and so worked against the tendency toward pretentiousness and exaggeration in Momoyama art. While palace walls were being covered with gold, life-size paintings of animals and landscapes, Rikyu chose not to decorate in anything like the manner prevalent at the time.

However, it would be unjust to claim that Rikyu's Way wholly thwarted this decoration. If that was his goal, he fell far short of it. I believe he sought to offer an intelligent alternative to the public display of wealth which everyone saw in the cities and buildings of the age. The decorative works of popular Momoyama artists tend to be sweet, perfumed, superficial, and grand in scale—as though size per se indicated mastery of medium. Rikyu thought most of the decoration to be of little meaning, while delightful, diverting. His own art form, however, was intensely personal, private, profound. He sought to rid tea of the carnival atmosphere, the solemn ritual aura, the master display tactics that had dragged it into the public arena so often in Japan's history. That he succeeded to any degree in an era characterized by gaudiness is remarkable.

Nobunaga questioned Rikyu closely on the master's service. When Nobunaga saw that Rikyu used the daisu in a way different from that taught by others, he sought an explanation from him. Rikyu explained the reasons to Nobunaga's satisfaction, and after that we read of Nobunaga's service as "learned from Rikyu."

It is possible that Rikyu and Nobunaga had met in the years before the 1570 meeting at the Shoso-in. Nobunaga had come into conflict with the rich merchants of Sakai and had resented their independence. The Sakai merchants were sufficiently wealthy to hire mercenaries to defend their city. No one had been able to break through this protection. Nobunaga, with uncharacteristic tact, sent his finest general, Toyotomi Hideyoshi, to negotiate with the Sakai people. The date was 1568. It is likely that Rikyu played a role in the discussions; he was well regarded for his quick mind, pleasant ways, and mastery of tea and the arts. Hideyoshi succeeded in bringing about an understanding between the merchants and Nobunaga. After the mission, Hideyoshi and Nobunaga had occasions to meet with the men of Sakai. They are known to have met with chajin in their Sakai homes, being served tea, examining the utensils of some of the richest men in Japan. Later, Hideyoshi encouraged the men of Sakai to take up residence around his sumptuous castle at Osaka just as Nobunaga had invited merchants to come to live by the great Azuchi Castle.

Nobunaga met death at the hands of one of his followers in 1582. En route to the western provinces he stopped at Honno-ji, in Kyoto, surrounded with but a few hundred men who were caught unawares while Nobunaga was having tea with friends. Their party was destroyed by the treacherous Akechi Mitsuhide, who had with him a force of some thirteen thousand. Nobunaga was spared the disgrace of being killed at the hands of his attacker; he committed suicide as the temple burned. He was forty-nine. His attacker lived for one hundred days following the incident, and was then assassinated by loyal Nobunaga followers.

Had the attack on Nobunaga occurred at another period of Japanese history, we might have seen Mitsuhide established as the supreme authority in Japan, but the times were turbulent. The Japanese accepted as ruler only the man who could back his word and rule with invincible force. Mitsuhide was neither efficient in his tactics nor apt in interpreting the reactions of loyal Nobunaga generals, most of whom immediately turned against him.

Nobunaga had been the leader of a movement in Japan that can only be characterized as masculine. Japanese arts, politics, and personalities for the whole of the Momoyama period were decidedly less feminine than they had been for a considerable time before Nobunaga's assumption of power. Strength of movement, quickness in decision, and a certain roughness replaced the more refined behavior of earlier Japanese. Nobunaga's immediate successor, Toyotomi Hideyoshi, carried this trend further.

The Rise of Toyotomi Hideyoshi

Hideyoshi had the respect of Nobunaga, that is certain, for he became first general to his chief and proved himself many times on the battlefield by defeating, by whatever means, the enemies of Nobunaga. They met when Nobunaga was but twenty, Hideyoshi eighteen, and their friendship and association extended from that time to Nobunaga's death. Hideyoshi learned from Nobunaga the arts of war, the tactics of diplomacy, and an appreciation of the fine arts.

If we are to take literally the contents of letters addressed to young Hideyoshi, he was called Little Monkey (*kozaru*). Like a monkey, he was quick and crafty. He married his sister to Tokugawa Ieyasu, Nobunaga's other great general, insuring the friendliness of the potential rival. His decisive actions at the time of Nobunaga's death assured his succession.

Hideyoshi is attractive to most Japanese because he is said to have been of very humble birth. The truth of the allegation is open to question on many counts, but he was not born a lord, inherited no territory, no staff of generals, no large fortune with which to hire foot soldiers. If he had had these advantages from the start, he would not have been attracted to working for another man, a lord who commanded his loyalty. Also, the man he chose to follow, Nobunaga, did not, at the time of their meeting, have one of the larger domains in Japan. Only later did Nobunaga emerge all powerful. So, we are led to conclude that Hideyoshi was forced by circumstance to ally himself with one of the lesser lords of sixteenth-century Japan. He chose his lord well, for no matter how insignificant Nobunaga was at the time of their alliance, he went on to become the strongest in the nation.

Nobunaga had been brilliant as a military commander; Hideyoshi was a genius. Where Nobunaga fell just short of unifying all Japan under one hand, Hideyoshi led the whole nation and sought lands abroad for his control. Seemingly capable of anything, Hideyoshi has inspired as many legends and tales as a score of other Japanese rulers before and since. He was a man given to poetry, architecture, politics, all the military pursuits, tea, drama, and pure scholarship. Whatever the depth of his involvements, he surpassed his predecessor in every respect and rendered dull his successors in power. This mighty figure wrote No plays (and performed in them), composed a few poems of merit, positively excelled in tea ceremony, and is said to have made dazzling arrangements of flowers.

It is no easy task to identify fact from legend in the records of Hideyoshi's life—most writers seem to have given up the effort and abandoned themselves to fiction. This writer has no claim to special wisdom, but has tended to rely on such things as inventories of Hideyoshi's possessions, eyewitness accounts of his activities, and examination of surviving relics of Hideyoshi's palaces rather than on interpretations of his attitudes. What these show is an independent man with taste and talent, an authentic hero, a kind of Renaissance man. The events of his personal life are inextricably intertwined with much fiction, no doubt, but they tell us that he occupied a unique place in Japanese history.

Following the tracings of Nobunaga, Hideyoshi built castles of magnificence; Fushimi-Momoyama and Osaka castles were the largest and finest palaces of the time. Osaka Castle may have been the largest building in the world of the sixteenth century. It required the full-time labor of sixty thousand men to complete and had walls covered in gold leaf, two moats, and scores of interconnecting structures. Jesuit missionaries on the scene reported its wonders to the Vatican, which must have served them as a basis for comparison. The missionaries reported that building stones of twenty feet by thirty feet were common sights on the river barges that made their way to Osaka.

The castle on Momo Hill at Fushimi was named Jurakudai. This too was a magnificent edifice, with a tall donjon that could be seen for miles, large decorative screens, fine woodwork, and extensive grounds. It was this site, Momoyama, that gave its name to the era in which it was built. But even in this gigantic castle Hideyoshi had a number of very small tearooms, fashioned with care and a respect for minute detail. In these rooms Hideyoshi served tea to close friends and associates, a humbling act for a magnificent man. The building sections that survive of his various structures indicate excellent taste in architecture. It seems he actually enjoyed building and that he built with two ideas in mind: there had to be some display of magnificence for the crowds outside the gates; and the interior had to contain places of privacy—tearooms and special chambers—to which he and his friends could retire for their own enjoyment. In all records of the time that make detailed reference to Hideyoshi's palaces and castles, there is constant mention of the duality of his architecture, the public and the private. Western writers, for the most part, tend to ignore the private, quiet, and tasteful elements of the buildings in favor of the grand, superficial outlines of the exteriors and public rooms. This is a serious mistake in judging Hideyoshi, for it is usually implied that he was a base character of low birth who cared only to display his wealth and acquired position by constructing bigger and richer works. Mere reference to lists of his gifts to others, purchases for himself, objects for which he expressed admiration, and tearooms and huts which he had constructed would be enough to confirm the quality of his personal taste. The numerous instances of his serving tea, at all hours of day or night, confirm that he was no mere collector of utensils but had a significant interest in the art form, perhaps in the Way itself.

Hideyoshi and Tea

Hideyoshi first got permission to serve tea in 1578, while serving Nobunaga. Only certain generals were given this permission, thus those who were so honored had obviously attracted the admiration of Nobunaga for their personal qualities as well as for their military accomplishments. Surviving records of the occasion tell that Hideyoshi employed a famous Jo-o tea bowl, a painting of the moon by Mu Ch'i (a Chinese artist active ca. 1200–1250 whose works were greatly admired by tea men), and other excellent wares. None of these would have been handled by a neophyte, for that would have been comparable to a new dancer's electing to star in *Les Sylphides* as his first stage appearance.

Hideyoshi's influence over tea was even greater than Nobunaga's—perhaps, as in other things, reflecting a desire to overshadow the latter's accomplishments. Hideyoshi greatly enlarged the body of chajin by encouraging Japanese to practice the art of tea. Under Hideyoshi's rule many activities formerly of importance were thoroughly discouraged, leaving tea and other favored practices to thrive without competition. Ceramics especially thrived under the influence of Koreans brought to Japan during the Hideyoshi campaigns to conquer foreign territory. Architecture assumed a worldly grace in palace construction, and a restrained simplicity in the building of tea huts. Opulent painting, spirited design in lacquer works, and splendid gardens flourished in the Momoyama period. The Japanese were beginning to find their own style. Tea was so much a part of this style that Takigawa Kazumasa, a Nobunaga commander stationed in the provinces, is quoted as saying, "I have fallen into hell," having no one with whom to share tea ceremony.

During this time the priest Ranjo wrote a small work entitled *Shu Charon,* a discussion of the relative merits of tea and sakè. As far as much of the general public was concerned, tea was still a subject for entertainment, as was the rice wine. Tea was favored by some because it did not leave a hangover. Also, while drinking tea, the imbiber was left free to converse or compose as suited the occasion. It is noted, however, that there are certain advantages to sakè not to be found in the world of tea.

The need for tremendous quantities of tea utensils provided the impetus for hundreds of craftsmen to devote all their talents to cha-no-yu. Utensils were given by Hideyoshi as rewards for service; this kind of reward was politically more satisfying to a man like Hideyoshi, for these gifts involved no loss of land or of the power which accrued to those who controlled enormous areas and the people thereon. This practice raised the price of utensils to unparalleled heights and cultivated a respect for the utensils among the Japanese people, as illustrated in the events surrounding the battle of Hideyoshi against Mitsuhide, Nobunaga's assassin. As Hideyoshi attacked the castle of the Akechi family, the rebel leader stood in the castle tower and declared it was not his desire to see the family treasury of tea utensils destroyed in the conflict. So saying, he placed some sixty pieces in a cushioning brocade and lowered them to the attackers at the foot of the wall. By this action several rare utensils were saved, including the justly famous

"Chidori" incense burner. The "Chidori" was known in that time all over Japan. It had a fine glaze and excellent form and is the subject of many tales.

Hideyoshi himself inspired countless artists and craftsmen with commissions. He had an enormous Buddha erected in Kyoto, to rival the seated figure at Todai-ji in Nara. Of course, the Kyoto Buddha was made larger than the one in Nara. Hideyoshi's was 160 feet in height, contained within a 200-foot-high building at Hoko-ji. Hideyoshi was exasperated by the natural forces which seemed to oppose the Buddha he had made. Earthquake, lightning, and the like played havoc with the finished building and its contents. An aside to the enormous undertaking is the antipathy of Hideyoshi to Buddhism with the exception of the Zen sects. Contemporaries said that the final destruction of the Buddha by natural disaster was the Buddha's way of getting back at the "wicked" general. Again, what we witness in Hideyoshi's construction of the great Buddha is his public side, his boastful and powerful political expression for the masses of people.

There were always two sides to Hideyoshi's emotions, also. On one hand he could be uncommonly kind in pardoning major offenders in his realm, while on the other hand he took unnecessarily cruel positions in cases of minor offense. Yamagami Soji, a former pupil of Rikyu's, made a mistake while serving tea to the great general and was punished for confusing the informal with the insultingly casual service of cha-no-yu by having his nose cut off and being sent into permanent exile.

Hideyoshi and Rikyu

Imaginative, hard-working, gifted, and capricious, Hideyoshi must have appealed strongly to Rikyu, a man of no small achievement himself. Rikyu would not hesitate to spend a small fortune on a utensil he liked, as Hideyoshi took an almost childish delight in having a tearoom of gold. But both men were known to have used simple vessels, rough ware, when suited to the occasion. Both men were practical and direct. Their differences, as Komiya Toyotaka points out, were those of necessity. Hideyoshi was ruler of Japan. Rikyu was, no matter how highly regarded, a servant of the ruler. What made both men differ from prominent personalities of previous and of future eras was the remarkable freedom of mind that both evidenced.

Hideyoshi considered tea as very special. The *Matsuya Kaiki* (dating from 1533), the *Tennojiya Kaiki* (from 1548), and the *Tsuda Sokyu Kaiki* (1554 on) are accounts by chajin of tea meetings of their times. Hideyoshi plays a prominent part in many of them. One mention of Hideyoshi in 1581 lists the general as serving tea to Rikyu. At that time Nobunaga was still alive, and Hideyoshi's serving his master's tea master speaks well of the ability of the general. The utensils he used were fine, and he used them well. Hideyoshi, even then, was no mere imitator of others' rules and ways. He is known to have improvised where he thought appropriate. He used many of the same utensils again and again, not because he had to, but because he enjoyed what he was using. Rikyu must have found the independent qualities of Hideyoshi the chajin admirable.

As Hideyoshi assumed more and more power, he took Rikyu with him into battle. Notes, letters, diaries, and recorded conversations confirm their attachment for each other. Apparently he used Rikyu for business purposes, certain military matters (usually having to do with diplomatic stratagems), and matters of state. They surely met frequently. Rikyu could be most useful to the general in dealing with other generals who were being instructed in tea by the grand master, as he could communicate battle instructions through Rikyu's letters. Hideyoshi also placed the famous General Date Masamune (1565–1636) in Rikyu's charge, following Date's arrest for resisting Hideyoshi's unification plans. Fujikawa says in *Chanoyu and Hideyoshi* that Hideyoshi's forgiving the arrested general was probably the result of Rikyu's intervention on Date's behalf.

Hideyoshi sought out Rikyu, as Nobunaga had done before, not for his name or position, but because of his ability. He could accept Rikyu's own democratic leanings, making the tearoom a space for the meeting of all men. At the same moment he would cautiously strike down aspects of liberalism in his own government. He did much to encourage Neo-Confucianism in Japan, paving the way for the ruling Tokugawas of the next century and their severe controls on the population.

With Rikyu and Hideyoshi working together, tea reached a golden age. The sixteenth-century tea was golden in a literal and figurative sense. Hideyoshi had a golden *chashitsu* (tearoom) constructed. He showed the structure on many occasions to visitors, whose accounts indicate that they were suitably impressed. The only objects in the hut that were not made of gold were the linen cloth, the bamboo whisk, and the wooden ladle. All else—post, walls, ceiling, bowls—was gold. This rivals anything in the Japanese world of the time, and with this Hideyoshi rose to a new height of ostentation. He showed the room to the emperor and served tea to him in the yellow light; it must have been blinding. Yet this golden tea contrasts with other types of tea in which Hideyoshi was involved.

In 1583, Hideyoshi held a tea at Sakai, Rikyu's home town. Rikyu served the invited townsmen. That he was one of them contributed to the success of the event and of Hideyoshi's plan to secure merchants' backing for his ventures. Rikyu apparently was willing to accept this from Hideyoshi, as he was loyal to his ruler. On the other hand, Rikyu insisted that his kind of tea be served, and Hideyoshi in turn accepted this. He named as his favorite tea hut the one Rikyu built for him at Yamazaki (midway between Kyoto and Osaka), site of the great battle in which Akechi Mitsuhide was defeated. The hut is but two mats, plain in every feature. He stated that he felt most at ease in Rikyu's grass-hut-style setting, and it is the Tai-an hut at Yamazaki that is the outstanding example of it. Unpretentious, the small hut holds with comfort one or two guests at most. Again, at Jurakudai a small chashitsu of Rikyu's style was installed and Hideyoshi served tea there very often. This room passed to the Sen family of Kyoto, and a replica of it is still used. Rikyu was told he could use the room as often as he liked. Hideyoshi had several portable huts built. Carried into battle, these served to hold the tea meetings the general favored even in times of danger. On the battlefield he took tea according to the dictates of Rikyu—simple tea in the grass-hut style. This is expressed by Rikyu's poem: "A house is to keep out rain, / Food is to prevent hunger, / This is the Buddha's teaching / And the true spirit of cha-no-yu."

Of all the important moments of tea for Rikyu and Hideyoshi, the crowning moment was the "dai Kitano chakai" (Great Kitano Tea Meeting). Kitano was a pine grove in Kyoto. The area is overrun today with shrines, temples, shops, and houses; then it was a beautiful spot. We do not know which of the men first conceived the idea of staging a magnificent tea for everyone in Kyoto and surrounding areas in a single spot, but we can guess that it was Hideyoshi. This kind of gesture suited him, as he took delight in great affairs. Whoever thought of it, Rikyu surely planned the presentation, down to details. It remains a fantastic idea even to those accustomed to large affairs. Hideyoshi had posted invitations stating that everyone was welcome, even foreigners. He prohibited any display of wealth and called for economy and simplicity, whatever one's condition. In addition, he promised to display much of his vast collection for everyone to see. He asked anyone who so desired to come, without regard to rank, and even urged the serving of barley, if one could not afford tea. He stated that participants could wear whatever they pleased. The caution against luxury is noteworthy; it again reveals the Hideyoshi who did not depend on wealth in his tea.

In late 1587, some eight hundred tea huts of varying kinds were erected, with all manner of ingenious devices used to shade the setting. Many stories come out of the great meeting through letters and notes taken on the spot, but none are so informative of the nature of the event as those of Rikyu. They show that he was acutely conscious of being in charge and that he accepted the responsibility with willingness and eagerness. Chajin from Sakai, Nara, Kyoto, and distant places met in the fields at Kitano. It was like a county fair (on an aesthetic level) with all participants delighting in the rare scene. The similarity between Rikyu and Hideyoshi is nowhere more evident than in the surviving literature on the Kitano meeting, which was to have lasted ten days, but closed after a single glorious one on account of Hideyoshi's having to rush to the rescue of a general faced with rebellion. The contrast between the portable, spontaneous tea of many men in one place, on one occasion, and the strict formality of indoor tea must have been keenly in the minds of everyone attending. The great welling up of spirit among the participants was unprecedented in Japan to that time. It showed an abundance and a liveliness which indicate the excitement of the blossoming movement.

Almost all contemporary writers in English speak ill of the affair. Gouverneur Mosher in his book *Kyoto: A Contemplative Guide*—excellent as it is—does a gross injustice to the scene at Kitano by stating, "It was as if, by massive mockery, he [Hideyoshi] meant to drive this art [tea ceremony] right out of Japan." Mosher misinterprets the intention of the tea when he chides Hideyoshi for inviting the whole of Kyoto; for the fine art of refined men to be made available to an entire population, on a democratic basis and with no restrictions, was surely not a wanton act of destroying tea. It was the first time that the art was fully presented to every class of Japanese society, and it was in a spirit of free and spontaneous exuberance that the Kitano meeting was held. It symbolizes the enormous variety in tea which began at this time and spread all over Japan.

Other writers suggest that the Kitano tea was held by the shogun to secure, by trick, fine utensils which he desired. But in the first place Hideyoshi had a fantastic collection of his own and hardly needed more. In the second place, if he really intended to get certain utensils he could have found excuses for seizing them without such public display. In the third place, Hideyoshi, though receiving gifts on the occasion, did not collect the famous pieces displayed or used at Kitano. These facts lead us to a position quite contrary to the usual interpretation of the event. Political display and stunning show were almost always a part of Hideyoshi. We must recognize that he was a gregarious man given to gestures of kindness and sincerity as well as avarice and greed.

The Great Kitano Tea Meeting was the turning point of Rikyu's career. His letters of the time indicate how important he considered the event, and apparently he saw the affair as the opening of a new era in tea, art, and connoisseurship. Hideyoshi also saw the event as a turning point for himself, and perhaps by intention forever linked his own name with cha-no-yu.

Early works such as Walter Dening's *A New Life of Toyotomi Hideyoshi* pay very little attention to tea and the relationship of the proud general with the art. This is unfortunate, for by record we have a great quantity of information associating this major figure of the Momoyama period with chado. Dening's virtual ignoring of the relationship is perhaps due to his own reliance on the opinions and research of the English historian F. Brinkley. An appendix to the Dening work (written in 1888, but subsequently released in three different editions) cites the art of tea in most uncomplimentary terms. Dening concludes that chado is not likely to survive in go-ahead Japan. Since his 1888 statement, tea has grown to unparalleled heights of public participation and has achieved the very incorporation of all classes so eagerly sought by Rikyu. Brinkley criticizes chajin for their love of odd shapes in ceramics and chides them for lack of taste in art. What he means by taste is the brilliantly colored export pieces made by Japanese for shipment to European markets, and which tea masters shunned. The gross, overstated works had no place in tea and the stern rebuke of tea artists must have stung Brinkley as mere authoritarianism. At any rate, we can forgive the two writers for their treatment of tea; both lived in an era when Japanese Buddhists were called "pagans."

Rikyu was *mekiki,* connoisseur, of all Japanese arts for Hideyoshi and for the host of men who counted him master. He was easy in his authority, and perhaps the Kitano affair led to a position which otherwise might have escaped him. The position and the staging of the great affair thrust him into such conscious authority in the minds of his contemporaries that not long thereafter rumors began to circulate of his unwillingness to compromise, to receive advice, or to remain aloof from political involvement. As he was during his own time by various chajin, Rikyu has been accused by later historians of taking financial gain through his position as sado. Of course one must recognize that Rikyu received from Hideyoshi some three thousand *koku* for one year's service. (Approximately six thousand square feet of land would yield some ten koku of rice. Therefore, Rikyu's stipend equaled the income of a landowner possessing one million eight hundred thousand square feet of land.) This payment, judged considerable today, was a substantial fortune in his time and subjected Rikyu to the envy of less fortunate chajin. Rikyu's stipend amounted to more than most artistic officials received in later times, especially during middle and late Edo, when a tea master received an average of ten koku per year (cases are frequent of a master receiving only one koku for a year's service). The great stipend placed on Rikyu by Hideyoshi, together with Rikyu's own well-known collection of valuable utensils, permitted stories to circulate about the integrity of the sado. It may be that Rikyu did profit to some extent from the myriad transactions he effected for his students, but if this did occur, it is a blemish on his career and a serious contradiction of the ideals he taught. He had sufficient funds to carry on a life of considerable ease, but his own restraint would indicate a position vis-à-vis finance that was less important, not more. Rikyu did act as frequent go-between for Hideyoshi as the latter acquired more and more treasures.

A letter of Rikyu's of 1588 asks a prominent family to sell a scroll, tea caddy, and pot to Hideyoshi. The letter is somewhat threatening in tone and could leave Rikyu open to charges of bullying Hideyoshi's subjects. For his manner there can be little excuse except that Hideyoshi was an insistent man and meant to get his way, perhaps setting the tone of the exchange himself. At any rate, the letter—and there must have been others as well—was rightly resented by the recipient. We can sympathize with Rikyu in wanting to advance his art through the highest circles, but we can be critical if he abused others in attaining that end. The sharpness and fast dealing of various tea men of Momoyama is revealed in many records. Covetousness, avarice, greed, and desire for display were commonplace. The world of tea after Nobunaga was a world of collectors, good and bad, men of taste and those without, men of sincerity and of bad faith. All elements mixed at once, that is the excitement of Momoyama, a time of contrasts, most of which were lost forever when Rikyu died.

Rikyu and Zeami: *Wabi* and *Sabi*

Junzo Karaki, in his brilliant *Sen no Rikyu,* points out that the two peaks of Japanese culture are Rikyu and Zeami—Rikyu in founding the complete art of tea, Zeami as founder of the complete art of No. Karaki distinguishes between the two in their respective achievements of *wabi* and *sabi,* difficult aesthetic terms referring to specific aspects of Japanese art.

Wabi expresses the presence in a thing or setting of that which makes it harmonious with other things, a kind of ultimate naturalness. This poem by Basho is often quoted as an example of wabi: "On a withered branch, / a crow, in the autumnal evening." The scene evoked by this poem leads directly to similar experiences of the reader's. There is a sense of poverty in it, but not a poverty of which one is ashamed. The poet acknowledges an insufficiency in the poem, but he is satisfied with what is. It is enough, even in its insufficiency. Rikyu's wabi tea was based on this spirit: man cannot prolong a short life, nor can he dramatically enrich it with effort, for basic experience is beyond his control. To yield to this fact of existence is to confirm one's own naturalness, to achieve peace with what is at best a difficult situation—not to be ashamed, but to be aware of what men have to be humble about.

Sabi refers to that well out of which unique creations arise. Sabi is beyond any aspect of personal control; wabi can be created, or induced. Rikyu created a tea that was wabi; sabi tea could not be made to happen. In Rikyu's wabi tea we are induced to look within to see the short-lived snails we really are. He caused people to act. In Zeami's No an actor goes through successive stages until, without rationale, there emerges something greater than the combined limbs and efforts of the man on stage. Comparing them, the present Urasenke grand master said: "Wabi is going uphill, / Sabi is going down." That is, as good as any definition one is likely to get. Junzo Karaki states that Zeami, before his death in 1443, achieved the perfect state of sublime art, sabi. He further maintains that Rikyu achieved the state of wabi, but the implies that this is somehow less than sabi. In most instances of modern usage the two words are treated synonymously; "loneliness," "irregularity in form," "aloofness," "a vague sadness" are common descriptions. Older uses were more distinct, the terms being applied to different situations and states.

The man of wabi is one who is always prepared for a guest, who raises himself by awareness above the irritation of unexpected encounter. The wabi man is wakeful, watchful. Perhaps wabi exists only in opposition to something—the grass hut preferred to the golden palace. If the hut is preferred to the palace, there is some resistance implied in the man facing his situation.

The man of sabi senses no irritations, and resists nothing. When Zeami was exiled on the death of his patron, he did not resist, but went willingly into exile. In exile he continued to create, achieving the perfection of his art. It did not matter to him in what condition he found himself or where. Exile and resistance ceased to have meaning for him.

Rikyu resisted; his writings are filled with warnings to his disciples. He resisted movements that were contrary to his Way. He was concerned for his time, his place. Zeami was a man of no resistance, no hesitation, no friction. Rikyu met friction with a forceful mind, resisted with great ability, and struggled against contrary forces. Wabi spirit prepares for the guest known to come. Sabi spirit prepares with no thought whatever for a guest.

Picasso has said that he tried to do the least expected in his art. This idea was put forth by Zeami some five hundred years before. He instructed his actors to be especially brilliant when the audience was dull and listless, that they might suddenly be illuminated from the stage performance. When the audience was least attentive, the most was required. As Rikyu said:

"Show them a single morning-glory when they are expecting nothing."

The unexpected is always a slight deception. The more sophisticated the audience, the more subtle the deception, the more delighted the reaction. An obvious deception can be immediately detected by a good audience. An audience enjoys subtlety because it creates a spiritual tension. Zeami and Rikyu led their audiences to greater awareness by masterfully playing on the interests and abilities of the disciples who studied with them. Both masters taught that grace and beauty were not requisites of birth. Devotion to the task, sincerity, and constant practice were necessary before one could achieve greatness in art. These teachings were revolutionary in Japan, and they changed the Japanese art world.

Criticisms of Rikyu

Michelangelo was the object of much jealousy during his rich lifetime. He was required constantly to fight in defense of himself and his art. As a young man he completed the *Pietà* only to have his contemporaries praise the work but doubt that a man so young as he had done it. The distressed artist crept into the niche where the *Pietà* was displayed and chiseled a phrase on the sculpture indicating that he had made it.

Rikyu has suffered a similar fate in the writings of various Japanese. Some contend that Rikyu merely drew together the works of many people, calling the finished art form his own. The pettiness and jealousy that plague artists of great stature in every age also attacked Rikyu. Some chajin are said to have hated him for the complete hold he had on the world of tea during his lifetime. The gossip and slander about him may in the end have contributed to his death, but he does not appear to have suffered the paranoia of other artists who spent their lives in bitterness and insecurity. Until his death he remained a forceful personality with firm control over his faculties. Zeami and Rikyu were both subjected to unusual pressures, for they moved in the circles of power. They associated intimately with men who commanded life and death, and they risked all to establish their art in the highest circles of Japan. They were bound to suffer—Rikyu in being sentenced to death, Zeami in being forced into exile. Being artists, they were fiercely independent, an unhealthy attitude for those who serve the masters of state.

Rikyu did not have to live a wabi life, he elected to. Perhaps his cultural background led him to contrast the refined with the rough, the privileged with the insufficient. In his statements on wabi there is often a hint of longing for the days of palaces and leisure while accepting the grass hut. We sense a bit of the friction, the submerged conflict of the rich and the impoverished, in his writing. But Rikyu chose the way of the simple life—he knew the rub (it is the cotton that snags the silk).

The huts in which Rikyu served tea were shelters from the rain, quiet places where men of like mind could come out of the rain. The meals served to satisfy hunger, no more. But Rikyu was a man, his authority subject to the time in which he lived, and to the will of the ruler he served. There is no doubt Rikyu did contribute organization to some of Hideyoshi's outlandish schemes, gaudy displays, and the like. It is unthinkable that Rikyu did not share in the planning of some of the stupendous events of Hideyoshi's imagining. That the ideas of the two men clashed on many of the occasions is certain, but Hideyoshi was ruler, Rikyu servant. Even the most faithful of Rikyu followers accept the humanity of the man and the compromises he surely made because of Hideyoshi's ostentation. It is his profoundly human quality that is so admirable today. That he lived a long and extremely successful life as mentor to the powerful of his land, while changing the entire world of tea, is a human triumph. The world of gold that invaded his wabi tea from time to time was his failure. Obviously, he did not convince everyone all the time. He reminds us of Gandhi who, when told he was to be assassinated, said: "If I am killed with a gun, by one of my own brothers, then it is I who have failed him."

Soetsu Yanagi, noted for his writing on Japanese folk arts, takes Rikyu to task for being a politician, economist, connoisseur, and chajin at once. He says they are mutually exclusive. We may disagree with Yanagi's conclusion, but certainly Rikyu did play all these roles and more. Yanagi accuses Rikyu of catering to the tastes of the wealthy and the powerful, saying that Rikyu debased himself and his art in seeking the support of the powers of state. This criticism is petty and largely unsubstantiated. Too numerous are the cases in which Rikyu publicly took his wealthy patrons to task for their attitudes and practices. Better had Yanagi said that Rikyu risked his life and the destruction of his Way by daring to challenge the establishment. There is too much documentation of the Japanese lords and merchants seeking out master Rikyu for his instruction to put much value on Yamagi's accusation that Rikyu sought to establish himself with his disciples. If we may read between the lines of Yanagi's writing, we can assume that he is reacting to the excess of praise that has been heaped upon Rikyu, until the man has been beatified. If this is Yanagi's point, then he deserves some credit.

Rikyu, the Man and His Legacy

Many statements that have been credited to Rikyu, including some of the near-sacred *Namboroku,* a compilation of Rikyu's teachings by his assistant, Nambo Sokei, must be dismissed as attempts to bolster his reputation. The serious scholarship of men such as Tadachika Kuwata continues to cast doubt on certain aspects of what is currently said to be Rikyu's own teaching. The strong Neo-Confucian vocabulary of the *Namboroku* suggests that parts of it were written much later. What we do have as conclusive evidence of Rikyu's work are some extraordinary tea huts, especially the above-mentioned Tai-an; tea utensils used by him; and writings in his own hand. Adding the accounts on Rikyu of his contemporaries, we picture the man, his faults, and his teachings with some accuracy.

Among his own utensils, simple things were preferred. We find he was very fond of ready-mades, naturally formed objects. He used things found at hand. He did not rely on expensive imports, though he did have occasion to use them. His gardens were simple in design, small in size, flowerless. These things give us an outline of the master's beliefs, the manifestations of his practice. We cannot know for certain why he was forced to commit *seppuku* (ritual suicide by disembowelment). The details have been obscured by the centuries.

We are drawn to him partly because he remains something of a mystery, partly because we of the West have never had anyone quite like him. His inconsistencies are similar to those that afflict most of us. He embraced his time; he was committed. He lived in a gorgeous era of palaces and gold, yet he sought to interest men in the Way of the grass hut. The elegant Rikyu was a constant threat to the wabi tea master. The master Rikyu was a constant threat to the wabi tea master. The master Rikyu was a constant threat to the servant Rikyu. He lived in delicate balance. Hideyoshi often challenged him to see if the balance could be upset. Following the previously cited incident of the single morning-glory, thoroughly appreciated by Hideyoshi, the general presented Rikyu with a golden bowl, a bucket of water, and a very large branch of cherry blossoms, asking him to arrange the elements as a *tokonoma* (art alcove) decoration. Without hesitation, Rikyu poured the water into the bowl, shook the blossoms from the branch into the water, placed the bowl in the tokonoma, and served tea to the amazed general. The simplicity of the "arrangement," so swiftly executed, was perfect for the challenge. The naturalness of what Rikyu did appeals to wabi chajin.

Rikyu insisted that his students learn two poems: "Looking around, this autumn evening, / there are no flowers, no maple leaves, / at this hut by the sea," and "To one who looks forward to cherry blossoms, / how I wish I could show the grass amid the snow / of this mountain village." Rikyu said the first poem was recited by his teacher Jo-o as a perfect example of the spirit of wabi tea. It is by Lord Fujiwara Teika (1162–1240). Jo-o told Rikyu that the cherry blossoms and the maple leaves were comparable to the elaborate reception-room tea of the Ashikagas, and that the rough hut by the sea was the wabi tea he espoused. But, he said, one can only come to the hut after being saturated with the cherry-blossom and maple life, or the experience would have no meaning.

The second poem, by Fujiwara Ietaka (1158–1237), draws attention to the profound beauty of the everyday, the common, the anonymous. The snow of the poem contrasts beautifully with the cherry blossoms, the grass contrasts with the other wonders of spring. In both poems there is a sense of longing, an undercurrent of sadness. Truth, Rikyu wanted to say, arises without spectacle most often, it is found quite simply among natural, unforced, undramatic life.

Lord Teika was famous for his technical innovations, but his meanings are not always clear. The poem might be interpreted as meaning that though there are neither blossoms nor maples, the landscape by the sea is attractive, or that the landscape is so attractive that it needs neither blossoms nor maples. He seems to imply that beauty rises from the double negative. He gives us the flowers, only to say that they are not there, and that real beauty is the beauty of nothingness. The poem alludes to the book of "Akashi" in *The Tale of Genji,* especially to the passage: "The shades of the leaves that grow in no particular pattern are often far more graceful and elegant than the cherry blossoms in spring and the crimson maples, flourishing in the prime of autumn."

Other accounts tell of Rikyu's instructions to gardeners and carpenters. He would decide on a spot for an object and expect the thing to be exactly as he ordered. Invariably things were slightly shifted and invariably Rikyu would require his helpers to move them again and again until all elements were perfectly placed. He had the Zen insight to see that he was as much a part of nature as earth and grass. He never felt he manipulated a scene in an unnatural manner, any more than he felt himself manipulated by the sun beating on his forehead. He sought to be at peace among the elements and to allow what qualities he felt he possessed to react to his setting. The environments he created were not overworked and his hands were not everywhere evident in the handiwork.

Rikyu felt that the world of man is a world lacking in perfection. He saw in himself an insufficiency, and the code of his tea strongly suggests awareness of the insufficient. He saw time and man and object and flower and hut and friendship and tea and paper everywhere changing, everywhere endlessly going on, naturally, and his tea sought to bring that awareness to significant height. He did not have need of the elaborate tea of Yoshimasa and the teachers of the past. He wanted only to be at peace among the simplest pleasures. It was his feeling that too many trappings stood between man and natural life, and that in taking the old idea of a mountain village hut he was not playing at being poor. He was a man of means and power, but he saw all of it, all of the glory of those close to the mighty, as so much vanity. He understood it would have been a kind of vanity for him to be rid of everything and retreat in smug self-confidence to a reclusive death. That was not what he sought. He hoped to be able to develop his senses to such a point of awareness that anywhere and under any conditions harmony would prevail. His life was not one of denial but an embracing of the possibilities for oneness. One of the rules he is supposed to have left instructs us not to fret over utensils for serving tea but to use what we have, and serve the best we can. Nothing, he said, was entirely sufficient, least of all the man serving tea to his guests, so it is better not to bother too much about anything. We should just try to live the Way without taking ourselves too seriously and be aware of the pitfalls of vanity and useless clutter in our minds. It was good tea that held the interest of Rikyu, not senseless clatterings over utensils.

Karasu Mitsuhiro was a chajin living about the time of Rikyu and studying under one of Rikyu's disciples. His sayings on tea reflect something of Rikyu's attitude: "If you keep calm and untroubled by anything in creation, making your friends of the flowers of springtime and the tints of autumn, and taking a drop of liquor when you feel inclined, you need not regard the world as such a bad place. Just sit down quietly and arrange a flower or two, burn a stick of good incense and sip a cup of fine tea, with some old books as company; and if a congenial friend does happen to drop in, you may find it very comforting to chat with him about all sorts of people from ancient times to the present day. Some say this kind of life is best achieved by retiring to the hills, but however far away you live you will find no peace of mind if you still harbor egoistic thoughts of honor and profit. So you may just as well live right in the middle of the city without changing your style or choosing any particular locality. Monk as monk, layman as layman, the flowers are bright and the willow is green. Whether you are enlightened or not, if you regard the mind of all things as the same, things are quite well as they are."

Rikyu was willing to let life happen and to take his part in it, with all the awareness he could achieve. He did seek to teach what he believed, what he observed, what life taught him. He respected man. When he worked in his garden he sought to be one with the plants, trees, and stones he found. More than anything, it is the quality of respect for life that most distinguishes Rikyu's teaching: for guests, for seasons, for utensils, for the Way.

With Rikyu's sensitivity to showiness, the question invariably occurs: during his advisership to Hideyoshi how could Rikyu have permitted the golden tea which is in such contradiction to the Way? There is no document extant which truly associates Rikyu with the golden tearoom, but we must assume he did contribute to the situation. He was master of tea, sado. Perhaps Rikyu saw in all men a side which tended toward display and allowed for this in himself. We cannot know his reaction, but we can assume that for whatever protest he might have made, he must have participated to some extent in the incident. The Momoyama atmosphere was heady, and it is doubtful that even the restrained master could have survived it without being affected. He may not have taught or encouraged grandness, but it was part of the time. Maybe Rikyu, who had lived through the extreme rationing of tea under Nobunaga and had seen tea flourish as an immensely popular practice, saw a chance for tea to grow through this grandness. He may have seen the golden tea merely as a reaction to the austerity of Nobunaga. It is possible that Rikyu saw in the golden age of tea the possibility of reaching out to include everyone. Surely he must have recognized that if tea were to be for all men, great differences were unavoidable, and many methods would have to develop to suit diverse chajin. Is it possible that golden tea did not bother him at all? Is it just possible that his attitudes were sufficiently tolerant that even in his own "sacred" precinct he could allow the very antithesis of what he taught! If so, then surely he is the outstanding pragmatist of his time. If not, perhaps he paid with his life for his opposition.

Rikyu's Death

The reign of Rikyu as complete master of all things in tea was brief. If we date his emergence as complete authority from the Kitano affair in the fall of 1587, he remained in the position for but three years and a half. He died in February 1591, ordered to perform ritual seppuku by the direct order of Hideyoshi, his old and close friend, his student and ruler. It was a heavy price to pay for involvement.

The specific reason for the order is not known to us, but many stories purport to hold the truth. They are interesting in revealing what a variety of sources take to be reasonable explanations. In all probability none of them is true, and we have an unresolved mystery. All tea masters (and most laymen) have their favorite versions of the stories. They love to discuss, as people in the know, the termination of one of Japanese history's most enigmatic relationships.

The most popular account holds that Hideyoshi passed a young woman on returning from a cherry-blossom-viewing party in Kyoto, and, attracted by her, made inquiry. Upon being told she was Rikyu's daughter, he asked him for her. The master refused, commenting that her husband was recently deceased and that she was in no mood for affairs, not even with the general. In anger at the refusal, the story goes, Hideyoshi forced Rikyu to commit suicide. This version, though a good story, is hardly verifiable. It is interesting to note however, that Rikyu's daughter died, also a suicide, on January 18, 1591. Her father followed about five weeks later.

A second version has it that Rikyu was discovered dealing in utensils that were faked, which he vetted for profit. This version is patently false. Records exist of Rikyu having bought and later destroyed objects which proved to be forgeries, lest others be taken in as he had been. It is certainly difficult to accept any such version as fact in reading Rikyu's own writing. In surveying the attitudes of those who knew him, he appears to have been a man of outstanding courage and honesty, and one who continually received unsolicited praise of his integrity. Rikyu instilled sincerity in cha-no-yu. It seems unlikely that he would have thrown over all he had strived to achieve merely for gain in a personal fortune which, as previously mentioned, was already considerable. One aspect of Rikyu's integrity is revealed in the account of his suggesting to Hideyoshi the purchase of a particular vase at a very high price. The owner from whom Hideyoshi did acquire the piece was delighted with the master's recommendation, especially since he was a known enemy of Rikyu. To commemorate the occasion he sent Rikyu fine gifts and publicly acknowledged Rikyu as the instrument of his good fortune. With customary directness Rikyu returned the gifts with a note stating that he had recommended the purchase in light of the obvious quality of the piece in question and, having great differences with the former owner, did not intend to buy friendship by such means. He preferred to let things remain as they were before the exchange.

A third version of Rikyu's death stems from an actual historical fact: a wooden statue of Rikyu was carved and installed in the upper story of the famous Sammon gate at Daitoku-ji, Kyoto. This was a common practice, and various patrons received such honors from temples, but it does indeed seem brazen to allow it to be so prominently placed. This position would have meant that Hideyoshi and all the nobles would have had to walk under the statue of Rikyu when entering the temple, and this is said to have so angered Hideyoshi that he ordered Rikyu's suicide. When Rikyu was confronted with this evidence of his own conceit, he is said to have offered no defense of the action, while all the time knowing that some apology and act of contrition could have made amends. Hideyoshi was proud, Rikyu stubborn, and the possibility of conflict is evident when the sculpture question is raised in any version of Rikyu's death. Further credence is lent the story by the fact that Hideyoshi had the head cut from the statue and publicly displayed it on the day of Rikyu's death. The sculpture was subsequently thrown into the Kamo River in Kyoto, from which it was recovered by the Sen family. It now stands in the Urasenke shrine to Rikyu, the Rikyu-do.

Priest Kokei of Daitoku-ji plays an important role in this account, for he was the abbot of the famous temple at the time of the incident. He had long been a close friend of Rikyu. Incredibly, Kokei owed his position, and perhaps his very life, to Rikyu's having him pardoned for a minor offense some years before, which had so displeased Hideyoshi as to have resulted in Kokei's banishment. Kokei had come from Sakai to Kyoto in 1573. He was known as a friend of Rikyu and other chajin from the time of his residence in the port town. He had also been a close friend of Hideyoshi—he was the only priest among twenty-six guests served tea by Hideyoshi himself on one important occasion. He was exiled in 1588 by the general, and only after Rikyu made a bold statement of sympathy for him did Kokei receive a pardon.

Kokei returned to Kyoto in 1589, at which time Rikyu was completing a gift of the upper story of the famous gate. Rikyu's wealth was such that he could afford a magnificent gift, and the gate stands today as witness to his generosity—without the sculpture. Kokei owed much to Rikyu and, in a display of his affection and respect, he directed the statue to be executed and mounted. When word reached Hideyoshi of the events, it is possible that Rikyu so feared the quick wrath of Hideyoshi that he thought the temple might be destroyed. He remained silent, accepting blame for the act of his friend priest Kokei. If this is true, Rikyu's death was indeed as silly a case of mistaken revenge and innocent evil as is recorded. What a fate, to be brought down by one's own friends in their attempts to act on one's behalf. It is too absurd, and therefore perhaps true, that Rikyu permitted his own demise.

It does seem unreasonable that Hideyoshi could have been sufficiently aroused in anger over any of the events as to kill one of his closest and most respected friends, one with whom he had so successfully collaborated. A most ridiculous reason, advanced recently, is that Rikyu was caught by Hideyoshi in a plot to poison the general while serving tea. One wonders why Rikyu would have sought to destroy the very man upon whose patronage he depended. Many other considerations in their relationship lead us to dismiss this version as impossible. Rikyu was extremely powerful in Hideyoshi's circle, whether or not he elected to use the power politically. His disciples included not only the general, but Toyotomi Hidenaga (1541–91), Hideyoshi's brother, and nearly all important retainers and administrators of the regime. His authority in his field extended to the far reaches of Japan. Anywhere men met for tea they did so in the name of Sen no Rikyu. The devotion of these men, added to the obvious favoritism with which Hideyoshi treated the master, must have provoked some envy among the ones not so close to Hideyoshi. Some of their testimonies remain for us to read. The *Choandoki,* a collection of tea anecdotes written in 1640, says: "He was a good chajin of Sakai, but not well informed in worldly affairs and his acquaintances never recommended him. Whatever one could have said of him, he was not good looking and did not care whatever coarse words he used. People hated him." If nothing else, the description shows that some people didn't care at all for the master.

Hideyoshi became a changed man at the time of the death of his son and supposed heir, in 1591. When a second son was born late to him, he had already promised to leave his position to another relative. He changed his mind at the time and systematically opposed any threat to the young boy's right to inherit all of Japan. He became increasingly suspicious of those around him and many fell victim to these suspicions, reasonable or not. In this atmosphere it was difficult to live at close quarters with the powerful figure. Rikyu was constantly thrust into contact with the man. That the independent Rikyu dared to criticize Hideyoshi may have been accepted in spirit and humor at first, but later it became a dangerous practice. Adding to the little irritants which we might note as conceit, the relationship must have suffered over the years of association. Rikyu's friendship with many Christians also may have been suspect to the court of Hideyoshi supporters, but hardly reason for Rikyu to fall into complete disfavor.

The real reason behind Rikyu's death probably lies in the man himself. We can obtain evidence of his dissatisfaction, after years of fighting the world of ostentatious tea, at the very center of his power. His passionate resistance to any power which corrupted tea certainly did not earn him favor. The idea of grass-hut tea was truly his and he meant to implement it as the Way. Perhaps Hideyoshi came to resent the strictures of Rikyu's tea and the restraint put on himself. In any case, Rikyu saw life clearly and sensed his jeopardy in his years. On a winter day in 1589, two years before his death, Rikyu said to an associate: "The real Way of tea has degenerated in the hands of so many who seek to use it as a toy, a plaything of their prosperity. What we see now coming is a shallow tea, and if I live long, I alone will enjoy the tea of the grass hut, and no one will come to share it with me. How sad it is."

These words are not the spirited statements of a young man, vigorous in his belief and crusading in his teaching. They are the words of an old man, recognizing the cruel reality which touches those who outlive the revolutions they make and turn away from their former ideals. By 1589 his passion was spent. The old man was worn to the point where he willingly accepted death. When, in conflict, Hideyoshi's own wife and mother offered aid in getting Rikyu a pardon, he refused—surely an indication of his independence and of his unwillingness to rely on others to save him. More, the situation indicates Rikyu's readiness for his fate. When Hidenaga died, four days after Rikyu's daughter took her life, the critical loss of support no doubt hastened the inevitable.

On February 13 Rikyu was confined to his home in

Sakai by order. He remained there about ten days, eventually making his way back to Kyoto, where he stayed at Juko-in. Rikyu was not surprised by the order to commit seppuku, and even refused help offered by Oribe, a prize pupil and later sado. He also refused the aid of Sansai, another of his seven famous disciples. He entered the small tearoom of Juko-in and prepared for his last tea. He gave away some utensils to friends and students and then made tea for a few friends invited for the occasion. The calmness with which he performed all of this is documented. We can imagine his accepting the fate in a calm, Zen spirit. He served tea and wrote two poems in customary style, one Chinese and one Japanese. The Chinese: "Over seventy years of life, / What trouble and concern! / I welcome the sword which / Slays all Buddhas, all Dharmas!" And his Japanese verse: "The sword which has ever been / close at hand, now I throw / into the sky." He wrote on the lid of the box containing the tea caddy which he had used for this last tea: "That which I always dreamed: / to be beyond this bothersome life, / in the true reality."

Rikyu was seventy years old. On the twenty-eighth of every month a service is held in Kyoto commemorating his death, and on the twenty-eighth of February, Juko-in holds a sutra reading with the grand master offering a ritual tea to the spirit of the founder of the Way of Tea. Following the service, tea is held inside the room Rikyu supposedly last used. His grave lies a few yards from the room, beside one of the most beautiful gardens of Kyoto.

Rikyu's property was seized. His family went into hiding, but Hideyoshi later restored funds and treasures to the survivors. Rikyu had been born into a chaotic time and, by his genius, rose to unequaled authority in tea—a position no one has held since his death. Through all schools of tea one learns something of his art. Even among those who least follow his teaching in their own practice, the spirit of Rikyu is respected. All chajin consider him their *chasei,* tea saint. Anything which can be claimed to have been his, approved by him for use, or influenced by his artistry has value beyond ordinary utensils. He was unique, and his death must have been something of a mystery to the men of his time, as it is to us.

Rikyu was inevitable in tea. There had to arise in his time a complete master who could finish the work of development spread over many centuries. Rikyu awakened in all sincere chajin a sparkling capacity to live in the moment through tea. That he died for some infraction of his conduct, or for no reason at all, is simply part of the story, part of the Way he brilliantly taught. He made his life of a very fragile thing: a cup of tea. When he was old and weakened by the pitch of chaotic life, he died for the same fragility. He had hung in the tokonoma an old verse dealing with the evanescence of things. Surely his life and death fit this idea perfectly.

Rikyu brought the qualities of his mind to work in tea but, of equal importance, he brought the genius of his fellowship for all men into the tearoom, establishing for all time an attitude in tea ceremony which does not allow for class distinctions. Though this innovation did not always withstand the fortunes of time, it has continued as a basic force of wabi tea until the present day. Wherever wabi tea is served there can be no distinction among men, according to class. All are equal in the room.

4. The Later Years

After Rikyu

Hideyoshi continued to serve Rikyu-style tea. He constantly referred to his master's teachings in his recorded attitudes on flower arrangement for tea and on architectural construction for tea ceremony. It is said he expressed grief at the death of his beloved tea master.

Hideyoshi had exhibited Rikyu. A special honor for a guest would have been to have Rikyu serve him tea personally. Rikyu had been present and in charge of the great tea held at Daitoku-ji and again was master when Hideyoshi presented tea for Kamiya Sotan, a very wealthy merchant of Hakata, a port town in northern Kyushu. When Sotan visited Hideyoshi at Osaka Castle he recorded detailed impressions of tea events in a diary begun in November 1586. He describes the scene and comments, with what modesty he has, on the honors heaped on him by Hideyoshi. He had what is described as a beautiful tea from Rikyu's own hands, and was allowed to examine all the utensils. While he was taking this tea, Hideyoshi's men were moving toward Sotan's land, attacking a Kyushu lord. Hideyoshi saw that the wealth of Sotan would provide excellent backing for his exploits, and he flattered the merchant into compliance.

Hideyoshi used tea but loved it. He served excellently, and various diary authors express their surprise at his skillful performance of tea. He was also adept in tea flower arrangement, *chabana*. This delicate art consists of placing one or two flowers in a small container and presenting them in as natural a way as possible. Sotan records that Hideyoshi achieved perfection in this. He records, in *Sotan Nikki,* that he visited Hideyoshi for tea of a morning about four o'clock and found him busily engaged in all preparations with Rikyu at his side. The tea of the occasion was in a two-mat room in the mountain village *(yamazato)* style.

Hideyoshi was up at four in the morning to present tea to a merchant in a room barely six feet square. To all of the accounts that picture Hideyoshi as insincere in his tea, this and many similar occasions afford direct contradiction. If Hideyoshi meant merely to flatter Sotan and other guests, or merely to use tea for political devices, he could have found an easier way to do it, a more comfortable hour for serving, no part in the preparations himself. But he rose and worked on many occasions of the same nature—serving tea with his own hand, continually receiving tea instruction from the master. Hideyoshi also prepared and arranged the meals he served his guests. He was deeply involved in Rikyu's tea and meant to master the art for his own pleasure. Had he not been the ruler of Japan, he could well have been an outstanding master of tea. He had the persistence and love for the art which come only from a sincere interest. To those who decry Hideyoshi's nature of display, we show the two-mat, simple tea he often practiced. Each of us has a Christmas-tree side, and Hideyoshi enjoyed his Great Kitano Tea Meeting and his golden tea service, but he was sincerely a man of the tea which Rikyu taught.

These lines Hideyoshi wrote and gave to Rikyu as an expression of his feelings about tea: "If the water of our tea / Is drawn from the depths of mind / Then we have true cha-no-yu." Even in his cruelty and crudity, even accounting for the evil that was part of him, this poem is a sensitive expression of the wabi idea. Nobunaga too, for all his interest in Rikyu, would never have put up with so much austerity at the hands of his sado. Hideyoshi enjoyed meeting in the salt huts by the shore and often praised the simple miscanthus-thatched chashitsu. He liked Rikyu's son Doan. He took tea by Doan's hand and praised the wabi spirit of its service. The ostentatious displays of Hideyoshi in tea are few compared to records of his wabi tea, but of course the famous teas are the bigger ones and he is most noted for them. He could be a man of great restraint and taste. No one could read Mrs. Fujikawa's account of the records of Hideyoshi's tea (*Chanoyu and Hideyoshi*) and leave with an impression other than that he was so sincere as a man of wabi tea that he forbade anyone to serve other kinds; only a man of Hideyoshi's power and gall could have done that!

Oribe, Rikyu's Successor

Rikyu had turned to one man following the Great Kitano Tea Meeting and thereafter constantly referred to him as a great spirit in tea. The man was Furuta Oribe (1544–1615). It is curious to consider the relationship of the two men. Their personalities as expressed by those things which they left us indicate great differences, something like the relationship of Hideyoshi and Rikyu, with respect to Hideyoshi's golden tea. Oribe was an early favorite of his teacher—that much is certain from letters and comments of their contemporaries. When Rikyu was asked once who would be his successor, he responded: "Oribe!" This comment is strange, for we know that Rikyu's own son was a gifted and famous chajin in his own right. In fact, Fujikawa states that he was more a wabi tea man than his illustrious father. However, Rikyu seemed to believe that his son Doan did not have the personality to serve everyone with equal taste. He did believe Oribe had these qualities. Their relationship was so close that Oribe, together with Hosokawa Sansai, another chajin, were the only men who went to Rikyu on the occasion of his brief exile, before he returned to commit suicide in Kyoto. Oribe was highly placed in Hideyoshi's court and acted for the general as an important commander, but we have evidence to the effect that Oribe was inept as a soldier.

We read that after the Kitano affair Rikyu turned more and more to Oribe for help. In 1590, Rikyu wrote to Oribe from a battlefield, "I have never felt more comfortable among the people of the world which you now inhabit, and here [on the battlefield] my only comfort is killing flies—and if I did not have such tricky business to do I should perhaps be on the battleground myself." Oribe, a soldier from the start, responded to Rikyu's wit with similar examples of his own. He was a brash man and a little like Hideyoshi in his impetuosity and proud manner. After Rikyu's death he in no way followed wabi tea but turned his considerable energy to the grand tea of lords. He left an enormous influence on tea utensils and architecture, reflecting his taste—or lack of taste. He inherited a tradition from Rikyu, but attempted to create his own, glamorous way. The difference between his tea and Rikyu's is that Oribe's was static in its offering, heavily weighed down with style. Rikyu did not stick to imported wares but sought to use Japan's Bizen, Ise, and Raku pottery. Oribe was the same in this respect. He created a series of important styles for his school, and they remain significant contributions to Japanese ceramic art. He was fond of eccentric shapes in tea bowls, water jars, and rooms. When Rikyu had used a straight post for the tokonoma, Oribe introduced dramatic curves to augment the arrangement. The effect is not unpleasant, as it relieves the austere straightness of Rikyu's structure. In the end, however, his tea is playful, and a whole school of "toy tea" descends from this man. Many tea men will say that tea is no more than an amusement, and that is the sum of Oribe's school, but it would be a mistake to include this as part of the Way of Tea as founded by Rikyu. If Rikyu had lived on to witness Oribe's effect on tea, he would have had much more cause for complaint than at the time of his death. A modern observer of tea, Soetsu Yanagi, has this to say: "The true chajin is one who has a deep relationship with common people. The Way of Tea is the way of salvation through beauty. Hence the chajin must make a paragon of himself so as to preach laws like a religious man. He must have a profound love for beauty, high discernment of truth, and deep experience in practice. So far as cha-no-yu is a Way, spiritual discipline should come first. An old saying is: 'To learn tea is to learn Buddhism.' The saying is true, for chado is one of the Eastern Ways that are completely Buddhist in basis. Chado is in fact a Buddhist's Way in the country of beauty; for this reason it embraces discipline—it is something more than merely pleasant." Oribe's tea was to a large extent the antithesis of what Yanagi says. He passed on his instruction to Kobori Enshu after learning tea from his father and from Rikyu. Perhaps Oribe merely elected to follow the inclination of his time when he turned away from the austere methods of his master.

As a general too, this man was not especially appreciated by his superiors. On one occasion he was visiting the front and noticed bamboo battlements being constructed. He made his way over to them hoping to fashion tea scoops from some of the smaller pieces, but as he reached out to touch the bamboo a sniper wounded him in the finger. Visiting Tokugawa Ieyasu later, he announced that he had been wounded in the service of his lord. Ieyasu, knowing the full tale, replied in despair, "Oribe is the kind of man who will die from a fishbone stuck in his throat." The remark was greatly resented by Oribe and later he plotted, in a tearoom, to overthrow Ieyasu. The Tokugawa forces learned of the plot and permitted Oribe to commit ritual suicide.

Oribe is said to have begun the practice of cutting up fine pieces of old damask to make *kofukusa,* small cloths for tea. Oribe would cut valuable and beautiful pieces into patches and make new squares using several different patterns. In doing this he ruined sections of exquisite cloth. Sensitive tea men of the time predicted Oribe's death would result from violence to beauty.

Enshu and His Influence

Oribe was replaced in the highest circles of Japanese tea by Kobori Enshu, who died in 1647 after establishing a style of tea close to Oribe's in grandness. Enshu was aristocratic and his tearooms are all of a highly refined character, reflecting their designer's excellent taste, the Mittan tearoom of the Ryoko-in, a Daitoku-ji subtemple, being the outstanding example. The room known as Bosen at Koho-an, also a subtemple of Daitoku-ji, is certainly beautiful, but it is technically a reconstruction by a later, very brilliant tea man, Matsudaira Fumai. Enshu taught the Tokugawa shogun Iemitsu his Way of Tea and the style became highly popular for a while, enjoying Tokugawa support.

Many of Enshu's contemporaries praised him as being greater than Rikyu, but he rejected their praise, stating that if Rikyu were described as heaven, he himself would be mud. Rikyu had maintained an independence which got him into trouble; Enshu never remained so aloof, freely participating with the nobles in their sumptuous teas. He said that when anyone visited Rikyu, the great master would express an honest opinion of the worth and character of displayed vessels, but that he, Enshu, always managed to say what the visitor wanted to hear, rather than lose favor or offend the guest. He added that Rikyu was the complete master and that wabi tea was the true tea. The modesty of Enshu and his exceptional ability make him interesting to us, for although he held a significant position with the Tokugawa establishment and affected the arts after Rikyu—as much as Rikyu had during his own lifetime—he remained disappointed with own style. His writing indicates that he longed for Rikyu's wabi spirit, but went on his own path—that is, with *daimyo cha,* the tea of the lords. He did not attempt to change them but to serve them. He survived his teacher Oribe by thirty-three years, making no mistakes in his dealings with Iemitsu. He enjoyed great respect among his contemporaries.

Today in Kyoto many temples boast "Enshu" gardens—the most famous being the fine Nanzen-ji "Leaping Tiger" arrangement. However, few records exist to prove his hand in most of the gardens attributed to him, a singular exception being the garden of Konchi-in, a subtemple of Nanzen-ji. His calligraphy, architecture, and gardens place him among the finest artists of Japan's history. Along with Koetsu and others, he was a most versatile master.

Tokugawa Rule

Furuta Oribe, Kobori Enshu, Honami Koetsu, Sen no Sotan, Katagiri Sekishu, Matsudaira Fumai, Hosokawa Sansai, Kanamori Sowa, and Yamada Sohen were among the most important chajin after Rikyu. Their careers in tea coincided with the Tokugawa rule, Japan's period of isolation. Each added to the art of tea, and all left important contributions. It is significant that all but one were men of daimyo cha—Sen no Sotan being the exception. He was the constant wabi chajin.

The establishment of a kind of feudalism as a firm and concrete governing system by the Tokugawa family meant that the status quo was to be maintained at all times. Any attempt to introduce levelers in the class society were put down. Everyone's place in society was firmly fixed and regulated by the edicts of the shogun. Hideyoshi had begun the process by confiscating arms, and by placing everyone in fixed classes. It is an irony of politics that Hideyoshi, an exceptional case of a Japanese ruler rising from relatively humble beginnings, should have been the first instrument of a policy which forbade the rise of a humble man to power. Hideyoshi, of course, instituted his policy to insure the continuation of his own house.

Tokugawa Ieyasu took a low posture in dealing with Hideyoshi, staying clear of involvements that would bring him into direct conflict with the ruler. He was Hideyoshi's ally, as he had been with Nobunaga, a powerful man with a large following. Crafty, able, and with complete confidence in himself, he lay back as Hideyoshi consolidated his own power. He waited for his chance to rule. It came in 1598 when Hideyoshi died, leaving as heir a son who was not sufficiently powerful to command the obedience of the lords. As it turned out, the best preparation Hideyoshi made for assuring the perpetuation of the Toyotomi family name was the construction of the mighty Osaka Castle. This unrivaled fortress, some eight miles in circumference, was protected with double moats, double entrances, and high walls soundly engineered. Ieyasu tried to assault the castle with a force in excess of one hundred thousand men. The assault failed, due largely to the superior protective devices inherent in the castle architecture. Ieyasu, seeing he would never crack the defenses, called for a treaty with the Toyotomi family. The agreement was to have been that the assault on the fort would be stopped if certain moats and defenses were filled in. Before the Toyotomis realized what had happened, Ieyasu filled in a far greater portion of the defenses than had been agreed to, making the fort's assault an easier affair. The castle was stormed and all the family of Hideyoshi met death. The Tokugawas were entrenched in power.

Ieyasu thereafter was primarily concerned with safeguarding his family's power. The laws he passed were aimed at the perpetuation of Tokugawa rule. He allowed certain lords to remain fairly autonomous within their own fields, but censors were sent into their domains to insure that hostile acts were not being plotted and that nothing contrary to Tokugawa rule was established. Laws therefore gradually came to be standardized throughout Japan, based on the Edo (present Tokyo) government of Ieyasu. As George Sansom points out in *Japan: A Short Cultural History*, the laws of Ieyasu were "minatory and repressive." They were the expression of a dominant lord in a state of war. It was military law that was established, though the times thereafter were peaceful. Ieyasu ordered the lords to sign a pact supporting his government. This pact had great effect among the honorable warriors and lords, for they would not go against it once they had signed, at risk of being discredited in the eyes of the people, fellow lords, and the protective government in Edo. Loyalty was defined as the principal virtue of the people in their relations with superiors and subordinates. Everything in the life of a Japanese was seen to be an aspect of loyalty, even filial piety. The government issued admonitions urging subjects to be faithful, loyal, and content. In the later periods of Tokugawa rule, crimes were punishable according to the standing of the guilty party. Samurai might be accused of "mistaken judgment," while commoners, for the same offense, might be judged guilty of "criminal action." The position of the soldier was extremely important. Under these conditions it is easy to see that the Way of Tea as practiced by the more democratic chajin would survive only with difficulty.

A tremendous burden was placed upon the farmers, though they were ranked higher than merchants and craftsmen. They produced rice for the soldiers, their superiors, but were not allowed to eat it themselves, being forced to make do with less elegant fare. One Tokugawa edict forbade farmers to drink tea or use tobacco. As the mercantile interest replaced the agricultural in importance, the merchants took advantage of the situation in manipulating the samurai and others. Osaka and Sakai were great centers of commerce during this period, with Edo overtaking and surpassing both in the nineteenth century. Edo became Tokyo and eventually came to be the largest city in the world, as Kyoto had been earlier.

The merchants were urged by the government not to be excessive in matters of dress and entertainment. These admonitions had little effect; the luxury of the merchants was much too old a tradition to fall before the ethical restraints of the Tokugawa government. When edicts were passed suppressing the outward display of wealth, merchants would wear plain cloth outer garments, but with linings of finest silk, meeting the letter of the law, and reflecting a bit of the ancient Japanese idea of exquisite restraint. The situation is very much like recent men's fashions in America, where custom puts restraints on a man's wearing furs. An innocent-appearing raincoat for a gentleman may cost thousands of dollars, and its value go undetected if one does not see the extraordinary sable lining.

In time, the fortunes of the samurai declined. They came to depend upon the wealth of the merchants, the townspeople. As their dependence grew, they freely mingled with the townsmen until by the nineteenth century their objects of desire, customs, and manners were indistinguishable from those of people who had been their inferiors.

Changes in Tea

Sansom, in the above-mentioned work, suggests that No entertainment disappeared as a dominating element of court and government because of the teachings of the Confucianist adviser Arai Hakuseki, who argued that No, long a preoccupation at court, had too strong a hold on the government bureaucracy and should be replaced with more ancient forms of music and dance. This was done after 1711 and No died as an upper-class amusement, surviving only through amateur efforts of commoners. Tea ceremony, he says, suffered a similar fate, being too refined for the robust soldiers and townsmen, too Buddhist for the government. Buddhism had gone into a steep decline following the assaults upon the various sects by Nobunaga and Hideyoshi. To state unequivocally that No and tea, sharing a common heritage, died in this period of peace, however, is overstating the nature of the decline. Crafts associated with tea were thriving at the time; masters were busy giving their lessons; chashitsu in great numbers were constructed, many of which survive. Much of the artistic work of the period was gaudy and ostentatious, reflecting the townsmen's wealth and attitude. However, this is the era of some of Japan's greatest artists: Koetsu, Enshu, Sotatsu, Korin, Kenzan, and others working in crafts. The long period of peace gave expression to the pent-up restraint of the people, who for centuries had been continuously warring. Small, highly portable articles of great value were elaborately decorated by master craftsmen, covered with rich incrustations of fine metals and materials. When money abounded, demand was great for exquisite articles, and they were produced in profusion.

Against this outpouring of richness the tea of Rikyu did not long hold sway. The finest era of tea had passed. The liberal spirit of Rikyu in matters of who should serve tea and the manner of their service was replaced by an extremely unrestrained decoration of utensils and extremely constrained manner of service. Discrimination focused on who should serve and to whom, not on utensils and manner of service. The liberalism of Rikyu was anathema to the Tokugawas.

An important change took place among the schools of tea and in their manner of gaining financial support. The Sen family no longer enjoyed unlimited support from the powerful lords. The institution of the sado, retained in name only, no longer assured family fortunes. Rikyu's stipend of three thousand koku a year was never given to family members. The sado served only to instruct the shogun in the formalism of tea, somewhat altered by the edicts of the Tokugawas. Extremely rigid rules of conduct were enforced upon all chajin, and they carefully adhered to these.

Tea masters were chosen because they were gentlemen descended from the nobles of the past. In Rikyu's age a man had usually been selected for his ability. With the coming of the Tokugawas there emerged the dominant idea that one was qualified because of his class. Katagiri Sekishu (1605–73), an extraordinary nobleman of fine taste, drew up a list of three hundred items relating to tea. This codified lords' tea. One treated guests according to their social standing and everything met the rigid standards of the Tokugawas. Tadachika Kuwata maintains that had tea not changed to the new standards of Confucianist thought, it would have died early under the Tokugawas, and that the new establishment in tea merely represented the ability of tea men to fit their times. In this we regretfully agree; tea was on a track from which it is only now being rescued, one of endless formality and distinction that hardly suits the creative spirit which it can be at its best.

The change from Buddhist to Confucian tea was effected by early Tokugawa. Teahouses built in the acceptable style and maintained according to Tokugawa etiquette became standard accouterment of the princely estates of Japan. As Hosokawa Sansai writes, "A good tea-lover means one who makes tea after he has secured armor, houses, and servants for his family, according to his rank." He meant that the gentleman ought to turn to tea for a complete life after he has established a secure social position. This is a far cry from Rikyu's simplicity and the spirituality of wabi tea.

Sekishu's writings are important for understanding the times. He maintains that among various tea men were some who claimed to be of the wabi spirit, but as they were nobles and wealthy, they should not pretend that they lack the means of a gentleman's life. Rather, he felt they should serve according to their rank. This was the ideal of Tokugawa tea. Sekishu represents the times aptly with his writing and tea performance. The order must be preserved and one should not pretend that he is of lower status than his position. In other words, wabi tea is out.

The foremost practitioner of this tea was the great lord of the town of Matsue, Matsudaira Fumai. He was licensed to perform tea when he was only twenty by the Sekishu-ryu Issa-ha (Sekishu school, Issa branch). Fumai studied Zen under Daiten and wrote *Mudagoto* (Idle Talk), a minor tea-theory masterpiece, when he was very young. He wrote about tea in terms of ruling a domain. He believed it would benefit the nation if each person fulfilled his position by being equipped through the study of tea. His area was peaceful and prosperous, he said, by virtue of his own tea spirit.

Fujiwara Sogen, disciple of Sekishu, mused that anyone who did a "good job" was a true tea man. We can sense the change of tea in Sogen's time from Rikyu's. The good job done by the tea men of the Edo period was not because of their pay. Kuwata points out that in the period under question a great lord's sado might get three hundred koku at most, and many of the lesser lords' tea men were paid much less. The average was about ten koku. One sado existed on one koku, according to Kuwata's research. Times had changed. The tea men had to look after their own welfare thereafter, and logically they turned to the men who had money. The townspeople, who were low on the social scale, became increasingly wealthy.

Among these people the schools of tea from the Sen family found their support and financial security.

Commoners' Tea and the Senke Schools

The close attention that the Senke (Sen family) schools had to pay to the townspeople led to the reestablishment of a popular, democratic tea. *Chonin cha* (commoners' tea), which alone maintained a semblance of the Rikyu spirit of wabi tea, continues in the Sen schools because Rikyu's immediate descendants were independent of the great lords and the Tokugawa family. Although Rikyu was posthumously pardoned by the government and his treasures were returned to his family, his son and grandson did not attempt to reestablish a relationship with the government. Rikyu had been stung by being too close to government. Shoan, the second son, and Shoan's son, the great Sotan, both kept apart from government but for rare cases of casual relationships with two of the more powerful families.

Sen no Sotan had three sons among whom he divided his houses and treasury: the eldest son, Soshu, founded the Mushanokojisenke school; the younger, Sosa, founded Omotesenke and was given the front part of the Sen property; while the third to inherit and found a school was Soshitsu. He received the back part of the family property and named his school Urasenke. Sotan retired to live with the youngest son. Aside from these sons, there was actually a fourth son, Sotetsu, who lived in north Kyoto at Shoden-ji. He died after having spent most of his life feuding with his father. There were two important disciples of Sotan: Yamada Sohen, whose splendid chashitsu can be seen in Kamakura, to which place it was recently moved from Kyoto; and Fujiwara Yoken. Both maintained distance from the government, having only minor relationships with officials. All these five tea masters depended on the wealth of Kyoto and Osaka, and from this townsmen's tea sprang a system of support based on respect for the traditions of the house of Sen.

Sotan was perhaps not a blood relative of Rikyu, because Rikyu had two wives and some suppose that Sotan was the second wife's son by previous marriage. Whatever the case, he was a wabi tea man in Rikyu's spirit. During his life he was known as "Beggar Sotan" because of his retiring life and the fact that he did not care for display and was not interested in impressing others with dress or rare possessions. He had lived in a temple at the time of Rikyu's death and was well liked by his colleagues. He is responsible for the reestablishment of the Sen family's fortunes through his own abilities as a chajin. When Sotan took over the house from the retired Shoan, Oribe was the center of attention in tea, the family of Sen being left to itself.

Sotan decided to protect wabi tea no matter how poor he might become in the process. His rooms at Urasenke are among the finest examples of wabi architecture. The Yu-in of Sotan is a plain example of a wabi hut without pretension. His chado depended on Zen and little else except the anecdotes of the masters of the past. Snow, the moon on a clear night—these were his teachers, and he professed a spirit called "shaded windows," no display of the bright or brilliant.

He was a close friend of the artist Honami Koetsu (1558–1637) and they shared a common tea. He and Koetsu had an extreme distaste for fancy tea and even went so far as to pretend illness when invited to share tea with a daimyo. Sotan hated pretension and was always careful that his designs did not reflect the daimyo spirit. His tea scoop design has a chip removed from the upper left side. He arrived at the design when he found that his scoops were tending to take that shape from constant use: the scoop scraped against the ceramic wall of the caddy with every drawing of tea from the vessel. This simple effect is characteristic of Sotan and is enough to sum up his attitudes.

His difference with Koetsu was one of religion, with Sotan strictly maintaining the Way, while Koetsu turned to a more popular form of Buddhism. Thus, Koetsu maintained a closer relation (in this respect) with the people than did the strictly trained Zenist Sotan.

When Sotan retired, Soshu was forty-eight, Sosa twenty-four, Soshitsu twenty-one. The Soshu house was some distance removed from Sotan's residence, but Sosa's house was merely the front section of the Sen dwellings. Soshitsu attended his father in the building in the back area of the property. Sotan lived first in the fine Kanun-tei, a shoin-style room containing exquisitely painted screens by Kano Tanyu (1602–74), a close friend. Kano Tanyu had seen the empty screens when the room was newly built and though barely out of his teens wanted to paint them for Sotan, who would hear none of it. Secretly he came to the house and stole into the room with his ink and brushes. He furiously daubed the screens with a scene of eight hermits. Nearing completion, he heard Sotan coming into the house and hurriedly finished the sketches. His haste was so great that he painted one of the figures with a left thumb on the right-hand side—a discovery made by the surprised Sotan. The "mistake" appealed to Sotan's wabi spirit, as it might to our own, and the screens are carefully preserved in the room today. On another occasion Tanyu was said to have been asked to paint a set of screens for a wealthy lord. He gladly accepted the commission and arrived at the scene carrying horseshoes, ink, and brushes. He dipped the horseshoes in ink and walked them across the panels, seemingly at random. The daimyo, seeing the process, complained that he had hired an idiot, and a sloppy one at that. Tanyu continued, but now with his brush, and made a fantastic scene of flowers and trees from the happenings of horseshoes, receiving the admiration, thanks, and apology of the lord. Like Jackson Pollock, he was not afraid to go further than a brush would take him.

The Kanun-tei is a room of eight mats, larger than Sotan found comfortable. He constructed an ideal four-and-a-half-mat room which he named Yu-in (further retirement). After that he lived there the rest of his life. In 1648 he constructed a one-and-a-half-mat tearoom and invited a friend who was a priest to join him for tea. The priest was late and Sotan, in anger, left word that the friend should return for his tea another day. When the priest finally arrived he was given the message and, taking up a brush, he wrote on the wall of the small room: "A lazy priest like myself / Can never be sure of tomorrow." Sotan immediately named the hut Konnichi-an (today hut). It is still used at Soshitsu's house, and the name of the small hut is synonymous with Urasenke—just as the famous Rikyu hut Fushin-an is used to indicate Sosa's school and house.

The *iemoto* system became the popular method of maintaining commoners' tea. The iemoto was grand master of a school of tea, No, flower arrangement, or some other Japanese art—and without his certification no one was supposed to perform the art. In tea, only the grand masters gave permits for teachers and students, in accordance with the teachings of Rikyu. In No, dance, certain schools of music, and tea the system still prevails today. It was used to preserve and maintain the schools and their methods of training. The Senke schools have come to cover the length of Japan through the tremendous patronage of the people who study under their system. The Sekishu school continued for some time, serving members of the court and the noble families. The Enshu school also served in the same capacity, but neither of these schools had a broad base of support, their clientele being strictly limited. The commoners' tea had no barrier by birth, so the Sen schools flourished. Local teachers were go-betweens in the tradition, joining the townsmen to the iemoto by means of a license from the grand master.

The institution of *hakogaki,* signing of utensil boxes that are for holding treasures, as well as the custom of an iemoto's naming various utensils became strong at this time, providing another source of income for the houses. Today a vessel signed by a prominent grand master is worth considerably more than a nearly identical piece not signed. A tea bowl whose box is signed by an important master, such as Gengensai, the eleventh Urasenke grand master, is a possession of great value because he was known to be a man of excellent taste, and because he signed only that which really pleased him. Any utensil can be signed, from screens that rest beside the portable brazier to bamboo tea scoops. The signing is usually done in a red lacquer on the box for the object, sometimes on the object itself. It is a dangerous practice unless the masters put their names only to really fine works that reflect their own taste—judging from some works that have been signed, masters have frequently lapsed in this.

The iemoto system of judging works of art has had great influence on craftsmen since the Edo period. Every craftsman who makes tea utensils of course hopes that they will be used. A sure way to guarantee the popularity of a new piece or design is to have it approved by signature of the reigning iemoto of the craftsman's school. The power of the iemoto among the crafts has been enormous, for they have been directing the progress of these arts since Rikyu first helped establish the Raku kiln of his friend Chojiro in Kyoto. One can visit some of the craft institutions and see evidence of the contemporary iemoto's favors. One pottery not far from Kyoto recently built a teahouse, but in fear of offending any of the iemoto, the room is a mixture of styles, a complex and unbecoming place for tea—that is, one part Urasenke, one part Omotesenke, and others.

When iemoto are men of taste and ability, the results in craft have reflected to the good of all concerned. Much of what we can appreciate among Japanese crafts stems from the balance of fine mind and excellent workmanship under the direction of various iemoto.

PART TWO

The Tea Setting

5. Tea Gardens

The Zen Landscape

When Zen introduced the concept of *mu,* nothingness, to Japan, Japanese art forms began to be scaled down; size came to be regarded as a contradiction of the idea of nothingness. The changes wrought by this idea on the Japanese are nowhere more evident than in the gardens of Zen temples.

Reduction in scale was a necessary concomitant of Zen teaching; diminution and simplification of gardens was a departure from Heian styles of magnificence. Temple compounds came more and more to incorporate limited designs. Restricted patches of green replaced expanses of rich planting. A few stones set in sand came to be all that was required for a first-rate garden. To stand before the simple Zen gardens today is a powerful experience. The richly worked European gardens seem pale by comparison—they are so over-expressed, so unrestrained, so tired.

When form is reduced there is a tendency to symbolize. This tendency has been strong among the Japanese, especially when it comes to Zen gardens. We find that guides, signs, and books are filled with prosaic symbolism for all the major *kare-sansui* (dry-landscape) gardens. It is difficult to resist giving meaning to matter, especially if we are aware that intelligent men created the sand and stone forms of a landscape. People often assume that the creators of the gardens had some object in mind, some representation: tigers, rowboats, cranes, mountains, and seas are said to be concealed within the arrangements. However, if the gardens represent forms, the depictions are fragile ones. The abbreviated forms are the very things that draw people into the pitfalls of symbolizing.

The traditional Heian devices of waterfalls, ponds, and flowering plants are replaced by sand and stone, spare plantings—all in relatively small spaces. The articles are carefully disposed in a dry landscape, suggesting much more by what they do not include than by what is actually present. Nonliteral representation is common in Zen. The directness of stones set in white sand recalls the Zen art of the late-Sung artist Mu Ch'i and the Japanese Sesshu (1420–1506), whose simple black-and-white paintings are not literally representational but suggestive. The stones of the gardens are like the black strokes of the paintings—perceived points of departure.

It is interesting to watch priests rake the sand. The sand is rotted granite gravel, 1/16 to 3/8 inches, about three inches deep on rolled earth. It is replaced regularly.

The garden of Daisen-in (1509) is an outstanding example of kare sansui. The Ryoan-ji garden is a more severe example of reduced form. These gardens should be seen under varying conditions: rain, sunshine, moonlight, and snow give special characteristics. Each kind of light plays with the forms in a sublime way, but under snow, that ultimate abstraction of nature, these gardens show their directness. Ryoan-ji is at once humorous and sad when snow obscures its forms. In that most brilliant of whites, nothingness sparkles.

The "Dewy Path"

Among the simplest of Zen-inspired gardens is the *roji,* literally "dewy path," the tea garden. The roji is not a natural abstraction but a functional path that leads from the garden gate to the tea hut. It was originally intended as no more than a passageway, but time broadened the idea. Rikyu's roji are considered definitive. He standardized the architecture of the path, but conceded that each man must adapt the basic plan according to the kind of tea hut and service required.

No two roji are identical, though they may include the same features. The roji of the Katsura Detached Palace is a greatly expanded form of Rikyu's simple path, which suggests a walk in the mountains or a country lane. At Tai-an, Rikyu cut off a spectacular view by planting a hedge that grows to a man's height. The roji at Tai-an is a way to the tea hut, not a place for a large landscape scene. This kind of garden is special, even in Japan. Tourists tend to walk right by a roji, hardly noticing the careful composition, and be attracted by the vistas of the palaces, large temples, and sumptuous homes, where paths take visitors from one splendid view to another.

A roji ideally has two parts, the *soto roji* (outer section close to the garden entrance), and the *uchi roji* (inner section close to the tea hut). The soto roji contains a *yoritsuki, roji-guchi,* and *soto koshikake.* The yoritsuki (also called *hakama-tsuki*) is a small place in which guests may change clothes or refresh them-

The main entrance gate, called "Kabuto-mon" (helmet gate), at Urasenke headquarters in Kyoto.

The stone entry walk and garden at Urasenke.

The end of the entry walk showing the front of the main building at Urasenke.

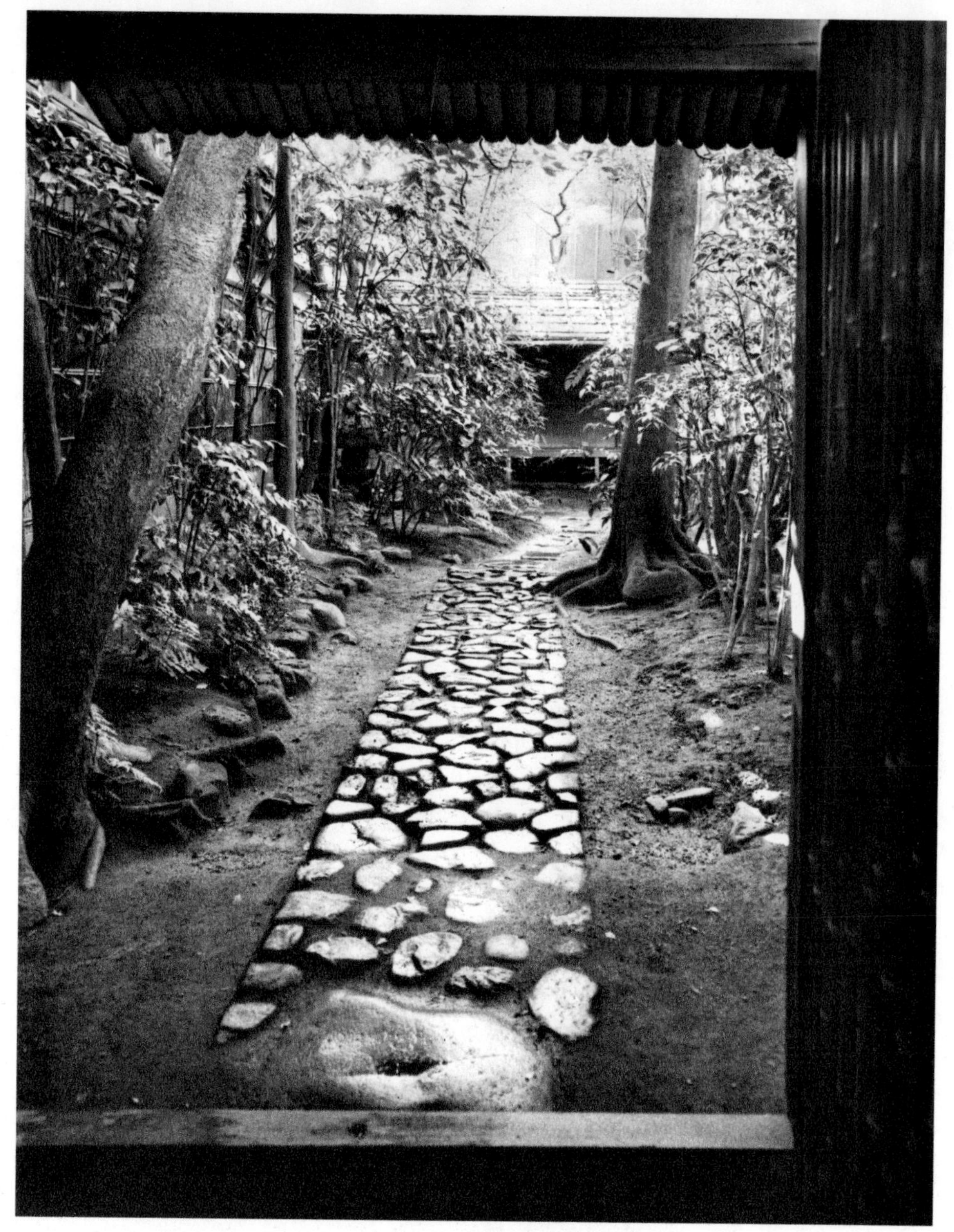

A *chumon* (middle gate) dividing an inner and outer *roji* (tea garden) at Urasenke. (Photo by Tankosha, Kyoto.)

A bamboo gate in one of the roji at Urasenke.

A roji and chumon at Urasenke. Note that this gate is hinged along the top and opens upward.

A *koshikake* (waiting bench) in a roji at Urasenke.

Uchi roji (inner roji) with *tsukubai* (stone wash basin) and *hishaku* (dipper for cold water) at Urasenke.

The uchi roji and *tobi ishi* (stepping-stones) at the Yu-in tea hut, Urasenke. (Photo by H. Ikeda.)

Tobi ishi in an Urasenke roji.

The Yu-in tea hut. Note the skylight in the center of the thatched roof, the broom hanging on the wall, and the *nijiri-guchi* (crouching entrance) in the lower right-hand side of the wall.

A lantern and tsukubai in the grounds of Myoki-an at Oyamazaki, Kyoto. (Photo by H. Ikeda.)

Rikyu's tsukubai at the Tai-an tea hut, Myoki-an. (Photo by H. Ikeda.)

A pond washing place at Katsura Detached Palace, Kyoto. This takes the place of the tsukubai and is called *nagare no chozu*. (Photo by S. Fujima.)
▼

Ensaki chozubachi (a stone wash basin at the end of a veranda) at Katsura.

Stepping-stones in the roji of the Shoko-ken tea hut at Koto-in. Note the open nijiri-guchi with mats visible inside. (Photo by H. Ikeda.)

Koetsu's fence design at Koetsu-ji, Kyoto. (Photo by H. Ikeda.)

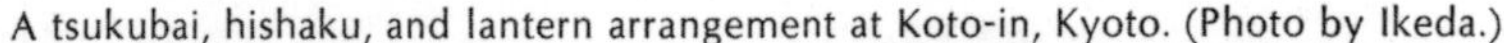

A tsukubai, hishaku, and lantern arrangement at Koto-in, Kyoto. (Photo by Ikeda.)

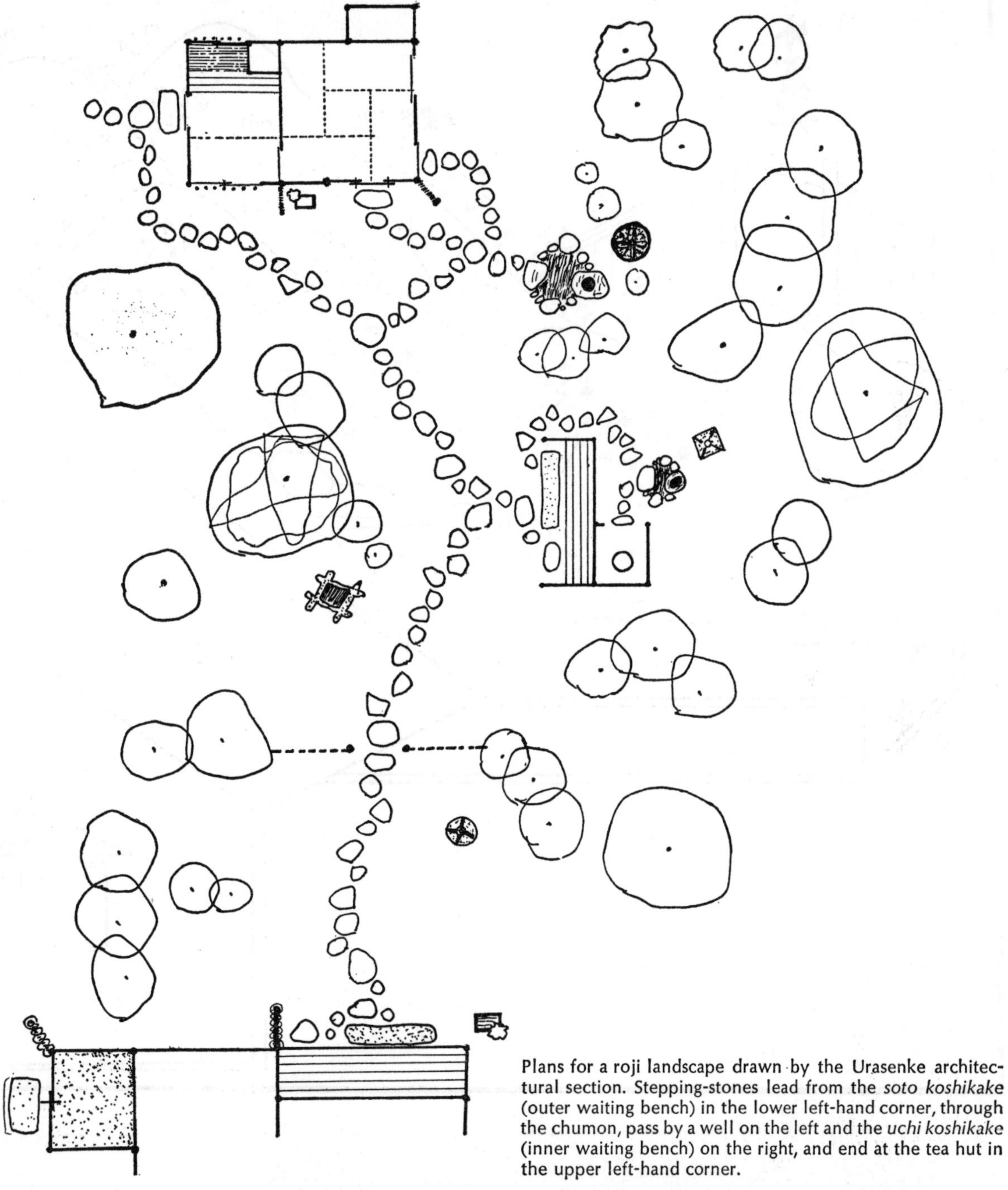

Plans for a roji landscape drawn by the Urasenke architectural section. Stepping-stones lead from the *soto koshikake* (outer waiting bench) in the lower left-hand corner, through the chumon, pass by a well on the left and the *uchi koshikake* (inner waiting bench) on the right, and end at the tea hut in the upper left-hand corner.

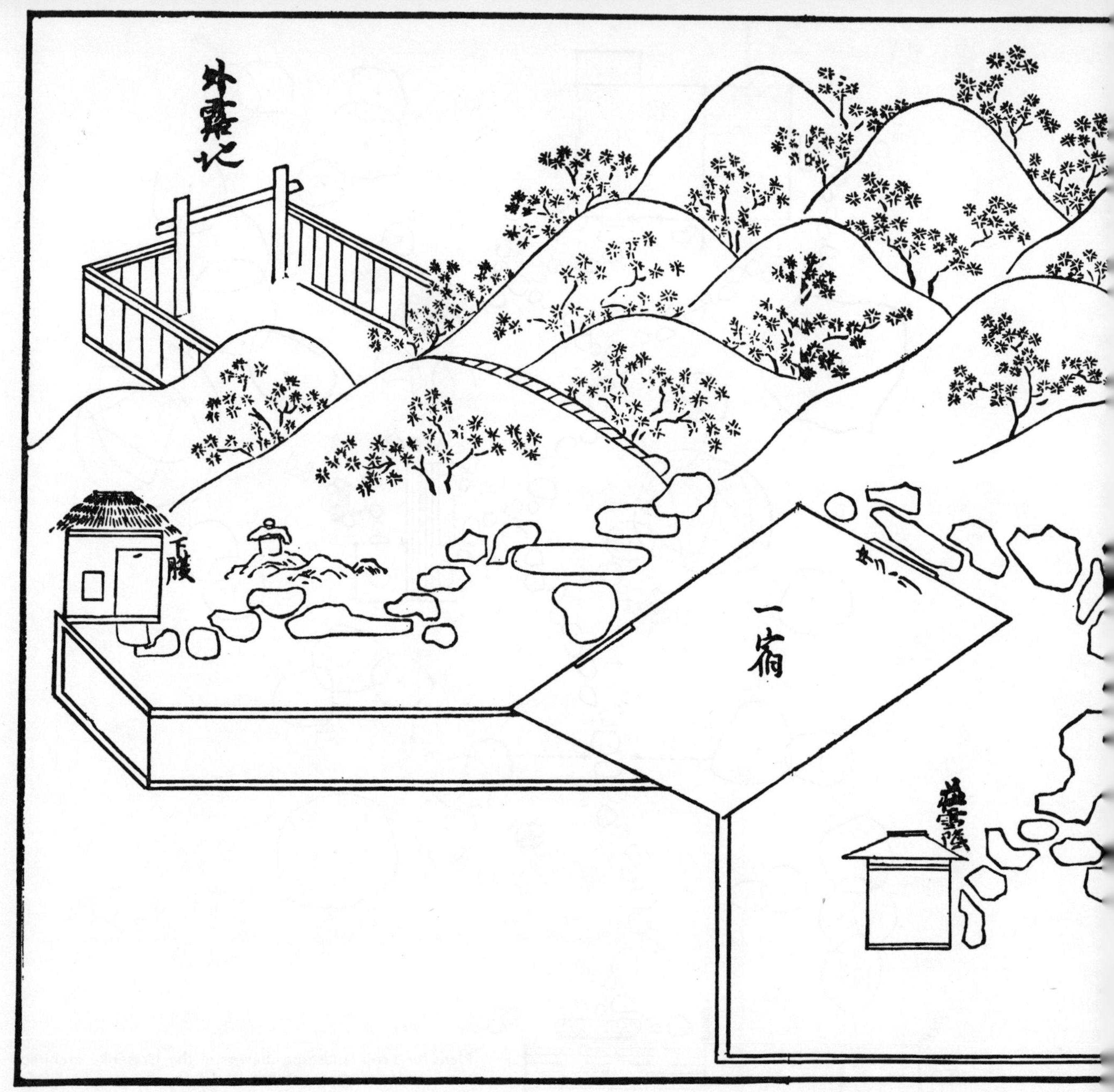
外露地
下腹
一宿

◀Roji plans from the *Kokon Chado Zensho*, a book published in Kyoto in the late Edo period, around the mid-1800s. (Courtesy of Yuichiro Kojiro.)

The standard complete arrangement of stones for the tsukubai:
1. *Yuto ishi* (hot-water stone). 2. *Teshoku ishi* (lamp stone). 3. *Mae ishi* (front stones). These were formerly called *kagami ishi* (crouching stones). 4. *Suimon* (water gate), where spilled water flows out between the mae ishi.
▼

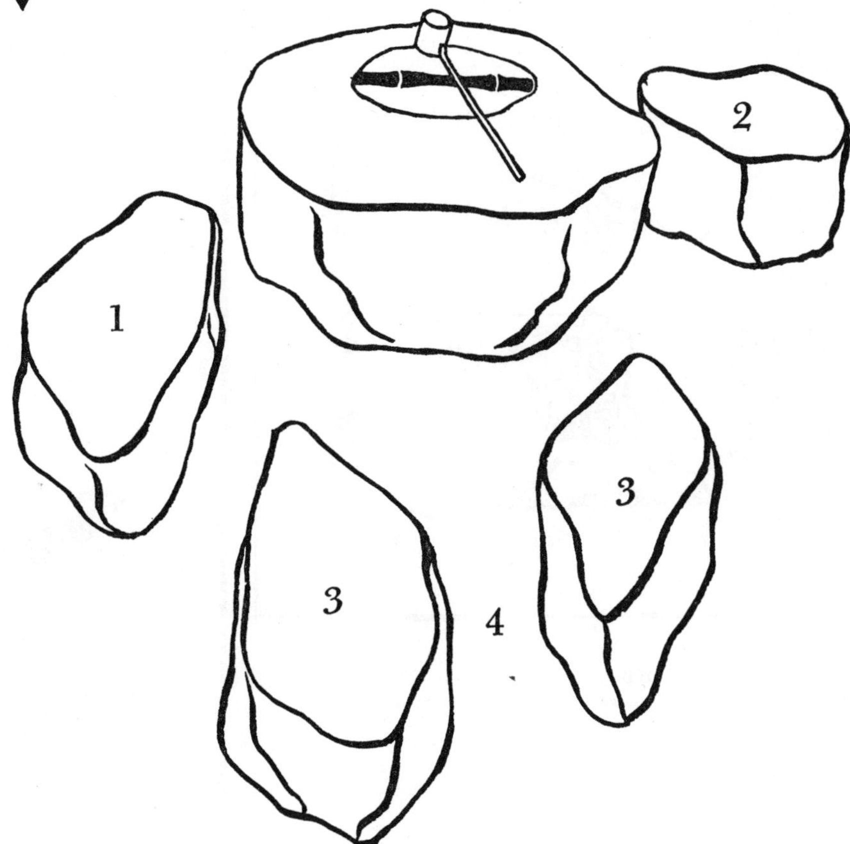

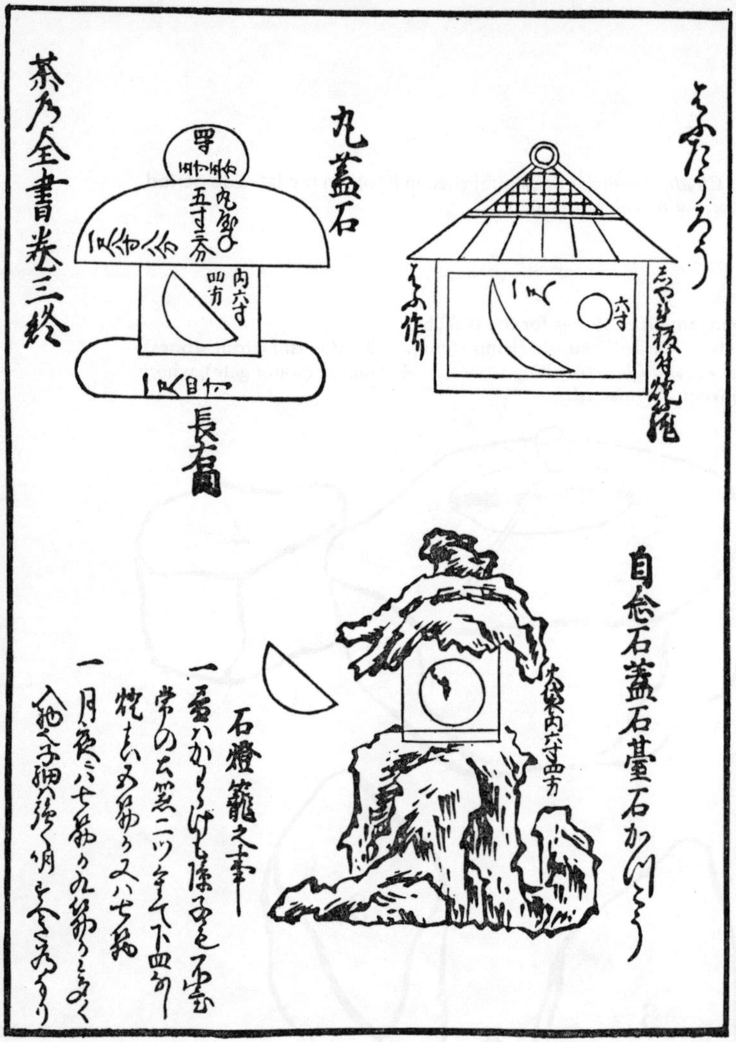

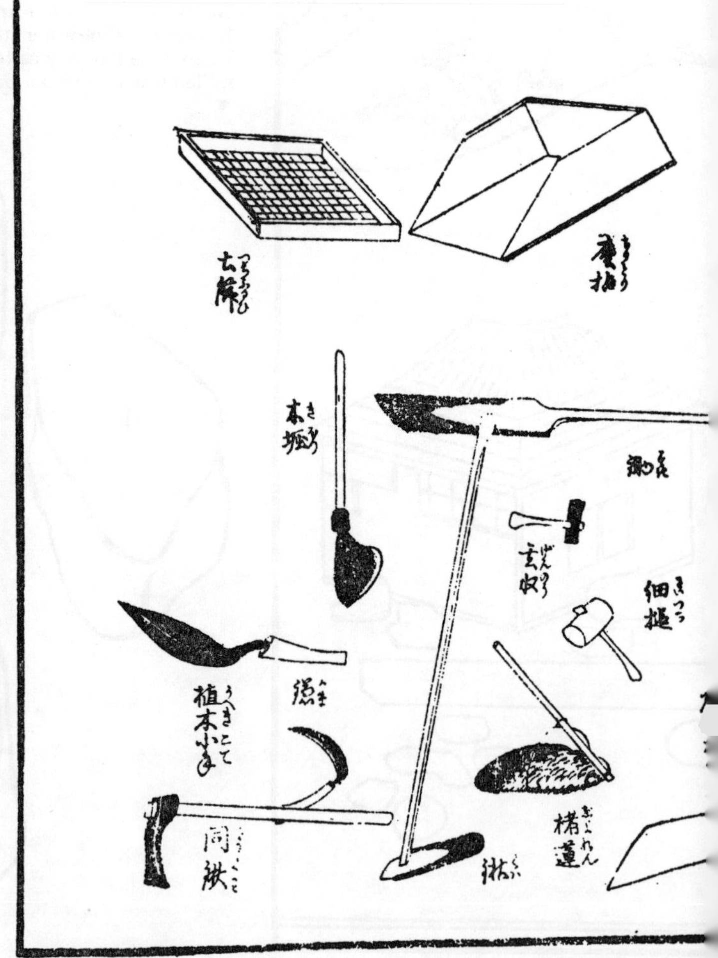

▲
Designs for lanterns to be placed in roji, from *Chaya Zensho,* an Edo-period book on tea architecture and landscaping. (Photo by S. Fujima.)

Illustrations from *Tsukiyama Teizo Den,* a book on gardening published in Kyoto in the late Edo period, around the mid-1800s. (Courtesy of Yuichiro Kojiro.)

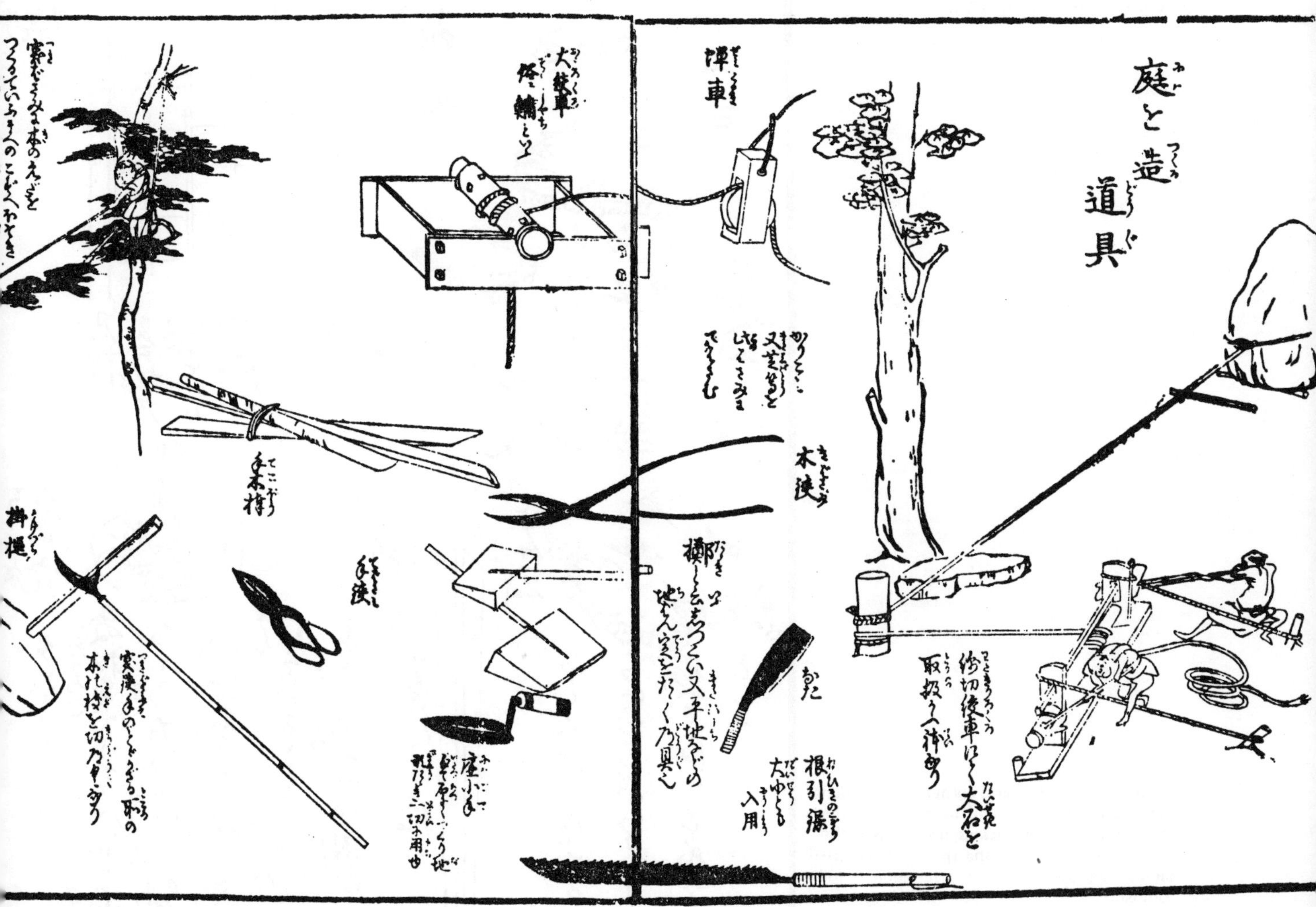

Seven illustrations from *Chado Hayagaten* (The Art of Tea: A Way to Quick Understanding), vol. 1. This two-volume work was published in Osaka in 1771.

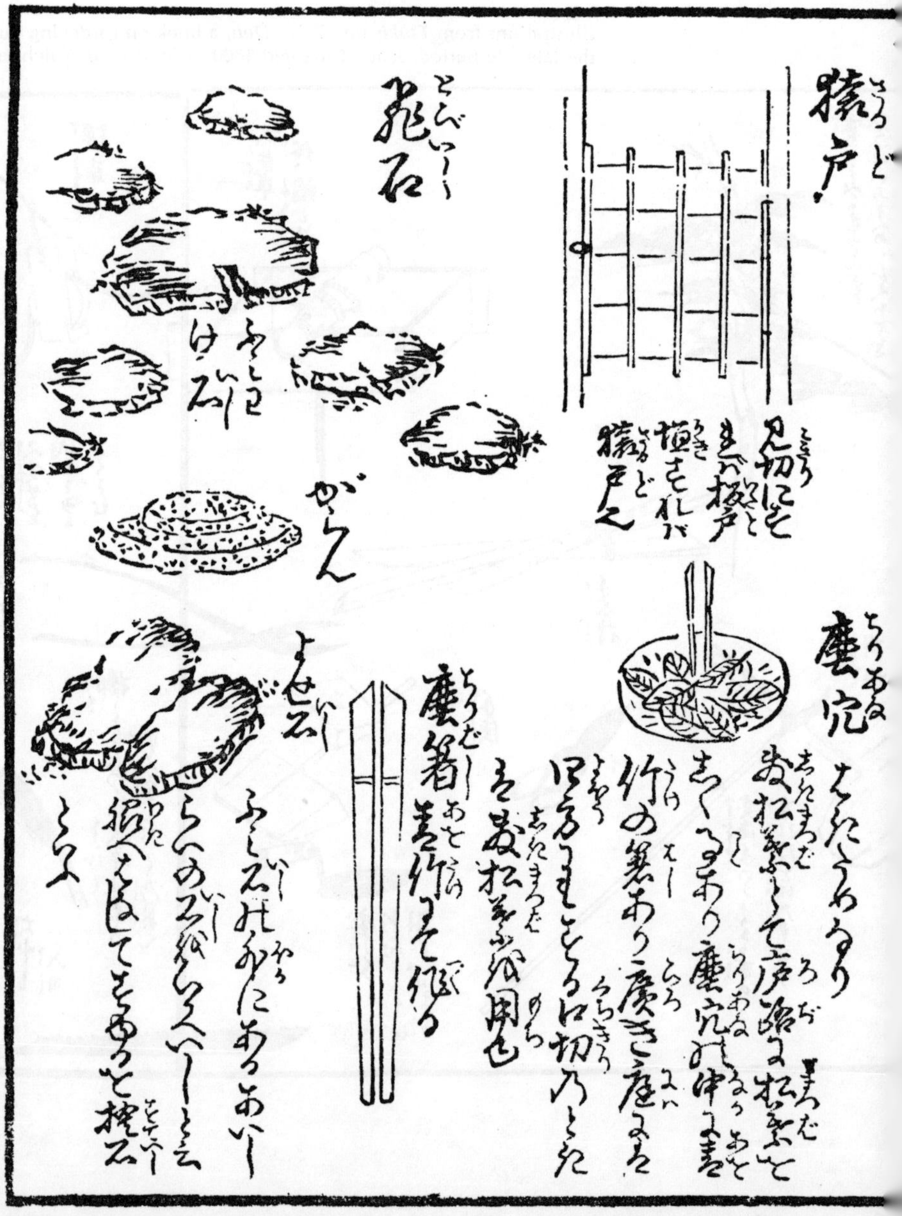

In the upper right-hand corner is a garden gate made of wood, and below it are the chopsticks used for picking up debris in the garden and the *chiri-ana* (prunings receptacle). On the left is an arrangement for tobi ishi.

In a general plan for the tea garden, the hut is shown with a waiting bench, *setchin* (toilet), tea hut, and middle and outer gates clearly dividing the uchi roji and soto roji.

荘雪隠　当代ハ小便所とも号

白きいしをまきたる大便所又ハ
あるひハ大便所へ下腹雪隠とも
中露路の外にあり他人を不浄
雪隠なからハ石雪隠なれども
内を荘られて下腹雪隠とする
ぶし下腹雪隠を壷とこそ
そくあり先踏板あり内雪隠
へ大便をる時先へ鼻紙抜つて内とかきのけ紙を多くしき
大便して上へ又紙をきせ鼻紙抜つて内をかきよせ多く

An overhead view of the interior of the setchin.

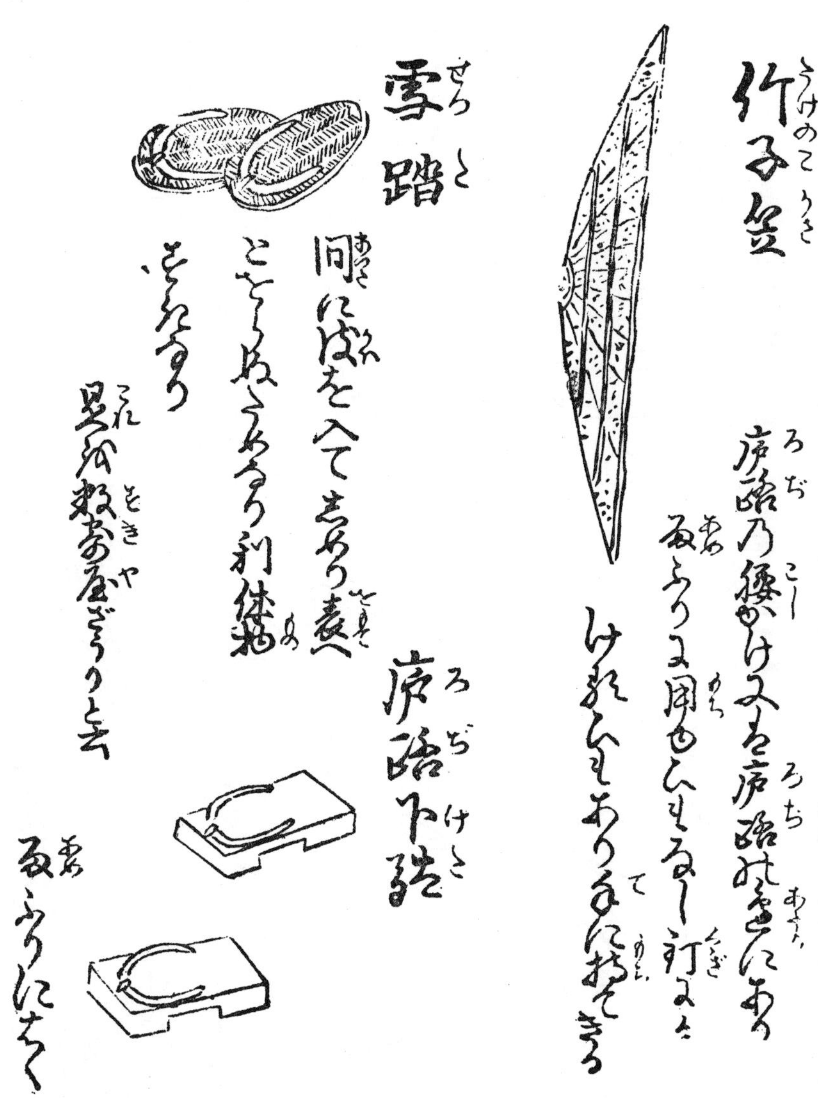

Articles of clothing for use in the garden include a rainhat made of bamboo sheath, *zori* (straw sandals), and *geta* (wooden clogs) for rainy weather.

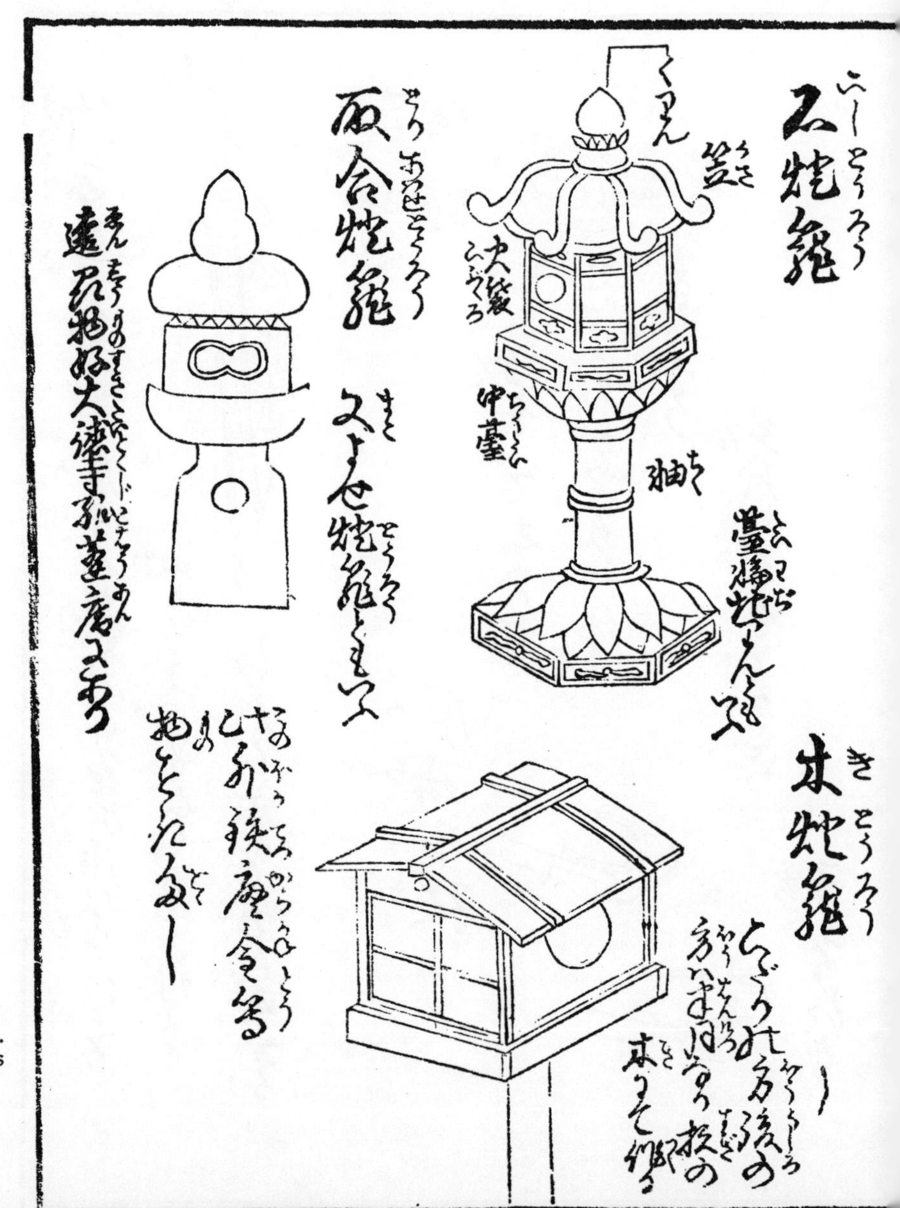

Three types of lanterns for the tea garden. The upper two are stone, and the lower is wood.

Tools for use in the garden include a board for sprinkling and arranging sand and a broom made of rushes.

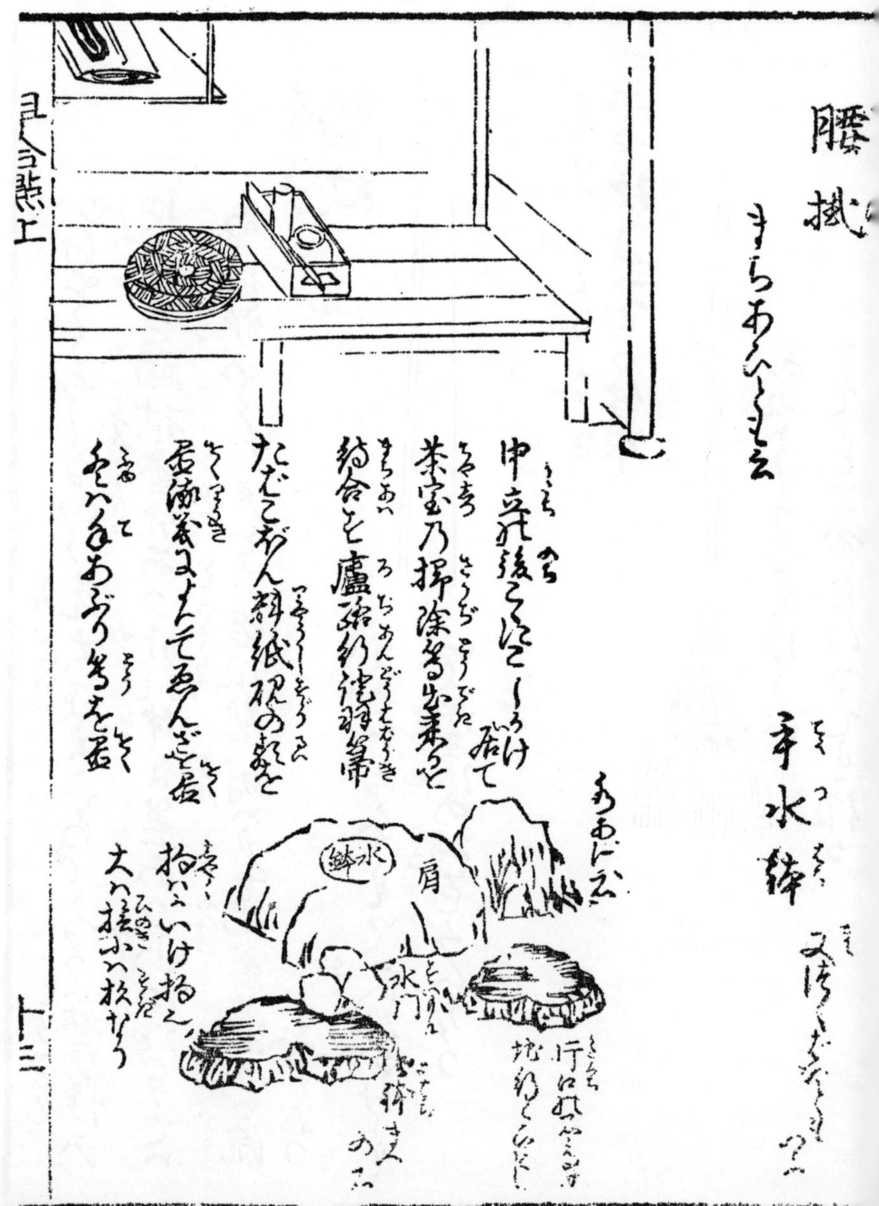

The upper part of the page shows a koshikake prepared with a tobacco box and round straw cushion. Below is the arrangement of stones for the tsukubai washing area.

selves before tea; the alternate name suggests a place in which to don the *hakama,* an outer garment for men that is worn over kimono. The yoritsuki is not often used today, tea tending to less formal arrangements. The roji-guchi, the entrance of the roji, and the soto koshikake ("outer bench"), the small covered bench where guests wait to be greeted by their host, complete the setting of the soto roji, except for the small toilet placed inconspicuously beside the waiting bench. The toilet, *setchin,* is a small enclosure, usually with a bamboo door. It is kept scrupulously clean, even attractive, though it is simply an arrangement of stones on an earthen floor. In days of old it afforded assassins a convenient hiding place. Perhaps out of habit, nearly everyone inspects the setchin.

The uchi roji contains an *uchi koshikake, tsukubai,* and the place for tea. Here too there is a setchin. The uchi koshikake ("inner bench") resembles the covered bench of the outer roji. Often a painting (not calligraphy) is placed in it, having something to do with the season or suggesting an appropriate theme for the occasion. The tsukubai is a small basin which ranks in importance with anything else in the roji. It was inspired by an arrangement of stones about a spring at Ginkaku-ji and is, according to most sources, Rikyu's invention. Hideyoshi had one made of wood for his tea hut at the battlefield of Hokosaki in 1587, but most tsukubai are of stone, chiseled, chipped, or natural. In the top of the stone a small depression called a *mizubachi* is hollowed out for water and is used for washing the hands and rinsing the mouth. This is not large—about eleven inches in diameter and ten inches deep; were it ample it would resemble a birdbath. It is low, on the ground, and smaller stones are placed around it. When a tea hut stands by a fresh lake or stream, water from natural sources is used. Stones are arranged for guests to crouch by the water (a good example is at one of the tea huts of the Katsura Detached Palace). The bowl of the tsukubai is constantly refilled. A bamboo pipe frequently leads directly into the basin, and water is allowed to overflow on stone and moss. In other cases, water is brought to the basin immediately before the guests arrive. Rikyu placed a pitcher of hot water to the left of the basin when he served winter tea, and this practice continues today. For evening tea, Rikyu placed a small lantern with a candle to the right of the basin, but today most chajin use stone lanterns, some equipped with electric lighting. The temporary lantern, usually of wood, is called *andon*. Permanent, stone lanterns are *ishidoro*. Rikyu never used stone lanterns in his roji, nor would he have used electric lights for tea. He would not have because the intensity of artificial lighting tends to fight against the night, while candlelight does not hide the fact that night is dark. Floor candlesticks, andon, or oil lamps are used.

Tsukubai descend from *chozubachi,* standing wash basins of stone, commonly found at the end of a veranda in a temple or public place. Chozubachi are properly called *ensaki chozubachi* ("veranda-end" chozubachi), a literal rendering of the position. The tsukubai is generally placed near the entrance to the tea hut, that is, in the uchi-roji, but the positioning is no longer strict. The custom is to place a lantern stone, *teshoku ishi,* to the right of the tsukubai, and a stone for a hot water vessel, *yuto ishi,* to the left. One or two stones, called *mae ishi,* are placed before the tsukubai. One crouches on these while washing his hands or rinsing his mouth. Between the tsukubai proper and the mae ishi is the *suimon,* or water gate, a water hole to contain the spilled water. This hole is shallow and filled with small pebbles, old roof tiles, or such. About this arrangement care is taken that the mae ishi are flat and smooth and not at an uncomfortable height above the stones of the path. The stones of the suimon may be held in place with cement or pounded in hard earth and are called *awakeshi* ("foam-preventing").

Other stones in the roji are considered with care. The *kutsunugi ishi* is placed in front of the entrance to the hut where one removes and leaves *zori,* common sandal-like footwear. This stone is smaller than one for the same purpose in front of the host's entrance. Both are just over a foot below the tatami level of the room, a few inches from the wall. It should be noted that all measurements here are approximate—allowance is made for the terrain in setting stones.

Tobi ishi, stepping-stones that actually form the path, have no set pattern. They are selected to afford easy walking, placed so that guests feel comfortable crossing them. These stones are usually placed about four inches above the ground, the greater part buried. They are four or five inches apart, some placed for aesthetic balance. A ratio of four for walking to six for balance was used by Oribe, but Rikyu preferred the reverse. When the tobi ishi lead in two or more directions—for example, when the path splits to go in one direction to the tsukubai and in the other to the hut—a junction stone called *fumiwake ishi* is placed, raised slightly above the other stones. This stone is also called *garanseki,* meaning snail stone or pedestal stone. When a path is closed, a *tome ishi* (also called *sekimori ishi*), detaining stone, is placed on the tobi ishi. The tome ishi is bound with black cord. A *katanakake ishi,* sword-rest stone, placed by a rack attached to the hut, was used as a step by samurai when putting away their swords.

Between the outer and inner roji a small gate, *chumon,* is often found. There is no rule for constructing this gate or for a fence to which it might be attached. The fence might be bamboo (as in the fine Urasenke chumon, designed by Sotan). It might be thatched or part of a solid wall (as in Omotesenke's outstanding chumon, a feature of which is a small sliding entrance similar to the door of a tea hut). The gates are rarely more than five feet high. The *shiorido* chumon, woven of branches, is lifted rather than slid open. The *hajitomi* is another form of woven gate. There is the possibility of no gate at all, or more than one.

Koshikake ishi are stones placed before the covered bench where guests may sit. A slightly larger stone is placed before the seat of the principal guest. The one who takes this seat is recognized first by the host. (The selection of principal guest is usually informal or else obvious. Young people invariably defer to older guests, but if all are friends and about the same age, they choose among themselves without much fuss.) The kinds of stones for koshikake ishi are many. Favorite stones in Kyoto come from the vicinity of Kurama, just north of Kyoto. These are black or red, but more common stones of other colors are also used.

Stone lanterns are made to order or selected from among the many old lanterns that one finds around Kyoto. They are usually from three to six feet in height for a small roji, but the ones for the grounds of a mansion are often much larger. They have many designs, but simpler ones are preferred for roji. Enshu's and Oribe's designs are especially favored, the lanterns of Katsura and of tea master Hosokawa Sansai's grave at Koto-in being models for many. Lanterns of stone combine three basic design elements: the square (earth), circle (water), and triangle (fire).

The plants in a roji should be found in the neighborhood—nothing unusual or especially fragrant being permitted around a tea hut. Pine, Japanese yew, cedar, oak, and maple are suggested for roji and, together with ferns, grasses, moss, and other green plants, make up the simplest kind of garden.

Oribe allowed brilliant flowers in his roji and others have gone further. Occasionally one sees streams, waterfalls, great stones, and contorted trees in a roji, but the effect is definitely not in keeping with chado as founded by Rikyu.

Garden Scope

Sakai, Rikyu's birthplace, was a crowded town. Great merchants set their homes close together. Gardens were usually small, pocket plantings. Perhaps this is why Rikyu's roji was purposely small. Possibly his path was based on the passageways close by the homes of Sakai merchants that led from the entrance of the house to the back or side where a small tea hut was placed. The limits of space in modern cities like Tokyo demand that roji be small. Houses are crowded together even in suburbs. The lack of ample space has certainly had an effect on Japanese architecture and landscaping in concentrating the forms a house or garden can take.

The distinguished critic Yuichiro Kojiro points out

that the amount of available land has always been limited for the Japanese people; gardens tend to be small. He traces the development of Japanese gardens through modern times, pointing out that the gardens of Tokugawa Japan during the period of isolation were especially diminutive. Today's Japanese artist must learn how to deal with large spaces, according to Professor Kojiro.

An important feature of tea-garden design is that architects will not include dramatic views in their roji, and will not use most of the devices that are their common trade. Also, if the roji is to be designed for a client rather than for themselves, every care must be taken to insure that the finished work precisely fits the attitudes of the chajin—no other personality must be present. This is difficult business. For most chajin then, the only solution is to design their own gardens, however much time and consideration that may involve.

Very recently chajin have begun to experiment more with tea gardens, forsaking old rules for new expressions. In a complex of tearooms such as at the school of tea at Urasenke, there is room for more than one kind of roji. Attached to the new Shinka no Ma, a large tearoom for students, is a sand and rock garden. This departure from the norm is important, and is justified by the Urasenke teachers on the basis of need for greater variety in a place where as many as five or six tearooms are in constant use. The garden is excellently done, with bamboo and a low stone wall.

The recent garden of Sutemi Horiguchi, among the most distinguished of Japanese architects, contains one willow, one stone, and some sand. Professor Kojiro states that it represents a significant departure from traditional Japanese gardening—something he feels needs to be encouraged. The Horiguchi garden is a place of loneliness—much needed in contemporary Tokyo. Architect Horiguchi, authority on Rikyu and tea-hut construction, is an accomplished chajin. His structures reflect the creative aspects of tea tradition. The Hasshokan inn in Nagoya, the additions to the Miyako Hotel, and the Tawaraya inn in Kyoto are representative of his work.

From the time of Muso Kokushi (1275–1351), Zen priest and designer of the gardens of Tenryu-ji near Kyoto and Saiho-ji, Kyoto's moss temple, the tendency in Japanese gardening has been to create a space, sharply defined, in which a limited number of objects are placed to greatest effect. The gardens for tea are in this tradition. *Yamazato no niwa,* mountain-village gardens, too, have influenced roji design. The simple, natural arrangement of trees and green is the appearance that a roji should have. Though the path is short, the roji should suggest a stroll in a small mountain village. The conventional Japanese gardens that feature distorted pine trees, dwarf maples, and other affected plants arranged in dramatic fashion are not found in mountain villages, nor are such plants grown in roji. Muso Kokushi did not use carefully shaped plants in his gardens, either. He too was a purist in this sense.

The Retreat Ideal

The small tea hut is seen ideally in a simple mountain garden of a few square yards. Since the hut is scarcely more than ten feet square, the garden should not be overpowering. Many chajin retired from active court or official life, moved into small huts, and lived in the simplest of styles. Dwelling in a small hut in a setting as natural as possible, a sensitive man could have tea in quietness and contentment. The palaces of Ginkaku-ji and Kinkaku-ji, where so little of the former magnificence remains, are set in mountain scenery. A simple path leads up a mountainside at Ginkaku-ji from palace buildings around the pond. Shoguns Yoshimasa and Yoshimitsu enjoyed the cool setting adopted thereafter by chajin and priests.

After the Ashikagas had built their palaces and gardens with a mountain-village feeling, Hideyoshi took up the idea in his *yamazato-an,* mountain-village hut or retreat. Hideyoshi and Rikyu certainly did not copy the plans of very early "retreat" gardens but they took inspiration from them. The early poets and artists who are said to have used yamazato huts were using them as retreats and as convenient, comfortable places for sharing sakè and conversation with friends. Hideyoshi and Rikyu must have admired the comradeship expressed in verse from the time. After Muso designed the Saiho-ji garden, there are numerous examples of his stone arrangements, and the pebbled paths found there. In this sense Rikyu was carrying on a trend begun long before his birth.

Surviving texts show gardens purported to be the designs of Jo-o, or Rikyu, or even Shuko, which were for viewing, not roji or paths. The plans show no pebble paths nor any stepping-stones; one is meant to view the whole, rather than enter into it as into a roji. The early gardens referred to must be related then to the residences by which they were placed, the style being *shoin-zukuri* (reception-room style), to be examined in the next chapter. Horiguchi, in *Rikyu no Chashitsu* (Rikyu's Tea Huts) points out that these early gardens reveal, already in late Muromachi, the origins of true roji styling when design turned to more simplified forms.

The yamazato gardens of earlier times were rather broad, though simply designed. As this tradition, favored by Jo-o, Rikyu, and Hideyoshi, proved less feasible in a Japan growing more crowded, everything was scaled down, while the tearoom itself was given much more attention in its immediate surroundings.

The attached garden began to be more than a mere section of a greater scheme. The independence of *chaniwa* (tea gardens) begins here.

Gardens of the Masters

The early gardens of Rikyu style were surrounded by clay fencing. Later this was replaced by bamboo, which is popular today. The early clay fences were about six feet tall, blocking any view that might disturb the guests. The succeeding forms also obscure the view. Fences were important to Rikyu; he constantly mentioned his fences, and took meticulous care of them.

In speaking of Shuko and of his insistent planting of pine inside his tea garden, rather than the customary willow, and of his other innovations, Horiguchi, in *Rikyu no Chashitsu,* says: "One may see in his attitude a manifestation of Zen spirit that admits no unnecessary hindrances, and also a proud expression of the tea which he was innovating. We learn from all of this that the tea garden had been started and was completed by other people than those who made shoin-zukuri gardens under the direction of Yoshimasa and others. Even though the tea garden had to admit some elements of the shoin-zukuri, it attained its final shape mainly because it overcame all the customs and conventions that had preceded it. It was this garden that eventually led to gardens such as that of the Katsura Detached Palace."

Rikyu's three-mat tearoom in Osaka had a garden with one pine and one oak. His son-in-law made a copy of this garden and the two, in their spare handling of details, reflect Jo-o's two-part, pocket style. Rikyu's garden too had very scant planting, possibly some fern and natural moss. Oribe put many pine trees in his roji, and other plants as well. He greatly increased its size. Set in a large area, the tearoom was comfortable and quiet. He used large firs also and placed an eight-mat independent structure some distance from the tea hut. This was a square building called a *dobuki,* where his guests could change clothes while waiting for their summons from the host. He spread pebbles about, and large stepping-stones led to the entrance of the hut. The Oribe Hasso-an, now in the grounds of the Nara Museum, is set in a grassy expanse beside a pond. Stones are set in a meandering row in grass, and lead to a gravel area near the tea hut. Around the hut the ground is pounded firm. Surrounding the whole is a hedge. The garden is certainly less attractive than anything Oribe would have planned himself. In recent times, aside from the very generous spaces around the mansions of some chajin, the trend seems to be a return to Rikyu's simplicity.

Horiguchi quotes the *SukidoTaii,* a mid-Edo-period

book on tea ceremony, architecture, landscaping, and tea attitudes: "As for the garden, the space in front of the four-and-one-half-mat room should not have any grass or tree planted, any stone erected, any sand spread, nor any stones set in a row, lest they distract the eyes of the guests; the guests must pay attention to the fine utensils." These statements are testimony to the desires of early masters to keep the roji plain. The gardens probably were mere pocket spaces, serving as passages to rooms inside houses set aside for tea, *kakoi* (distinguished from the chashitsu, which is a separate building). Horiguchi continues: "The tearoom had not only preparations which the other rooms of the house did not have, but also had a small gate (*naka-kuguri*) and waiting room (koshikake or *machi-ai*) for its own use. The traditional methods of gardening were admitted only where they were needed. At last there came to exist the roji—something for which some people felt it necessary to give a name more significant than the practical 'passage.' From the start the garden was aimed to be used, not to be seen, and in this it was nearer the [earlier] gardens."

Horiguchi points out that, in harmonizing the hut and path into one consistent whole, Rikyu founded a new style we might call *sukiya-zukuri,* a wabi tea style. Except for Tai-an, there is little left that truly represents the handiwork or design of Rikyu.

Eventually the simplicity of the path and the prevailing and more complex style of house gardens came into conflict. Thereafter we find the roji divided into two parts. One part reflected the shoin-zukuri style, the other, Rikyu's roji.

From Rikyu's letters we can be sure that, by his later life, roji already included the koshikake, water basin, and some kind of stone arrangement for a candle. Jo-o's tearoom had a double garden attached, in front and to the side. Both were pocket gardens. Apparently Rikyu sometimes used this form. Usual gardens of this kind measure about six by nine feet for the front, and not more than a narrow path eighteen feet in length along the side, making a bottom-heavy "L."

Outer roji today are sometimes sandy, covered in winter with pine needles, while inner roji are mossy and green. However large Oribe's or Enshu's roji became, they were distinguished from palace and large residence gardens by the absence of arranged stones and the lack of any significant body of water. Lakes or ponds of size were occasionally used, though small streams were favored.

In the outer koshikake and in the inner koshikake various things are provided for the guests: tobacco and ashtray, as well as charcoal lighters, paper and ink, and sometimes ceramic or lacquer hand-warmers containing charcoal. The Hasso-an of Oribe at the Nara Museum has elegant dressing and waiting quarters for distinguished guests. Provisions for creature comforts were considerably more grand in Oribe's dobuki than in the smaller koshikake.

Care of the Garden

The owner of a roji is constantly caring for his garden. He continually cleans, rakes the grounds, prunes the pines and plantings. Refuse from the roji is placed in the *chiri-ana,* a small hole to one side of the tea hut. Special brooms and rakes are used for Japanese gardening—bamboo, reeds, or rush, tied with black cord. These attractive implements perform their functions well.

While chajin always water their own roji, work in the garden, and take great care in the inspection of it, many have part-time gardeners who regularly tend the grounds. In the many gardens of Omotesenke and Urasenke, professional gardeners are constantly in attendance. When plantings have to be pruned, special attention is needed; the care of Japanese pine trees and shrubs is an art in itself. Chajin, however, are gardeners *par excellence.*

Priests of temples with important gardens are also expert gardeners. They spend hours each day sweeping their plots, cleaning up debris, and cultivating plantings. In the gardens which feature plantings, alternates are cultivated in special plots so they can be transplanted immediately, should garden plants die. The reserve plants or trees are pruned to resemble closely those of the garden proper. As transplants are made, it is inevitable that the gardens alter ever so slightly from generation to generation. This is the life of the garden, its naturalness. Old records show that a great cherry tree grew just outside the confines of the stone garden at Ryoan-ji, and that its branches hung over the wall. Today's Ryoan-ji has no cherry tree as backdrop, but there is no record from the time of the origin of the temple to indicate that the cherry tree was considered part of the design. On the flexible naturalness of Ryoan-ji, composer John Cage stated he felt the expanse of sand was sufficiently powerful to be able to support stones at any point. He implied that the man who planned the garden need not have placed the stones just as he did—that he could have put them almost anywhere.

Westerners View Tea Gardens

Josiah Conder's *Landscape Gardening in Japan,* written in 1893 and published in 1912, is one of the earliest English-language books on Japanese gardening. Conder had gone to Japan in 1877 and, with his student, John Scott Bradstreet (who arrived in 1886), left a great amount of material on the subject of Japanese gardening and crafts. Bradstreet established a Japanese craft center in Minneapolis, contributing much to the development of that city and to the popularizing of Japanese interior designs and arts. The work of these two men, and that of Morse, the Englishman Piggott, and Lafcadio Hearn, make up all that nineteenth-century America knew about Japanese gardening. Hearn wrote a widely read article on the subject for the *Atlantic Monthly* (1892). Conder's book makes reference to well-known gardens. He says that the Katsura Detached Palace gardens in 1893 were in sad neglect. He describes Rikyu's tea garden as "the lonely precincts of a secluded mountain shrine, with the red leaves of autumn scattered around." Of Enshu's tea gardens, he says, "The sweet solitude of a landscape in a clouded moonlight, with a half-gloom between the trees." Of Sotan's, he says, "Grassy wilderness in autumn, with plenty of wild flowers." According to Conder, the architect who arranged the grounds of the two great Hongan-ji temples of Kyoto studied the works of old chajin, restored their gardens, and advanced new ideas for roji.

Conder describes the tobi ishi and reports that the names for these stones are taken from the character for "flight of birds," saying that their disposition looked like birds in flight. He compares them to scattered islands. He states that the stones he saw were slabs of schist, slate, flint, and granite. He points out that the stones for an emperor were six inches above the ground; daimyo stones, four inches; those for samurai, three inches. Commoners' stones, he says, were but one and one-half inches above the ground. This conflicts, in part, with other records of the time and with current practice. Conder mentions several examples of path stones that combine the rough with the hewn: *chotankaku* designates a combination of small, rough stones and larger, shaped stones; *tanzaku ishi* resemble paper labels, laid lengthwise and overlapping 40 percent of their lengths; *obi ishi* are the longest stones used in constructing paths. The name comes from the wide sash of the kimono.

David Engel, in *Japanese Gardens for Today* (1959), states that tea gardens containing stone lanterns should have a natural, "found" stone close by—this combination of the hewn and the natural giving balance to the garden. Stones, he says, should be laid apart according to their widths—the wider the stone, the wider its separation from others. Engel also says that tobi ishi should be placed two or three inches above the ground with five to twelve inches of the bulk being buried. *Nobedan,* inlaid rock, if used, should not be placed so that there are cross-joints. The effect is weak.

Engel mentions the presence of wells in roji. There are some famous wells in old roji, such as at Urasenke. These are covered with bamboo lattice or stone or wood to form a square. The lids of these wells extend slightly beyond the sides.

The Unplanned Element

Many of the most important aspects of a roji cannot be planned. If one's neighbor has a grove of pine trees that grow and alter over the years, this will affect the garden. The Japanese garden concept of *shakkei,* borrowed scenery, has long been the foundation of some of the finest gardens. Entsu-ji in Kyoto has a moss and stone garden that is bounded by a low hedge above which rises Mt. Hiei. The mountain is seen through the small grove of trees that back the property. The effect is marvelous, but too dramatic for a roji. At Shinju-an's Teigyoku-ken tea hut, a low wall blocks the street from view but once permitted guests to see distant Hiei. Now that many buildings have been constructed close to Shinju-an, trees have been planted that completely shield the mountain from sight. Whatever limits a chajin might impose upon his roji, a distant view of beautiful and historic Hiei could not be resisted. Serving tea at Urasenke, I have often found my eyes wandering across the low walls and fences to look at the trees of neighboring gardens. I remember once seeing a cat jump the fence of the same garden, the birds that came to rest on pine branches, and noises of the city drifting into the garden—all these things, if only for a moment, becoming part of the spontaneous life of the roji.

One of the most neglected areas of Western gardening is sound. Sound has long been a part of Japanese gardens. Special devices for scaring away wild boars and crows are still to be found in such gardens as Saiho-ji—bamboo devices that fill and empty themselves of water, making a clacking sound. This and the sound of water flowing from a bamboo pipe into a tsukubai are obviously important to a small garden, but equally important are the sounds made by birds, people, and bicycles. A roji must be able to accommodate these. It must not be a place where natural, everyday sounds are forbidden. When the wind is high the tall bamboos clack together, leaves rustle, and the wind soughs in the pines. A roji would be poorer without these sounds of life.

Other unplanned happenings in the roji are snow, rain, the light of the sun and moon, lichens, moss, falling leaves—each contributing to the whole. The balance of all this, as Engel says, is occult, not evident, in a Japanese roji. What we have in the roji is a partnership with nature, a humanized garden where light and dark, positive and negative, living things and dead are found. New York's Central Park is primarily a place for view; Paley's vest-pocket park with waterfall is primarily a place for sound.

Roji as small, sceneless gardens offer a stunning variety of colors, textures, and sounds, in spite of the attempt to keep them spare. They are cleaned so that their simpler, truer natures are revealed, but not so thoroughly stripped of decaying natural debris as to be lifeless. The lines of the garden are not sharp or angular. When the trees are pruned it is done with the thought in mind of allowing some of the dark of the trunk to be seen, but also to let sunlight penetrate to the lower branches and the ground beneath. Guests in these roji find a refreshing patch of earth, nothing overwhelming. That is all that is intended in the path that leads from gate to hut.

6. Tea Architecture

Space

"Empty space is imperishable." Werner Blaser's statement strikes at the heart of tea architecture. The architects of tea huts have eliminated everything but that which is aesthetically and structurally indispensable. They have created superb spaces by omitting nearly everything that is architecturally important in the West; walls, massive supports, and furniture, as we know them, are not present. Instead, the chajin have created empty spaces bounded only by corner posts and crossbeams of matching thicknesses, lightweight ceilings of woven rush or bamboo, removable mat flooring, and walls of paper or mud.

The space of a tea hut is so perfectly formed that furnishings are all but unnecessary. Space itself is what the masters wanted, the product of light and shadow, slender beams and reed. The space of a tearoom requires only the addition of people, not trappings, to be complete. The articulateness of Japanese tea masters in achieving living space for human beings is perhaps unparalleled in the history of architecture.

In the first place, a chajin sits *on,* not *in,* the room; that is, he places himself in direct, bodily contact with the room, he sits directly on the flooring, designed specifically to accommodate the human form in length and breadth. The mats, *tatami,* form the basic module of the whole structure; a door is just as wide as one mat, a ceiling is a little over one mat in height, the length of a room is measured in mats, corresponding to the number of people who can fit comfortably. It is the humanity of this Japanese architecture that first strikes us. The rooms are warm in feeling; they are ever-changing spaces that seem to live.

The tradition of this architecture goes back centuries, but Japanese traditions tend to be part of the present. Tea architecture lives in Japan, even in the most advanced creations of contemporary architects. Tea architecture was developed for the sake of living, not for the sake of architecture—therefore, it is as relevant a style today as at the time of its inception. Geoffrey Holm, in his introduction to Jiro Harada's *The Lesson of Japanese Architecture,* says this development in Japanese craft and architectural arts led to the shaping of a house and its contents as the expression of a philosophy or religion.

Japanese have long stressed the lower areas of dwellings, rather than the upper. Little attention was given to the illumination of the upper reaches of a room. As Kojiro has said, *fusuma,* the paper-covered sliding panels that divide inside areas into rooms, were heavily painted on the lower parts, light and airy elsewhere. Part of this can be explained by the fact that the Japanese were always seated low, on the mats, and the eye level was correspondingly low. In Western homes, eye level is always considered to be something over five feet above the floor, that is, corresponding to a standing position. In a Japanese house, and especially a tea hut, rooms cannot be understood, cannot be well seen, unless one is seated on the mats. Fashions in American interior decorating have encouraged the placing of works of art on a much lower line between floor and ceiling, perhaps in tacit acknowledgment that more of our time is spent in a seated rather than a standing position. This brings us somewhat closer to the Japanese.

Western architecture tends to stress the vertical, while Japanese stresses the horizontal. Even in decorations or paintings, the Japanese paint along walls, not up and down them. In the great mural tradition of the West, our artists have always placed their more important depictions higher, toward the ceilings, and the murals are to be seen as vertical.

Japanese painting on fusuma follows definite patterns. In a Japanese house the most important rooms have fusuma paintings in black and white; adjoining rooms have lightly colored portraits; outermost rooms are brightly painted with flowers, animals, and grasses. None depict heroic or epic struggles. As in tea, there is no climax, no dwindling in these paintings.

It is significant that the Japanese have only severe black-and-white paintings in their most important rooms. I feel that we of the West tend to place our most colorful paintings in the central rooms, not our ink sketches, pencil drawings, or watercolors. The Japanese have no fixed artwork in the tearooms, the innermost chambers where men gather to talk and sip tea. In our libraries and sittings rooms, where we gather with friends for conversation, are found fixed articles of attention—supports for conversation and reflection, trappings for personality expression. In the West, the furnishings supply the finish to our conversational setting: in Japan the space itself is the setting, the people are the finish.

As we might expect, rooms for tea have come to be standardized. But however high the degree of standardization, there is as much variety in space and construction as there are tearooms and chajin. The basic elements are so finely conceived that an infinite variety of combinations is possible.

The Chinese prefer symmetrically balanced structures, even numbers of doors and windows and wings. The Japanese prefer the odd to the even. A Japanese will not have his entrance squarely in the heart of a facade; he will not have evenly spaced and perfectly proportioned fenestration. The Japanese love of the unbalanced is almost an obsession, but it is a positive aesthetic expression. In a garden, the Japanese will place fifteen stones, not fourteen, three trees, not two—it is the love of *suki*. Suki is variously translated as meaning "odd numbers," or "love of odd things." It is most often applied to the architectural style of simple tea huts, sukiya-zukuri or sukiya.

The term sukiya was not used in Rikyu's time, but came to be adopted at a later date as a technical name for an architectural style; the tea hut itself is called chashitsu; tea place is *chaseki*. Sukiya is associated with individual tastes, special likings. Compared to the temples, shrines, and palaces of Japan, sukiya are plain and small, almost rickety. They are not made to impress, outwardly or inwardly. The strongest are visibly affected by the wind.

Tea huts are made of local woods, earth, paper, and straw; they are wholly part of their environment. What appears to be the most substantial thing about them is the roof, which is thatched or of tiles. The uprights are joined directly to the roof; this combination unifies the whole structure.

There are two basic styles of chashitsu: the retreat hut and the attached hut. The former is completely separated from other buildings, the latter is an extension of a main edifice, usually a family dwelling or temple. Both Muso and Shuko had separate huts for their retreats; Rikyu carried on this idea. The attached huts are reached through the main buildings by covered passageways, or entered from outside through doors in the outside walls. Enshu and Sekishu were especially fond of attached huts, and brilliantly led the way in joining tea huts to houses.

The *So-an* and *Shoin* Styles

Within the two kinds of chashitsu there are two stylistic divisions: *so-an* and *shoin*. So-an means "grass hut"—a small thatched shed of simplest construction. Shoin means "writing room" or "study"—a room that has a built-in place that serves as a desk. The so-an is the less elegant, less formal of the two. Shoin-zukuri is a style of elegant construction, usually translated as "reception-room style."

So-an huts have no provisions for treatment of guests according to rank; everyone shares a common floor level, common mats. The shoin style appealed most to the nobility, who chose to make distinctions according to rank and social standing. The shoin temples received noble patrons who contributed to the support of the temple. Tea was served by the priest in surroundings they were accustomed to. Shoin rooms often have lacquered boards instead of plain wood, shelves for the display of art pieces, and other accouterments of a gentleman's dwelling. So-an rooms are devoid of special decoration. Many more old tearooms of the shoin style survive than of the so-an because their owners had the wealth to care for their buildings, insuring that they would last, and also because they were extremely well made. Though Enshu died in 1647, many of his works survive either in original or replica. So-an huts, though exceedingly well made, are by nature not permanent. I remember sitting in Rikyu's Tai-an when a train passed some hundred yards away; the small windows rattled, the walls seemed to shake in the wake of the train's passing. I thought then what a wonder it was that this so-an had survived. On another occasion, I sat in a superb Enshu shoin, now perilously close to a road. As trucks and cars passed by a few yards from the building, I felt totally secure, almost oblivious to the traffic. The sturdy shoin, elegantly combining both strength and delicacy, was 250 years old when auto traffic was born.

The so-an is a place of humility, where man is constantly reminded of his temporariness; the shoin is a place of dignity, where man is reminded of the enduring arts. One would be hard put to find better examples of the two styles than in Rikyu's Tai-an and Enshu's Mittan, the former built in 1582, the oldest of the simple Rikyu-style tea huts. The room for serving tea is but two mats, but a third, separated from the main room by a track for fusuma, can be used to enlarge the room for more guests. Hideyoshi is said to have sat on the third, outside, mat as Rikyu served tea. The walls are rough, the windows small, the ceilings supported by woven bamboo. If one includes all three mats, the room is but a ten-foot square.

Enshu's Mittan, located in the Ryoko-in subtemple of Daitoku-ji, was built between 1606 and 1608. The room is a beautifully proportioned four and one-half mats, with a three-quarter-mat extension. In it are two tokonoma, one designed for conventional use, the other for displaying the Mittan calligraphy which gives the room its name. There is a set of shelves to one side of the conventional tokonoma; exquisitely arranged, these shelves are made of the finest woods; above and below are cabinets, the lower ones being painted. The *shoji* (papered wooden sliding windows or doors), of this room are crossed with very slender lacquered pieces, doubled and superbly spaced. The whole room is an expression of the most refined taste in architecture, unpretentious but supremely elegant.

The principal differences between the two types of sukiya, so-an and shoin, are these: the so-an depends for its construction on logs, rough woods, and a few cut pieces of common woods; the shoin depends on finely hewn lumber of excellent woods. So-an structures are a skillful blending of the natural. Shoin structures are a skillful manipulation of the natural to make the whole a product of man's conscious intellect. Shoin grew out of the *shinden,* a tenth-century form of private dwelling. Shinden's literal meaning is a palace for sleep. The shoin were rooms for audiences and for the reception of nobles. Traces of early shoin can be found even in countryside dwellings of commoners, but it was with Enshu that the style achieved its perfection. It may also descend from Buddhist structures, or perhaps from early guest houses attached to the main buildings of a compound. The round columns of earlier buildings became square late in the Kamakura period (1185–1333), and sliding doors were introduced. The shoin is less functional than the so-an, but more simplified and practical than the earlier shinden. Hence, in the Momoyama and succeeding eras, it replaced the elaborate shinden as the most popular form of architecture for samurai and men of distinction. Too, the shoin follows stricter patterns than the so-an; the so-an's informality is less regular, The so-an has no porch or veranda; the shoin usually has a wide veranda, called *hiro-en*. The so-an has no shelves, as a rule, for the display of art objects, whereas the shoin almost always has *chigai-dana,* ornamental shelves, arranged asymmetrically. Lastly, the shoin has its namesake, the built-in writing desk. One of the earliest can be seen at the Togu-do, at Ginkaku-ji. There the desk is built into a windowsill, an arrangement that was to become common. Eventually, shoin were more elaborate, never returning to the precise elegance of Enshu. Enshu developed a fondness for the rectangular, the slender, the long, in his designs, and these characteristics are found in perfection in Mittan.

The simplicity of the so-an and of the restrained shoin of Enshu is the result of the philosophy of a people who saw the enduring in the economical. The Shaker communities of America went far along the same path of simplicity, but in their work and attitudes toward life is found little of the pleasure that the Japanese experience. The Japanese sought only to strip away the unnecessary; they did not seek to deprive themselves. Enshu's brilliance as an architect of shoin was that he used materials so skillfully. In other hands, the angular posts, sharp corners, and rectangular forms would have been harsh. He combined these so well that the effect is soft, inviting, and restful.

Rikyu did not favor the shoin style over the so-an,

but he did create a number of rooms that have shoin elements. The justly famous Zangetsu-tei of Omotesenke is such a room. It is a large tearoom, *hiroma*, with a two-mat tokonoma, built in or about 1587. The ten-mat area is unusually generous, and there is a windowsill desk.

Momoyama Architecture

Architecture of the Momoyama period is distinctive for several reasons. The first is that religious buildings are not features of the era. The Japanese concentrated on the construction of castles, private dwellings, and tea huts. In Momoyama Japan, the largest and grandest buildings were built (Osaka, Azuchi, and Momoyama castles, and Juraku-dai), and the smallest, least grand (Tai-an, Fushin-an, and the tea huts of Rikyu and his disciples). Again, the phenomenon of the extremes: a public style that was overwhelming, a private style that was unprepossessing. Castle fortifications, shoin dwellings and rooms, and so-an tea huts are strikingly dissimilar, yet all were produced in an era that barely spans a generation.

Hideyoshi was a hero in Momoyama, and built on heroic scales the most magnificent buildings of the time. With Rikyu, he made cha-no-yu a popular art, and stimulated the building of some of the most sensitive of Japanese structures, and though they are almost flimsy, these tea huts are definitely masculine, daring, and free. The whole age was one of bold people, clearly opposed to strict class distinctions and old traditions. The leaders were inventive, imaginative artists who relished the opportunity of innovating in every form of art and craft. Whatever the characteristic of boldness in the architecture of Hideyoshi and Rikyu, their simple chashitsu reflected the same spirit found in the earliest forms of Japanese architecture, the early Shinto shrines such as the Grand Shrines of Ise. The simplicity they espoused in tea is the same as that found in the thatched wooden buildings of indigenous Japanese architecture. It should be noted that the Momoyama chashitsu were concerned primarily with man; they, together with the castles and shoin, were the principal architectural concerns of the era.

Architectural Plans: *Okoshi-ezu*

The highly specialized architects of tea huts employ standup paper designs for their plans, called *okoshi-ezu*. The standups are exact models of famous tea huts, carefully pasted together in such a way as to fold flat, fitting into sleeves or envelopes. A set of accurate okoshi-ezu is a valuable architectural item, much sought by students and architects of tea. The good sets were designed by men who devoted years to the study of tea, the most recent example being the currently available set by Sutemi Horiguchi (accompanying it are photographs, drawings, and notes; the set is divided into several categories).

Horiguchi and other Japanese architects of the traditional school have recently experimented with new materials in chashitsu; plastics, alloys, and various synthetics have been incorporated in their new designs. These departures have caused a stir among antiquarians but they are certainly within the scope of a living chado.

Tea architecture is bound to change in the near future. Costs, the introduction of new materials, and spirited innovators will have their effect on the future of chashitsu. Most likely, we will again find the tearoom moved back inside the house proper, renewing the old kakoi style. From day to day there is less room in the cities of Japan, yet more chajin; lack of space alone dictates some sort of consolidation in living structure and tea hut, scenic garden and tea garden. At present, Isohachi Yoshida, Yoshiro Taniguchi, Kiyoshi Seike, Junzo Yoshimura, and Sutemi Horiguchi lead the revival in tea architecture. Their homes, restaurants, hotels, and exhibition spaces indicate they are headed in a new direction with old materials. Again, Japan's traditions live in the present, serving the Japanese, showing the way to the rest of the world.

The Roof

The most arresting feature of a chashitsu is its roof; this is perhaps true of all traditional Japanese architecture. The combination of graceful curves and straights in a thatched roof is beautiful. The roofs have several forms: *kirizuma,* or gabled; *yosemune,* or hipped; and *hogyo,* or pyramidal. Materials for roofs include straw, reed, bamboo, bark shingles, metal sheets, and tile.

Temples and tea huts having roofs of tile are common sights in today's Japan. Some temples have enormous roofs of tile; Todai-ji, Nishi Hongan-ji, Higashi Hongan-ji are examples of larger temples that have roofs of tile. The tremendous weight of tile places a great burden on the structural posts. As a consequence, a severe jolt can cause them to fall. Another weakness of this construction is that the walls offer little support, and walls of tea huts are easily cracked or broken by a jolt. At the same time, the structural independence allows the frame of the building to roll with the earth, especially important in an earthquake. Regardless of drawbacks, Japanese tile roofs have a subtlety and beauty hardly found in Western buildings with weighty roofs. The immense tile roof of Nishi Hongan-ji is slightly curved along the spine; this, with bowing ends, makes the form light and attractive.

Thatch roofs are perhaps the most attractive of all, but they are highly susceptible to fire, difficult to thatch in an age that produces few thatchers, and increasingly expensive. As far as size is concerned, tea huts with thatch roofs are larger in appearance than those with shingle or tile, but they have a much lighter feeling. The exterior of a thatched hut is a comfortable sight, inviting and pleasant. Because the straw gives a slightly irregular line to the eaves, takes on an invariably interesting color, and its whole body repeats the shape of a hill or small mountain, it is ideal covering for a tea hut. Regardless of size, it is a style of roofing to which we easily relate.

Bark shingles have a nobility as they age. The infinite repetition of small shingles across the space of a roof provides a contrast to the irregular patterns of windows, walls, and posts of the lower parts of a hut. Their color blends well with dark woods and trees. It is the most delicate covering for a chashitsu and is still often used.

In these three materials—tile, thatch, and shingle—are excellent colors for a wabi hut; the gray tile, yellow thatch, and brown shingle harmonize with any clay, wood, or bamboo that might be used for other sections of a chashitsu. The overlapped tiles shimmer in the afternoon sun and evening moon, resembling the scales of a fish. The moss which often grows on the shingled hut adds color to the expanse of deep brown; this has a cooling effect. On thatched roofs we see grass sprouting from seeds blown there by the wind. The grass makes the roof belong to the countryside.

A roof of thatch will last longer than twenty years. Many householders who now have thatch roofs are covering the whole with metal sheet, which retains the outlines of the roof but loses much in attractiveness. The most common thatch is a grass called *kaya* (miscanthus). Rush is also used, and a marsh reed called *yoshi*. Beneath these roofs is an underpinning of bamboo and timber. The tile roof usually has a mud base, with heavy timbers for bracing. Thatch is first bound with bamboo, then beaten into place. When well matted, the outer bamboo is removed and the sides are trimmed. Thatch provides excellent covering for huts and houses, but rodents and insects eventually make their way into the matting. The covering is three feet thick and usually extends well beyond the posts and walls of a building's sides.

The eaves of all Japanese houses are important; they are especially important to the tea hut. Jiro Harada has said that the eaves are the triumph of Japanese architecture. They allow a broad overhang that protects the interior from rain and sun. In large temples the eaves are complicated structures that help distribute the weight of tile roofs. The abundant supply of cypress, hemlock, cryptomeria, and pine permitted Japanese architects to create strong eaves, great roofs, and large buildings. Nowhere is the grandeur of Japanese architecture better seen than in tall buildings with immense roofs and complicated eaves. These buildings seem to be literal products of stately forests. The Grand Shrines of Ise too seem born of the forest in which they stand. The Ise site is a magnificent forest, a sacred preserve for the most important of all Shinto shrines. The buildings are the finest examples of indigenous Japanese architecture; serenely simple, they have stood for centuries in their great forest. Until World War II the buildings of the shrine were reconstructed every twenty years, in exact duplication, by the priests and craftsmen of the shrine. The present buildings represent the fifty-ninth reconstruction—a living tradition with over a thousand years' history. The simplicity of the Ise buildings is unparalleled; plain wooden structures on piers, thatch roof, and gravel plots with plain wooden fencing comprise the whole of the central shrines.

The quality of Japanese tea huts, like the quality of the Ise Shrines, is a product of the superior craftsmanship of Japanese artisans. Wood is fitted and joined with only the eye as gauge. Today one can witness a master carpenter at work on a tea hut, instructing workmen from the ground, using only his eye as he directs the placing of posts and supports. Because of the central importance of the post, walls can hold as many windows or as few as the architect decides, and they can be placed anywhere on the wall areas. Doors, in like manner, can be placed where convenient or pleasing. Oribe often placed six or eight windows in small ten-foot-square huts. Windowsills and thresholds are never painted in a tea hut, nor are any other wooden surfaces, unless they are lacquered. Japanese chajin have a special fondness for the grains of woods, they prefer to let them show. The aging of *hinoki,* Japanese cypress, is beautiful to watch: first the wood is brilliant yellow, in time it turns dark golden, then brown, then gray. The abundance of this wood is a treasure in Japan and it has been used with distinction. Just after the war, rooms and houses were scarce in Japan, and many American army personnel used old tea huts and shoin structures for housing. To the lasting horror of Japanese owners, superb woods were often painted with the thought of brightening up or preserving the flimsy structures. This bewildered and saddened the Japanese, who value the patina of old woods. At the same time, one young GI wife was shown the small dwelling which had been rented for her use and, upon seeing the unpainted surfaces, fragile shoji, and loose-fitting fusuma, was heard to remark that she didn't come all the way to Japan to live in a beach house. Such are the differences of East and West.

It is notable that only rarely does one encounter reflective surfaces in cha-no-yu huts. The soft-textured mud walls, natural woods, and tatami absorb light. In the narrow confines of a tea hut anything strongly reflecting light would cause discomfort to the guests and not be conducive to contemplation. The only mirror surfaces in a tearoom are water and the polished metal of kettle lids—everything else has a dull finish.

The Post: *Naka-bashira*

Japanese architecture stresses the importance of the post, *hashira;* everything centers around the upright. Western architecture relies on the wall. The source of the importance of the hashira is probably the sacred post, *naka no mihashira,* that occupies the central position in the Grand Shrines of Izumo, Japan's oldest Shinto shrine. Izumo is dedicated to the spirit of Okuninushi no Mikoto. Sericulture, fishing, and medicine are said to stem from this spirit, making the shrine a place of veneration for the Japanese. The sacred post at Izumo has both religious and architectural significance, but the exact origins are unknown; perhaps it is a manifestation of the story found in the *Kojiki,* Japan's first national history, which tells of a deity's erecting a post around which he builds a palace. At Ise, the most important of Japan's shrines, the central post does not pierce the interior, but remains part of the understructure of the main buildings. It is significant that this post is fenced from the view even of those who enter the sacred precincts. When the twenty-year cycle of reconstruction is accomplished, this post alone is left untouched.

Other evidence of the importance of the post can be seen in Japanese literature. In *The Tale of Genji,* poems are attached to posts and inscribed on posts, and people lean against posts, not walls. Many references in other works mention the *Daikoku-bashira,* the kitchen post, which, while not the physical center of the house, is the point from which all plans evolve.

As an architectural idea, the central post is clearly stressed in most tea huts. In the tea hut the post takes the name *naka-bashira,* central post. This again is rarely in the center of the room, but is the spatial center of the small structure and certainly the center of attention. The naka-bashira offers little real support to the roof, as do corner posts; its function is primarily religious or aesthetic. This post is a Japanese reaction to space: it supports emotion, it is not a rational inclusion. Excellent examples can be seen in Oribe's Hasso-an, and in Enshu's Mittan, Sowa's Teigyokuken, Sochin's Toyobo, and Sansai's Shoko-ken.

The naka-bashira is made from a tree trunk; often the bark is left in place. This post is freestanding and placed by the *daime,* a three-quarter mat that extends beyond the conventional one-, two-, three-, or four-and-one-half-mat areas of the tearoom proper. When the daime arrangement is used, the naka-bashira is essential.

Oribe's naka-bashira most often include a curve about two feet off the base; this is graceful and serves to relieve the otherwise severe straightness of woods found in the chashitsu. Rikyu preferred naka-bashira that rise straight from base to ceiling. Enshu, too, liked straight naka-bashira, while Fumai liked a trunk that curves slightly.

Attached to the naka-bashira is an extended wall, the *sode kabe*. This device, always open at the bottom, is made of the same mud texture as the other walls of the chashitsu. An exception is the famous sode kabe of Jo-an, which is of wood. The reason for the lower part of the sode kabe being open is that this allows light into the area where the host sits, the same place where utensils are placed as tea is being prepared. Too, as the area is open, the guests may see all the movements of the host as he is sitting before the utensils. The sode kabe is usually about two or three feet wide; the width varies with the curves of the naka-bashira to which it is joined. A variation on this is the Doan kakoi style designed by a son of Rikyu who was lame. He did not wish guests to see his body movements so he built a small enclosure for the host—actually a wall that extends from the host's entrance to a point near the place where utensils are placed on the host's mat. A small arch is included in the wall. This arrangement is very unusual.

There are ample precedents for both the naka-bashira and the Doan kakoi in Japanese architecture. The following passage from *Tsurezuregusa,* a work written about 1313, is indicative of a peculiarly Japanese attitude toward such things: "When you build a house you should consider what it will be like in the summer. In winter you can live almost anywhere, but living in a badly built house during the heat of summer is unbearable. Deep water does not look cool, while a shallow stream appears very cool indeed. As for the interior detail, sliding doors give much more light to the room than one held with a bar. A room with a high ceiling is cold in winter and lights are not effective in it. I remember hearing people say that a building should have some impractical aspects which are both interesting to look at and which may be used for a variety of purposes." Both the naka-bashira with its sode kabe and the Doan kakoi fit the last remark of the passage. As for the rest of it, it seems clear that the Japanese have long been intent on preparing houses for the summer months—with the great shoji that slide open to gardens and cool the interior—while we of the West have striven to seal our houses against the winter cold, forgetting the summer heat.

Tatami

In old Japanese paintings and prints, elegantly attired ladies and gentlemen are seen sitting on mats about the room. The mats are forerunners of the tatami now found in Japanese houses, tea huts, temples, shrines, and even shops. Tatami are extremely important in the tearoom.

The mats, roughly three by six feet, are the modules for all standard dimensions of Japanese house architecture. They are uniquely Japanese, and after having been introduced in the fifteenth century they came into wide use throughout the country. At first they served as occasional pieces in a room, placed directly on a wooden floor of wide boards. Their use spread until they came to cover the entire floor space.

Tatami are cooler in summer than other flooring, and warmer in winter. They are a pleasant color, soft but firm to the touch. On them, hosts will often place *zabuton* (flat, square cushions) for guests to sit on, but in tea ceremonies these are, as a rule, not used. Tatami centuries ago replaced straw mats about the size of conventional cushions, their form being taken from the length and width upon which a man could comfortably rest. There is some variation in the size of contemporary mats; Tokyo mats are slightly smaller than those of Kyoto, and the mats in recent Tokyo apartment buildings are considerably shorter and narrower than the old standard in either city. Mats purchased recently in New York (at thirty dollars each) proved near the standard Kyoto measurements.

Originally tea was served to guests sitting in Chinese chairs that rested on wooden floors, but after the Muromachi period, tearooms had wall-to-wall mats as a permanent fixture. Tea is the better for it. Sitting "on" the room, with a relatively low ceiling, fine woods, and interesting textures is infinitely more satisfying than being braced by chairs, faced by tables, and, generally, being kept an alien of softness among hard elements. The two-inch thickness of the mat rests about eighteen inches off the ground, the tea hut floor being raised to provide ventilation. One literally floats when walking on these ingenious coverings.

Houses and apartments built in traditional Japanese style are advertised for rent or sale by the number of mats of floor area; a four-and-one-half-mat room is about ten square feet, a two-mat room six square feet, an eight-mat room a twelve-foot square. An eight-mat room is a generous size—there being no furniture to clutter the space. Of course, much larger rooms have been built in traditional style; I have seen a banquet hall of 250 mats in a Japanese inn, an immense area with no central columns to support the ceiling, which is hung from the spine of the roof.

The fact that the Japanese do not wear shoes in a house, not even in *roka,* which are wooden passages or halls, helps keep the rooms clean while protecting the tatami. Japanese hosts, wishing to be polite, will occasionally urge an unknowing Westerner to wear his shoes inside the house; of course, this should never be done. Recently in Tokyo a Westerner who is a long-time resident of Japan and who owns a Japanese-style house had as a guest the famous soprano Zinka Milanov. She came wearing sharply pointed high heels. The host asked her to remove the spikes before entering the tatami rooms. She refused steadfastly; stepping onto the soft mats she was heard to remark to her host: "But darling, I am nothing without my shoes!"

Mats are easy to clean; if something is spilled, it is wiped up. When powdered tea is spilled, the area is first wiped with a damp cloth, salt is spinkled, and then it is wiped thoroughly with a dry cloth. Mats are removed once a year, beaten, and allowed to air in the sun for one full day. At the same time, the underflooring is cleaned. The outermost layer of the tatami will last, with average use, about four or five years before it must be replaced. With the outer layer replaced two or three times, a mat can last about fifteen years. Prices for mats vary with the quality of the workmanship and materials that are used. Morse, writing in 1886, priced mats at sixty cents and at four dollars. Today's average is about fifteen dollars for one tatami. Each has a tape border along the edge of the two longer sides, about an inch and one-quarter wide; it comes in black or brown, and can be had in expensive materials—brocades and so forth. Tearooms generally have the following sizes: 1, 1½, 2, 2¾, 3, 3¾, 4, 4½, 6, 8, 10, or 12 mats, with most rooms being four and one-half mats. The mats are laid in patterns so that two corners abut the long side of a third mat; care is taken to avoid a meeting of corners that would form a plus sign. The custom of avoiding four corners in one place probably goes back to samurai days, when a sword could easily be thrust from below if four corners met in one spot. In tea school one is taught never to step on joining lines of tatami, nor on tracks for sliding screens.

Tearooms have eight basic patterns, the *hachi ro no ho,* a system of arranging mats around the *ro,* or fire pit. The style of a room is determined by the position of the ro. There are additional varieties, but nearly all rooms follow the basic patterns. There are two major categories of rooms that follow the hachi ro no ho: *hon-gatte,* basic style, and *gyaku-gatte,* reversed style. In a hon-gatte room guests sit to the right of the host. In the gyaku-gatte rooms, the position is reversed. The host always sits in the immediate vicinity of the ro, while the guests always sit opposite him.

From the hon-gatte and gyaku-gatte stem four variations: *yojohan-kiri* (four-and-one-half-mat), *daime-kiri* (latitudinal two-mat), *sumi-kiri* (longitudinal two-mat with corner fire pit), and *mukau-kiri* (longitudinal but with fire pit where the mats join). These four variations multiplied by the two basic styles are the eight patterns of the hachi ro no ho. There is a sufficient number of variations to satisfy most tastes.

After Rikyu's time, mats distinguished between places for the nobility and those for commoners. Nobles sat on the *kinin tatami,* fronting on the tokonoma, the traditional place of honor. This position affords a post against which one can rest in the course of an evening's entertainment. Kinin tatami are still seen in Japan, preserved out of habit. The kinin tatami are edged with a special tape, different from the rest of the mats in a room. There have been rooms in which these mats were raised to a position higher than others; this, too, can still be seen in Japan.

Other mats in the tearoom are *kyaku tatami,* or guest mats. The principal geust, like the nobles of the past, sits directly in front of the tokonoma; other guests

The approach to Rikyu's Tai-an tea hut at Myoki-an, Oyamazaki, Kyoto. (Photo by H. Ikeda.)

The tokonomo and a window of Tai-an. Note the wood-and-bamboo construction of the ceiling and the discoloration of the clay walls. (Photo by H. Ikeda.)

The Shigure-tei tea hut at Kodai-ji, Kyoto. Note the two-story construction. (Photo by S. Fujima.)

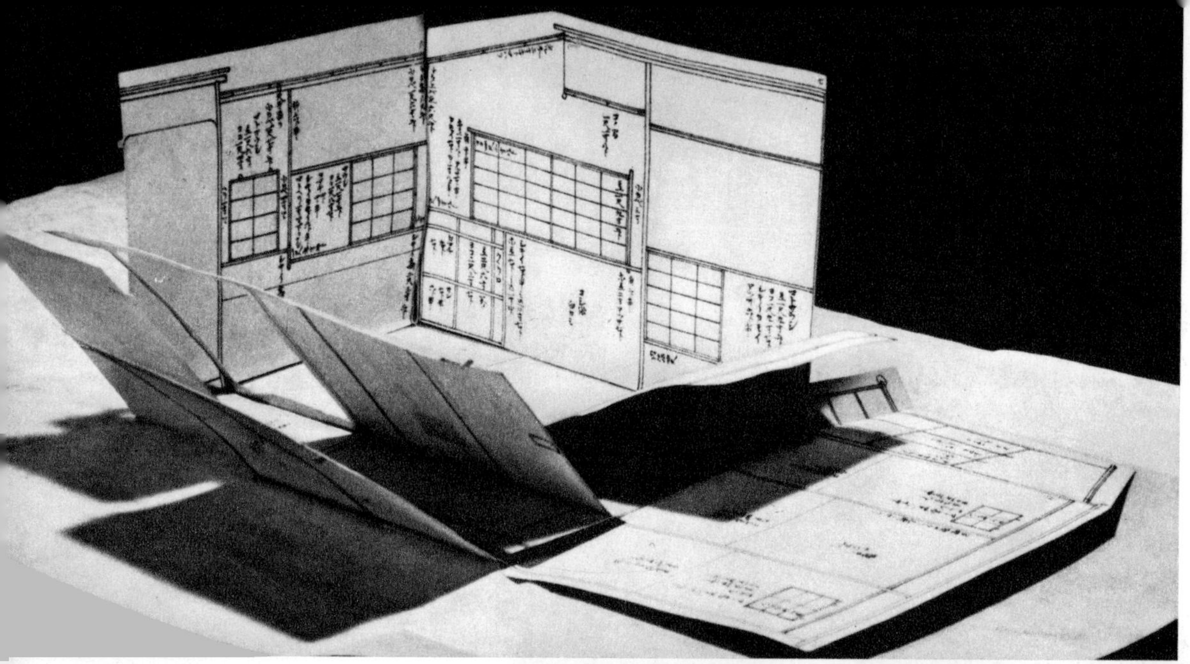

Okoshi-ezu (standup paper model of a tea hut) used by architects, showing the standing-up process. (Photos by S. Fujima.)

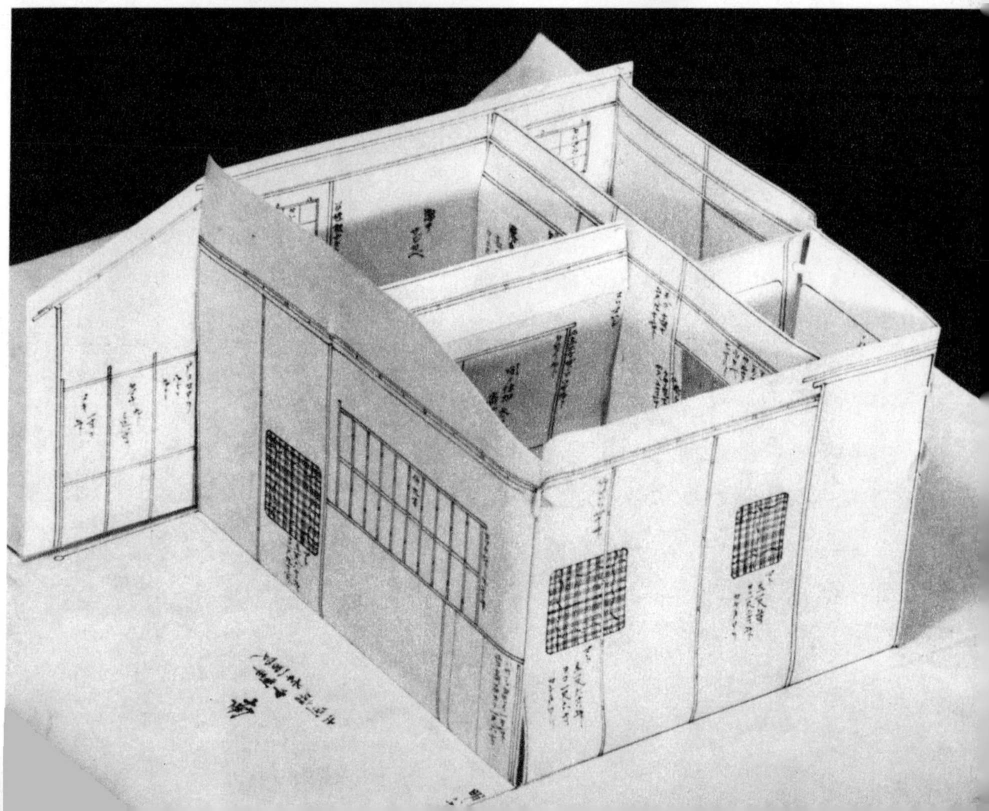

◀The open skylight of Yu-in at Urasenke, as it appears from the inside.

Detail of the lower wall and ventilation openings of the Shokin-tei tea hut in the grounds of Katsura Detached Palace. (Photo by S. Fujima.)

Detail of the ceiling, a window, and the eaves of Shokin-tei. (Photo by S. Fujima.)

▲ Sotan's design of the interior of Yu-in. Note the pattern of the ceiling.

Inside Shokin-tei. Shown are sword shelves in the upper left-hand corner, windows, and a post. (Photo by S. Fujima.)

Katagiri Sekishu's design at Jiko-in, Nara.

Two views of the interior of Enshu's Mittan tea hut. (Photos by H. Ikeda.)

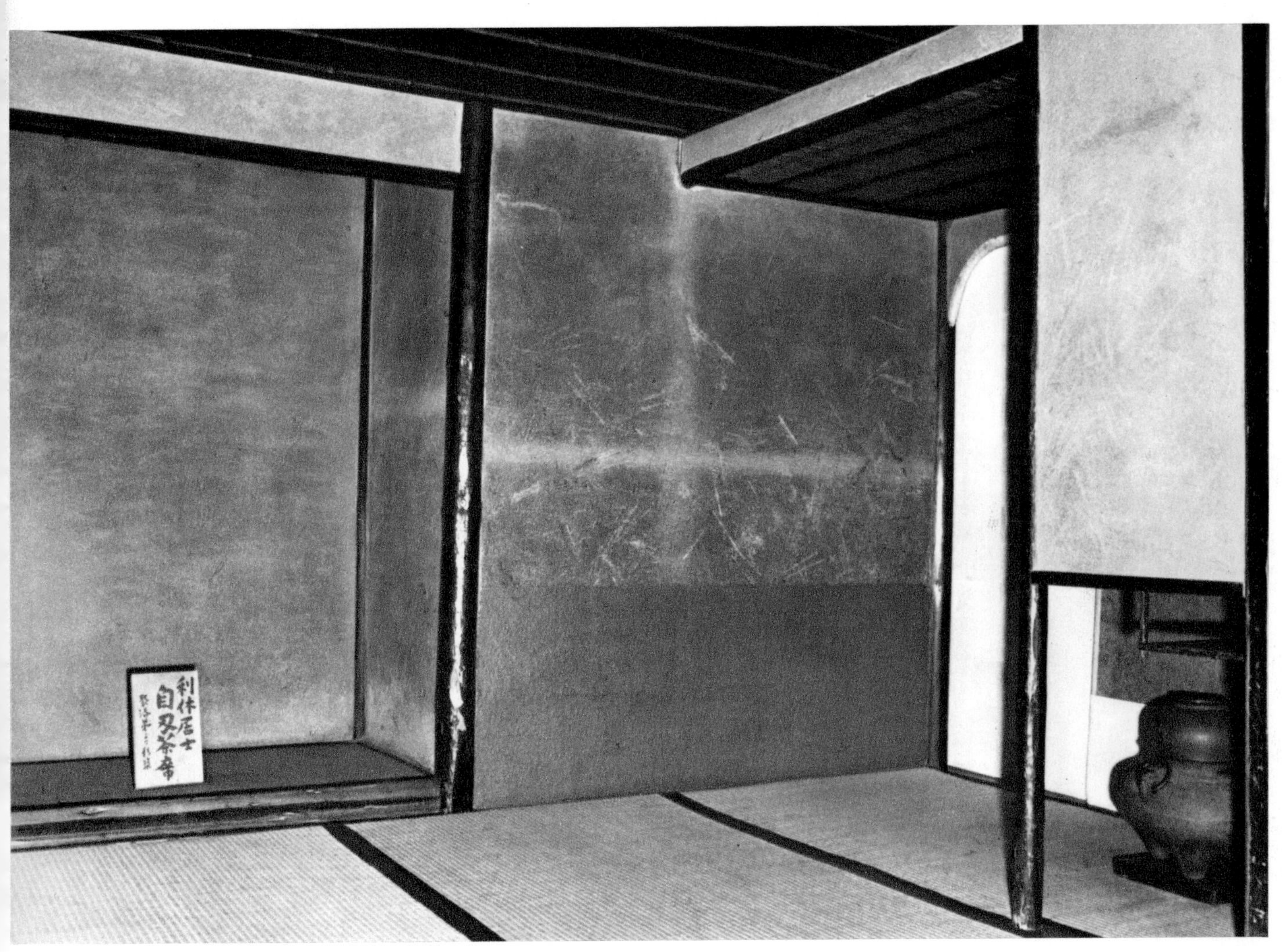

Interior of the Kan-in tearoom at Juko-in subtemple, Daitoku-ji. Note the *naka-bashira* (post) and host's entrance. (Photo by H. Ikeda.)

The Totsutotsu-sai tearoom at Urasenke, arranged for tea.

Interior of the Hasso-an at Konchi-in subtemple, Nanzen-ij, Kyoto; Note Enshu's curved naka-bashira design.

The host's entrance of the Konnichi-an tearoom at Urasenke.

A *mizuya* (preparation area) at Urasenke with all the utensils for the preparation of tea.

The Yu-in tea hut at Urasenke. Inside this hut is a single four-and-one-half-mat room and a mizuya.

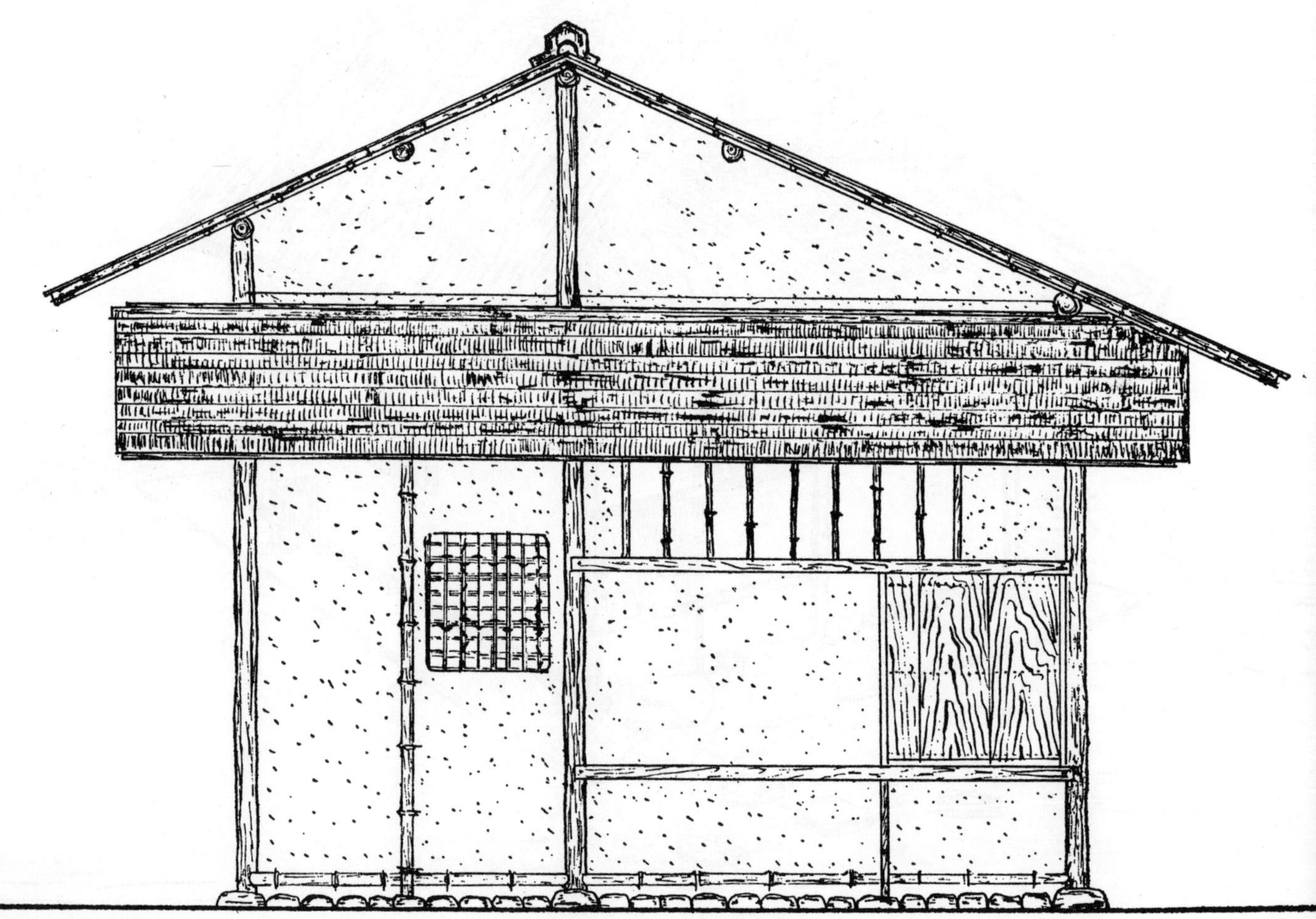

An elevation of a tea hut with a cedar roof.

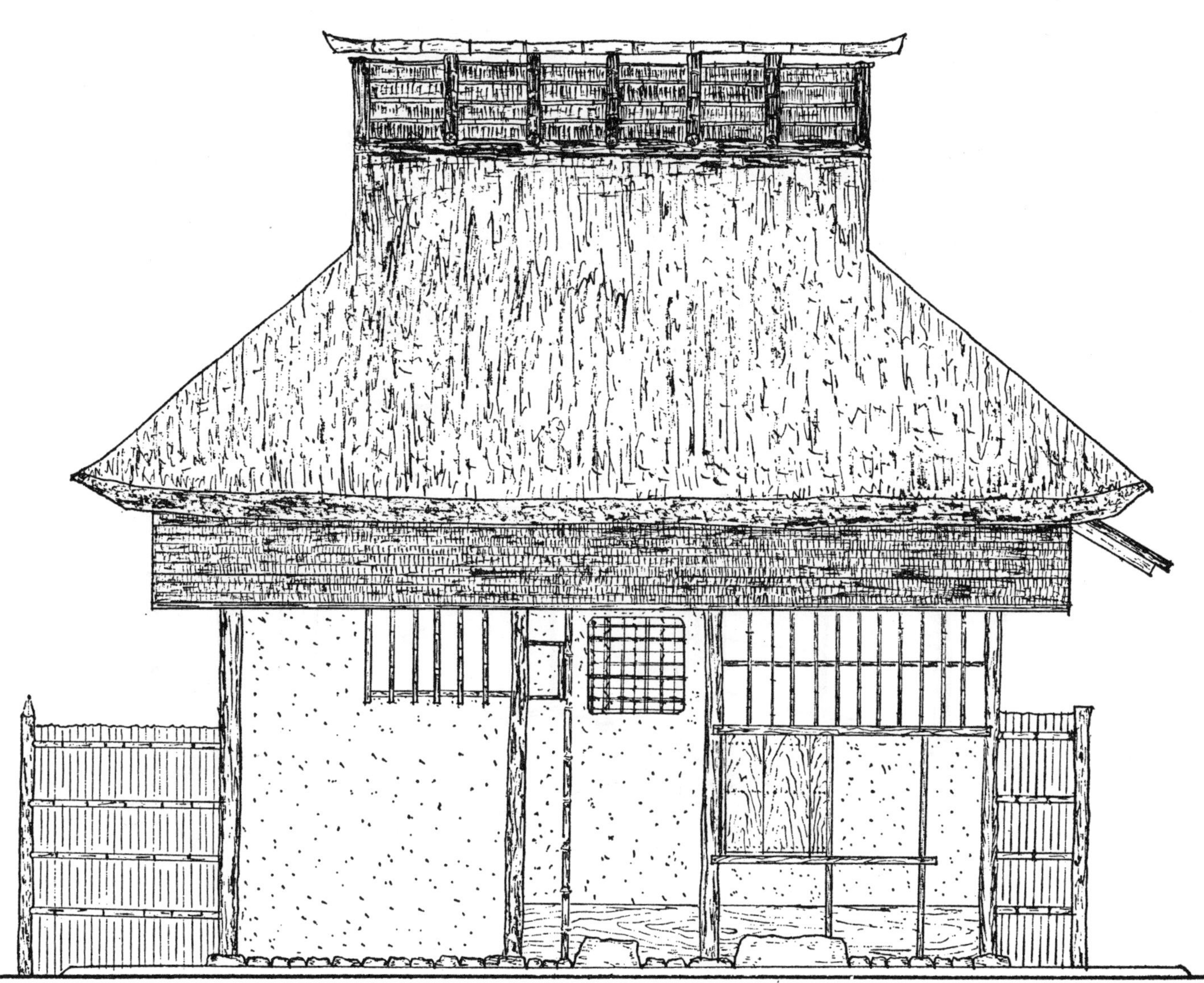

An elevation of a tea hut with a thatched roof.

The interior of a tea hut.

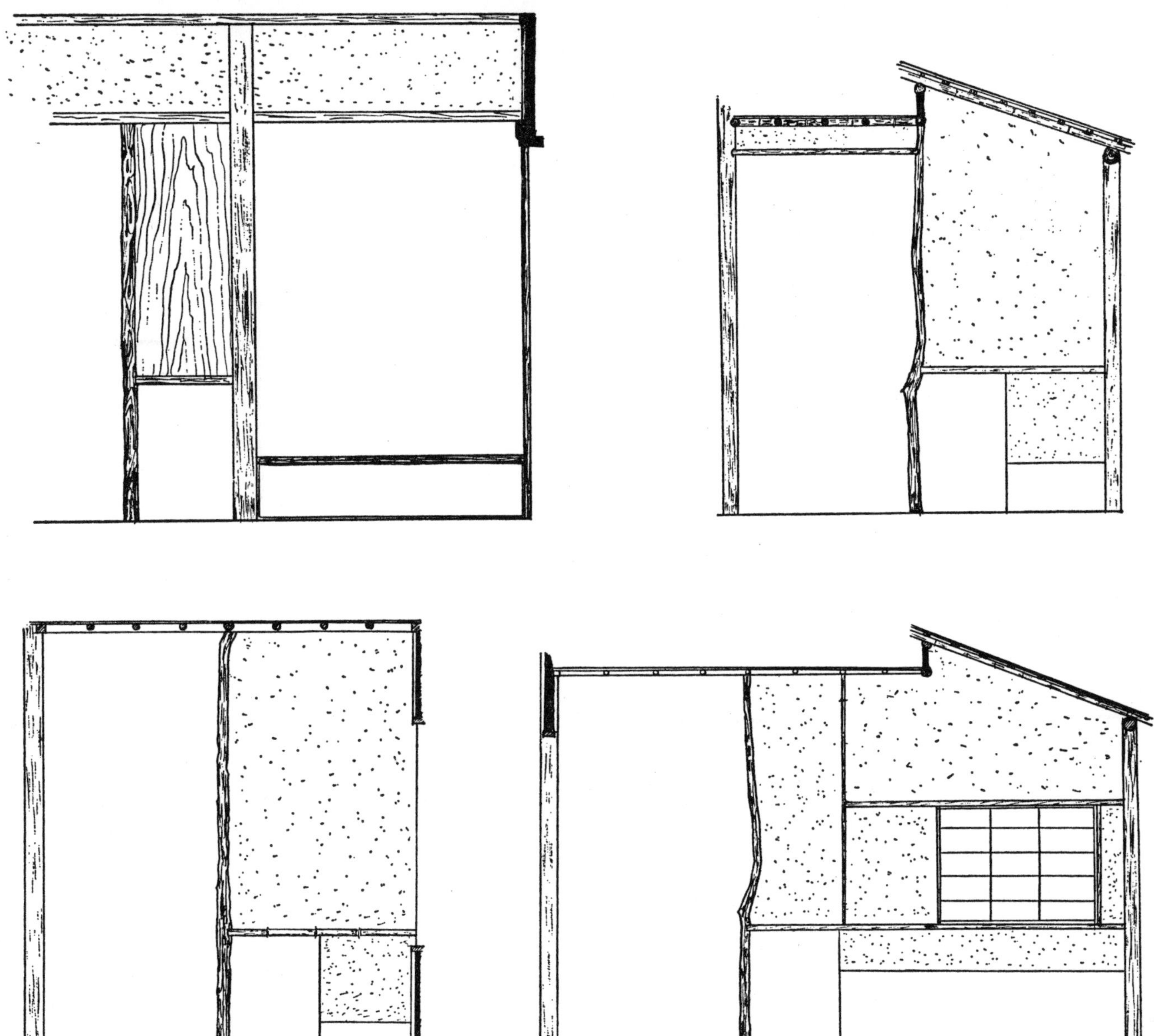

Four styles of naka-bashira.

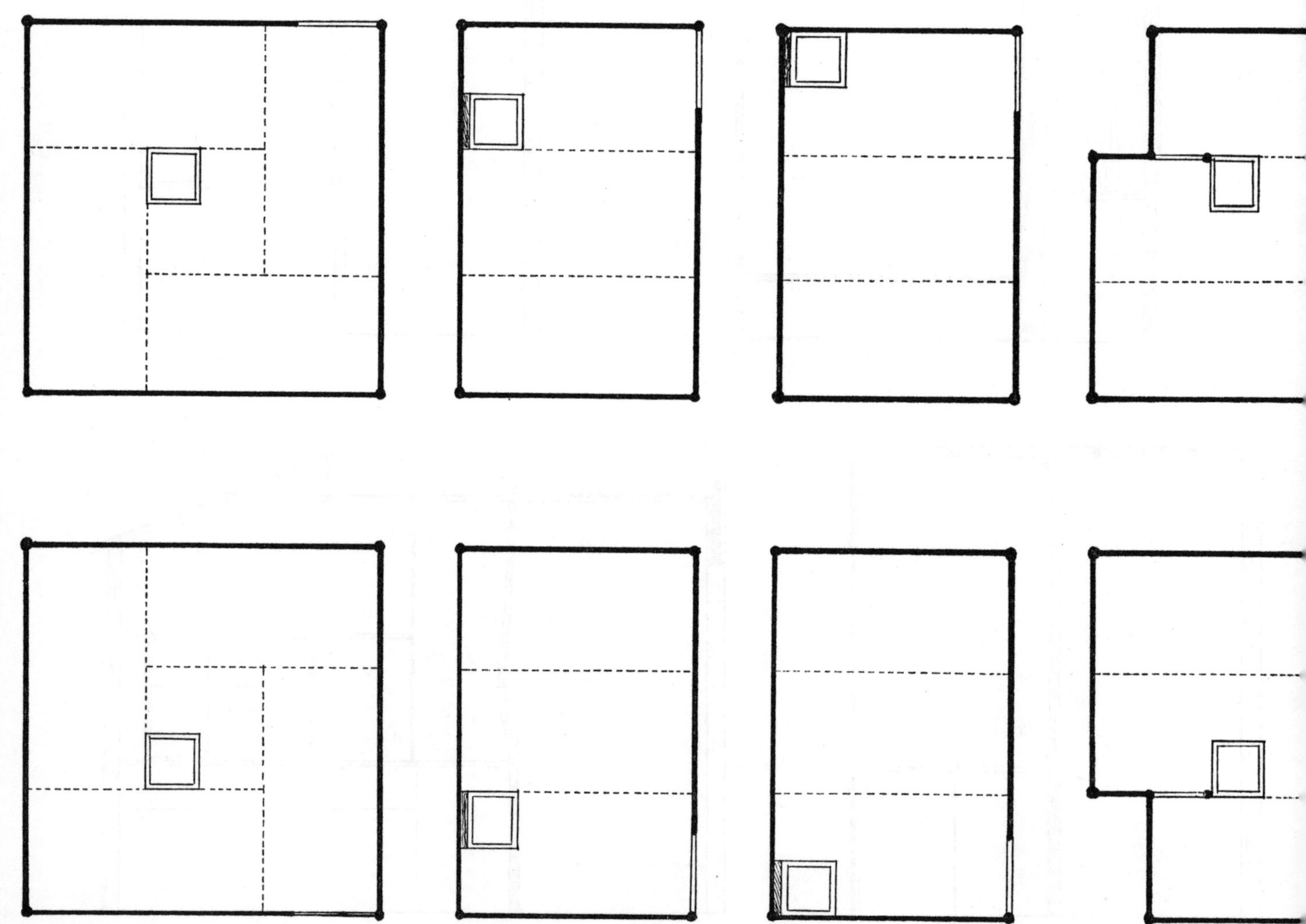

Hachi ro no ho, the eight basic ways of placing the fire pit.

Four designs for tea-hut windows.

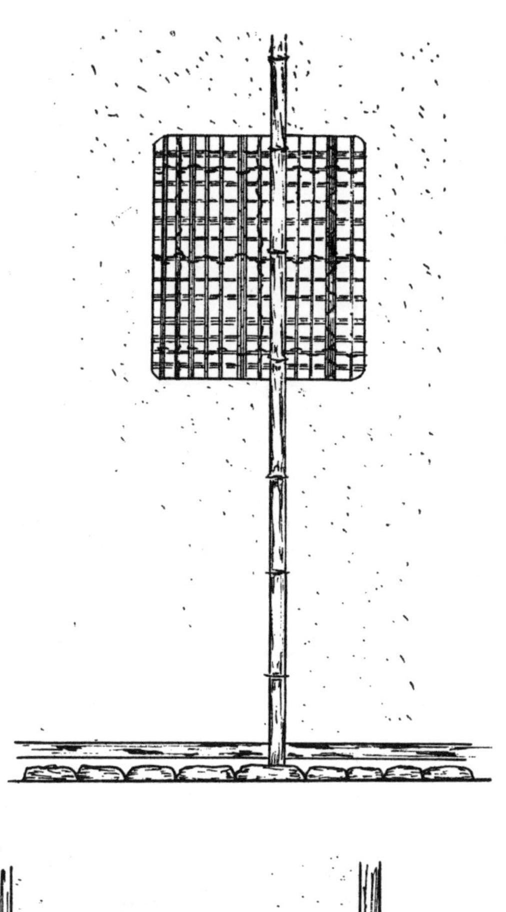

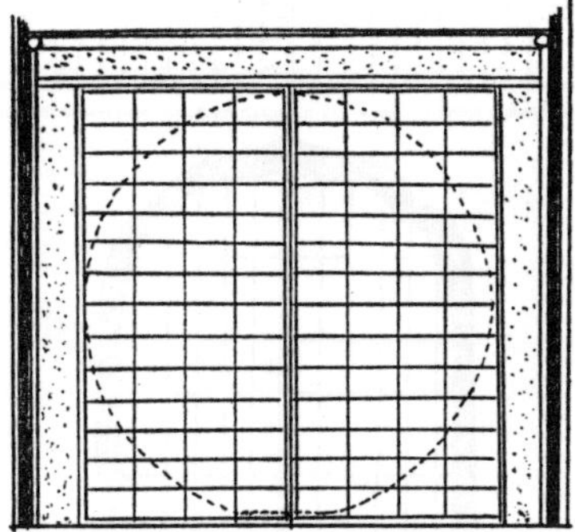

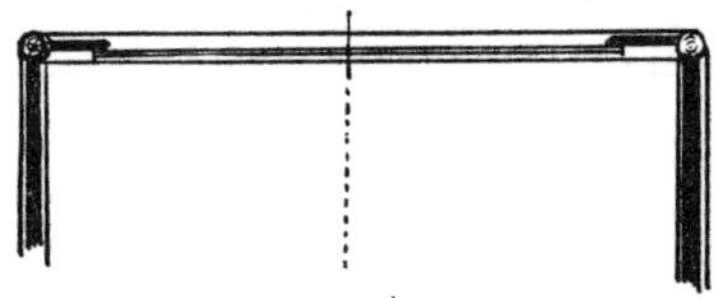

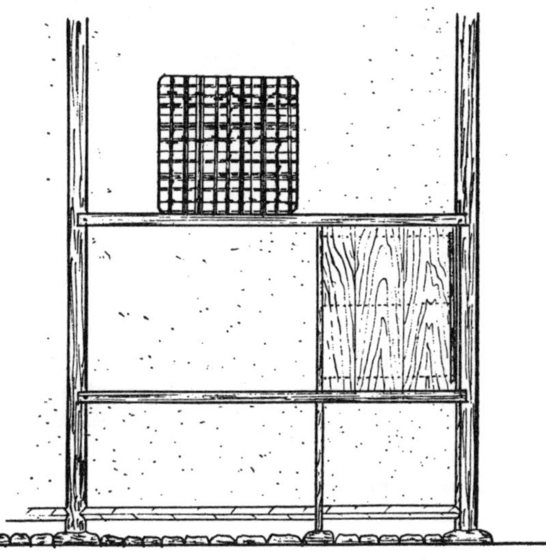

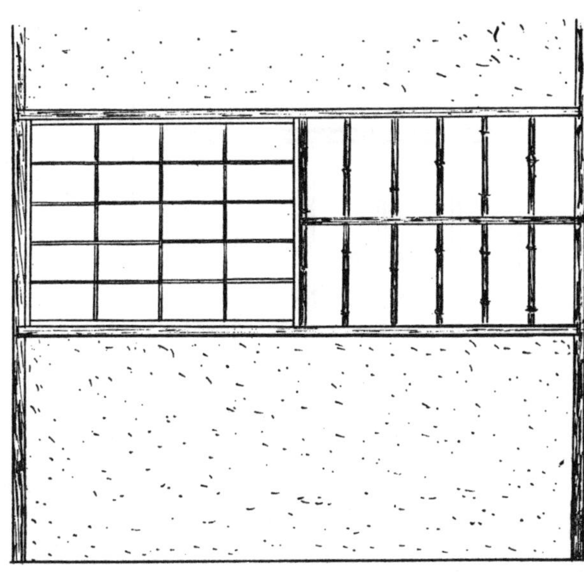

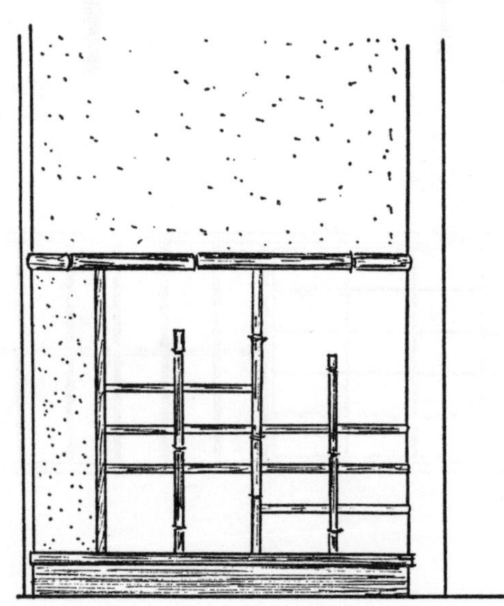
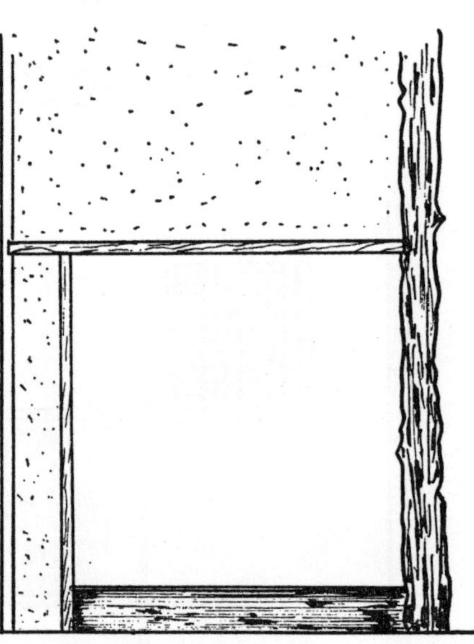

Above are two window designs for *shoin*-style tearooms; the left-hand window is above a *shoin* (alcove). Below are two side views of tokonoma openings.

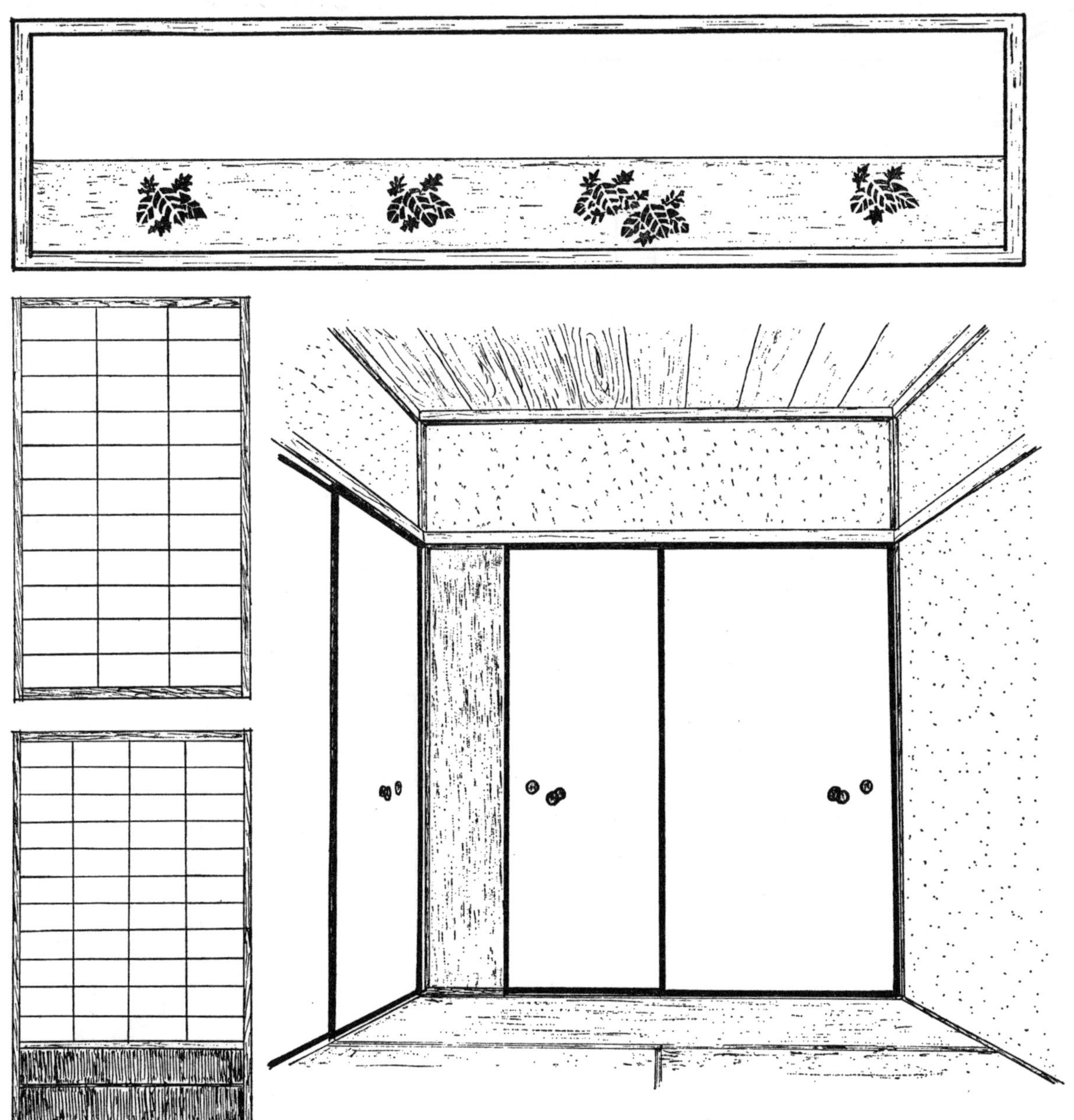

Above is Rikyu's design for the *ramma* (carved transom) of the Zangetsu-tei tea hut at Omotesenke in Kyoto. Below it, left, are the two types of *shoji* (papered wooden sliding windows or doors): *akari shoji,* above, and *koshi shoji,* below. Right is a design for the *fusuma* (sliding doors) of a shoin-style room.

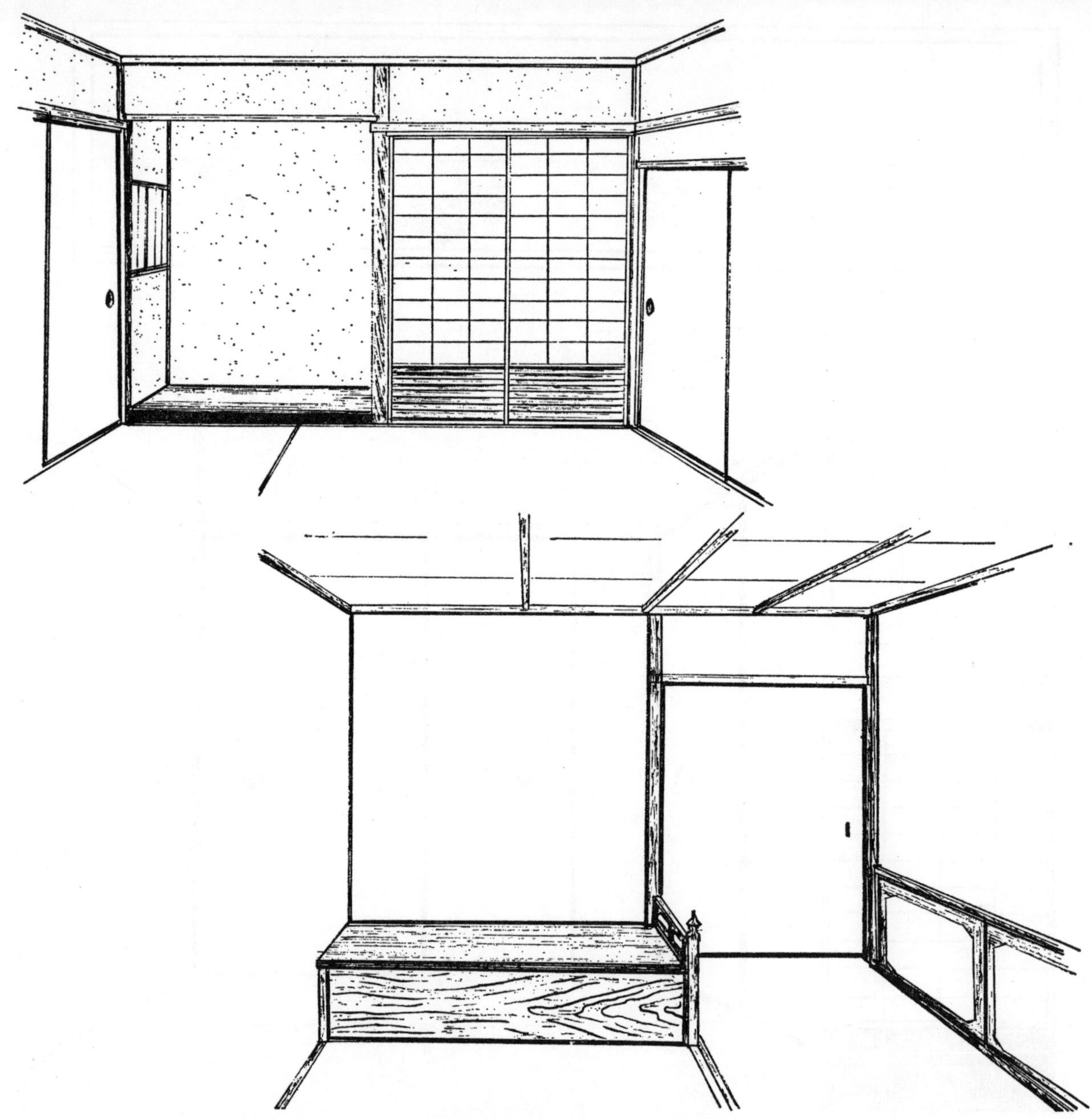

The upper design is for a conventional tokonoma in a large room. The lower one is the raised-platform-style tokonoma of the *kakoi* (room set apart for tea in a large building) at Manshu-in, Kyoto.

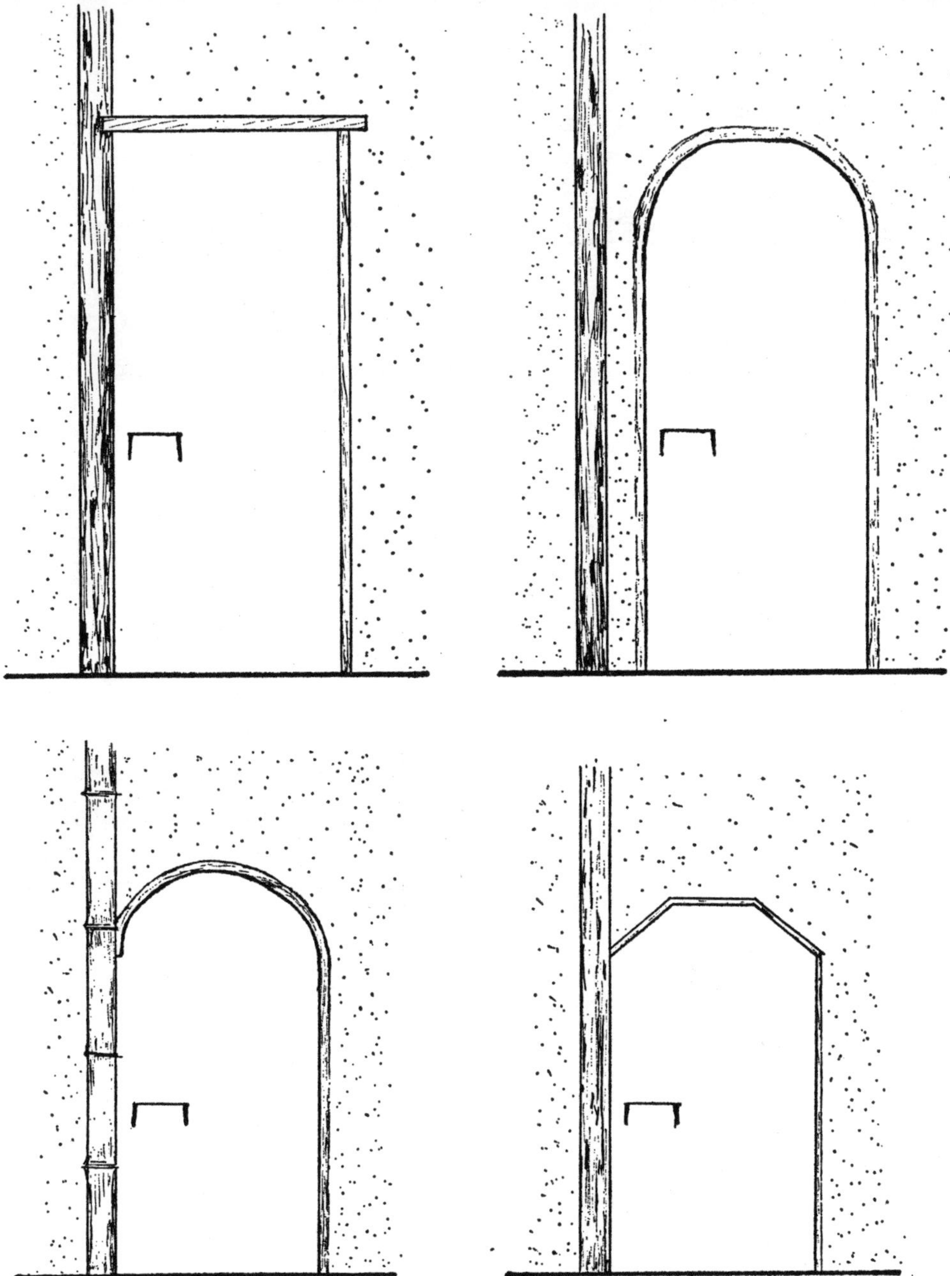

Four styles of host's entrance to the tearoom.

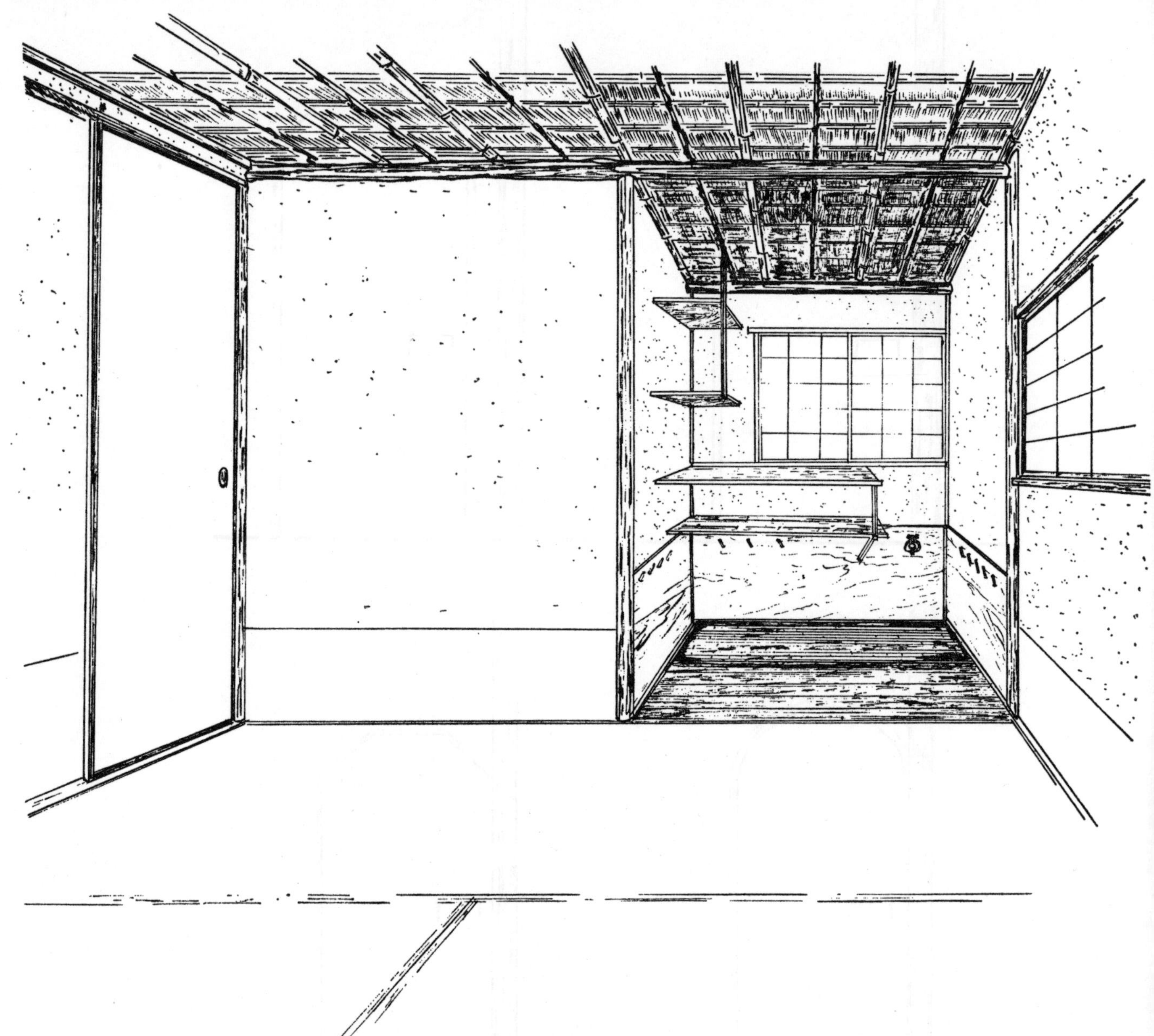

The *katte no ma* (preparation room) and mizuya. The shelves are for storing utensils. The mizuya has bamboo flooring that serves as a drain.

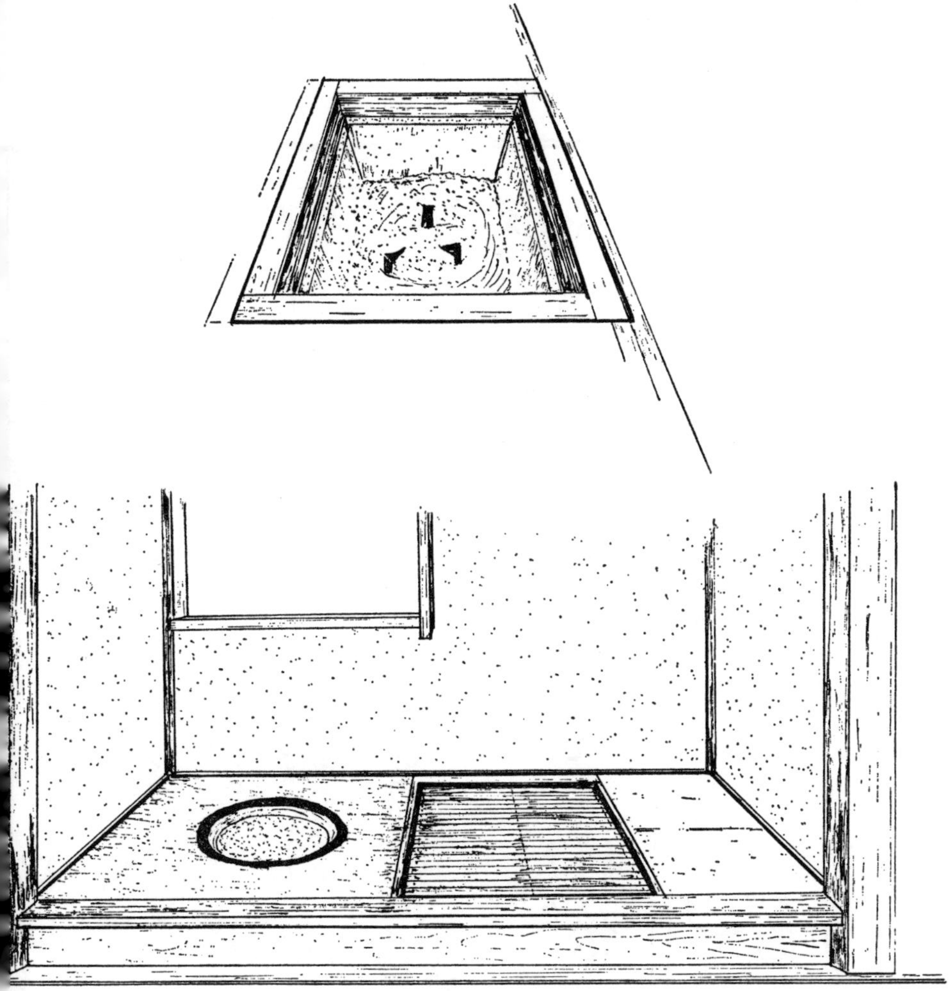

The upper design is for the *ro* (fire pit). Note the raked ashes and trivet in the center. Below is the mizuya's *ganro* (fire pit for heating water prior to the ceremony).

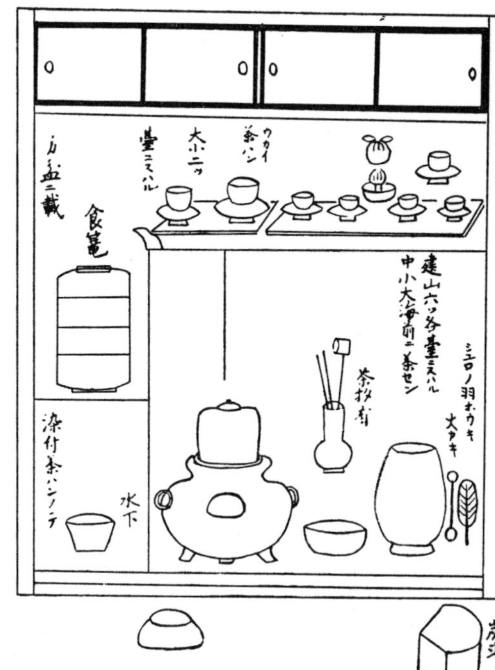

Arrangement of utensils in the mizuya, from *Chaya Zensho.* (Photo by S. Fujima.) ▶

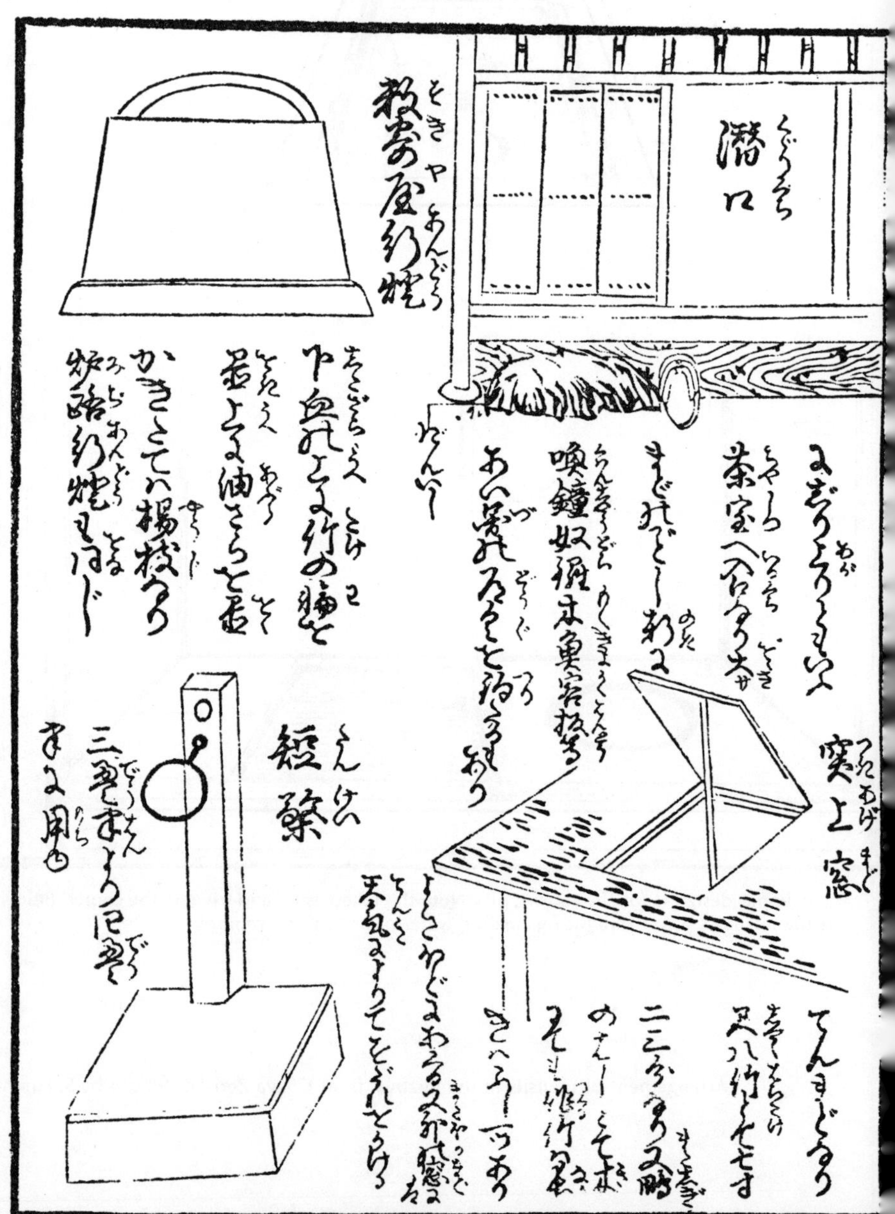

Illustrations from *Chado Hayagaten*, vol. 1. In the upper right-hand corner is the nijiri-guchi, and below it a skylight for moon or snow viewing. In the upper left-hand corner is an *andon* (wooden lantern), and below it a stand for an oil lamp to be used during evening tea.

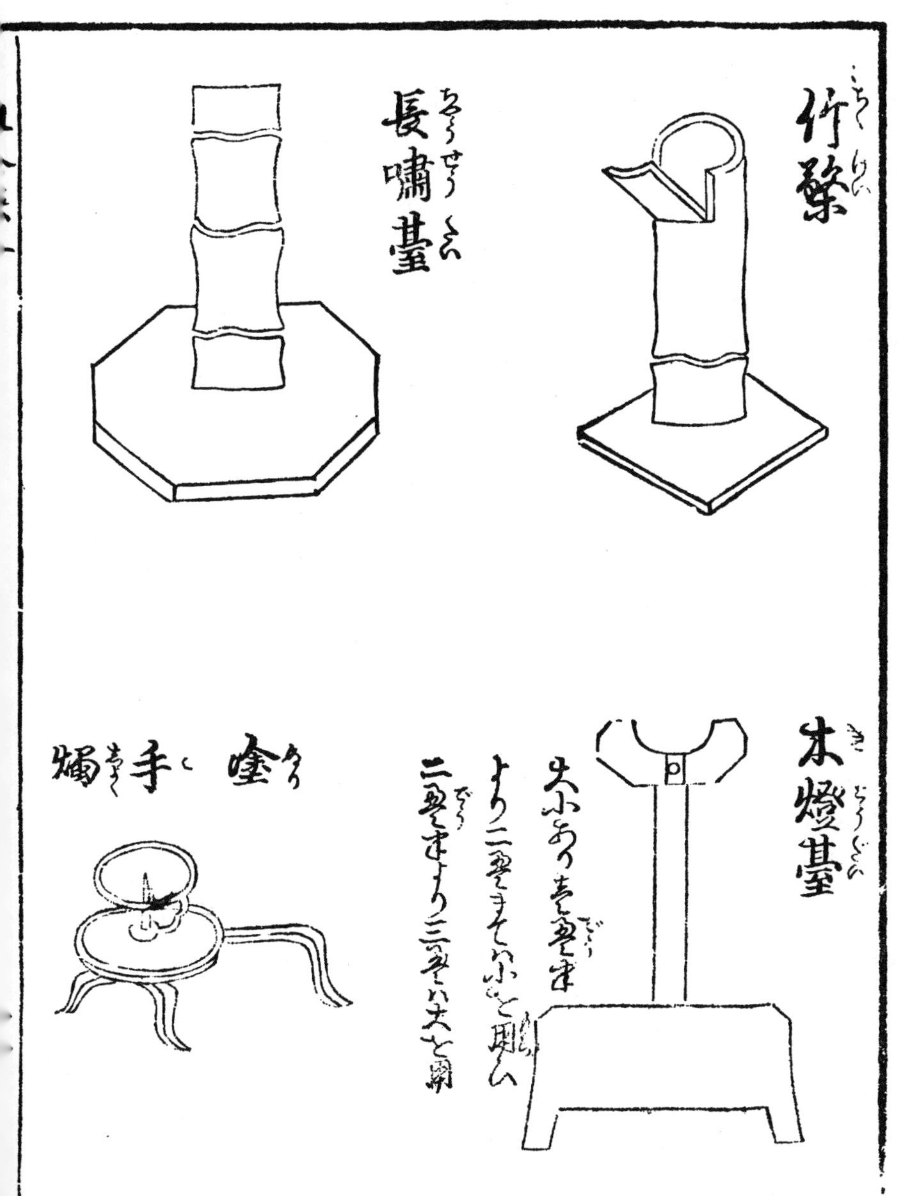

Various kinds of candleholders used for evening tea, from vol. 1 of *Chado Hayagaten.*

form a row beside him, the last guest sitting closest to the door by which they entered the room.

Fumikomi tatami is the entrance mat for the host. This is placed in front of the small, arched doorway that leads to the preparation room, and which the host uses when entering and leaving the room. The daime, already mentioned as being the mat by the naka-bashira, is the one upon which utensils are placed. Though not always present, the daime has long been an important element of the architecture of the tearoom.

The slight give of the tatami as they are walked upon, their texture, and their color make them ideal for tea ceremony. Utensils are most often placed directly on the mats. The mats prevent breakage and act as a soft background for viewing the utensils.

The Ceiling

The height of a tearoom averages about six feet or less. The ceiling is often divided into three sections, the lowest being over the place where the host sits. Ceilings have great variety; cedar panels in small squares, hurdled bamboo, matted rush tied with black cord and held in place with bamboo, and various braided materials. Ceiling borders are often natural woods with the bark left on.

An unusual ceiling is found in the Karakasa tea hut of Kodai-ji, Kyoto. It forms an umbrella supported by long bamboo braces. The nearby Shigure hut, connected by a passageway, also has a distinctive ceiling revealing the hipped roof that covers the hut. Both huts were removed from Momoyama Castle; they were experimental and cannot be compared with other huts of the era. Tessellated ceilings are common in larger tearooms, using woods of fine grain and color. Occasionally plain boards, usually of pine, cypress, or cedar, are placed with widely spaced bamboo supports. When natural boards are used, the lengths are cut and placed in sequence; grains match evenly, joints being covered by bamboo to give an appearance of continuous boards.

Before Rikyu, Japanese architecture long ignored ceilings. Rikyu paid great attention to all the details of his structures and, naturally, to the ceilings. He drew attention to the working of ceilings in all parts of the structure, even in the tokonoma. His concentrated vision—Buddhists call it *isshin tokudo* (complete concentration)—is similar to the dictum of Mies van der Rohe: "God is in the details."

The Hollywood attitude toward ceilings—that is, no ceiling—was anticipated by the Japanese artists who depicted countless palaces and houses in *emaki,* painted scrolls, which omit any hint of a ceiling. The perspective of these pictures is that of three-quarter bird's-eye; the whole interior of these Japanese dwellings seems open not only to the gardens which flank them but to the heavens as well. It was not that the houses had no ceilings, but that they were unimportant. Apparently, one never looked up at home. Rikyu inspired a new concern for architects when he chose to install ceilings of beauty.

Why the Japanese had not paid attention to the upper reaches of rooms is debatable. Perhaps it is the result of sitting on the floor rather than in chairs. Another consideration might be that the lack of bright lighting made the upper parts of rooms dark and difficult to see. Rikyu dropped the ceiling to a level of easy view and enriched the shrunken space by making the ceiling a highlight of the room. Most important early Japanese dwellings had high rafters which often left the roof itself in full view. We suspect that Rikyu installed ceilings so as to avoid the dirt that must have fallen from the roof. The cleanliness of the mats and the protection of articles that rested on them would have been a consideration too. Japanese must have been interested in protecting Buddhist sculptures from the soot of temple roofs when they installed mandorlas with the statues; these devices swoop up from behind the figure to cover its head and are often of fine craftsmanship. As an overhead cover, the mandorla can be thought of as a kind of roof.

Most tea huts in simple style have three ceiling heights; one for the host (the lowest), and two of different heights for the guests. The host's ceiling is of crude rush. The guests' ceilings are of boards or woven materials held secure by bamboo or skinned timbers. Rich materials, excellent craftsmanship, and subtle blending of elements make tea-hut ceilings worth imitating. Often the bamboo is very old, having been purchased from a farmer whose dwelling is being reconstructed or repaired. This is a dark purple or maroon, and comes from the kitchen ceilings of country houses where charcoal fires have slowly turned the ceiling bamboo to a deep, lustrous hue. This is purchased from brokers who search it out for bamboo craftsmen and sukiya architects.

In the seventeenth century, ceilings were sometimes trimmed with lacquer. The two-mat kakoi of Manshu-in, Kyoto, has a board ceiling of dark wood with brilliant red lacquer trim. This room has no windows, but the white plaster walls and red trim give brightness to the setting.

The Walls

Because tea-hut architecture is based on posts, the walls can be freely punctured by doors and windows. This makes for a most versatile structure. There is no architectural style in Japan as freely given to windows and openings as the tea hut; many are known by the number of windows they possess (Hasso-an, an eight-windowed hut; Rokuso-an, a six-windowed hut). In many tea huts, the windows are the most distinctive exterior feature. The walls are of a clay mixture with a rust, gray, or yellow coloring. Sometimes grass or straw is mixed with the clay, the fibers showing on interior and exterior surfaces; pebbles are also used in walls. Less often seen are smooth, plaster walls which have been papered or painted. Examples are the Togu-do tearoom, the kakoi of Manshu-in, and the Mittan of Ryoko-in. The brilliant white surfaces of the plaster is muted by the dark woods of the ceiling, windows, shelves, and shoji.

The sukiya-hut room differs from conventional rooms in that the sukiya walls are almost invariably permanently fixed on all four sides. The usual walls of a residence in Japan are movable, removable, and variable on one, two, or three sides. Conventional Japanese room walls are of fusuma or shoji. The space of the hut is defined by these walls, and it is interesting that, in the evolution of Japanese architecture, as the philosophical outlines of tea were broadened the physical setting of tea shrank to the absolute minimum, making the tearoom the smallest of all Japanese architectural modes.

The tea-hut walls are never painted. The architects of tea prefer the reddish clay of Kyoto, but clays of other areas also have special coloration which is attractive. In time, all clay colors change; the oil additive, which is also a binding agent, stains the surface. On the inside, walls are sometimes papered along the bottom; this area rarely exceeds two feet from mats to top of paper. The paper protects the lower surface, where people are seated and against which they lean, and is usually a soft color. The paper in some tearooms is black. The famous Jo-an had wall-base paper of old calendars. In the Konnichi-an at Urasenke, the base papers are from old sheets of paper on which the rules for various ceremonies had been written; these are a feature of the room.

The usual plainness of the walls is relieved by corner posts of natural wood or bamboo. In some of Enshu's rooms these are beautifully hewn logs of chestnut. In the Tai-an, Rikyu omitted a post from one corner; the wall is rounded in this corner, as it is in the tokonoma. The reason was perhaps Rikyu's desire to leave the fire pit—placed to the extreme side—unencumbered. For the corner pit, Rikyu often employed the hanging kettle, the chain forming a post, in effect. The roundness of the corner serves also to relieve the severe lines of the room.

The lintel, *kamoi,* of a Japanese house is usually about six feet above floor level, the underside serving as the groove for fusuma. Above the kamoi is a narrow board, the *ramma,* a kind of transom that is often carved. Designs for ramma have become famous, such as the paulownia carvings of the Zangetsu-tei at Omote-senke, and the chrysanthemum and geometric patterns of the Manshu-in. Outside ventilator covers, too, are expertly designed. The ventilators are located in the lower part of the walls and are made of bamboo in horizontal or vertical arrangements. As the walls rest on carefully placed stones, the combination of textured wall, stone, and bamboo makes the exterior attractive and provides fresh air for the understructure.

The Windows

Windows in the tea hut do not frame a landscape picture, but the windows of famous temples are often placed to afford the best possible view of a garden or natural scene. A good example is at Kozan-ji, in northern Kyoto. Tea windows are usually small, covered openings for light; if the windows happen to frame a good view, this would detract from the tea itself and, therefore, would contradict the spirit of the occasion. The splendid view from the hall of Kozan-ji—mountains across a deep valley and river—is planned to be seen from the temple buildings. The planning is perfect, for in all Japan there is hardly any shakkei garden of such beauty. The windows at Kozan-ji, shoji openings from floor to ceiling, are excellently conceived; the veranda, deep eaves, and dark interior of the room from which the view is best seen are perfectly proportioned—there is depth to the view. The windows of the tea huts have no depth, they are unframed, except in the cases of some shoin-style chashitsu.

Windows placed by guest mats are called *shitaji mado,* unframed latticework, or *renji mado,* with vertical sections of bamboo. These are at various levels, and are covered with small paper screens. On the outside wall, about two inches above the windows, are small nails that hold a bamboo screen hung to reduce the amount of light passing through. These windows often have some kind of vine entwined about the latticework. The paper covers are mounted in a track in the rooms of Tai-an, Shokin-tei, and Jo-an, but in others they hang by nails. When the paper covers are held in a track for their frames, the track is usually of exposed wood. The exposed wood, running along the inside walls, creates a pattern not unlike that of Mondrian's color squares and rectangles.

The windows near the *temaeza,* the host's place, often penetrate the lower areas of the wall, interrupting the base paper. The low windows allow light to fall directly on the utensils used by the host. These windows are *shikishi mado*. They appear singly or in unmatched pairs. These also often have tracks that allow the paper covers to be slid back for more light. The skikishi mado parallel the naka-bashira and sode-kabe arrangement.

On the second wall of the host's area there is often a *furosaki mado,* a window alongside the portable brazier. A shelf is frequently fixed to the back of the sode kabe; the furosaki mado illuminates the shelf (or shelves), *hibari-dana*.

Most of the windows, especially in the host's area, are placed low, near the floor. The effect of light falling directly on the mats is a good one; only recently have Western architects begun to think in terms of directly lighting the floor area. Westerners, however, have long held to the use of a skylight. This too is found in tea huts, and is called *tsuki-age mado*. It is used for snowy nights and for dawn. A small stick or length of bamboo is used to raise and hold the trap open. A famous example is in the Yu-in of Urasenke.

In large shoin or elegant tearooms, shoji are the major source of light. These are of two kinds: *akari shoji* and *koshi shoji*. Akari shoji are fully papered. They are placed on the side of a room that joins a veranda. Koshi shoji are papered except for a foot or so at the bottom, where they are boarded. The lower extremes of the koshi shoji are often fancily decorated with paper, bamboo, and other materials.

Shoji are among the most beautiful elements of Japanese architecture. Their latticework is severely simple, forming three or four rows of rectangles across the width, ten to fourteen in the height. The paper is usually plain, but paste-on repairs in the shape of leaves or butterflies can be seen throughout Japan. If the paper is decorated, it is usually with silk threads that have been kept on the surface, but real leaves and flowers occasionally find their way into the shoji of temples and palaces.

Enshu's shoji are different from most. His often have double lines of verticals and horizontals, creating very small areas of paper between larger rectangles. The double sashes are thin, about an inch apart, and lacquered in brown or black.

When fusuma separate a tearoom from other rooms of a temple or house, they are covered with fine papers, decorated with designs of the owner or of his school of tea. The hardware—finger catches for sliding the fusuma—are objects of attention among architects. Those of the Katsura Detached Palace are famous; arrows, rings, fans, and pine needles are among the designs often used.

Another form of hardware used in tearooms is nail covers. These are molded in flower forms or other interesting designs. Those at Manshu-in, in Kyoto, are in cloisonné.

Unusual windows in tea architecture are the *kato mado,* which is a window with a foliated arch, and the *yoshino mado,* a large circular window. In the area of the kato mado there is often a shoin, the writing desk made from the windowsill and upon which is placed the writing box. The yoshino mado is named for a famous woman entertainer who designed a round window for her own tearoom, and it has become fairly popular. A typical example is the window of the Iho-seki tearoom at Kodai-ji in Kyoto. There the window, backed by a bamboo grid, is about 5 feet 2 inches in diameter and covers nearly the entire wall area of one end of the room.

As Shokin Furuta has pointed out, the light of the tearoom must be different from that of the living room of an ordinary house. If too much light spills into the tearoom, the utensils look cheap and small, but too little light for a family or for reading and writing will be depressing. Each room has its own requirements of light, depending on its uses. When tea areas (kakoi) were used by chajin, *byobu,* which are free-standing screens, were placed around the area to cut off excessive light, as well as to add privacy. In tea an excess of anything is damnable, even light.

The *Tokonoma* and Shelves

Tea ceremony made the *tokonoma*, the alcove for art, necessary in Japanese houses. Buddhist-trained chajin inherited the tradition of placing flowers and offerings in a small niche. They made the niche the object of attention, for in it they placed their treasures in honor of the seasons, the occasion of a visit, or merely to be enjoyed. The tradition persists, though hotels and inns sometimes place a television set in the formerly sacred tokonoma.

The tokonoma of a tearoom is most often raised and made of tatami, but board tokonoma, flush with room mats, are seen. The tokonoma vary in size; some are less than three feet wide and a few inches deep, while others are greater than six feet by three feet. A small window is sometimes found to the side of the tokonoma or even at its back wall, this latter not being well understood today—was it to offer a view of the landscape outside or to make the hanging scrolls flap in the wind? To be sure, the side window of a tokonoma serves to give light to the flowers or scrolls that are placed for guests to view.

The *toko-bashira,* the post by the tokonoma, is made of a variety of woods, but pine and chestnut are common. Rikyu preferred leaving the natural bark on the post, while Enshu preferred his posts planed. Exceptional cryptomeria posts are found in the Kitayama area, north of Kyoto. There one can see tall, straight trees growing, cut, or prepared by families specializing in this architectural detail. The toko-bashira are expensive. Some are made by wrapping a growing tree with tight bands of metal which leave an impression in the wood.

The inside of the tokonoma has walls of the same clay used elsewhere in the tearoom. Now, in numerous new chashitsu, a light is placed above the spanning beam directed at the objects in the tokonoma. On the back wall is a nail or hook for hanging scrolls. The same kind of nail is found on most toko-bashira for hanging flower containers.

Shelves beside the tokonoma are staggered, like the cloud designs of Japanese fabrics. This is the common chigai-dana (ornamental shelves) design, but these shelves are called *tokowaki-dana* (literally, "shelves beside the tokonoma").

The tokonoma is not an ancient element of Japanese architecture. Rooms for tea such as the Togu-do at Ginkaku-ji have no tokonoma at all. Instead, shelves are placed to one side of the room and upon them objects are displayed. Some small tearooms of later date have a *kabe-doko,* which is a place against a wall where scrolls can be hung, but without the usual recess and floor area. When the kabe-doko is used, a small board is placed by the wall where the scroll is hung. This has been used often in very small rooms, such as the Konnichi-an, and at places of tea demonstration.

An unusual tokonoma is the *hora-doko*. This one is cavelike, deep, and dark. In front of the display space, a large arch extends from the floor to about two feet from the ceiling, joining the opposite wall in framing the tokonoma. A kakoi rarely has a tokonoma, but the kakoi at Manshu-in has a small, movable, boxlike platform which serves for displaying flowers and art. An *enso-doko* is a rounded-opening tokonoma; a good example of this is in the Rikyu-do at Urasenke.

The *kai-oki-dana* are shelves found outside the tearoom but inside the hut, for occasional use. Some are simply designed, others have exquisite carvings in their supports. These shelves are often suspended from the ceiling by a single piece of dark bamboo, attached at one corner; the other three corners engage the walls at a corner.

The *katana-dana* are exterior shelves, formerly used by samurai as a place for swords. These are used today by guests as a place to deposit anything they do not want to carry into the room.

Doors and Entrances

Aside from shoji entrances, referred to above, larger rooms have *kinin-guchi*, special guests' entrances. This kind was used by distinguished guests, and is always attached to a *hiroma,* which is a room of more than four and one-half mats, such as the above-mentioned room of Zangetsu-tei. Kinin-guchi allow one to enter a tearoom standing. These are papered to form, in effect, koshi or akari shoji. A kinin-guchi is always found in shoin-style tea huts, where rooms are large and furnishings elegant. The kinin-guchi is a radical departure from the *nijiri-guchi,* crawling-in passage, of Rikyu's design.

The nijiri-guchi is a small entrance, barely two feet in width and height, covered by a sliding door of wood. In Rikyu's time the tracks for the door were made of two boards forming a groove between them, but later doors moved on single-board grooves (this is one way of dating some chashitsu). By entering on hands and knees, even the proudest men are humbled by the nijiri-guchi. It takes a little practice to enter and exit without bumping one's head, but is easily negotiated by chajin.

Other doors inside the hut are the *sado-guchi* and *kyuji-guchi*. The sado-guchi, the host's entrance, has been described above in connection with the fumi-komi-tatami. Because it is often arched, it is sometimes referred to as a *kato-guchi,* arched entrance. This door is papered on both sides and is higher than the nijiri-guchi, but not much higher than five feet when arched. A kyuji-guchi is the entrance used by assistants when the host needs them.

Nijiri-guchi appear to be boarded windows, and are said to have been introduced by Rikyu when he saw a fisherman crawling into a tiny hut by the sea. They are always used for independent huts of less than six mats.

The *Mizuya* and *Katte no Ma*

Mizuya is the room or area in in which tea utensils are prepared, kept, and cleaned. The name is synonymous with *katte no ma,* meaning kitchen. A possible distinction between the room names is that the mizuya can be a distinct area of the katte no ma, which is generally thought of as a larger room. The mizuya contains an area of bamboo flooring, where spaces between the stems allow water to run through to the earth below. Above this are shelves of various sizes where utensils are stored. Again, it is Rikyu who is said to have made the first real mizuya and style of arrangement of utensils in his Fushin-an.

A large water jar is kept on the bamboo floor of the mizuya, and from this water is drawn for washing utensils before and after a ceremony. Formerly the jar held special water brought from famous wells that were said to provide excellent water for tea. The average mizuya working space is about two feet by four feet, a very comfortable arrangement for storing or cleaning utensils. Cupboards are generally arranged on the left side, and the utensils on the shelves above the area are for immediate use while other things are stored.

In front of the mizuya is a one-mat area where the host sits while preparing the utensils he intends to use. A covered window is generally found in the back wall of the mizuya, below or behind the shelves. Care is taken that the mizuya space is neat, easy to work in, and clean. Occasionally one will see cupboard covers painted with landscapes or other designs, but the mizuya is usually the simplest area, with no decoration at all.

In the mizuya or katte no ma is a *ganro,* a round fire pit where ashes and charcoal are placed for heating water before it is put in the kettle in the tearoom proper.

It is not absolutely essential for a tearoom to have a mizuya attached to it, and certainly not essential to have a full kitchen, as in some katte no ma. However, it is convenient and useful to have a small place set aside especially for tea preparations. If a meal is to be served with tea, the mizuya is a busy place, with courses laid out in order and food cooking.

Ro and *Robuchi*

The *ro,* a winter fire pit, is a Japanese invention, a permanent fixture set in the floor of most tearooms. When the ro is not in use its area is covered by a mat or wooden fixture. It is not used in spring and summer, when the portable brazier is used. The position of this pit determines the style of the room.

In many temples and farmhouses of Japan this kind of fire pit is used for warmth and for heating ordinary tea water. A kettle is usually hung from the ceiling directly above the pit; this is called a *jizai* arrangement. The farmhouse or temple fire pit is larger than the ro of a tearoom, which is fixed at one square foot, inside-rim, and one foot five and one-half inches, outside-rim. The pit used to be made of a special bronze, but now it is of copper, iron, or stone. The container for the pit is sunk directly into the flooring, the mat being cut away. Into the pit ashes and charcoal are placed, along with a tripod on which the kettle rests. The ashes are raked carefully, assuring an even draft for the fire.

Robuchi is the plain or lacquered rim of the ro. A small room generally has a robuchi that is plain, while larger rooms have lacquered rims, often designed by tea masters.

PART THREE
Tea Utensils

7. Connoisseurship of Utensils

The Price of Art

In prosperous times, masterpieces bring great prices and great attention. The age of undiscovered geniuses passed with the birth of systematic art scholarship and instant communication on a wide scale. Fashion continues to play an important role in determining art prices, but great works have rarely been cheap. This phenomenon has not been limited to the Western world. Tea utensils have brought fantastic prices for centuries in Japan. Since the days of Yoshimasa's importation of Chinese objects—and even before—the collectors of Japan met in a highly competitive market for ceramics, paintings, lacquers, and bronzes. Nobunaga, Hideyoshi, Rikyu, Oribe, and Enshu are among the connoisseurs who contributed to soaring prices.

Jiro Harada suggests that there are many good reasons for art to be expensive. Some objects, he says, have value as curios. They are old, odd, or rare. Others have historical value because important people have used or possessed them, or because they uniquely represent an era or attitude. Some are expensive because they took long to make or because the materials used in the making are valuable. An object fashioned by a famous artist or public figure—whatever its merit as a work of art—will be priced high.

To most individuals interested in purchasing a work of art the determining factor will be the subjective one of direct appeal. The intrinsic, subjective value of the piece will decide the purchase. But to the Japanese collector interested in tea utensils, another factor must be considered. This is the practical value of the object. How can it be used, for instance, in tea ceremony? A good bowl must be handled, and concerns of weight, glaze, touch, and size receive serious attention. In the area of practical concerns, the collector of tea utensils, then, differs from other collectors.

What is generally true about expensive art is that purchasers take good care of it. Carefully preserved expensive works tell us much about the tastes of an era and of the collectors who helped determine or confirm those tastes. Henry Clay Frick, we believe, had good taste in painting. Matsudaira Fumai had good taste in tea utensils.

The acquisition by museums of some of the best tea utensils has led to an upgrading of utensils on the open market. The museum phenomenon of the past one hundred years, together with the tendency for collectors to keep collections whole—never parting with any acquired piece, and giving the entire to established museums or creating new ones—has led to astronomically high prices for tea utensils by the greatest artists of Japan. To collect utensils actively, therefore, requires money, if one is to have good ones, and it also requires serious study of tea. Japan's centuries of involvement with tea have produced an abundant quantity of men and women who have both.

Where the Utensils Are

Outstanding utensils have generally remained in Japan. One has only to read catalogues of tea masters such as Matsudaira and search out the pieces named to know that this is true. Important American or European collections rarely contain any utensils of the first rank. Our tastes have not been cultivated in quite the same way as Japanese tastes, but this alone does not account for the inferiority of our collections; the best utensils have simply not been available for foreign purchase.

The government of Japan inhibited the export of Japanese works of art in 1931 by passing a law for the protection of national treasures and important cultural assets. This was a direct result of the purchase of the famed *Kibi Daijin Nitto Emaki* (the picture scroll of Minister Kibi, of the Kamakura period) by the Boston Museum of Fine Arts. Recognizing that foreign funds could quickly draw many important works of Japanese art from their homeland, the government took the step of stopping sales to foreigners. An unexpected by-product of this action was the dampening of international interest in Japanese art, for when the market became restricted the dealers, scholars, museums, and collectors turned their attentions elsewhere, namely to China. In Chinese art many who were originally interested only in the art of Japan found what they perhaps had suspected all along: Chinese art was the true source of the best art of Japan. They felt they had come in Chinese art to the *true* art of the Far East. In the process Japanese art somehow came to be labeled "imitative" and hardly worth studying. For these people Japanese art lost its appeal, a situation that continued until recently. The remaining lovers of Japanese art closed ranks and continued collecting, but few were interested mainly in tea and their collections show it.

Various Japanese have catalogued the famous utensils. Comprehensive classifications of *gyobutsu* (imperial properties), the important Higashiyama pieces owned by Yoshimasa, and *daimeibutsu* (special famous implements), masterpieces of Rikyu's age, have been made. Chajin Soami and Shuko published the *Kundaikan Sochoki;* The Matsudaira family produced the *Meibutsuki* records; and Kobori Enshu contributed the important catalogue *Chuko Meibutsu*. None of these is complete, but each provides important records of the times and tastes of foremost chajin; for example, the Soami-Shuko record lists T'ang, Sung, and Yuan objects and artists of interest to the Japanese of the period in great detail. The Japanese who catalogued utensils were all important chajin, often using the listed works in their own service of tea. Again, to judge well in the area of tea utensils one must have a high regard for the use of the objects. We often see what appear to be excellent Shino ware tea bowls in American and British collections, but they are excellent in appearance only. Often these bowls are too heavy to be of much use in a tearoom. There are exceptions, of course, in the Freer Gallery in Washington, D.C., in the Boston Museum of Fine Arts, and in other collections, but too often our connoisseurship falls short of the ultimate standard: practical use of the utensil in the tearoom.

One of the most unfortunate representations of Japanese crafts and arts is the displays of novelty shops that proliferate in Western cities. Trinkets and geegaws are sold as Japanese craft or art. These are usually made specifically for foreign consumption, are ill-designed, poorly decorated, and cheaply made. They plague the American market and seriously misrepresent Japan. It is the Japanese manufacturers who are at fault in this situation. They produce far superior works for home consumption. Their merchandisers have taken haphazard assessment of American and foreign tastes and have commissioned goods accordingly.

The architectural developments of the past twenty years have resulted in apartments and houses in the West that are perfectly suited to the use and display of fine Japanese crafts and art. The small, severely simple apartments of I. M. Pei, the houses of Philip Johnson, the rooms of Mies van der Rohe, are good settings for Japanese bamboo, ceramic, and lacquer works. Given the increase in travel to Japan, publication of books on Japanese arts, and a better knowledge of Westerners' tastes by Japanese designers, we should see an influx of excellent Japanese works to other nations.

The Fortunes of Tea

Whatever is sent, we can be certain that we will but rarely get first-rate tea utensils. The Japanese who have an interest in tea are so reverential before their possessions that nothing but the most extraordinary circumstances causes them to offer a work as a gift or for sale. Take, for instance, the story from Lord Tokitsugu's diary, *Tokitsugu Kyoki,* written about 1570. The widow of Isshiki Yoshitatsu refused to surrender a superb ceramic piece in her family's collection, saying it was a personal treasure so great that were it to be given up, she and her thirty retainers would commit suicide.

Others had their price. One man paid 3,000 *kan mon* (one kan mon is equal to the total production of a village household for an entire year) for Shuko's "Konasu" tea caddy. The "Seiko *tsubo*" (Seiko pot) sold for 500 kan mon. The great "Kazu *dai*" (Kazu stand) went for 2,000 kan mon.

These prices were generally set by tea masters, many of whom must have accumulated large fortunes by sending the prices of their own pieces to unreasonable heights. Yamagami Soji, for example, asked—and received—a 400-percent profit over the price he paid for a Jo-o ceramic.

One would think that the high price of utensils would have seriously dissuaded commoners from participating in tea ceremony. It did not. During the Genroku era (1688–1703), a greatly increased tea production caused the art to become more and more popular. Tea came to be a household beverage. As the tea-drinking base enlarged, so did the use of tea utensils. Terms like wabi and sabi were more widely used in Japan and popular architecture came to reflect more of the tea spirit than before. This had its good and bad effects.

Toward the end of the Edo period, about the mid-1800's, tea was the object of little serious attention, except for collecting utensils and following rules of service. The wealth of the great daimyos declined and support of the samurai was decreased. With the reduction in importance of these two classes, always prime supporters of tea ceremony, the art of tea came to be little more than a formality. Famed tea families failed to produce sensitive chajin. Kobori Masataka, descendant of Enshu and lord of Bitchu and magistrate of Fushimi, got into serious financial difficulties and was forced to sell his greatest treasure: the "Zaichuan" tea caddy. The price was one thousand pieces of gold, but it was not enough to save his subjects from severe taxation by the lord. In the end he was forced to relinquish his position.

After 1888, tea began to recover some of its lost prestige. This was a period of resurgent nationalism, and since tea was thought of as representing the old values of the nation, it was encouraged. This, despite an official put-down of Zen Buddhism by the Meiji forces, was sufficient to draw new blood into the ranks of chajin. Because of the government's somewhat harsh treatment of Zen Buddhists, tea became a secular practice at this time by decree of the grand masters.

It was in the Meiji era that some samurai collections

were placed on the Japanese market. The best things went usually to merchants, finally establishing them as foremost among collectors of tea utensils.

In late Meiji so many Western ideas and forms of art were introduced into Japan that there seemed to be a danger that the Japanese were giving up the art forms they had spent so many centuries cultivating. Again, Japanese works of art and craft from old collections were sold. To combat the export of valuable works, wealthy families banded together to systematically halt the outward flow. One group sent representatives to America to buy up whatever Japanese art of value came on the market. One important recovery was the "Donta" tea bowl, purchased for ¥4,000. This amounted to $30,000. The Meiji businessmen who made such purchases were men of fabulous wealth—the Mitsui and Iwasaki fortunes, for example, were increasing yearly by hundreds of millions of yen. At this time the center for tea-utensil collections moved permanently from the Kyoto-Osaka area to Tokyo.

The following are conjectured prices for tea utensils of the very highest quality and greatest fame, were they to be placed on the market. By far the highest prices would be for the tea bowls made by Koetsu. A brilliant bowl by this master would command $100,000, at least. Similar prices hold for Nonomura Ninsei's best work and outstanding Shino ware pieces. The great Raku ware master Chojiro's bowls would probably sell for $70,000, as would excellent Iga pottery. The very best Ki-zeto and Ko Kutani wares would cost $40,000. The work of Korin, Kenzan, and the finest old Bizen ware could command something like $25,000. Nabeshima and Ko Imari ware of first quality would probably demand prices of $15–20,000. So would the masterpieces of Donyu, a Raku potter, and Oribe, as well as excellent Shigaraki ware. Ten thousand dollars would not be too much to pay for the best wares from the E-garatsu, Seto-garatsu, and Ko-zeto kilns. The Imari ware popular with American tourists of means would be last on this list, but still would command $3,000 for the best bowls. The foregoing are all works made by Japanese. Chinese and Korean wares for tea, the great Ido-style tea bowls favored by Enshu and others, would perhaps equal the $100,000-plus figure for the bowls of Koetsu. Next among the foreign wares would be the much appreciated Temmoku and Korean celadons. These would likely bring $75,000. Mishima-style bowls would sell for about $10,000, with Ko Sometsuke-style pieces bringing a little less. Among living artistic potters the most expensive ware is by Toyozo Arakawa. His bowls bring prices of upward of $3,000. Not far behind Arakawa are the prices for the best works of Shoji Hamada, Munemaru Ishiguro, Toyo Kaneshige, followed by Sango Uno, Yuzo Kondo, Taroemon Nakazato, and others. In other crafts similar lists could be drawn of men whose works command very high prices, but first among them would have to be the remarkable lacquerwork of Gonroku Matsuda. His lacquer pieces sell for $5,000 and over.

Among works by Japanese painters most appreciated in tea ceremony one could not hope to obtain a first-rank Sotatsu or Sesshu for less than $75,000. Imitations, unvetted works, and inferior but genuine works certainly exchange hands every year for less. The best Koetsu calligraphy might go for half the Sesshu price. Taiga and Ikkyu calligraphy or painting might sell for $15–20,000. Rikyu's greatest calligraphy would perhaps bring $6,000, as would Hideyoshi's. Sotan's, Fumai's, and Enshu's calligraphy might bring as much as $2,000. Again, these prices are for the most part conjecture, as the best works of the great artists of the past rarely appear for sale. These prices are based on records of past sales and conversations with dealers, collectors, and museum curators.

8. Tea Bowls: *Chawan*

Basic Shapes

The term *chawan,* when used in daily Japanese conversation, means "rice bowl." The characters, however, signify "tea bowl," and it is this reading that is appropriate to tea ceremony. The prototype for the tea bowls in use today was the bowl used by people all over Asia in the course of their daily meals. Rice is eaten in the small bowl, and meals are often concluded by pouring hot water or tea into the bowl, a practice which continues to this day.

Asia's rice bowls come in a tremendous variety of shapes, glazes, textures, and weights. Ceramic bowls from China, Korea, and Japan have proved ideal vessels for serving tea in cha-no-yu. For this reason, old rice bowls of these nations of Asia are referred to as tea bowls. Contemporary Japanese rice bowls are thin and made of porcelain, unsuited to tea ceremony.

As tea-ceremony tea is neither brewed in a pot nor dispensed from another container, so the tea bowl must serve a variety of functions. First, it must be an adequate base for preparing tea. It must also be easy for guests to handle and, of course, contain the tea well. When a chawan is handed to a guest he should experience no difficulty in holding it and drinking from it. If the bowl is too thin the sides will be hot. If the walls are too thick the bowl will probably be uncomfortably heavy. A bowl of very rough texture will not drain well and will break tines from the whisk. All these elements—and many more—must be considered in selecting a tea bowl.

There are basically two kinds of bowls: large bowls, shared by guests in taking thick tea, and smaller bowls, used individually by guests for thin tea. These classifications are for the sake of convenience and are not strictly followed; one uses what he has to suit invited guests. These classifications have subclassifications according to the seasons: bowls of considerable depth are used in the colder months; shallow ones are used in warmer months. The reasoning here is that deep bowls tend to hold the heat of the tea for a longer period, whereas shallow bowls have a feeling of openness appropriate to spring and summer.

Tea masters believe that a bowl slowly comes to life through generations of use. Its value increases with use, not necessarily with age. This is especially true of bowls whose glaze is light in color. The Ido-shape bowls of Hagi ware, for instance, are felt to have an almost offensive brightness about them when new, but this disappears as successive hands hold and use the bowl. The glaze of such bowls takes on extremely subtle tones in time; the fine crackle comes to be revealed as it stains. Raku bowls have unusually rough clay that is often left exposed at the foot. The roughness of the clay wears down in time and the bowl becomes increasingly pleasant to hold.

The famous bowls seen in museums and galleries are often lifeless through lack of use. These bowls are interesting as specimens from past ages, but their beauty is specious. The very finest bowls are best seen under the circumstances of having tea from them. Then, only, can the qualities of the bowls be adequately judged. An artist who makes a tea bowl will say that his control over form and glaze is no more than that of the kiln, which often seems to have a will of its own. The same artist will also say that his bowls come to life only as they are put to the test of their purpose. While tea masters and potters express appreciation of the great bowls on display in museums, their real delight is reserved for the fine bowls in circulation.

Tea masters have divided bowls into three categories: Chinese, or *karamono;* Korean, or *Chosen;* and Japanese, or *wamono*. These, in turn, are categorized by various styles, glazes, shapes, and kilns. The Japanese category is subdivided into three kinds: Raku, products of the Raku family kiln and a few artistic potters working in Raku style; *Kyo-yaki* (literally, "capital fired"), pottery of Kyoto's vast number of excellent potters; and *kuni-yaki* (literally "country fired"), pottery from all other areas of Japan. These number in the hundreds of kinds. Raku ware generally comes in red, black, and, rarely, white glazes. These are preferred tea bowls. Their touch, superb glazing, and rightness of form for tea have long been acknowledged. Kyo-yaki tends toward the brighter color range in glazes. These bowls are often decorative, pleasing to the eye, carefully and finely made. They represent the most refined products of Japan's kilns. Kuni-yaki, provincial ware—i.e., from outside Japan's ancient capital of Kyoto—is the most varied of the three. This kind embraces Bizen, Takatori, Shino, Ki-zeto, Kuro-zeto, Hagi, and a host of others.

On the subject of tea utensils more has been written

about the tea bowl than any other. This might be because of a special Japanese love of pottery. Or it might be because the bowl is the most intimate of utensils, touched not only with the hands but with the mouth.

The shapes of bowls are as varied as their kilns. Perhaps the oldest shape in tea bowls is the *Temmoku-gata* ("Temmoku shape"), a distinctively formed bowl of narrow base and broad rim, made at the famed Chinese kilns at Chien-ming in the north of Fukien province. These bowls tip easily and usually require a stand when used. Such bowls are employed in the most elegant ceremonies. The *Ido-gata* ("Ido shape") is one of a high base rim and flaring sides. It is a pleasant bowl to use, for its shape accommodates the whisk nicely. *Wannari* shapes come directly from old rice bowls. *Kutsu-gata* are eccentric forms that resemble horseshoes. These were the delight of Oribe, who purposely distorted rims by crushing them inward. *Tsutsu-gata* are a tubular shape; these are ideally used in cold months. Others are: brush washer, *hissen-gata;* low and wide, *hira-gata;* sharp, high-rise sides from a well-defined base, *sugi-gata;* three-sided, *sankaku;* squarish, *yomo-gata;* half-tube, *hantsutsu-gata;* horse bucket, *uma-darai;* tight waist, *dojime;* and many variations and combinations of these. This list is by no means exhaustive, for rare shapes have particular names or designations. No one knows all the names, but an astute observer of Japanese life and artifacts would perhaps be able to guess that a bowl with a smallish mouth and bulging sides takes its name, *shioge-gata,* from the salt bucket that once was common in Japan.

Qualifying these are further classifications by base type. The base, *kodai,* of tea bowls is a distinctive feature. In base nomenclature we find some thirty headings, which I shall refrain from giving in Japanese, but here is a sampling: round and high, round and low, square, whirlpool, uneven, four-legged, split circle, cherry blossom, see-through, outwardly inclined, straight-falling, recessed, no-base, and so on.

During the Kamakura and Muromachi periods the most common bowls were Korean or Chinese. These were Temmoku, misty green celadon (*seiji*), and pure-white *hakuji*. They were possessed from the start by the most powerful officials, priests, and families in Japan. The priests who traveled to China brought back bowls for their own use and as gifts to their patrons, or to sell. As these bowls were rare and of excellent form and glaze they were imitated by Japanese potters. Moreover, Chinese and Korean potters were brought from their homelands to produce such bowls for their masters.

Shuko and Jo-o did much to alter the interests of the Japanese, preferring domestically produced bowls to those of foreign origin. This helped promote a local artistic pottery, in which the Japanese craftsmen soon excelled. Shuko and Jo-o liked the common rice bowls they saw in the countryside around Kyoto. These were adapted to their style of tea service. These men and Rikyu saved Japanese pottery from becoming mere imitation of the great *Higashiyama Meibutsu,* the collection of Yoshimasa and the Ashikaga family at their silver pavilion estate in the Higashiyama section of Kyoto. Ashikaga Yoshimasa's collection consisted mostly of Chinese pieces, and these were the most highly regarded by Japanese chajin until Rikyu's time. In establishing the Raku tea bowls as his favorites, Rikyu effectively ended the Chinese wares' monopoly in tea ceremony. His patron, Hideyoshi, also contributed. The Korean campaigns of Hideyoshi strengthened Japanese tea-bowl artistry by introducing new forms and new blood into its community.

The tea-bowl form has been broken down into components, each with a name. The *kuchi-zuri,* mouth of the bowl, is the component which is thought to unify a bowl. It is generally considered the single most important aspect, carefully and lovingly shaped. It finishes the bowl, caps the potter's efforts. Perhaps because of its importance, the mouth is often given a poetic name according to its form; *gokaku,* "five mountains," a rim with five slight mounds about it, is the most common of these. On some bowls the mouth has a decidedly inward cast, others incline outward. Some are in a line with the sides of the bowl. A few bowls have mouths without distinctive shape.

The inner rim of the bowl is the *chakin-zuri,* so named because the linen cloth, *chakin,* touches this area of the bowl in the wiping process. The middle inner part of a bowl is known as the *chasen-zuri*. The whisk passes over this area when the tea is whipped. The bottommost part is the *mikomi,* and at its center is the *chadome,* over which the tea scoop drops the powdered tea.

The outside of the bowl, too, has its various parts named. The *do, koshi, kodai waki, kodai,* and *tatami mitsuki* are, respectively: body, middle area, base side, whole base, and mat-touching areas. The last, tatami- or mat-touching, is of considerable interest for the variety of styles it takes: regular, round, polyangular, and double-folded. Attention to this detail is important for a potter. He must construct a base which supports the bowl well while resting on the mat but which also sits well in the hands.

Chinese-Style Bowls

Some particular bowl types warrant discussion. The famous Temmoku bowls were originally called "Kensan" by the Japanese. In the earliest period of their importation, only special Chien-ming wares bore this appellation. In time the term Kensan was applied to any bowl having a Temmoku shape. The original Temmoku have an iron-content glaze, charcoal-brown coloration, and a hard surface. These are heavy for their size and have thick bottom areas and small base rings. The prized glaze effect was one of stripes that flow vertically from the rim to a line just above the base, where the clay is exposed. Color variations and slight changes in shape found in some Temmoku bowls are the result of unexpected temperature changes in the kiln.

Yohen Temmoku, iridescent glaze of bluish green with frequent starlike points or rays, is highly prized among Japanese tea men. Of these the incomparable Yuteki glaze seems to contain silvery stars scattered among various colors like drops of oil on water. An extremely fine Yuteki is in the possession of the Ryoko-in subtemple of Daitoku-ji, Kyoto. This work has been displayed in museums from time to time. It is a masterpiece of a bowl that continues to have life.

Hare's-fur Temmoku is fairly common. These bowls are characterized by deep green or purple colors radiating on a soft-brown ground. The radiance gathers in a pool at the inside bottom. The magnificent Kaki Temmoku ("persimmon Temmoku"), is popular with Japanese collectors. The richness of the glaze coloring is the result of ash sprinkled onto the surface before firing. A contemporary Kyoto potter, Uichi Shimizu, works with this technique. There is also a yellowish Temmoku, the Ki Temmoku.

Another unusual Temmoku is the Kishu kind. Kishu is the blackish-brown color of tortoiseshell. Over this is laid a lighter, yellowish brown. The finished glaze has a mottled effect. These bowls have rather thin bodies and small rings for kodai. On this kind of bowl one sometimes finds flower designs.

The Chinese and Korean celadon bowls enjoyed popularity in the earliest stages of the development of tea ceremony. This choice, aside from the superb craftsmanship which went into their making, is difficult to understand. The celadon color is not suited to the rich color of green tea. The appearance of celadon, too, is rather cold or stand-offish. It is not an inviting, warm color. The glaze has a cold touch and the surface of a celadon bowl tends to make handling difficult. In spite of these things, the celadons flourished. Aside from tea bowls, celadon was much liked for incense burners and boxes and for vases.

The Japanese term for celadon is seiji. The Chinese call it *ch'ing-tz'u*. Sung celadons were especially prized, and they appear to have influenced Korean potters as well. The Korean products have fine light grays and blue-greens. The Japanese today prefer wares from Lung-ch'uan for their superior crackle. The mallet-shaped (*kimita-gata*) vases are seen commonly in reproduction throughout Japan in tea huts and schools.

Blue-and-white Ming ware bowls were imported to Japan, but these did not prove wholly satisfactory to chajin. They were often thick and ungainly. However, the very ungainliness appealed to some Japanese. They favored the cloud-palace designs on bowls with poorly shaped mouths. The designs of these bowls were frequently heavy in cobalt blue of a violet or grayish hue set off against a sharp white background. The Ming ceramics, as René Grousset points out, are somewhat less spiritual than the Sung; the potters slipped from the heavenly to the earthly realm. The earthliness of these must have attracted the Japanese.

The Chinese use of underglaze provided a new challenge to Japanese potters. The yellows, greens, and reds careened off the white porcelain with dazzling speed. The rich blues were mixed with three and four other colors on the same bowl. In this category the Japanese most liked the *shonzui,* bowls made for export. The famous "Goro Daiyu Go Shonzui" is a bowl of distinction in this category and is often reproduced in tea books.

Korean-Style Bowls

Korean bowls grew in popularity as tea acquired wabi spirit. Among tea masters there is a decided preference for three wares: Hagi, Karatsu, and Raku. And of the three, two are directly influenced by Korean pottery.

The first of the three, Hagi, makes fine Ido bowls. The distinctive conical shape, like a deep morning glory, is covered with a pasty glaze that varies from pink to yellow to a bluish purple. The name Ido may come from a site of the same name in Korea, or it may, as Sherman Lee of the Cleveland Museum of Art and others suggest, come from the Japanese word for "well." A common story about the origins of the name has it that a man at Kofuku-ji in Nara named his bowl Ido and the name spread with the fame of that bowl.

Ido bowls have considerable variety. Some are wholly glazed, with the glaze spilling over the base and across the ring. Some have especially thick bodies, sides cut down with a spatula, and bamboo-joint (*take no fushi*) bases. Commonly Ido bowls have a sharkskin glaze, *kairagi,* produced by a shrinkage of the glaze in firing.

The Ao Ido (blue Ido) have thick bodies and a soft, mat finish. The finest Ao Ido were made in the fifteenth century or before, in Korea. Among the others: Ko Ido bowls are of translucent glaze; O Ido are similar but have a thicker body than Ko Ido; Kokan-nyu bowls have a thin glaze, good crazing, and are made of hard clay.

In *Cha no Kaikaku,* Soetsu Yanagi devotes a chapter to comparing Ido and Raku bowls. His belief, as set forth in the book, is that the Ido bowl and the kata-tsuki (the high-shouldered caddy) were made essentially for home use. The beauty of these common objects was recognized by Zen masters and incorporated into tea. A significant part of their beauty, he goes on, lies in the fact that they were first made for daily use. He, therefore, prefers the Ido bowl to the Raku. Rikyu, he feels, was on shaky aesthetic footing, and he accuses Rikyu of intellectualizing in commissioning Raku bowls expressly for tea ceremony. This was unnatural. With a scholar's hauteur he states that the common people who made everyday objects were incapable of making anything which was not natural, and the natural object is preferred for tea. Enshu, too, had often stated his preference for the Ido.

Hideyoshi's Korean campaign is sometimes called the "pottery campaign." Hideyoshi was a devoted chajin and while in Korea searched for utensils and potters who might serve him in cha-no-yu. He and many of his daimyo captured Korean potters and brought them to Japan where kilns were erected for the purpose of making tea utensils. The influence of these imported potters was great, especially in northern Kyushu.

The second ware of Korean influence, a kiln established by a daimyo, is at Karatsu, a small village on the west coast of northern Kyushu. There are excellent potters there today, continuing to work in vigorous styles adapted from Korea. The site is close by Nabeshima, noted for its porcelain production. The Karatsu kiln was created by Terazawa Shimonokami, lord of Karatsu. The site was chosen for its excellent—though coarse—clay. Karatsu glazes are grayish, off-white, and brown. E-garatsu (painted Karatsu) is popular for its simple underglaze drawings. These works are masculine, strong of form and color, and have a fine crackle in the glaze.

The more somber Karatsu pieces have a good appearance on the mats of a tearoom. Sazo Idemitsu, a well-known oil man, has an outstanding collection of Karatsu and E-garatsu wares. He displays these—along with other treasures, notably the paintings of the Zen monk Sengai—in Tokyo's Idemitsu Art Galley, which is in the building housing the Imperial Theater. The gallery, designed by Yoshiro Taniguchi, is a perfect setting for the Idemitsu collection. It contains what is undoubtedly the finest demonstration tea-ceremony room in Japan.

Also among Karatsu wares are Shiro-garatsu (white Karatsu), Madara-garatsu (dappled Karatsu), and Seto-garatsu, which has white glaze, a large rim that flares outward, and large crackle. These bowls have two subdivisions: Honte-zeto-garatsu and Kawakujirate, the latter being an elegant "whaleskin" type; and Chosen-garatsu, an appealing ware in Korean style, of very coarse clay with a high iron content.

There are other Karatsu-like wares. Among these are Karatsu Mishima (Karatsu in the form of the Korean-style Mishima bowl), which will be discussed later; Kuro-garatsu, which has black or deep brown glaze; Agano, from a kiln founded by Hosokawa Sansai and listed by Kobori Enshu as one of the "seven kilns of Japan"; Satsuma, the wares of many kilns in the Satsuma area of Kyushu (present Kagoshima); Ryumonji, an old kiln still operating near Kagoshima; and Takatori, a site near modern-day Fukuoka, but which was originally a kiln of the Karatsu area. Takatori is also one of the kilns selected by Enshu, and its bowls are refined, with varied glazes.

Glazed pottery in the Karatsu area did not come into its own until the split-bamboo sloping kiln, *nobori-gama,* was introduced. This is an arched chamber, divided many times along its length, set into a hillside. This kiln technique was adopted quickly throughout the area around Karatsu, eventually spreading to Seto and the rest of Japan. This kind of kiln is remarkably more effective than the cellar kiln, *ana-gama,* used in Japan at the time. The stairway of chambers up a hillside created a natural draft and greatly increased the efficiency and production of the potters. Prior to its introduction, most Japanese ceramics were Sue ware, a more sophisticated advance over the crude Yayoi-period ware, Haji, that had been the domestic mainstay. Sue ware was fired at a relatively high temperature, about 1200° F, and has a firm body of gray or ash green coloring. Hugo Munsterberg suggests that Bizen, Tokoname, Iga, Tamba, and Shigaraki (to be discussed) are outgrowths of that technique.

Another influential Korean import, though not one of the three favorite tea wares, was the Mishima bowl. These were produced in vast numbers during the Li dynasty (1392–1910) at a site in southern Korea. Ko Mishima are those bowls brought to Japan before the Tensho era (1573). These bowls, of olive coloring and with a bamboo-joint base, are especially prized in tea circles.

Other Mishima bowls are the Hana Mishima, having an interior and exterior floral design on a rust-gray surface; Sansaku Mishima, with brush marks decorating the walls of the bowl; Hori Mishima, shallow bowls with a cypress-fence design etched into the surface. The inside bottom is stamped with chrysanthemum designs in white, and the bowls are made of thin clay of reddish hue, and glazed with a translucent white or slightly bluish color. These last were mostly made to order for certain Edo tea men and came to be prized in that area. The Raihin Mishima are stamped with the characters for Raihin, a temple.

Southern Korean bowls with clear brush strokes in their glaze are called Hakeme. These graceful, cool bowls were made in the Li dynasty also, and were very much admired by Rikyu. The brush strokes were made with a white clay, and the bowls are shallow and light in weight.

Bowls made in Japan following Korean lines are very difficult to distinguish from their Korean prototypes. Reevaluation of tea bowls is constantly going on however, and many bowls that have long been said to be of Korean origin are now thought to be by Japanese hands. The glorious three-colored bowls in the Shoso-in, once thought to be Chinese, are now definitely labeled as Japan made. Because of the interactions of the three cultures it is probably impossible ever to know for certain the origins of many of the best bowls.

Seto, traditional site of the founding of the Japanese pottery art and industry, is near Nagoya. There, kilns still operate in profusion. A legend of the area states that Kato Shirozaemon Kagemasa, known as Toshiro, went to China with the Zen master Dogen. Upon returning to Japan he is supposed to have established the Seto kilns. His family continued in the area for twenty-eight generations. The last of the line, Kato Soshiro, known as Shuntai, died in 1878.

Many great chajin have visited the Seto kilns. Nobunaga spent considerable time at Seto and designated six of the master potters for special honors. Some works of these men survive today. Nobunaga's recognition of the Seto masters was an early example of Japan's honoring her craftsmen and artists by ceremonial visits and the conferring of official honors. Seto potters of Nobunaga's time carefully copied Chinese and Korean wares, but with Rikyu's ascendency these men turned to indigenous forms and glazes, giving the Seto kilns new life.

Another important influence upon the Seto potters was Furuta Oribe, whose contribution to Japanese pottery is significant in terms of its wide spread, although the finest Oribe products were all made during his lifetime or in a very short period following his death. Oribe ware developed out of Shino styles, another of the Seto products. In Oribe ware, figures and designs are engraved on a white paste covered with a brown slip. A white or slightly reddish white glaze is laid over the bowl, and the finished product is russet colored. The same characteristics could be said to apply to Shino, but Oribe style dictates that a touch of green be added to the surface. It is a bold, almost luminous green. Momoyama and early-Edo Oribe bowls have a childlike quality which is attractive.

The earliest Oribe wares frequently did not include any green glaze. They are therefore almost indistinguishable from Shino and are called Oribe Shino. Oribe potters did work with red glazes at one time. They are strong and beautifully glazed, and it is unfortunate that this Oribe strain did not continue.

A masterpiece of the Seto kilns was the "pull-out black," *hikidashi-guro*. Notes on this technique call for the bowl to be removed from the kiln when white-hot and thrust into water. As it was a favorite of Rikyu's, another name is applied: *Rikyu-guro,* "Rikyu black." A spatula was used in shaping the sides of the hikidashi-guro, giving it a masculine feeling. A potter's wheel must have been used in making these bowls.

The Ki-zeto (yellow Seto) was a common product of these kilns. For the most part, Ki-zeto ware was made for household use. The pieces were used in cooking but were not roughly made. They usually had a floral design, covered in green, on their surfaces. This was later incised and the green glaze merely laid over the design area. The effect of tea bowls in this style is graceful and soft. This glaze is instantly recognized in Japan as a first-rate Seto specialty.

The Shino bowls of the Seto kilns continue to have a host of exponents in contemporary Japan. Foremost among them is the potter Toyozo Arakawa, designated a Living National Treasure for his superb preservation of Shino and black-Seto techniques. Arakawa's best Shino bowls rank with the best of all time. His research into the origins of the Mino kilns has won wide recognition for him as a scholar. His bowls and water jars are vigorously formed and delicately glazed.

Most Shino work is roughly formed, lending a vigor to its shape which is rarely equaled in bowls of other kinds. The Shino glazes run from pure white to bluish, with a strong strain of gray. The gray Shino, Nezumi Shino, is well represented in public collections abroad. The best Nezumi Shino are not tea bowls but shallow plates or dishes used in meal service accompanying tea.

Japanese-Style Bowls

Kyo-yaki is the traditional pottery of Kyoto artists. Kakiemon Ninsei, who was active in the second half of the seventeenth century, is regarded as the founder of this significant movement. Kyo-yaki potters were masters of the *rokuro,* potter's wheel, and a characteristic of these potters that becomes apparent immediately is that their works have particularly fine bodies. A well-modeled, smooth form was necessary to contain the exquisite designs they showered on the surfaces of the bowls and vases for which they have been noted. Kyo-yaki is the most highly refined of all Japanese ceramics, perhaps reflecting the taste of patrons. Ninsei's patron was the chief priest of Ninna-ji, an elegant temple in the western part of Kyoto, and Ninsei's kiln was constructed at the temple.

Some records seem to suggest that Ninsei was instructed in tea by Kanamori Sowa. This is a possible explanation for the kind of taste shown in the shapes and decorations of Ninsei's bowls, which are most important in that they are purely Japanese. Ninsei's style, together with those of Oribe and Raku, represents a radical departure from tea utensils of Chinese and Korean influence.

Ninsei's glazes were unique, gathered from a variety of sources, and his tradition was followed by all the makers of the Kiyomizu, Awata, and Omura wares of Kyoto. The elegant designs, fine painting, and colorful glazes that always cover Ninsei utensils were attractive to the Kyoto aristocrats. Thus Ninsei's presence in Kyoto gave tremendous encouragement to Kyo-yaki potters, and for the first time potters became established members of Kyoto's artistic community. They began to mark their wares with personal seals, and a genuine style was born.

Ninsei had studied with Seto potters, making his

way to Kyoto in the latter half of the seventeenth century. The exact dates of his life are unknown, but a few of his pieces were dated and signed during the second half of the seventeenth century. An important Kyoyaki piece is his large tea jar at the Nezu Museum, in Tokyo, dated 1688 and decorated with a rich mountain scene in overglaze. Judging from the quality of the work we can assume it was made during his mature period.

Kiyomizu ware generally refers to pieces with colored enamel. Enameling was a technique taught to Ninsei by the potters of Hizen, a porcelain center in northern Kyushu. Ogata Kenzan (1663–1743), the famous potter and painter, developed the art of enameling, fashioning a distinctly Japanese decoration. Kenzan and Ninsei are thought to have worked together, but records proving this are lacking. Kenzan was probably inspired by notes and works left by Ninsei, and he refined Ninsei's decorative ideas. His bowls are strong, and less luxuriously decorated than Ninsei's. But Kenzan must have admired the magnificent tea jars of wisteria design. He made his own products more dramatic by making their designs simpler. Kenzan's older brother, Korin, had achieved fame for his outstanding decoration long before. Later the two brothers worked together on various commissions. Plates made by Kenzan and designed by Korin are among the most celebrated collaborative efforts in art history. Korin's great mentor was not Ninsei but the painter Sotatsu, ca. 1596–1623. It is assumed that Korin worked with Sotatsu, but this is no more supported in fact than the assumption that Kenzan worked with Ninsei.

Following the deaths of these great decorators, the art of enameling continued in Kiyomizu pottery until the Meiji era. Then the potters turned to porcelain and only the Awata kiln remained in the tradition.

Asahi pottery is made on the slopes of Mt. Asahi in Uji, a village near Kyoto. This kiln was begun in the Shoho era (1644–48), but the earliest works bear no stamps or dates for identification. The surface of Asahi is uneven, the color bluish or scarlet, and the bowls tend to be heavy. The Asahi clay is coarse and mixed with sand. Enshu selected this as one of the seven great kilns, but recent products have not achieved the quality of those of his time.

Akahada bowls date from early Edo and have a red glaze. These bowls resemble Hagi ware but frequently have colorful paintings on the outside.

Tamba is one of the five oldest kilns in Japan. The site is in the Kyoto area but did not enjoy the renaissance of the Kyoto pottery world when Ninsei, Korin, Kenzan, and Koetsu held sway. During this time Tamba ware continued to be a simple, undecorated pottery. The clay used in Tamba is porous, giving the ware a coarse and thick appearance. This pottery is dark brown, very masculine, and reflects nothing of the feminine sensibilities of Kyoto.

Shigaraki is another of the five oldest kilns in Japan. The kiln has produced mostly water jars and tea caddies. The bowls tend to have a surface that is too rough for easy handling. All Shigaraki products are fired with an ash glaze covering a portion of the surface.

Bizen bowls are comparatively rare. The kiln shares with Tamba and Shigaraki the distinction of being the oldest in Japan in continuous use. The oldest products, of the Kamakura and Muromachi periods, are the most highly prized. The dark clay is unglazed. If a Bizen bowl is old and its rough surface has been smoothed through use it will make a good tea bowl, but Bizen is most highly prized for its flower containers, especially those in the shape of *ohaguro tsubo,* tooth-blacking pots.

At one time in Japan there were as many as ten thousand kilns operating. Many of these made utensils for tea, especially tea bowls. The discussion could go on and on, detailing the kilns and their products, but the major producers of tea bowls would not extend much beyond those already listed—with the important exception of the Raku kiln.

Fourteen Generations of Raku Ware

Of all the kilns engaged in the making of tea bowls, Raku is the greatest. The Raku family has been associated with the leading schools of tea since the sixteenth century.

Raku ware is not made with the potter's wheel. Rather, it is fashioned with the clay resting on an unattached block of wood that moves with the master as he works the clay into shape. I had the pleasure of spending considerable time with the present Raku master, Kichizaemon, the fourteenth generation from the founder. Born in 1918, he is a graduate of the Tokyo Art School (now Tokyo Art University). His work has the quality of solidity evident in the bowls of his father. I watched him make two bowls in the course of an afternoon.

The master works quickly to center the clay on the block. His tools are simple and he uses them sparingly, mostly working with hands and fingers. He uses red or black glazes and does not experiment with new forms and techniques but rather has mastered the family tradition. He continues to supply discriminating chajin and the masters of the Sen schools with excellent products. Raku is still the bowl preferred by tea men.

An exhibition of the works of the Raku family was held in Tokyo in 1967. An exceptionally authoritative, detailed catalogue for the exhibition and conversations with the master are the sources for my information on this ware. The exhibition was attended by tens of thousands, preventing any of the pieces from being studied for more than a few minutes. At the same time documents, letters, and calligraphy were shown that had some relation to the Raku family.

The earliest record of a Raku work is dated 1574, though some kind of production is likely before that date. The object (a lid) to which the note of 1574 refers was made to order by Chojiro, the first-generation Raku potter. He may have been a Korean with a Japanese mother, but on this there is too little known to make definite assertions.

Most scholars assume that when Chojiro received the order cited he was a tile maker, a new profession in that time. Tiles from that period are extant, including those made with the characteristic Raku clay and glazes. It is likely that Chojiro came into contact with Rikyu and Hideyoshi through his tile business, for commissions must have been handed out for Hideyoshi's palaces and public buildings.

Whatever the case, the *Tennojiya Cha Kaiki* records that it was about 1580 that Chojiro began to make bowls for tea ceremony and later, about 1586–87, these bowls came to be listed as Raku chawan, i.e., they were an accepted, discernible style among the tea bowls of the time. As the Chojiro bowls were made at Rikyu's request and according to his dictates, they are listed in tea diaries and on boxes as "Rikyu form" or "Rikyu bowl."

Chojiro died in 1589 but he left in the span of a few years a great many superb bowls and objects. The early "Koto" and "Dojo-ji" bowls of Chojiro have a flaring rim not characteristic of his later work. For this reason they are given an extremely high value. The beautiful glaze flows down the sides in a wave which leaves exposed a small section just above the rim foot. But the quality of the bowls to which one always returns is the distinctiveness of their shape. Beginning with the rim, uneven and slightly turned out, and continuing to the very small base, the roundedness of the chawan invites cupping with the hands.

More characteristic are the "Kaburo" and "Omokage" bowls. These have rounding waists, as do most Raku bowls, and in this sense are representative of the Raku tradition. The grandest bowls are those such as "Shunkan" (literally, "moment"; even the name is grand) and "Gantori"—superbly straight but not stiff, they seem to lift from their diminutive bases to summon the eye. Some of the Chojiro bowls have tightenings at the waists: "Kimori," "Hayafune," and "Toyobo" are representative of this kind. These are pleasing and seem perfectly suited to fit the hands.

The Chojiro glazes are slightly brown, while later-generation bowls are black due to higher temperatures during firing. The Raku bowls are made from a formula of white lead (100 parts) and hinoka quartz (40 parts), finely strained through silk and mixed with seaweed size and water. For black glaze two parts iron scales and one part impure Chinese cobalt are used. Stones from the Kamo River are ground into fine powder. Those from its upper reaches are considered best.

Chojiro's bowls do not have the gokaku (five

mountains) rim shape which was later favored as a characteristic of the family. His red bowls, inconsistently colored and thin in glaze, are different from later works. The unusual "Koto" and "Dojo-ji" bowls are exceptions to the Raku rule that the glaze must fully cover the bowl body. Having established the rule, Chojiro was sufficiently gifted to break it.

After Chojiro, confusion leaks into the family records of Raku. A man named Tanaka Sokei made some excellent ware which is much in the style of Chojiro, but which is obviously not of his hand. The name Tanaka had been used by the Sen family and it is possible that Sen no Rikyu gave this Sokei his own family name in recognition of the potter's outstanding work. Some critics would have us believe Sokei was Rikyu's son, but this is just a guess based on the fact that Sokei had among his possessions a portrait of Rikyu. It is more likely that Sokei was a talented assistant taken on by Chojiro and liked by Rikyu and the Sen family. But in the final analysis, the facts of his background are unknown, and things are better left open.

There are seven pieces said to be by Sokei: an exquisite incense box in three colors called the "Sansai Shishi," which is signed and dated the fourth year of Bunroku (1595), and six tea bowls. Three of the black bowls resemble the work of Chojiro, as they are finely shaped and glazed, but no real evidence exists to determine Sokei's hand in them. The other four are surely Sokei's, whoever he may be.

It is likely that Sokei had two or more sons. The first is thought to have been Somi, but of his work nothing exists that has been verified. The second son, Kichizaemon (or Jokei) lived until 1636, at which time he is said to have been seventy-five. It is supposedly from this son that the Raku family descends.

In documents of the time Kichizaemon is called *tenka ichi,* "first under heaven," among potters. Koetsu sent him letters, some of which survive, and he kept among his possessions a *noren* (a short curtain for a shop entrance) with the characters for *chawanya* (tea-bowl shop) written on it. Copies of this noren are used today outside the Raku house in Kyoto. Kichizaemon is said to have been especially favored by Hideyoshi's son Hidetada, and from the latter's grave a box for incense was removed bearing the name and seal used by this second-generation Raku potter. The famous Maeda family, too, is said to have favored him.

His work has great power and masculine appeal and he even made bowls in a white glaze that resembles the famous Temmoku. These are magnificent in every respect. He also made this kind of bowl in red, and neither of these kinds resembles works made by typical Raku family potters. His other bowls are also distorted slightly, eccentric but never distasteful. His clay, from Juraku, contains much iron and is charcoal-brown and viscous. His bowls often have spatula marks; this adds to their masculine quality.

Donyu, the third-generation Raku potter, was also

known as Nonko. Born in 1599, thoughout his life he maintained close relations with Koetsu and Sotan (of the Sen family). Koetsu said of him that his work would endure and be appreciated throughout the ages, but added that he was noted for having financial difficulties as well, and was in this sense a "real artist." He died in 1656 and left a great number of outstanding bowls, especially blacks. His blacks are extremely thin, with the glaze often seeming to be the entire thickness of the bowl. His glazes were poured so thickly that they hang like a curtain over the thin clay, running in soft undulations around the base line. He never repeated a theme, even if it had been successful. He began the Raku family practice of placing exceptional works and specially designed works on the altar or shrine of the family.

Donyu's son was Ichinyu, known as Kichizaemon after he inherited the family kiln. He married the daughter of a lacquer maker and she made ceramics under the name Myonyu. He adopted the son of Ogata Sanuemon, uncle of Korin and Kenzan. Born in 1640, he died in 1696, five years after he had shaved his head and changed his name to Ichinyu.

Ichinyu's techniques with subtle reds are superb, though he made blue-black and brilliant-red bowls as well. The brilliant red is known by the special name Shu Raku. He used glaze so heavily on his pieces that they are usually wholly covered, and often no stamp appears.

When Ichinyu died, his son (adopted from the Ogata family) moved the kiln closer to the Ogata home. This son, later known as Sonyu, had been adopted when two years old (1665), and was six years younger than Korin, one year younger than Kenzan. Being contemporaries of the same family and living next door, they must have seen a great deal of each other. This is suggested in *Raku Daidai* (Raku Generations), the catalogue of the Raku exhibition held at Mitsukoshi department store in Tokyo in 1967. The author, Fusenji Isono, further suggests that Kenzan became a potter because of this relationship—not a completely supportable thesis. Isono's assertion that Kenzan did not make monochrome ware for fear of competing with the Raku family works also lacks verification in documents.

Sonyu's work is thick and big and lacks gloss; his blacks are subdued and silvery in feeling. The work of his adopted son, Sanyu, on the other hand, is gentle and deliberate. Sanyu was fond of copying other people's work—especially Koetsu's (who could blame him?). His "Koetsu" are so good that they passed for years as the genuine article.

Sanyu's fame was overshadowed by his natural son's. Chonyu's work is most highly regarded by all who appreciate Raku ware. He was born in 1714 and died in 1770. His wife was also a potter; she maded *ama-yaki,* white "nun's ware."

Chonyu is regarded by many to have made the finest

of all Raku, excepting that by Koetsu. His bowls are distinguished by five-point rims that turn slightly inward. They have full bodies and are generous in size. Most common are Chonyu's blacks, which have a deep and powerful color. His kiln must have been fired at a higher temperature than most, for his reds have a distinct blue tone. The curtain glaze, *maku-yu,* is not often found on his pieces, thus a great many bowls attributed to him must be of another's hand. Nor did he use the snake-scorpion glaze, *dakatsu-yu*. He is known to have distorted rims and walls of some of his bowls—much in the style of Oribe—but these pieces are rare.

The succeeding master was Tokunyu. He was a frail man and yielded the title to his brother Sojiro. Tokunyu's work departs in no respect from that of his forefathers.

Sojiro, later known as Ryonyu, was an active potter who had a long life. At the time of the celebration of the two-hundredth anniversary of the kiln he made two hundred pieces of red Raku and distributed them among his friends and clients. He inherited the title when he was fifteen; his brother died four years later. This potter was a gifted man and an interesting one. He seems to have led a full life: his interests are listed as being fishing, divination, Shinto thought and practice, poetry, tea, calligraphy, and painting. When he retired it was said of him that he left to enjoy the "wind and the moon." We know that he fired fifty pieces in 1818 and seventy in 1825 (when he was seventy). Very prolific, this man was popular in his time with all Kyoto, and when his house burned in the great fire that destroyed the emperor's palace and nearly burned out the center of Kyoto, he had no trouble building the whole back and starting again. Many treasures of the Raku family were lost—including, significantly, all of the old clay which had been preserved since the time of Chojiro. Today's master has much old clay that he keeps carefully in bins by the kiln house. These clay collections are a valuable heritage for the young potters that succeed to the Raku title.

Ryonyu was a *meijin,* a distinguished artist who was also an authority in his field. He made so many pieces that there is an abundance of his work available. He was experimental in the extreme, considering some of the spatula markings on his work, but at the same time he produced very conventional works. Some of his reds are light and yellowish, resembling Koetsu's. Some are crimson, and he used the curtain and snake-scorpion glazes. Where Sanyu had imitated others without injecting his own personality, Ryonyu always allowed his own sense of proportion to intrude—making his imitations of Koetsu, Chojiro, Nonko, and Oribe quite distinctive. Some of his pieces were painted by others, some decorated by himself, and he was fond of signing the pieces by incising his name and the date on the side.

Tannyu was the second son of Ryonyu, the elder having died young without gaining the title. He worked as a young man in the established kiln of the Kishu Tokugawa family; as an assistant there he made many works.

This family gave him a stamp, marked "Raku," which he used as his own. Prolific, he made one hundred special pieces in 1829 and two hundred fifty in 1838, when he celebrated the anniversary of Chojiro's death. The two hundred fifty were all black and bear the same stamp. He died in 1854, nine years after his retirement.

Keinyu, eleventh-generation master of the Raku kilns, suffered the fate of seeing the family house destroyed again by fire. He rebuilt the house in 1857, and it is this house which survives. Keinyu made some fine original pieces, a set of thirty red and black bowls, a *mizusashi* with twelve scenes from waka verses painted on it, and the famous "Unkakubun *hibachi*" (ordered by the emperor and painted by an artist of the late Kano school), and a tea bowl for the emperor's use, before retiring in 1871. He was adopted into the Raku family when he married the Raku daughter, and his name was changed at that time.

He lived briefly in Hagi and visited Bizen and Izumo, where he made tea utensils. He avoided Kyoto because of his role in the Meiji Restoration, but returned to be appointed special potter for the Kyoto government and museum. He retired at seventy but continued to be active (that year he gave some twenty tea ceremonies) and two years later he held virtually continuous tea ceremony from December through June of the next year. At eighty-one he visited Tokyo and the surrounding areas, making bowls and tea scoops. He died in 1902 at eighty-five, while serving tea.

His bowls reflect his active life; he was agile, his bowls are facile. His glazes are sharp and appealing, splendid in appearance. Every one of his works is tasteful and elegant.

His only son, Konyu, had a difficult time following in his illustrious father's footsteps. He served as an assistant at the tea ceremonies of the Tokugawa and Mitsui families and worked hard at his own creations, but he kept a certain vitality only through his early thirties, going into patterns of repetition after that. He never gave a tea himself—perhaps because of the work he was forced to do for the exalted families—and he died in his retreat in 1932.

The thirteenth-generation Raku master, Seinyu, was close to the Sen family and worked for them in various capacities, especially as chief of the "Senke Jishoki" (Ten Jobs Relating to the Sen Family). His work is marked by strong Oribe, Shino, Bizen, Karatsu, and Hagi influences.

The present-generation master was born in 1918. As he is still young, a summation of his important work cannot be set down here in detail. Suffice it to say that he exhibits qualities of strength befitting a man living in the time of Japan's maturing as an economic power and artistic force throughout the world.

Among the many potters who have worked in Raku

styles—there are thousands of amateurs in today's Japan who devote themselves to this—the greatest of all was Koetsu (1558–1637). A man who considered himself an amateur, this great artist was perhaps the finest single spirit that ever graced the Japanese art world. He was an eclectic who could use any idea, from whatever source, to his own advantage in art.

Koetsu was fiercely independent as a man and as an artist. He had his favorite themes and things, and these he pursued with passion. He acknowledged little of his great ability except in the field of sword and sword-furniture connoisseurship (his family had traditionally served the nobles of Japan in this field). He retired in his seventy-sixth year and went to Takagamine to live in his hut, the Taikyo-an.

He had followed a simple life and on retirement he gave away all his famous possessions. He objected to the gaudy tea which took over after Rikyu's passing and refused to toe the Tokugawa line. He was supreme as a calligrapher in Japan, and to see any of the many examples of his work in this art is to acknowledge the reputation as deserved: original, sweeping, forceful, and inventive, his calligraphy persuades with versatility. He was perhaps the first artist-craftsman in a land of craftsmen-artists. No one in Japan, save perhaps Rikyu at his best, surpassed Koetsu in synthesizing Japan's diverse arts and tastes into a workable and beautiful whole. He made, for example, excellent *kama;* one is preserved by Hompo-ji, his home temple, and another is at Koetsu-ji, a temple in the vicinity of the hut to which he retired.

Koetsu copied some two hundred No plays in his flowing script, and these were printed as woodblocks and are still used by many. His work always refreshes, in whatever field. The stories growing up around the man and his work are numerous. When he made his most famous bowl, the magnificent "Fuji-san," he gave it as a gift for the dowry of his daughter—wrapping it in old material and saying that he had nothing else. It is a noble dowry for any woman, priceless in the finest sense. One must see the Raku works of this extraordinary artist; description does them no justice.

9. Other Major Utensils

Iron Kettles: *Kama*

The Japanese imported many of their original tea utensils from China and Korea. Japanese missions to the continent returned with lightweight objects of great value, together with ideas and learning. Reischauer's *Ennin's Travels in T'ang China* verifies the interest of Japanese in Chinese things that were easily transported for good profits.

The *kama,* or iron kettle for tea, is a case in point. So popular did it become that tea shops came to be identified by signs carved in the shape of a kettle, and a special celebration, the *kamabi,* "kettle (or tea) day," was observed.

The Japanese consider the kettles made at Ashiya, a town in northern Kyushu, to be the finest and oldest of Japanese make. Old Ashiya kettles survive today and are the model of what the best tea kettles should be. Next in appreciation are the Temmyo kettles of Sano, Tochigi prefecture. Kyoto kettles are called *Kyo saku* ("made in Kyoto"), while those produced in the area around Tokyo are called *Kanto saku* ("made in Kanto").

The classification of kettles is usually made according to the area in which they are produced. There are hundreds of shapes and kinds: crane-neck, arrow-notch, square-mouth, Daruma-like, hailstone, devil-face, etc. The term *kansu* is sometimes applied to kettles, but it is probably a reference to water kettles from Han China. As late as 1712, the name o-kama (the "o" is honorific) referred to a cooking kettle. This is made clear by the *Wakan Sansai Zu-e,* a 105–volume illustrated encyclopedia published that year. An earlier work, the *Tsutsumi Chunagon Monogatari* of the twelfth century, refers to a hanging kettle, *sagari.*

This is the one that came to be used for tea, the one we refer to as the kama of cha-no-yu. Kettles of this kind have been excavated in both Korea and China. From the encrustations of their surfaces we know that the Korean and Chinese kettles, especially the type called *hirakumo-gama,* were hung over open fires. A second kind, *bumbuku chagama* (chagama means "tea kettle") is sometimes seen with the hirakumo-gama in illustrations dating from after the twelfth century. Many kettles resembling the bumbuku chagama have been found in recent Korean excavations. These resemble Chinese Han-dynasty kettles, and one can suppose their design came from China. A few such works have been found in Japan, and their source is thought to be the Koreans who came to Japan at an early date.

Earlier the priest Myokei was mentioned in connection with a kettle upon which the "ten virtues of tea" were inscribed. The date of the inscription was 1201–3. The kettle was an Ashiya, which would indicate that Ashiya kettles were relatively well known at the time. Judging from the quality of this kettle it is obvious that some Japanese kettle makers had made masterful advances in the art of metalwork and kettle creation.

Tesshi Nagano, far the most authoritative scholar on the subject and himself the foremost living kettle maker, lists forty-seven basic designs for kettles in his *Cha-no-yu no Kama*. Among them are these examples: standard, *shinnari;* flat spider, *hirakumo;* helmet, *kabuto;* cloud-dragon, *unryu;* jujube, *natsume;* high shoulder-tube, *katatsuki-tsutsu;* armor, *kirikake;* wide mouth, *hiroguchi;* pot, *nabe;* Mt. Fuji, *Fuji-san;* and gourd, *hyotan*.

Master Nagano was first attracted to the study of kama when he judged a craft exhibition as a young man. He passed over two kama which had been entered in the show. The men who made them were elderly and careful craftsmen who resented being neglected in the awarding of prizes, so they verbally attacked Nagano. To defend himself from their charges he began to inquire about the process of making kettles. The old men explained the difficulties of their craft. Their explanations were so compelling that Nagano took up the study of kama. The young Nagano soon discovered that little research had been done on the history of tea kettles.

Today, some fifty years later, Tesshi Nagano has succeeded not only in ordering the complex history of Japanese tea kettles but has also created the finest tea kettles of recent times. He laboriously deciphered the notes, records, and box writing (*hakogaki*) that comprised the history of the Japanese kettle. He classified the oldest Chinese, Korean, and Japanese kettles in a system which reveals the origins of styles and techniques. His many books, pamphlets, catalogues, lectures, and exhibitions have done much to lay a scientific groundwork for anyone seriously interested in the study of kama.

Nagano points out that the surface, materials, shape, ears, and lids are basic elements in appreciating kama, and are keys to the verification of types. The surfaces of kama are divided into eight basic types: dragged, *hiki-hada;* raked, *sasara-hada;* cloth, *nuno-hada;* brushed, *fude-hada;* flicked, *hajiki-hada;* crepe, *chirimen-hada;* and irregularly roughed, *ara-hada*. The dragged surface is created by turning the kettle mold while holding an implement against it. The raked surface is that which has had a *sasara,* an implement resembling a whisk, drawn across it. The cloth surface is obtained by impressing a wide-weave fabric onto the mold. A specially designed spatula called *bobera* creates rougher surfaces. A variation on the spatula is a stamp which can be pressed into the mold surface, but the most interesting rough surface is made by simply flinging wet clay onto the smooth mold, giving the final product an irregular texture.

Chikuzen Ashiya, the modern city of Fukuoka, is the designation for the earliest Japanese tea kettles. These were designed with a spatula or bobera and in the Kamakura period the sasara, too, was used. Chikuzen Ashiya kettles are purplish-black unless heavily rusted, and occasionally they are decorated with a stamp that produces a hailstone pattern.

Echizen Ashiya kettles are made of hard steel and they rust to a slightly yellow color with age. Ise Ashiya are dull black. Hakata Ashiya are wine colored; Nagano thinks the iron used in them came from the Philippines. Banshu Ashiya have either a reddish tint or are black; this coloration may suggest a change of location of the makers.

Other outstanding kettles come from Iwami, Hizen, Temmei, and Odawara, but these frequently duplicate the colors and designs of Ashiya. The imitation of Ashiya designs complicates kettle history, a history already bothered by dislocation, changes of patronage, and loss of records. In judging kettles it is important for a student to be exposed to a variety of styles and makes before attempting any identification. And even after considerable experience, identification frequently remains uncertain.

In examining a kettle the first feature to be observed is its mouth. Kettle mouths exhibit great variety: scooped, *kuri-guchi*; steaming basket, *koshiki-guchi*; round, *wa-guchi*; old woman, *uba-guchi*; folded, *ori-guchi*, etc. For the most part, early kettles have round mouths. Later, especially in the Edo period, kettle makers who specialized in tea utensils made mouths that were octagonal, square, and hexagonal. With the advance in technical proficiency, artistic merit declined as the number of designs increased. Kettles made in late Edo were garishly designed and the craftsmen became facile in their medium.

In the beginning, the usual kettle shape was round. Korean excavations reveal kettles made from the late-seventh through the mid-tenth century that are decidedly bulbous. Earlier Korean kettles of the fourth century were rather squat but still rounded. After the Muromachi period, Japanese kettles appear that are tall and squarish, more fitting to tea service.

Chinese Han-dynasty kettles have a ring of metal around the middle called the *kemuri-gaeshi,* or smoke rejector. This ring continues to be found on early Ashiya works. Below it is an area called the *hi-zoko,* or fire bottom. In old kettles the original hi-zoko rarely remains today, having been replaced long ago.

The ears of a kettle are called *kantsuki* and form the receptical for the rings, *kan,* which are used to lift the kettle to and from the base. Because of the care with which they are made, the beauty of their design, and the importance attached to them by tea masters, kantsuki are highly regarded by collectors and scholars. Much has been written about them, and they come in a variety of kinds. Chinese kantsuki are elegant miniature sculptures. A favorite was the monkey-face kantsuki, a form which descends from Han sculpture. Chikuzen Ashiya kantsuki, however, form the basis for all Japanese styles. When the forms were not sculptural they were knoblike though still decorative. The peculiarly Japanese forms are called *wayo kantsuki,* and these are often shaped like pine cones, shells, bamboo joints, and waves. Location seems to account for form: a beach area such as Odawara nearly always produced shell kantsuki; Ise kettles are famous for their drum-shaped kantsuki, *shogomini,* perhaps because of the use of drums in the Grand Shrines at the same location.

Kettle lids, too, have many forms. For expensive kettles there are two lids: *tomo-buta,* a kind of special or occasional lid, and the *kae-buta,* replacement lid. The use of two lids was a development of the time of Jo-o and Rikyu. Rikyu had a passion for lids, spending hours selecting them for his utensils. He had a habit of using lids that did not fit his wares, which annoyed some people, but was no doubt another example of his spirit of insufficiency.

The finest kettles have always been made by a sand-casting process. The Japanese came early to sand casting and became wonderfully adept at it. The first step in the process is to form a clay mold. Before the clay dries a design is etched or drawn onto the surface. This is done by hand, whether it involves an elaborate design of pine trees or a simple geometric pattern repeated across the whole surface. Once in Yamagata I was permitted to watch Master Nagano transfer a delicate design from paper to the surface of a mold. He had made many drawings of the pine branch he had chosen before selecting one that would lend itself to the kettle he had in mind. The translucent paper on which he drew was the precise size of the mold wall. He wetted the paper and smoothed it over the clay. Then, using a thin or broad spatula as needed, he traced the design. This was done quickly and surely, for the clay dried in a short time. When he was finished the mold was allowed to dry. The top and bottom were then bound together and holes were fixed in the mold for pouring the molten iron and to allow air and steam to escape. Each step is performed by hand and requires considerable physical effort. The mold must be perfectly formed; spaces into which the molten iron is poured must be uniformly thick. If this thickness varies, the iron will form uneven walls that will crack. When the iron is poured into the mold the craftsman requires two assistants. The pouring process is the most exciting part of making a kettle, for the brilliant red iron spews out from the mold like exploding lava. While the iron cools, the caster goes through a period of tension. Molds are used only once and if something has gone wrong, the work of weeks will have come to nothing. We were with Master Nagano when the mold for his pine-branch kettle was opened. The kettle was superb, of uniform strength, harmonious design, and excellent coloring. The kettle was brushed and cleaned, later to be displayed in an exhibition of tea utensils at a Tokyo department store.

As with many traditional arts in Japan, many people will inform the visitor that the art of casting kettles is dying. They will say that Tesshi Nagano is the last master of an ancient art. This is simply not true. Today there are fifteen master casters in Japan, a comfortably large number for such a difficult and time-consuming art. The tradition has been going on for hundreds of years and is not likely to die soon in such capable hands. Junichiro Tanizaki, the novelist, once remarked that the survival of the Awaji puppet theater was most unlikely. Today, forty years after his observation, the Awaji theater is performing with the same regularity and vitality it had when Tanizaki announced its coming extinction.

Tea masters have developed strong attitudes toward the kettles they use. These include proper care: the exterior must be carefully washed with fresh water and scrubbed with a brush after every use. Young people must not touch the sides of the kettle with their hands for to do so would leave a deposit of oil which makes the kettle glossy, while the mat finish is considered best. Older people have less oil on their hands and can touch the kettle without seriously affecting the finish. Old kettles that are well made have an interior encrustation that makes a pleasant sound when water is boiled. This is the *nari* effect, and it is something to be cultivated, but nothing should be placed in a new kettle to produce this sound artificially.

On the appreciation of a kettle Tesshi Nagano has this to say: "See as many kettles as you can. Learn to enjoy them by yourself. Trust no dealer, no book, no writing on containers. Trust only the beauty of the kettle in front of you. Work hard; this is no easy art."

Small Kettles: *Tetsubin*

Small, hand-held kettles for tea ceremony are called *tetsubin*. These are most often of iron, made in the same manner as the larger kama. Tetsubin have spouts which allow water to be poured directly into the tea bowl. Therefore, the tea ceremony in which they are used employs no water ladle. The tetsubin ceremony is considered less formal, and perhaps for this reason few tetsubin are included in major exhibitions of tea utensils. There is little information available on this utensil, an unfortunate omission, for it is the tetsubin which students first learn to use. Tetsubin are the only kettles ever made for ordinary use in silver or gold.

The Brazier: *Furo*

As is true of so many other utensils for tea, the portable brazier, *furo*, was first imported from China or Korea. This object is constructed to contain the charcoal fire over which the kettle of water is placed. It is used for the warmer months of the year, usually beginning in April or May and continuing through October. There are three common varieties of brazier: iron, bronze, and earthenware. During the ceremony, fine ones are usually placed on a lacquer board, *shiki-ita*, while others rest on a tile, *shiki-kawara*.

The furo was the only fire container for tea ceremony used in the early period of development. The first were of two designs only. One allows the kettle to rest directly on the brazier sides, fitting the kama to the furo as a lid to a jar. The other requires the use of a trivet which stands over the flame; the kettle rests on the iron trivet, free from the furo wall. In the case of the kettle-supporting furo, the charcoal fire cannot be seen from above, but only through a small opening in the front that allows air to reach the fire. This design is called *kirikake*, and the kettles used with this are equipped with small rims of metal, something like a belt course, which secure the kettle.

The furo that require a trivet are of three designs. The Doan style has an ample horseshoe-shaped opening at the front that permits guests and host to view the raked ashes and charcoal fire beneath the kettle. A second design has a broad, ovoid opening in the front of the furo. The third is an inverted arch, again with an ample opening onto the ashes and fire. Each of the three kinds of furo that use trivets require that the ashes be raked for the fire in different ways.

Beginners are always taught to use a plain iron kirikake furo for basic ceremonies, but the simple tray tea is introduced with a ceramic furo, *tsuchifuro*. The tsuchifuro rests on a coarse-grain board, *arame-ita*. Ceramic furo, some of which are highly decorative, are available in a large variety of glazes, the most common being red Raku and Oribe.

The Fire Pit: *Ro*

Ro is a shortened form of the word *irori*, or a fixed fire pit inside a house. Many Japanese houses of traditional design come equipped with a ro, often fitted into a half-mat area of a tatami room. The ro is used during the winter months because heat is given off from the open structure more freely than from a contained structure such as the furo. In cold months the heat that rises from the open pit is no small dividend in a room where no other heating arrangement is provided.

In old Japanese temples, shops, and houses there is rarely any heat except from a charcoal fire. If the room is used for tea ceremony one can expect a good charcoal fire in a ro, but the usual meeting of host and guest is over a *naga-hibachi*. This beautiful device is sold in America and Europe as a coffee table or planter, but in Japan it is the center of attention as heater, ashtray, kettle warmer, cigarette lighter, and winter "sandbox." Many pleasant hours can be spent in conversation around the naga-hibachi and its small fire of charcoal. If the host is a scholar or priest explaining points of Japanese art he may reach over with the *hi-bashi*, metal chopsticks used to manipulate coals, and draw a character in the fine ashes, much as one would do in sand by the shore. Aside from the naga-hibachi, *kotatsu* are used to heat a conversation or dining area. Kotatsu are low tables under which is placed an electrical or charcoal device for heating. From the sides of the tabletop hangs a quilt under which one places his legs. Hands, too, are warmed beneath the quilt.

The ro in temples and old farmhouses is the dining area. The family and members of the household sit around the open pit. A large kettle is often suspended over the fire. This device has been adapted to tea ceremony and represents an original Japanese addition to the art. The tea-ceremony ro is bordered by a wooden frame, *robuchi*. In rooms of four and one-half mats or smaller the robuchi is plain, grained wood and is called *kijimono*. In large rooms the robuchi is lacquered, most often in *maki-e* style, gold-design lacquer. The robuchi is a work of superb craftsmanship and bears the seal of the maker. An extraordinary robuchi painted by Tessai can be seen in the famous Tessai temple, Seicho-ji, at Takarazuka. A more recent example of an excellent robuchi is one designed by the Urasenke grand master in Kyoto, decorated with a ship in gold lacquer; a witty case of a ship surrounding water. This robuchi is a standard one foot five inches square.

During the coldest month of the year an enlarged version of the tea ro is used at Urasenke. An outsized fire is laid in it, and the room temperature rises to a very comfortable degree.

Using the ro calls for a special arrangement of utensils, special position for the host, and special handling of the water ladle. With the ro one places utensils in an arc and turns to a three-quarter position in front of the guests. This attitude makes for a more intimate tea. As opposed to the relatively complicated variety of positioning of the water ladle in furo ceremonies, the host always handles the ladle the same way while using the ro.

Chajin have always been fond of the ro; it has been a fixture in traditional Japanese architecture, an object of admiration and of fond memories. Anyone who has experienced the intense cold of Kyoto or of a farming village in northern Japan cannot but appreciate the role the ro has played in Japanese life. Its presence in the tea ceremony is quite natural.

At this writing the use of the ro outside of Japan is strictly limited. The Urasenke school in New York is not equipped with a fixed fire pit, due to architectural requirements and regulations against open fires indoors. However, an *oki-ro,* a small ro raised from the floor and mounted on a platform, is now in use.

Tea Caddies: *Cha-ire* and *Natsume*

The original *cha-ire,* ceramic tea caddies, were medicine bottles from China by merchants and priests. These small pots were also used in their native land for holding cosmetics and seasonings. Tea was contained in them because it was commonly regarded as a medicine. Eisai is said to have brought the "original tea seeds" in one of the more famous cha-ire. These seeds from China were used to introduce cultivated tea to Japan.

The bottles came to be wholly associated in Japan with koicha, powdered tea for the thick-tea ceremony. Cha-ire were in great demand because of their high value and light weight. Next to the bowl and kettle, a tea master most prized his best cha-ire. These were often offered as rewards for outstanding service to generals and officials, as mentioned previously. The cha-ire brought from China were much copied by Japanese craftsmen.

Like tea bowls, cha-ire can be classified by area. Those from China are called *karamono.* Products of the Southeast Asian islands are *shimamono.* Seto and Mino are from the kilns of those areas in Japan, and those made in other areas are called *kuni-yaki.* The shapes are distinguished as follows: high shouldered, *katatsuki;* apple, *bunrin;* eggplant, *nasu;* gourd, *hyotan;* bulge bottom, *shiri-bukura;* sculptured form with low waist, *ruiza;* handled, *tsuru-tsuki;* crane's neck, *tsurukubi;* rounded with short neck, *marutsubo;* bulbous ("big sea"), *taikai;* "smaller sea," *naikai;* and a shape resembling a long-necked flowerpot, *anko.*

There are still more classifications and variations upon these. Pots imported from other countries are not similarly classified. They are too few in number and their shapes do not easily fit into the established categories of Chinese and Japanese ware. Cha-ire from many countries can be used. Some excellently shaped pots from ancient Persia are just the right size for cha-ire. These, fitted with ivory lids, are used by chajin in Kyoto. In selecting an imported cha-ire it is only necessary to pay attention to size, glaze, and surface. The size must be sufficient to hold a few ounces of powdered tea. The glaze should be subdued. The surface should be relatively free of texture because the outside of the cha-ire is wiped with a piece of silk, which would catch on rough surfaces.

A good variety of cha-ire can be seen at the Boston Museum of Fine Arts in the collection assembled by Morse, which includes almost every known shape and kind from Japan. The Metropolitan Museum in New York also has a fine elongated caddy which has been put on display from time to time.

The ceramic caddy has many named parts: lip, *hineri-kaeshi;* shoulder, *kata;* body string, *dohimo;* glaze line, *kusuri-giwa;* exposed clay part, *tsuchimi;* thread cut or bottom line, *ito-kiri* or *soko;* dew edge or snow-slide, *rosaki* or *nadare;* tray or mat point, *bon-tsuki* or *tatami-tsuki;* skirt, *suso;* body, *do;* and neck, *koshiki.*

The whorl on the underside of a ceramic caddy usually serves as a quick indication of the country of origin. If the whorl center is to the left, the caddy is Chinese; if to the right, Japanese. There are three other kinds of marks on a caddy bottom which assist identification: string-cutting marks, concave whorls, and rough removal marks and spatula cuts. The finishing techniques often reveal its origin.

For a thick-tea ceremony the caddy is filled almost to the brim. All the tea in the caddy is used, unlike thin-tea service, in which powder remains in the lacquer natsume. The tea is drawn from the ceramic caddy with the scoop and placed in a large bowl. The same bowl is used by all guests. Thick tea is pasty, not frothy, and is taken in small amounts.

Most ceramic caddies are given poetic names by their owners. These names often point out the special characteristics of the caddy, such as shape, origin, previous owner, kiln, and so forth. Of the greatest cha-ire the name "Matsumoto kata-tsuki" comes to mind. It is a very special caddy, at least seven of the greatest names in tea having owned it, the first being an early tea man whose name it bears. From his family it passed to the shogun Ashikaga Yoshimasa. It is a piece from Ming China, brought to Japan by merchants. Yoshimasa gave the caddy to his tea master, Shuko, who passed it on to Furichi Sanei. The next owner was the most important tea devotee of his day, Matsuya Gensaburo, and he passed it to the powerful

Shimazu family. Today it is in the collection of the Nezu Art Museum, Tokyo, where it can be seen in special exhibitions. A chance to see the Matsumoto kata-tsuki should not be missed. Perfect in form, color, and weight, this cha-ire is a standard against which the very best cha-ire can be judged. Legend says that Hosokawa Sansai was so taken with the caddy that he attempted to take it from the tearoom in the folds of his kimono.

Accompanying the Matsumoto kata-tsuki are four bags used to dress the caddy for various ceremonies. They are *donsu,* damask silk or satin, and *kinran,* cloth of gold. The bags are drawn tight with small golden or purple cords. Such bags are called *shifuku* or *fukuro* and always accompany ceramic caddies. The Matsumoto kata-tsuki has a separate bag for each season, but most caddies have only two. The bags are displayed with the caddy in the course of the ceremony.

A good caddy has a series of wooden boxes in which it and the bags are kept. These often have inscriptions on them, with successive owners adding box upon box, complete with his own messages and testimonies.

The best caddies have mouths that are fairly generous, so that the tea can easily be drawn out. The Bizen ohaguro tsubo that are adapted for tea ceremony as caddies have the largest mouths. Recent Bizen caddies are light both in weight and color. Old Bizen tends to be heavier than necessary, but its qualities of color and shape more than make up for this defect.

Seto products are most popular for caddies, which have been a specialty of the kilns for centuries. The lustrous brown glaze, relieved by touches of blue or green, is ideal for a formal thick-tea ceremony. The surfaces of the Seto cha-ire are smooth, more easily handled than new Bizen.

The lid of a ceramic caddy is usually ivory or plastic. But certain caddies are fitted with lids of lacquered wood or—rarely—ceramic. The underside of these lids is covered with gold leaf, just thick enough to make the lid fit snugly.

Thin-tea ceremonies require *usuchaki* or *natsume.* The latter is the most common name for lacquered tea caddies, but others are *usuki* and *chaki.* The earliest lacquer caddies were most likely plain black. After the Momoyama period many were made with gold, red, blue, green, or yellow designs drawn on their inner and outer surfaces. Carved lacquer and mother-of-pearl, *raden,* were also popularly used for natsume. Floral patterns and family crests—especially those of the Tokugawa and imperial families—were laid on natsume sides and lids. Black line drawings on red lacquer have recently been popular, but it is the plain black lacquered natsume that is best suited to contain the brilliant green tea. The lustrous, deep black is perfect for tea and unrivaled in its beauty.

Hira-natsume are wider than they are high; *ko-natsume* are higher than they are wide; *chu-natsume,* the most common form, are middle-sized; *dai-natsume* are

A *chagama* (metal kettle for tea). (Courtesy of Urasenke.)

A round chagama.

Chagama.

A small *tetsubin* (iron kettle) used for tray tea. (Photo by S. Fujima.)

▲ An Ashiya tea kettle.

A wooden *furo* (brazier). (Courtesy of Urasenke.) ▶

A chagama as it is placed over the ro. Note the lacquered *robuchi* (wooden frame). (Courtesy of Urasenke.)

Various kinds of metal furo. (Courtesy of Urasenke.)

"Aoi no Ue," Kenzan's famous bowl, upper left. A Hagi-ware bowl with *himo-ana kodai* ("cord-hole" foot), upper right, and a Ko Hagi (old Hagi) bowl of the rough-surfaced *oni* (demon) type, lower left. The bowl on the lower right is of Taishugohon (an area of Korea) ware, with *dan kodai* (stepped foot).

A Kosobe bowl in Enshu's design, upper left. A Ko Bizen (old Bizen) bowl, made before 1600, upper right. The bowl on the lower left is of Shodai ware with *ninajiri kodai* (shell foot) and the potter's seal on the bottom. A Temmoku-ware bowl in Kensan style is shown in the lower right-hand picture.

The seals of the Raku potters.

A black Raku summer tea bowl by Ichinyu, fourth generation (top), and a Raku bowl by Chojiro, the first Raku potter (bottom).

Four Raku bowls. On the upper left is a black one by Keinyu, eleventh generation; the upper right is red, by Konyu, twelfth generation; the lower left is red, after the Hagi style, by Konyu; and the lower right is Urasenke Grand Master Tantansai's design. Tantansai was the father of the present grand master.

Koetsu's famous tea bowl "Fuji-san." (Courtesy of Tadamasa Sakai; photo by Tankosha.)

A shallow, summer tea bowl from Korea. ▼

Two views of a black Oribe-style tea bowl.

A *natsume* (lacquer caddy for *usucha,* thin tea) of the type preferred by Tantansai, left, and a Momoyama-period natsume of yellow Shunkei lacquer, right.

Three types of natsume, one containing tea as it is prepared for use in the ceremony.

▲
A natsume with its box, showing *hakogaki,* the writing of a grand master, on the side and lid.

The "Matsuya *kata-tsuki*" (Matsuya high-shouldered tea caddy). (Courtesy of the Nezu Museum, Tokyo.)

A *cha-ire* (ceramic caddy for *koicha,* thick tea) of the kata-tsuki type, with ivory lid and brocade bag.

Silk brocade bags for various shapes of cha-ire.
▼

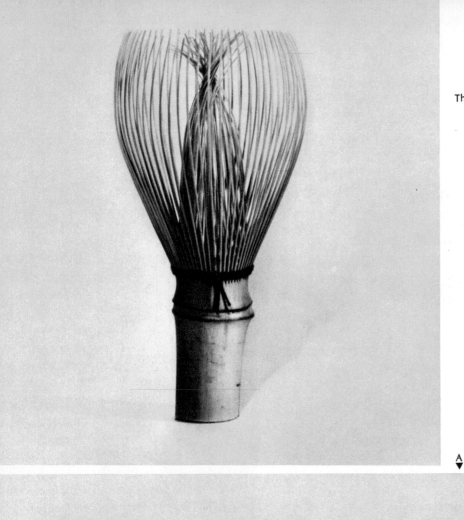

The standard form of *chasen* (tea whisk).

▼ A *hishaku* (water ladle) for use inside the tearoom.

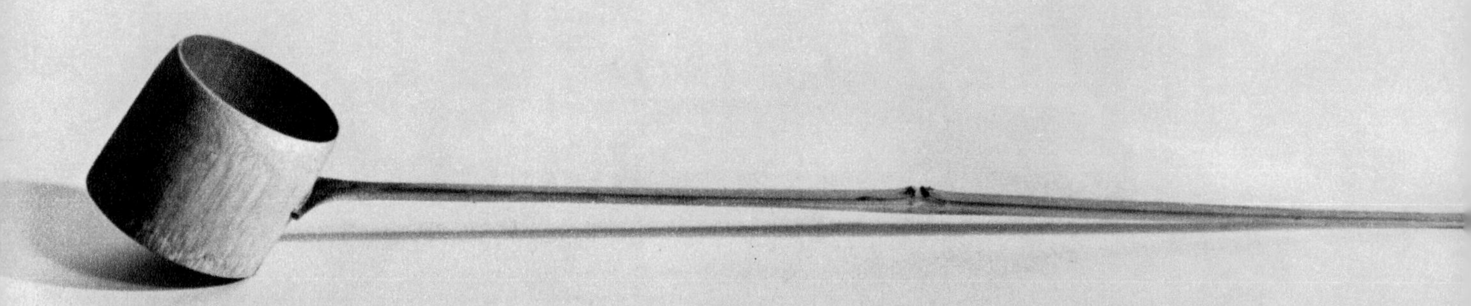

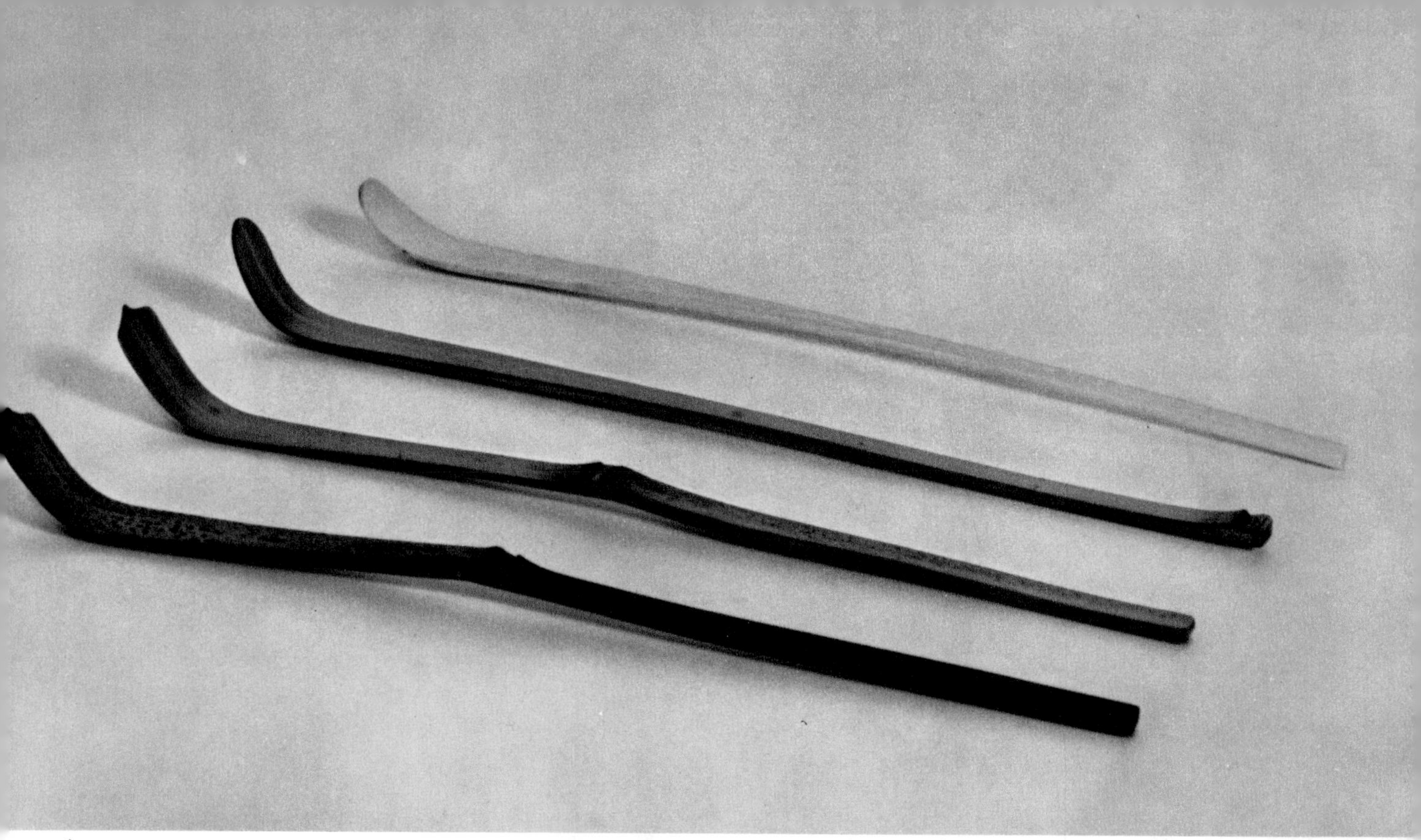

▲ Standard types of *chashaku* (tea scoops). The uppermost one is of ivory; the other three are of bamboo.

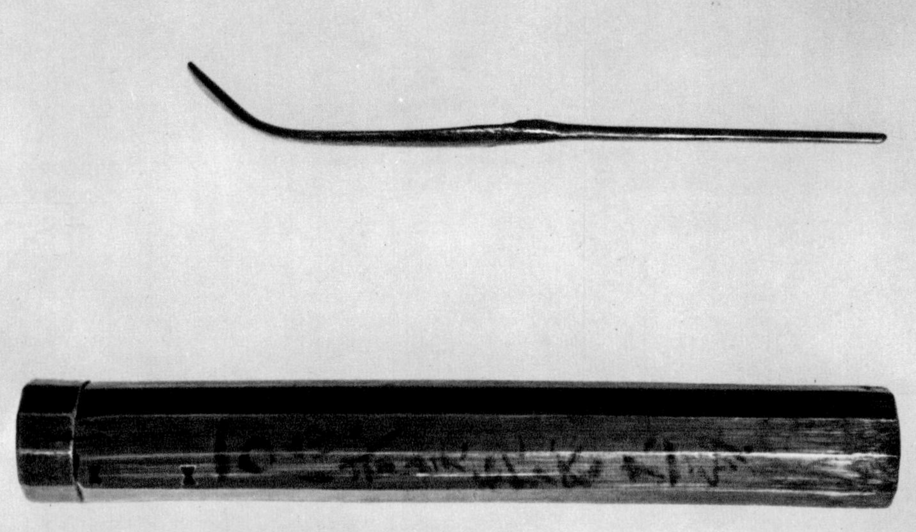

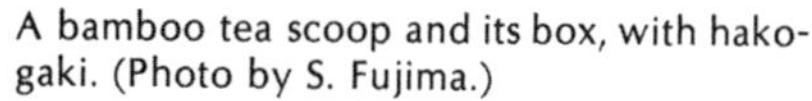

A bamboo tea scoop and its box, with hakogaki. (Photo by S. Fujima.)

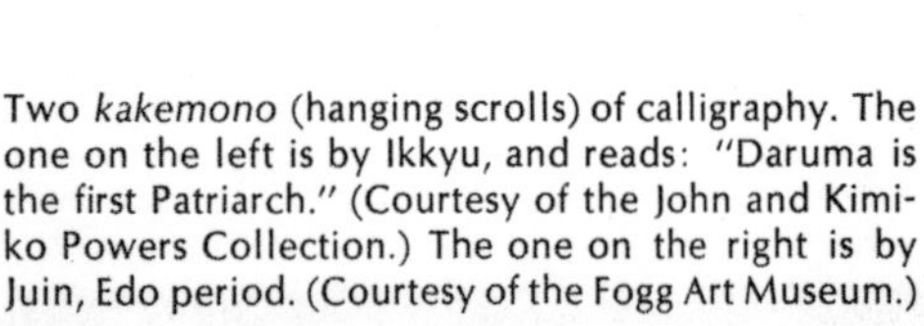

Two *kakemono* (hanging scrolls) of calligraphy. The one on the left is by Ikkyu, and reads: "Daruma is the first Patriarch." (Courtesy of the John and Kimiko Powers Collection.) The one on the right is by Juin, Edo period. (Courtesy of the Fogg Art Museum.)

A bamboo wall vase with a camellia arrangement.

▲
Four types of *kogo* (incense containers), of wood, lacquer, and ceramic.

A brown Raku *hana-ire* (flower container) in a boat shape, with box showing hakogaki.

Shown here are the small implements a guest takes with him to the tea ceremony. In the upper left and lower right corners are two types of *fukusa-basami* (cloth carrying-cases), that on the left for the *fukusa* (silk napkin; upper right), and that on the right for *kaishi* (paper napkins; lower center). In the lower left-hand corner is a *yoji* (pick for eating sweets) and its carrying-case, and in the upper center is a small *sensu* (folding fan). (Photo by Tankosha.)

▲Two types of *mizusashi* (water jars). That on the left is Bizen ware, and that on the right is an imitation of a Korean ware. (Courtesy of Urasenke.)

An incense container by Nonko, third-generation Raku.

A *kensui* or *koboshi* (waste-water jar) of the type preferred by Tantansai.

Arrangement of utensils on the *daisu*, stand, for the most formal style of tea ceremony.
▼

Futa-oki (lid rests) of the seven styles selected by Rikyu, and one of bamboo.

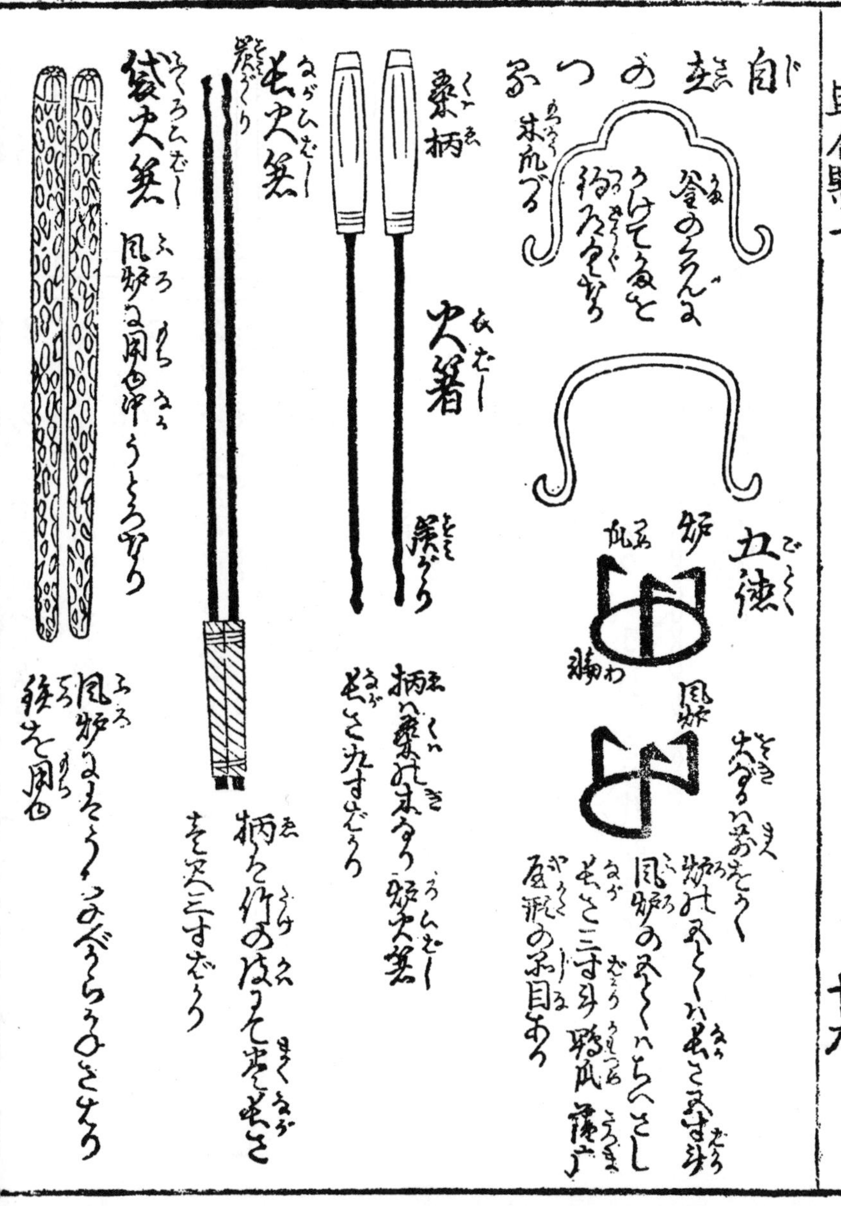

Three types of metal tongs for arranging charcoal in the fire (left) and trivets used for large kettles (right), from vol. 1 of *Chado Hayagaten*.

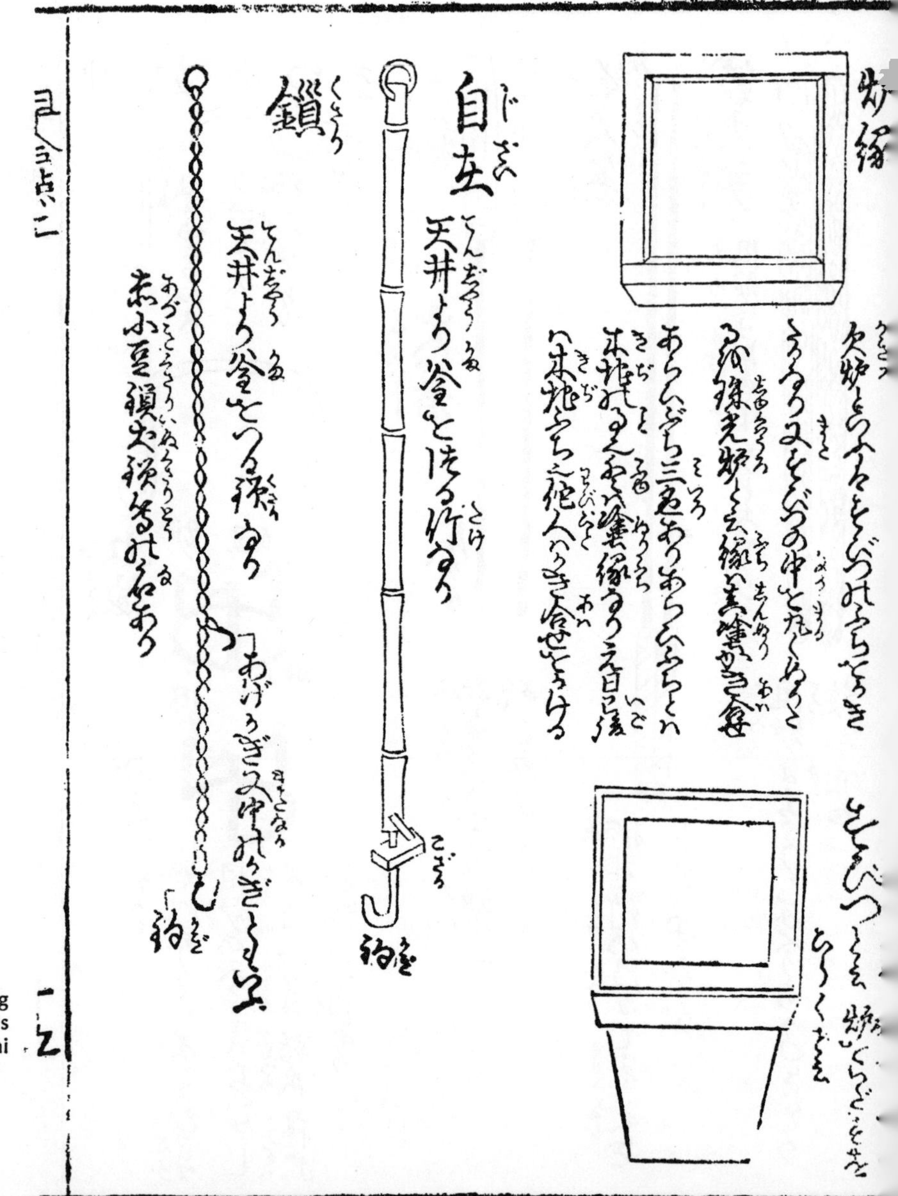

Bamboo and chain devices for suspending the kettle over the fire pit when a trivet is not used (left) and two designs for robuchi (right), from vol. 1 of *Chado Hayagaten.*

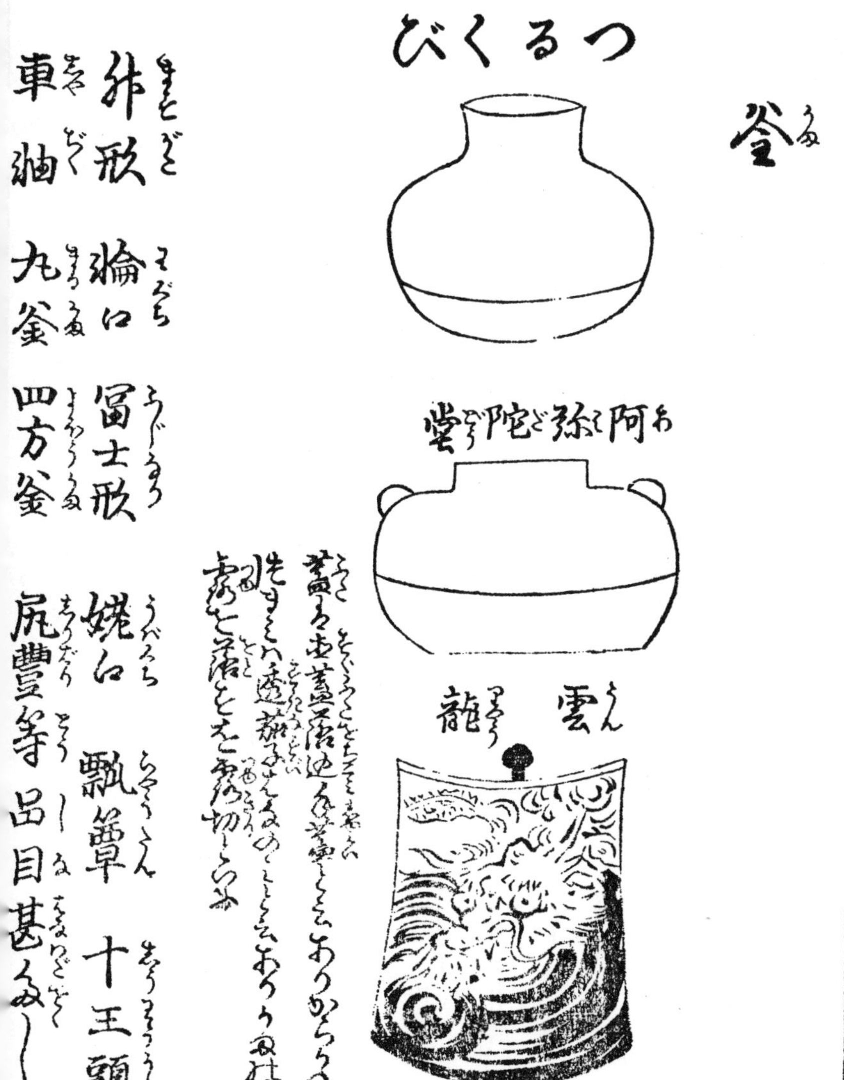

Three kettle designs, from vol. 1 of *Chado Hayagaten*.

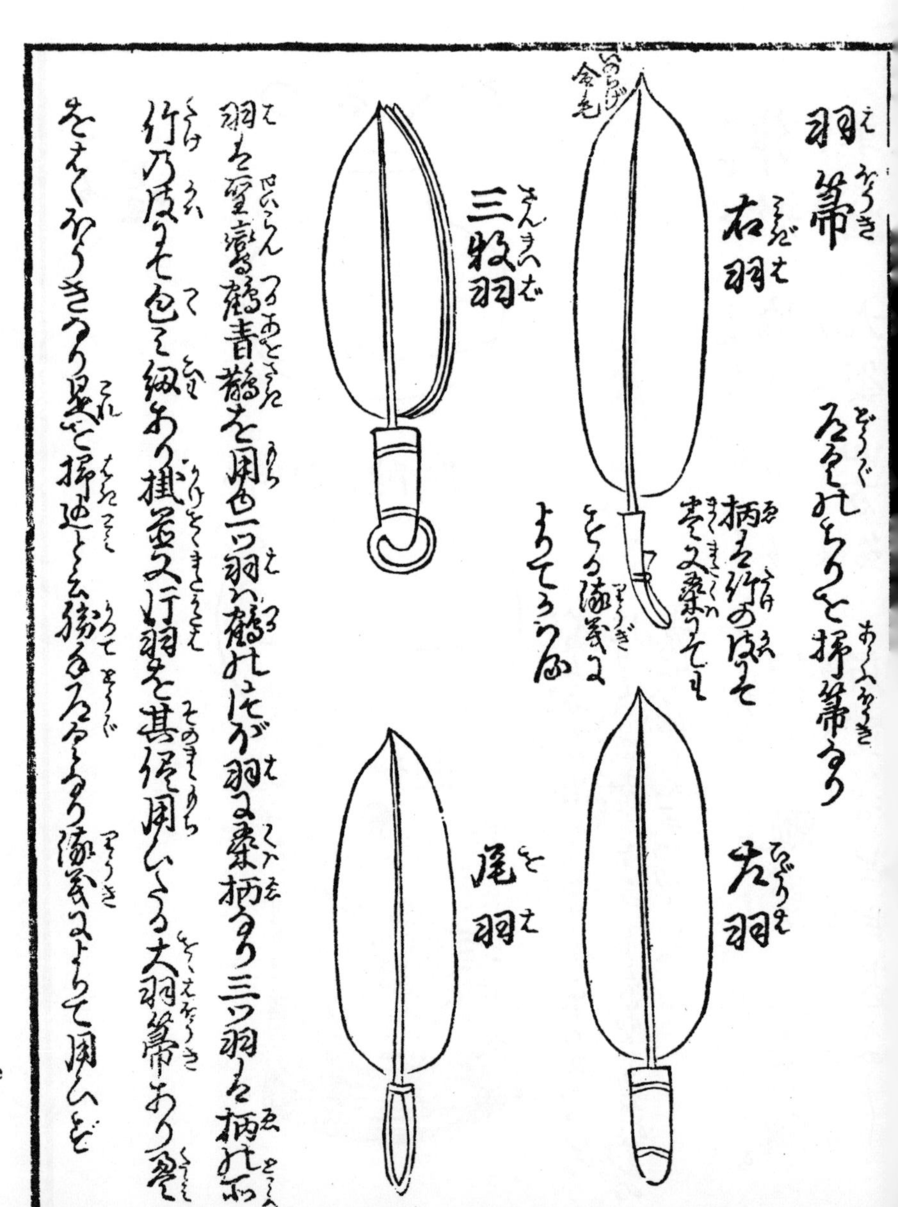

Feather dusters for removing ashes from the robuchi, from vol. 2 of *Chado Hayagaten*.

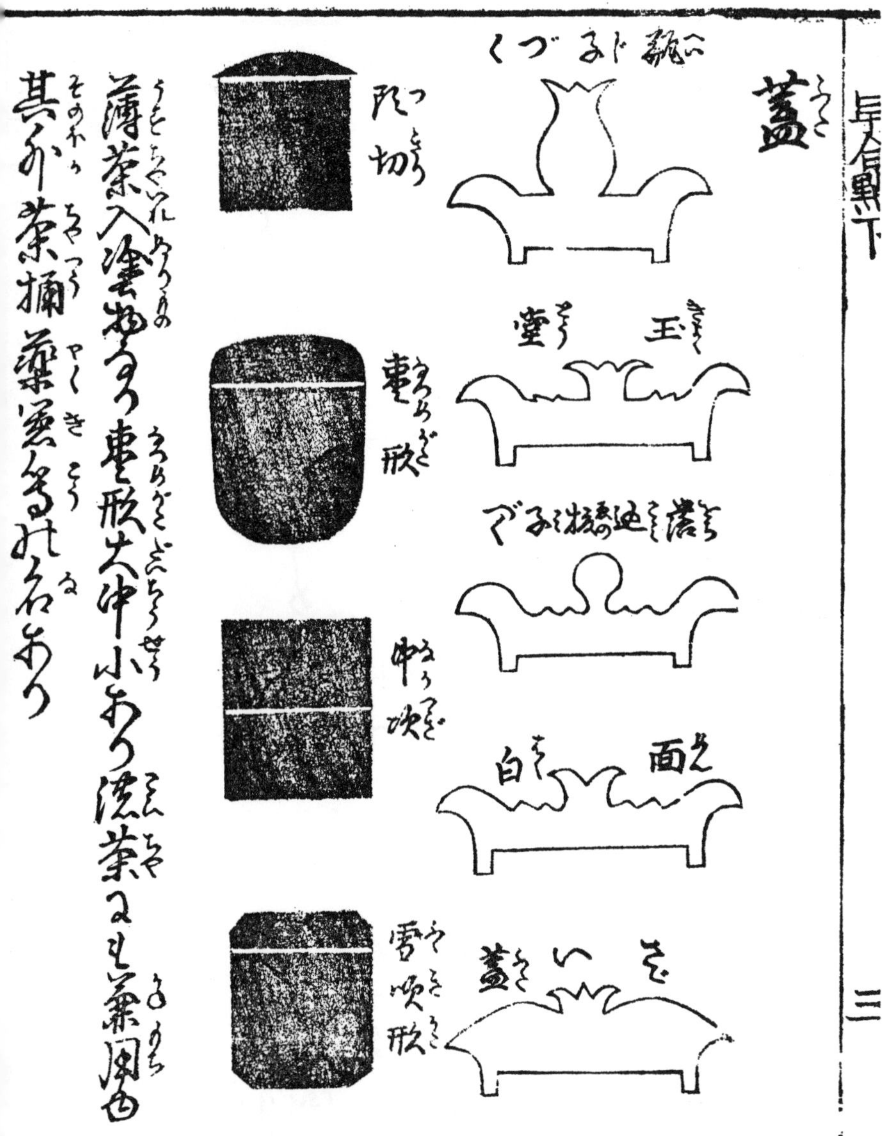

The four standard shapes for natsume are shown on the left, and on the right are cover designs for cha-ire. From *Chado Hayagaten*, vol. 2.

Two standard designs for cha-ire, from *Cha-do Hayagaten*, vol. 2.

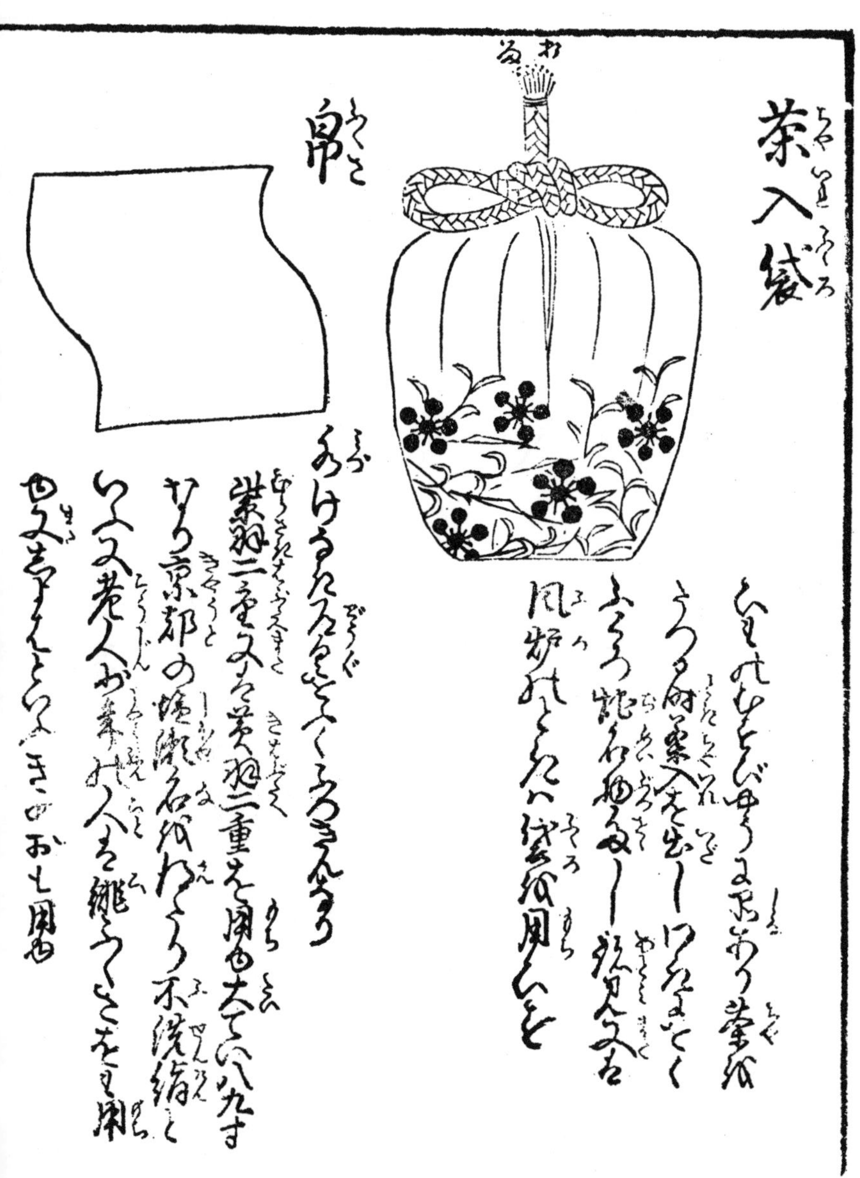

On the left is a fukusa, and on the right is a brocade silk bag with drawstring for a cha-ire. From *Chado Hayagaten*, vol. 2.

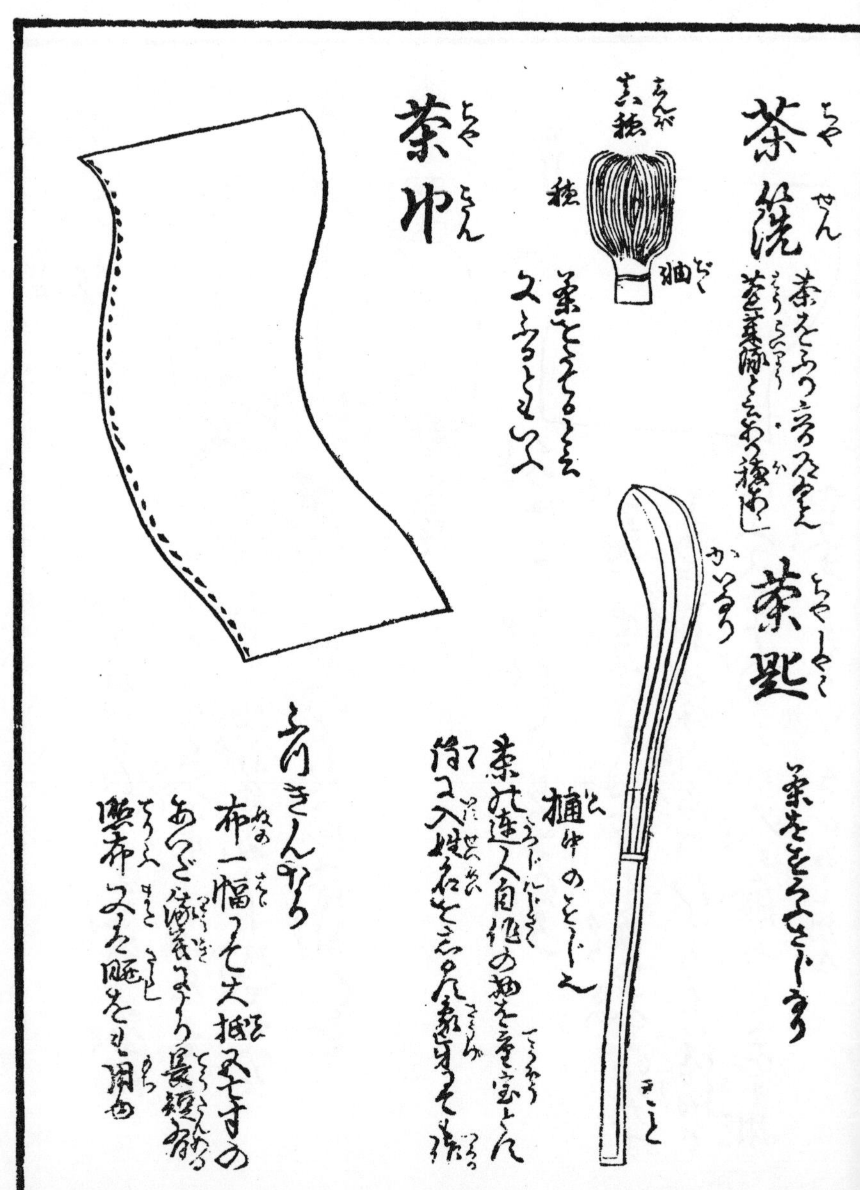

In the upper right corner is a chasen, and below it is a chashaku. To the left is a *chakin* (gauze cloth used for wiping tea implements when they are wet). From *Chado Hayagaten,* vol. 2.

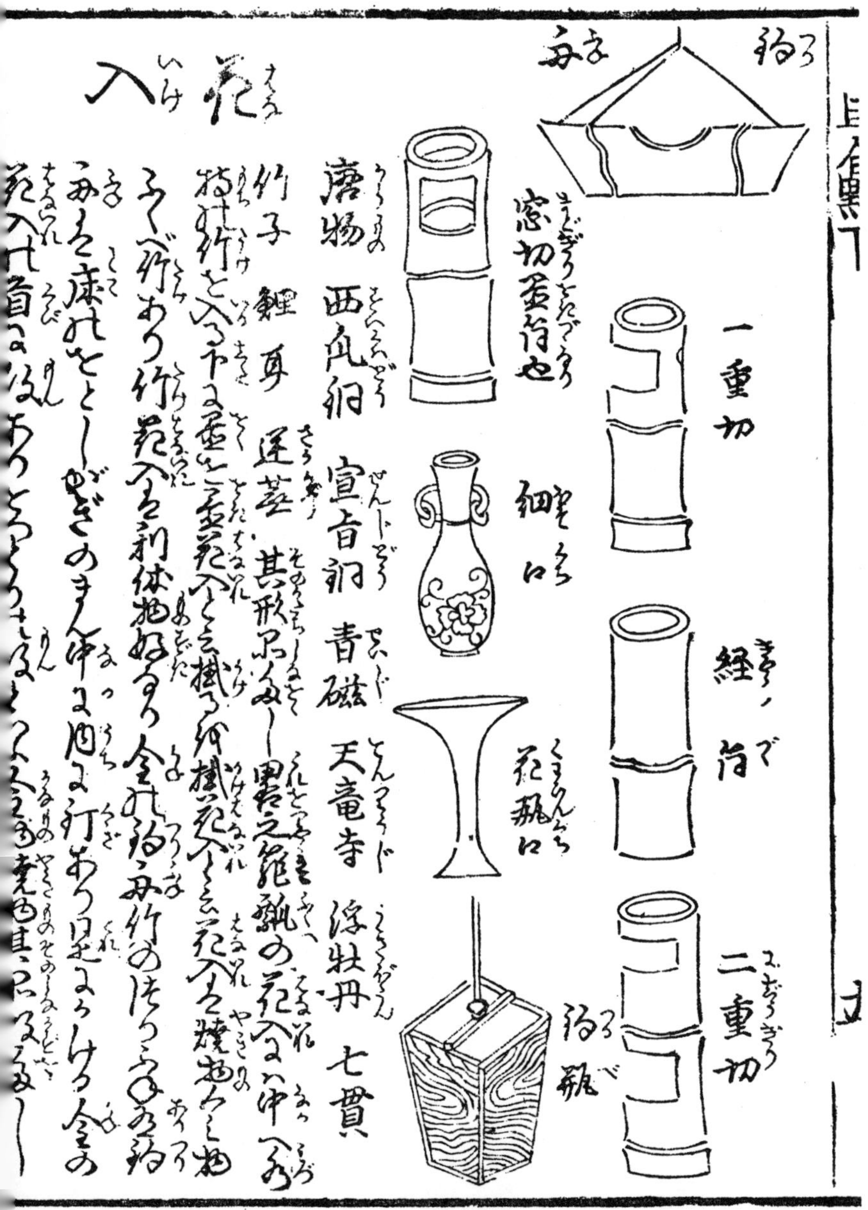

Various types of hana-ire. They are made of bamboo, ceramic, and wood, but bamboo is most common. From *Chado Hayagaten*, vol. 2.

the largest made. The size one uses on a particular occasion depends upon the number of guests and one's own preference.

There are many other containers that are loosely called natsume, but strictly speaking they are not. Natsume means jujube, the name given because of its resemblance to the plumlike fruit. The *naka-tsugi* and *kinrinji* have forms different from the genuine natsume: they are squarish with sharp sides. Other containers for thin tea are made of plain bamboo or wood.

Lacquer caddies by master craftsmen cost hundreds or thousands of dollars. They are the products of many tedious hours' work. A lacquer master of genius, such as Hoshin Matsunami, does not make many natsume in the course of a lifetime, and consequently they are in great demand.

Lacquerwork has been an important art of Asia for thousands of years. In India, China, Korea, Thailand, Burma, Vietnam, and Japan there is a long tradition of national styles and techniques. The Western world, owing to lack of knowledge and unsuitable climate, has never developed a good lacquer artist. Today Japan certainly has the greatest concentration of master lacquer craftsmen.

Base materials for lacquerwork include wood, bamboo, metal, porcelain, leather, hemp, cloth, paper, and chemical compounds and synthetics. If the base material is wood, chances are the piece will alter its shape if transported from one place to another; this is true even in Japan, where lacquer pieces do change shape—and color—if carried from, say, Kyoto to Tokyo. Needless to say, if this kind of lacquer is taken from Japan to a place like the United States the lacquer will probably be irreparably altered. Hisashi Yamada of the New York Urasenke school of tea was given an exquisite natsume, the work of a famous lacquer master in Japan, which began to split apart within a very short time of its arrival in New York. The dryness of New York and the effects of central heating will not permit the best lacquer to survive unscathed.

Lacquer artisan Gonroku Matsuda has experimented for years to develop a lacquer-on-wood process that will not warp. He took his research to the deserts of Africa and claims success with a wood base that is specially treated. Bamboo changes less in different climates. Synthetic materials hardly change at all from place to place. This is a good reason for using only less expensive natsume outside Japan.

I spent considerable time with Mr. Matsuda discussing the process of making fine lacquer pieces. It is slow and demanding. If wood is to be the base, it is first thoroughly dried by artificial means. The wood is made to conform, generally, to the shape of the desired object. After this the wood is scorched. Then three coats of lacquer are applied; each is allowed to sink into the surface. After a certain length of time cloth is pasted to the surface and a foundation lacquer coating is applied. This coating is a mixture of lacquer and stone powder. It is sprayed evenly over the whole surface. The base is then sealed in an oven at 176° F for eight hours.

If the object loses its shape at this stage it is discarded. Changes in shape may result from moisture that remains in the wood base. Now the long and difficult part of applying sixty, seventy, or eighty successive coats of lacquer begins. Each is allowed to dry, each is polished separately. Fine-grain charcoal is used to polish the lacquer coats, and the whole process takes months. If complicated designs of many colors are used the piece may take as long as a year to finish.

Master Matsuda has lacquered whole rooms (the imperial chambers of the National Diet Building), automobile interiors (the first was for the American ambassador in Tokyo), and ships' cabins. If well treated, lacquer lasts in perpetuity—Mr. Matsuda reported seeing lacquered bedsteads and ceremonial objects in China that are at least two thousand years old.

Tea Whisks: *Chasen*

The tea whisk, *chasen,* is among the finest objects crafted in Japan. The whisk is so perfectly suited to its task that no significant changes in its design have taken place in several hundred years. It is ideally conceived, finely made, and thoroughly useful.

The chasen is always made of bamboo, a material much underestimated in the Western world. Bamboo is one of two thousand kinds of grasses and has a tensile strength greater than that of steel. Long-lasting, pliant, light, and odorless, bamboo whisks have not been displaced by plastics or any other materials. The whisk is always handmade, yet it is inexpensive. It is doubtful that a university of engineers could improve upon its design.

The abundance of bamboo in Japan makes the material a natural one for craftsmen, and a large body of artists works with this material. The kinds of bamboo used in Japan's bamboo craft are: *awa-dake, ma-dake, ha-chiku, moso-chiku, me-dake, shi-chiku, kan-chiku, hotei-chiku, narihira take, iyo-dake,* and *okame-zasa,* but other strains are used as well.

Bamboo grows in groves, usually along hillsides and on the slopes of mountains, where it is cultivated for household use or grown for the commercial market. It is used extensively in construction work. Once every sixty or one hundred twenty years Japan's entire crop blossoms. When this happens all the bamboo dies. It takes about seven years to develop new groves. In 1967, Japan saw bamboo blossom for the first time since 1847. Thousands of acres bore the leafy decorations, like wreaths of death.

Aside from the chasen, bamboo is used in the making of flower containers, tea scoops, incense containers, water ladles, and boxes: all utensils for tea.

The first important chasen craftsman was Takayama

Sosetsu, who lived in Nara during the Muromachi period. He appears to have known Murata Shuko. Perhaps it was Shuko who showed one of Takayama's chasen to Emperor Go-Tsuchimikado. At any rate Takayama's work became famous at this time and his family was permitted to change the initial character of its name from one that meant "hawk" to one that had a more lofty meaning, "high." At one point there were fifty-six branches of the Takayama family engaged in making chasen, but by the Meiji era this number had dwindled to sixteen. Today there are five: Tango, Izumi, Shinano, Chikugo, and Iki.

There is a good variety among today's chasen, more than at any other time in history. Prices, too, have increased but not by very much. Whisks are available from about sixty cents to four dollars. A record of 1711 states that chasen were available for sums ranging from the equivalent of about twenty-five cents to three dollars.

Usually the bamboo used for a whisk is awa-dake, cut in the cold season, from December through February. This bamboo is boiled for one hour, exposed to the sun for a month, and stored in a dry barn for about a year before working.

New Year's chasen are customarily made of ma-dake. The finest chasen are made, however, from *susu-dake.* Susu-dake is bamboo that is two or three hundred years old. It is the bamboo which has served to cover the ceilings of farmhouse kitchens.

Susu-dake has a deep purple color, the result of centuries of charcoal smoke flowing across its surface. Fine susu-dake is difficult to obtain in any quantity. Brokers serve as scouts, crossing and recrossing the countryside in search of old farmhouses that are being remodeled or are about to be torn down.

The cost of susu-dake is high, but this alone does not determine the high price paid for good bamboo craft. An artist such as Chikuunsai Tanabe spends a long time creating a single bamboo work of susu-dake. In Japan his baskets and containers sell for as much as two thousand dollars. His work has been shown several times in the United States and in Europe, but Westerners are rarely willing to pay so much for a craft they little understand or appreciate.

The front of a chasen is regarded as the face on which the black knot that holds the tines is fixed. This is the side that is always turned up when the whisk is resting in a tea bowl. Aside from the knot, however, a bamboo whisk is the same all around.

An important quality of bamboo is that it is odorless. For this reason it is used not only in making chasen but in lining such objects as the drums which are used to roll, stem, or dry tea leaves. It does not readily absorb odors.

The name "chasen" probably refers to the fishing basket, *sen,* or to something which is related to the Japanese character meaning practical. The Chinese referred to some kind of whisk as early as the Sung dynasty, but we suspect that this was one used for cleaning kettles and kitchen utensils, a kind of brush.

A standard chasen is about five inches long: three inches of tine, two of handle. The parts of the chasen are not fitted together from separate pieces. It is a single length of bamboo that almost always includes a joint along the length of the handle. The diameter is about an inch. As a rule the host supplies a new chasen for guests.

Kinds of chasen are determined not only by the type of bamboo used but by the number of tines they have. Kazuo whisks are the finest, having some fifty tines. Nakaho have forty-six, and the coarse Araho have thirty-two. For thick tea the Araho or Naka-araho, another coarse variety, is used. Long-handled chasen are used with deep bowls, shorter ones with shallow.

The Omotesenke school prefers the use of smoked-bamboo chasen; Urasenke prefers plain. Some chasen have a mottled effect. This is caused by sprinkling bamboo with water and firing the surface with a blow-torch or flame. The wet areas remain light, the other areas are burned to a deep brown.

Tea Scoops: *Chashaku*

The *chashaku* is a tea scoop or measure. It goes by other names as well, such as *sashaku* and *chasaji*. The history of the chashaku goes back at least to Sung China; Sung records refer to spoons for tea made of gold, silver, iron, and bamboo. Chashaku for tea ceremony are most often of bamboo, though wood and ivory are also relatively common.

Scoops of ivory are for formal occasions and are called *shin* chashaku (most formal). A bamboo scoop with no middle joint bears the same label. Those of mulberry wood or bamboo that have a joint about midway along the handle are most common. These are used for most kinds of tea ceremony. If a bamboo joint is at the very end of the handle, the scoop is used for intermediate-level ceremonies.

Metal scoops are shunned for tea because they endanger the ceramics with which they come into contact, and because they tend to give off a metallic taste. In the early Edo period a man sent a silver spoon to Sotan, but wabi Sotan had the article labeled "for kitchen use," refusing to employ it in his tea ceremonies. The *Isei Teikin Orai* enumerates various kinds of old chashaku, including some of tortoiseshell and lacquer, but these are too rare even to be seen by most chajin. Bamboo seems to have come into fashion after the Temmon era (1532–54), about the time of Jo-o. With the popularization of tea and the increased use of bamboo for chashaku, specialists came to be known for their craftsmanship in carving them. Names such as Shutoku, Sosei, and Soin, men noted for their carving of chashaku, survive to this day in the literature and tradition of tea ceremony. The strong personalities of the great Momoyama masters led to distinctive styles of scoops, and in the Edo period scoops came to be objects of special attention during *haiken,* that part of the ceremony during which objects are closely examined. It became the custom for tea men to carve their own scoops, endowing them with special characteristics. The scoops of the famed chajin are especially appreciated today, and many contemporaries copy examples from the past.

Like all utensils in tea, chashaku can have very special significance. Attending a special tea ceremony to commemorate the eight-hundredth anniversary of the birth of Yoshitsune, at Kurama-dera in north Kyoto, I witnessed a tea performed by the present grand master of Urasenke. Master Sen used a scoop on that occasion which had been carved by his father from the wood of an old tree in the temple precincts. Present also was an elderly woman who had attended the ceremony at which the scoop was first used. All the guests were moved by the special significance of the occasion for this woman, who was able to recount the precise origins of the scoop.

At Urasenke there are fifteen styles of scoops currently in use, one for each of the generations of masters. The styles of these scoops differ most often in the treatment of the bowl, *kaisaki*. Considerable variation can be achieved by dexterous manipulation of the short length of bamboo, width, curve, length, and treatment of bowl being the most obvious areas of difference.

Rare or unusual chashaku are placed in silk bags, boxed, and signed. These most often have historical significance and serve as prototypes for others. The boxes for chashaku are usually made of a single piece of bamboo, the end being cut away to form a cap. An outer box is called *tomo-zutsu,* and when there are two separate boxes, the inner box is called *tomo-bako*. On these a maker or owner will write his name. Scoops of plum, pine, cherry, and those decorated with gold lacquer are placed in a tomo-zutsu of bamboo.

Though Jo-o popularized bamboo scoops, and Shuko is known to have used the same material, neither is thought to have paid much attention to them. Rikyu followed them in his attitude at first, but later he carefully saved his scoops and treasured them. Rikyu's scoops were masculine and rather sharp. Sotan's scoops were almost amateurish, but this was their wabi character. Enshu's were slender and elegant, almost feminine in their attractiveness. Sekishu combined the diverse qualities of Rikyu's and Enshu's in making what are considered the perfect chashaku, and of course these are rare and highly prized. Doan and Shoan copied Rikyu's practice of leaving knife marks on the bottom sides of bamboo chashaku. A very distinctive scoop is that by Taiso; it is extremely thin and has a bowl in the shape of a bamboo leaf. Ito's is sword-shaped on the end and very thick. Master Tantansai's scoop bears a pointed end, with rather sharp curves. Nineteenth-century master Gengensai made thick and powerful scoops, as masculine as those of Rikyu and Ito.

Kobori Enshu would not use plain bamboo, and always selected special qualities and colors for his designs, but Sekishu cautioned against using bamboo that was too decorative, preferring plain white bamboo. In naming the scoops, Enshu used selections from old anthologies of poetry, but common practice today is to select a name that accords with the season or is taken from the literature of Zen.

A note of caution should be introduced in regard to appraising old chashaku. Any box for a chashaku that purports to bear Rikyu's signature is certainly doubtful, the practice of signing tomo-zutsu being a much later addition to tea. Further, it has long been the habit of chajin to copy the works of masters whom they especially admire. As a result, numerous scoops which seem to date from Momoyama or before—the patina, material, and design resembling known works by the masters—most likely are copies by students or disciples or later admirers of Momoyama chajin.

Scroll Paintings: *Kakemono*

Kakemono (also called *kakejiku*), scroll paintings hung in the tokonoma, are an important complement to the tearoom. Scrolls for tea are most often done in ink on paper or silk. The subject of a kakemono for tea is usually calligraphy by a noted tea master or a landscape in the Chinese manner.

Tea scrolls hung in the rooms of the famous tea masters have been carefully recorded in diaries and letters for hundreds of years. Vigorous works by such painters as Sesshu have long been those most admired. Sesshu's *haboku* (splash ink) style is as popular today as during the Muromachi period. The works of later, and lesser, painters were popular during the late Edo period—works of detailed landscapes on gorgeous panels of red, green, blue, and gold. These, however, were exceptions in the history of tea taste.

The most popular Chinese scrolls for tea are by the incomparable Mu Ch'i, a Zen priest and painter of the first half of the thirteenth century. His *Six Persimmons,* birds and flowers, and landscapes appear in many records as having been the kakemono of important ceremonies. Hideyoshi was especially fond of using works by Mu Ch'i, but Ma Yuan (ca. 1190–1224) and other Chinese masters shared honors with him.

Whatever the taste of any period's tea masters, the kakemono occupies a central role in the tea ceremony, for it is the focal point of the room and the first object to which the guests turn as they enter. Disagreements have often taken place among chajin as to what kind of work is appropriate. Rikyu said that care should be exercised, such that if the guests had just come through a field of flowers on their way to the tea hut, it would be most inappropriate to hang for them a painting of a field of flowers. Rikyu also said that the seasons should be observed; for example, no one wants to be reminded of how cold the snow is outside on a wintry morning—a cheerful work with a cozy feeling should be hung. Matsudaira Fumai, brilliant master and lord of a territory in north-central Honshu, said that much time and effort was wasted in the careful selection of paintings and that the best advice was to simply choose one straight away and be done with it. Yoshino, daughter-in-law of Koetsu, invited her guests on a fine snowy day and provided a blank paper so that each could fill in his own impressions as best suited the time and feeling that they shared.

Calligraphy is still the preferred decoration of a tea hut, though paintings are sometimes used—usually, however, paintings are hung outside in the small waiting arbor. The stated preference for calligraphy goes back in origin to the gift of a piece of fine writing to Shuko by Daitoku-ji priest and imperial son Ikkyu (1394–1481). On presenting the piece he told him that "even in tea there is Buddhist enlightenment," and that by contemplating the written verse, Shuko could attain the enlightenment. Calligraphy was also valuable to priests and student priests, for it was in writing, the *inkajo,* that they were given official notification or approval of the state of their knowledge, an ancient form of the contemporary diploma.

From the beginning, letters from one's teacher, notes from great masters, epigrams, poems, and other writings were used as kakemono for tea ceremony. These were usually related to Zen, but many other kinds were used as well. The handwriting was thought to reveal some degree of mastery. This too was important. Contemporary calligraphers such as Koso Sakamoto and Shiryu Morita, who are representative of this attitude, have come to be known and appreciated even outside Japan.

Because of the temple's long association with tea, the works of Daitoku-ji priests, such as Ikkyu, have been highly regarded in tea ceremony. A list of calligraphers for tea would include the following: Eisai, Dogen, Daio Kokushi, Sekishitsu Zenkyu, Kokan Shiren, Jakushitsu Genko, Daito Kokushi, Muso Kokushi, Ikkyu Sojun, Sen Sotan, Sen Rikyu, Tairin Soto, Shorei Shukin, Shunoku Soen, Kokei Sochin, Tairin Soto, Gyokushitsu Sohaku, Takuan Soho, Kogetsu Sogan, Tenyu Soka, Seigan Shuyu, Honami Koetsu, Koun Soryu, Jiun, Matsudaira Fumai, and many more. Some of the painters whose works might be used are Shubun (fifteenth century), Sesshu, Taiga (1722–76), and Buson (1716–83) of the *nanga* school, Hakuin (1685–1768), and Sengai (1751–1837). The Enshu school of tea prefers to use Enshu's calligraphy; the Sekishu school prefers Sekishu's. American tea men seem to have a strong preference for the writing of Zen master Daisetz Suzuki, perhaps because he came close to being "father confessor" to so many American students of Zen and Japanese art.

A number of Americans are presently involved in practicing Japanese calligraphy. One such is Gerow Reece, a former student of Shiryu Morita. Reece's works range from ancient Japanese characters to roman lettering. His calligraphy in English is fluid but strong. In an exhibition of the Bokubi calligraphers' association in Kyoto, Reece's work stood up well alongside that of many of Japan's foremost artists.

In the future it will probably be necessary for students of tea who reside outside Japan to use works other than kakemono for their tearooms. I would suggest that photography is a good place to begin to look for the kind of work that might be an effective substitute for calligraphy and black-and-white ink painting. George Holton, Harry Callahan, Werner Bischoff, and Aaron Siskind have done superb work that seems suited to an apartment tearoom. Drawings and lithographs are other possibilities.

There is precedent within the history of tea for not using strictly phrased and mounted calligraphy. Jo-o was fond of using old calligraphs that were in fragments, *kohitsu-gire*. He also used damaged or incomplete versions of poems by Lord Teika, as well as fragments of old *kana* (phonetic alphabet) syllabaries, *jodai-gana*.

The ancient *Kokinshu* and *Manyoshu* poetry anthologies were often sources for poems used in tea ceremony scrolls and writings. Poetry was a likely selection for Japanese tea men, as it played an important role in their daily lives. The calligraphy of the old poets was thought to have balance between what was said and how it was said. Many kakemono in today's tearooms are copies of poems and sayings by the old writers. The quality of the paper was a consideration, too. The *shikishi* (originally a kind of pamphlet, later a single thin sheet of reinforced paper) of noted poets, calligraphers, and chajin are still used by some. These are not mounted in the usual fashion; that is, they are not on a scroll but are fixed to a framework which allows them to be placed in the tokonoma.

A curious note on the history of *kaishi,* the small paper used by all during a tea ceremony for sweets or for cleaning a bowl, is that it was first carried to tea for purposes of writing waka verses. Apparently an emperor once wrote a waka on kaishi, and this started a trend among aesthetes which continued for some time. Poems on this paper have an immediacy and a fresh quality not found in the kohitsu-gire, nor indeed in any of the other forms.

The paper came, eventually, to be more and more fancy—gold and silver filaments were sprinkled across the surface—and conventions grew up around the practice which limited the number of characters to be written. From Edo times there are many surviving examples of this practice.

Certain haiku poems have been popularly used for tea ceremony, and these were written on long strips of paper, made perhaps by cutting kaishi into several pieces. To begin with, they too were plain white but time and convention changed them to more decorative forms. Unlike the shikishi, these were mounted as kakemono, for the paper was pliable and easily worked onto a silk surface. These bore signatures, except in the case of emperors.

The shikishi seen today are descended from the Muromachi period. The papers are hand dyed or watermarked. The designs of Koetsu are still popular, and are often seen even on inexpensive store-bought papers. These are similar in use to the old-style letters of Momoyama; such letters from Rikyu, Oribe, Enshu, and the famous chajin are valuable for the special relationship they sometimes revealed of a leading tea man to his kind of tea or to a disciple. Some really outstanding examples of this work are found in the Maeda collection, which was shown in Kyoto in the spring of 1967. Included are letters from Rikyu, Oribe, and Enshu which are magnificently mounted. Rikyu is quoted as having favored paper mounts for kakemono, but his letters, so treasured, have but rarely been so treated. Such letters are called *shosoku*.

The precision paintings of the early Chinese were made fashionable by Yoshimasa, and this style of colorful art dominated tea during the Muromachi period, to be replaced by the dictates of Rikyu and those who followed him. The great Higashiyama collection of Yoshimasa remains a Japanese national treasure and it has served to instruct generations of Japanese in the fine skills of Chinese-style painting. Some portraits, mountain scenes, and seascapes were used by the Muromachi leaders and by those who followed; these, together with pictures of birds, flowers, and grasses, were the standards against which the Japanese judged their native works. When Japanese painters such as Sesshu went to study in Ming China and returned with a vigorous black-and-white style, the colorful works were displaced in the minds of the chajin in favor of the splash-ink style more compatible with Zen, which was then in ascendency.

The most that could be said about contemporary taste in subjects for kakemono for tea is that a liberal spirit has been loosed; the *sanjurokkasen,* thirty-six poets, the most famous classical Japanese poets prior to the eleventh century, are used, *hakubyoga,* white drawings, are used, and even oils. The Japanese have no difficulty in adjusting to the contemporary abstract style of painting, for it has been with them since Muromachi, and the future holds much more of this for purposes of tea ceremony tokonoma decoration.

Flower Containers: *Hana-ire*

Flower arrangement for tea is a demanding aspect of tea ceremony and is treated elsewhere as a special practice. The *hana-ire,* containers for flowers used in tea, are divided into three categories: most formal, *shin;* less formal, *gyo;* and least formal, *so.* Within these categories is a wide variety, of which only the most important are considered here.

For shin ceremonies the flowers are arranged in very formal fashion in vases of old copper or bronze, celadon, or old blue-and-whites. The mallet-shaped celadon vase is appropriate to this style. The *kyo-zutsu,* sutra container, form is also used. The magnificent bronze, copper, and brass bowls that were brought from China have traditionally been thought to be especially suitable to shin tea ceremony because of what are felt to be its Chinese origins. Some of these containers were made with ears, but the masters of tea in Japan since Rikyu have designed vases based on Chinese designs that do not have ears. Among the designs are four of bronze: golden, *kin-sahari;* silver, *gin-sahari;* Korean, *Chosen-sahari;* and the inexplicable "southern barbarian," *namban-sahari.*

Among the favorite celadons for chabana are the previously mentioned mallet-shaped container and the *Tenryu-ji-de,* Tenryu-ji type, which was a later development than the mallet shape, and of dark coloration and heavy design with elaborate impressions. The native Japanese celadons are less successful. These include the seiji of Nabeshima, Sanda, and Zuishi. However, these are probably to be preferred over the Shichikan, having a more recent history than the Tenryu-ji kind. The Shichikan are covered with a transparent glaze and a crazed surface. In this connection, some Japanese have long used the Nanking vases of the Ch'ing dynasty. These too seem out of place in the quiet of a tearoom. Common Ming ware and imitations of this were much in use during the Edo period, and can be seen today. For very special occasions of celebration, the Ming painted reds (*aka-e*) or gold-painted (*kinran*) vases are employed. The contemporary potter Hajime Kato produced some excellent works of this kind for shin ceremonies. The Ninsei products and some of the Ko Kutani (old Kutani) wares, too, are used.

Gyo-style containers are most often ceramic, with some copper or bronze used. Shino, Hagi, and Chosen-garatsu fit the gyo requirements well. Excellent containers in the form of *tsuri-bune,* fishing boats, are found in this category. This is the smallest category of the three.

The style having the greatest variety of container forms is the so, the least formal style. So tea is exemplified by Rikyu's concept of wabi, and the containers are accordingly simple. Unglazed pottery and bamboo comprise most of the containers in this category. Iga, Bizen, and Shigaraki hana-ire are appropriate as they are roughly made, of coarse clay, and contain no prominent coloration.

So-style bamboo containers are either cut pieces or woven baskets. *Ichiji-giri* are made of a single piece of bamboo into which a single opening has been cut.

Those with two openings are called *niji-giri,* and those with three openings are *sanji-giri*. One of Rikyu's best designs for so tea was the *shakuhachi* (flute) container of bamboo.

Baskets for chabana can have any shape: gourd, with handles, handleless, flattened, tall, crudely woven, bird's nest, vaselike, etc. Though most chabana baskets are bamboo, some others are of bark or vine. Takeno Jo-o is recorded as having been especially fond of Chinese bamboo work; Chinese bamboo is more pliant than Japanese, and this perhaps accounts for the extraordinary delicacy of some of their pieces. Rikyu liked to use fish baskets and traps for his tea. These were roughly made and are rarely seen in today's tearooms.

Many of the baskets are fixed for hanging—as are other hana-ire—with flower arrangements that cascade. Some are made so that they can be attached to the back wall of the tokonoma or to the post. Bamboo containers are placed directly on the floor of the tokonoma. Most other containers require stands of plain or lacquered boards.

The flower containers for *ikebana* (conventional flower arrangement) are referred to as *kaki, kabin,* and *hana-ike,* but these names are not used to describe the hana-ire of chabana. The *oki-hana-ire,* containers that rest on the mats; *kake-hana-ire,* containers that are hung from a nail in a wall or on a post; and *tsuri-hana-ire,* containers that are suspended by a chain, are for tea ceremony.

10. Minor Utensils

Fukusa The *kofukusa* is a napkin, six by six and one-half inches, of fine brocade that serves as a pad upon which objects are placed for examination by guests during a ceremony, or when objects are on display. It is carried, folded diagonally with the upper corner tucked into the obi, by all guests, though the host invariably provides a kofukusa of his own for their use. A translation of the character for "ko" in kofukusa indicates that the cloth is to be antique, but in practice this is not the case.

The kofukusa is folded in half, making it the size of the folded sheets of kaishi paper that are also carried, and placed in a *fukusa-basami,* a small carrying-case. During the period of examining tea scoops, caddies, and incense boxes, the kofukusa is taken from the carrying-case and used as a pad for each object. When thick tea is served the kofukusa is always used as a pad for the tea bowl as it is passed from guest to guest, unless the bowl is from the Raku kiln. (The precise reason for its not being used with Raku bowls is obscured by time, but we suppose that the smoothness of Raku kodai makes a kofukusa unnecessary.)

The most popular patterns for kofukusa are taken from the textiles in the Shoso-in and tend to be elaborate and of gaudy color, gold being the most commonly used thread. Many of the old kofukusa are patchwork, almost designless in appearance. This is thought to be a result of Oribe's fascination with cloth fragments. He is claimed to be responsible for putting together small bits of unusual fabric to form highly individualistic kofukusa, and his enthusiasm extended as far as cutting up whole cloth to obtain interesting pieces. For this he was roundly condemned by contemporaries and later tea masters.

Another suggestion for the origin of the patchwork kofukusa is revealed in a story about old priests and geisha. Buddhist devotees made a practice of presenting fine brocade to their priests from time to time. This brocade eventually showed up in the costumes of various geisha, so donors began to patch the brocade they gave to priests. This effectively prevented priests from giving the brocade to their geisha friends, as geisha costumes must be made from perfect cloth.

A third suggestion—the least colorful of the three, but the most likely explanation for patched kofukusa —is that the more prominent tea families had quantities of old cloth fragments in their possession and simply put various pieces together. If this is the explanation, it is a ridiculous practice today to make patched kofukusa from all new cloth.

Textiles as such were evidently of interest to chajin from the Muromachi period on. Records exist cataloging the famed fabrics (*meibutsu-gire*) that were brought back from China by the priests of such temples as Tenryu-ji. Kamakura traders returned with Yuan and Sung materials of great variety. These were picked up by Muromachi chajin and used in tea ceremony.

Imported fabrics had great influence on Japanese textile makers. Their designs were—and are—copied widely. The disastrous Onin War, which ensued upon the assassination of Ashikaga Yoshinori by militarist Akamatsu Mitsusuke, and which devastated Kyoto, also destroyed many of the original Chinese imports. But the industry was by then widespread and so it quickly recovered. The textiles of this time were much more subdued than those of Heian Japan, and they reflected independence from complete reliance on Chinese and early Japanese models.

The popular kofukusa of today are the kinran gold brocade, a damask weave called *donsu,* and a striped weave called *kanto*. The designs for these materials can be seen repeated in mounting fabrics for kakemono, in bags for caddies, and in sashes for kimono. The most common patterns are the familiar Oriental themes of dragon and cloud, pine with plum and bamboo, chrysanthemum and stream, crane and pine, and the tortoiseshell hexagon. Whether it is plain or with design, the kofukusa reflects the taste of the owner. Class, age, and marital status are said to be signified by one's kofukusa, but the exact requirements of design and material for each are extremely complicated.

During the Edo period severe restrictions were placed upon all classes of the Japanese population. They were informed of the kinds of fabrics and designs that could be used by what class and on what occasion. These restrictions were so severe that real ingenuity was required by weavers and kimono makers in meeting the demands of their clients. This proved a boon to the technology of the weavers. Their methods and styles consequently improved vastly during the time.

The basic fabrics that one must know in tea ceremony can be learned in a matter of several months' study, but the subtle aesthetics of putting a collection together takes years. One learns to take into account the mounting on the kakemono, the shifuku brocade, the fukusa, the kofukusa, sashes, and kimono materials when preparing for a ceremony.

The *fukusa* is larger than the kofukusa. It is a square about ten and one-half by ten inches. Made of silk, it serves as a napkin for cleaning certain utensils in the course of a ceremony. The design of the fukusa is supposed to have been originated by Rikyu's wife.

It is folded in one simple manner several times in the course of performing. Young men invariably use a deep purple fukusa. Old men use any subdued color. Young girls favor floral patterns of bright colors, while older women use subtle hues of blue, green, or brown. Grand masters may use whatever color strikes them as appropriate to the occasion, but they alone are allowed to use pure white fukusa, and then only for a formal presentation of tea at a temple or shrine.

Paper, Picks, and Fans

Kaishi were the first paper napkins. Pads of folded kaishi are used to hold sweets. The paper is packed thirty sheets to a pad, and comes only in white, but there are several qualities. The paper is stiff and slightly coarse. Kaishi for men are slightly larger than those for women.

Kaishi are always taken to tea and are sometimes used to wipe the rim of a bowl after drinking. Soiled paper is deposited in the sleeve of the kimono, or in a pocket.

Kuromoji and *yoji* are small, hand-cut wooden picks that are used with *omogashi,* delicious sweets that are soft and juicy. Kuromoji are served, one to a guest, for use in cutting sweets. They are placed on individual plates of ceramic or porcelain, or on lacquered trays. If sweets are served from a large bowl, two kuromoji are used. Especially when sweets are served from a bowl, it is advisable for guests to carry a small yoji with them to tea. Some picks are made of ivory, silver, or now even stainless steel. These are somewhat more durable than yoji of wood. Kuromoji takes its name from Japanese allspice, from which tree it is made.

The *sensu* is a fan taken by each guest to the tea ceremony. The fan for a man is about eight inches long; a woman's is about five inches. The paper covering is usually white for a tea fan and decoration is kept to a minimum. Special fans containing inscriptions are given as gifts by priests and tea masters. Some of these are valuable. Department stores sell fans on which tea maxims or calligraphy have been printed.

Fans must have been used for cooling at one time but they are never opened for that purpose now. However, they do have a practical use. When a guest enters a tearoom he places the fan behind him. There it serves as a kind of place card. The fan is also used—

though rarely—as a tray for receiving a gift. It is opened and given to the host, who places his gift on the fan and returns both to the guest.

On important ceremonial occasions special fans are made and presented to guests. The host of the occasion often inscribes these with his own calligraphy and seal.

Guests always place the fan in front of them, between themselves and objects they are admiring. Tea students place the fan directly on the mat in front of them when thanking a teacher or beginning a lesson.

Chakin

Chakin, plain white linen rectangles, are used to clean the tea bowl. The linen is folded and placed in the bowl when the host enters the tearoom. It is damp when used and serves to clean dust and stains from bowls before and after they are used. The chakin is a little less than a foot long, and about five and one-half inches wide.

In most formal tea ceremonies individual chakin are folded and presented to each guest on a lacquer box. After they are used, the chakin are dropped into the box through an opening.

When tea was first presented abroad, at an international exposition in Europe, the Urasenke grand master designed an all-red chakin for use by women who wore lipstick. This practice has not taken hold in Japan unfortunately.

Incense Containers: Kogo

The *kogo* is an incense container, an attractively made object that is displayed on a shelf or handed directly to guests for their inspection during a tea ceremony. The material may be wood, lacquer, metal, bamboo, or ceramic. The kogo used for winter tea should be of lacquer or earthenware. The incense for this season is kneaded, and a mat of camellia leaf supports the incense inside the box. Dry incense is never placed in a ceramic box, but rather is used only with metal or lacquer containers.

Kogo were first used by priests to carry incense that was meant to cover unpleasant temple smells and also to supplicate the gods. The interest in incense has been greater in Japan than in almost any other country. An incense game has persisted as a pastime until recently.

Japanese incense favorites come from Java, Sumatra, and India. *Byakudan* (sandalwood) has been used in tea ceremony since its inception. Japanese regard for incense in earliest times is underscored by the presence in the Shoso-in of an incense log. The *negoro* (red and black lacquer) incense containers that were brought to Japan from China are still copied by Japanese craftsmen.

The Water Jar: *Mizusashi*

The tea-ceremony water jar, *mizusashi,* is a simple pot with a a lid. It resembles a common cookie jar in shape. The overwhelming majority of mizusashi are ceramic, but jars are also made in wood and metal. The wooden ones are quite like buckets or small tubs. The metal mizusashi are often of gold or silver and are used primarily in the temple and shrine ceremonies of grand masters.

Perfectly fine American ware is available for use in tea ceremony, without special commissioning. In the antique shops and auction houses of New England, a good variety is available. The old bean-pots of earthenware are ideal if they have lids. Some English ware, and Dutch or Italian ceramics also serve the purpose, if the containers stand about six inches high and are compatible with other utensils. Mildred Johnstone of New York sometimes serves tea with a crystal jar as mizusashi. It has no lid, but Mrs. Johnstone covers the flaring rim with a large leaf. This is a good idea for summer tea and is perfectly consistent with Japanese practice. A leaf cover is called *ha-buta,* leaf lid.

A few designs for water jars include two small ears near the rim or mouth, but such protrusions tend to make the jar difficult to handle. The mizusashi should not be heavy or awkwardly shaped.

Lids for water jars are customarily made of lacquer or of the same material as the jar. In some cases two lids are provided. Regardless of the material, the mouth of the jar should be ample. Taller mizusashi are used in winter, shorter ones in summer. Mrs. Tomiko Sen frequently serves tea with a very low, large-mouthed water jar of blue Kyo-yaki. From the guest's position the water appears deep and cool. In Kyoto's hot summer the sight is welcome.

Stand Utensils

Kensui—or *koboshi,* as they are sometimes called—are containers for waste water. Originally kensui were part of a set of utensils of the same material, used with a stand, *daisu.* The other pieces of the set were the lid rest, *futa-oki;* water jar, mizusashi; and a tall container for the water ladle, *shakutate.* Today the tradition survives most frequently in the special sets of utensils made for temple and shrine service. The entire set was called *daisu kaigu.*

Common kensui resemble nothing so much as the spittoon, and are often made of copper. The elegant *hyo* kensui is in the shape of a gourd. It is slightly taller then the *efugo,* spittoon-shaped, kensui. Other varieties include the *yari-no-saya,* which is tall and spearlike, slightly resembling a flaring vase. The *bonosaki* version looks like the shaped end of a fence post. *Hira-kensui* are broad, flattened waste-water jars. All of the above are usually made of metal. Some of them can be found of cypress or cedar wood. Cherry-bark kensui are also seen.

Ceramic kensui are commonly Bizen, Tamba, Raku, and Karatsu. Their textures need not be smooth, as in the case of cha-ire or chawan, for kensui are not cleaned in the presence of guests.

Futa-oki, rests for the lid of the kama, were grouped by Rikyu into seven forms, and these have become standard. Many others have been added to the list of acceptable shapes since Rikyu's time. His list comprises: chimney, *hoya* (originally an incense burner); trivet, *gotoku;* "leisurely man," *ikkanjin*; three dolls, *mitsu-ningyo;* top shell, *sazae;* trefoil, *mitsuba;* and crab, *kani*. The one requirement of all futa-oki must be that the top has a surface sufficient for resting the bowl of the water ladle and the lid of the kettle. Rikyu's selections are all made of metal, usually bronze. Various writing tools have been used as lid rests: ink stands, *bokudai;* lamp stands, *yagaku;* seals, *tsukune*. None is more than two or three inches high.

Far the most common futa-oki are of bamboo. When using a ro, the rest is made of bamboo two and one-quarter inches long, with a joint in the middle of its length. Furo tea requires the joint of the rest to be just below the top. On New Year's, the rest is made of freshly cut, bright green bamboo.

The Water Ladle: *Hishaku*

The *hishaku,* water ladle, consists of two parts of dried bamboo: the bowl, *go;* and the handle, *e*. The free end of the handle is cut in one of three ways, each signifying a particular use. The handle cut square on its end is intended for display, but such ladles are sometimes used in winter or summer, with either furo or ro. A second cut, on a bias away from the end, top to bottom, denotes a ladle intended for use in the ceremony at the furo. The ladle for the ro is cut on a bias, bottom to top.

Like the chasen, a new ladle is used for each ceremony with guests. In actual use, the hishaku occupies a prominent place on the kettle throughout the service portion of the ceremony. It is used to ladle out hot or cold water for preparing the utensils and for mixing the tea. The hishaku handle is about a foot long, and requires considerable skill in handling.

There are also several other types of ladles used in tea. Ladles used with water basins differ from those used with a kettle. Water-basin ladles are usually made of cedar wood. These are always placed with the side of the bowl resting on the basin. Cypress ladles, used in toilet facilities, are placed mouth down in tea gardens. *Kaigan,* ladles used in the preparation room, have larger bowls than those used in the tearoom. *Mizukoshi* are ladles equipped with strainers; these too are used in the preparation room for cleaning and filling the kama. The mizukoshi is an essential utensil of the preparation room, along with the *kamashiki,* a wooden square on which the kettle rests, and the *kiriwara,* a tightly bound brush of hemp fiber used in scrubbing the kettle.

PART FOUR

The Practice of Tea

11. The Nonprofessional's Study

Alan Watts wrote in 1963 that Zen artists no more paint from a natural setting than poets write from a landscape. He added, however, that these artists were trained in techniques so formal, so complete, that it would seem impossible that their work would have anything left, in the end, of what we call life. It would seem that the works of the Zen artists would have no "personality." Yet, where is there an art more spontaneous, less studied, less labored in effect!

The thoroughness of training in tea would appear to be so formal that nothing spontaneous could be left in, yet it is the training in technique that gives certainty to the art.

Lessons and Equipment

In Japan today the most common way of learning about tea is to study with a teacher accredited by one of the tea schools. Some of the older schools have been associated with a particular clientele: Enshu and Sekishu schools are noted for instructing the aristocracy, while Urasenke is known to be a school for commoners. But the reforms of the Meiji era and the United States occupation lowered many of the barriers of class, and all schools serve all ranks of Japanese society today.

In every city of substantial population, and in most fair-sized villages, there are tea teachers. Men and women who make their living instructing students in tea constitute the largest body of tea professionals. Most of their students never become professionals.

As lessons are carried out, the teacher will offer advice on selection of utensils, discuss the origins of certain aspects of the ceremony, point out important journals that should be read, and relate anecdotes about the great tea masters.

The teacher is expected to be familiar with the following: architecture, landscape gardening, flower arranging, ceramics, textiles, incense, scroll mountings, ironware and metalwork, lacquerware, woodwork, bamboo, painting and calligraphy, cooking, and dress. These are in addition to a knowledge of Japanese history, language and customs, Zen Buddhism, and the lives of the great tea masters. The teacher must also know the order of service for the seventy-five or so tea ceremonies he is likely to encounter in his professional career. He must closely supervise the students as they prepare utensils, lay the charcoal fire and rekindle it, and serve the tea. Obviously a great deal of what must be known has to be learned from books. There is simply not enough time to present so much in the course of weekly lessons spaced over a period of years. Most students will take tea lessons for a few years only. Their time is spent being introduced to tea. The professional spends his entire life in study, if he takes his role seriously.

Students gather at the homes of teachers, who supply most of the utensils for lessons. The classes are usually about an hour or two in length. Each student performs the service he is working on at the moment, with others in his group serving as guests. There are usually five or six students in the tearoom at a time. The teacher sits by the host student and offers instruction and criticism as the ceremony progresses. In the student group there are likely to be two women to every man. The chances are fifty-fifty that the teacher will be a man. Most students attend these classes once a week. Fees are paid for each lesson or once a month. The amounts vary according to the fame of the teacher, standing of the student in tea instruction, and income of the student. In these respects tea lessons are similar to lessons on the piano in America.

Many Japanese universities and schools have tea societies. Large institutions often have paid instructors, who may or may not have private students. If the institution has a special association with a tea school, chances are there will be a tea hut or room donated by the tea master. These societies make field trips to museums and galleries, visit temples and shrines, and attend special performances by grand masters.

There are tea clubs aboard Japanese ships. Officers of the military are known to have performed tea before and after the battles of World War II. The present Urasenke grand master supports a large number of tea societies at home and abroad.

Though all students of tea at one level will study the same movements of a ceremony, considerable latitude is allowed by teachers. The physique of a student, his personal likes and dislikes, and the utensils he uses are taken into consideration. The order of a ceremony is the same and the elements are the same, whoever is performing, but the individual student must reach an accommodation of all these aspects in his progress toward a natural, personal tea.

Whatever the service, all ceremonies have some movements and utensils in common. The basic movements are involved with handling the utensils. The commonly used utensils are: individual cake plates, water jar, tea bowl, tea scoop, tea whisk, linen cloth, waste-water bowl, lid rest, water ladle, and tea caddy. These articles are brought into the room by the host. Those already in place before the guests arrive are: brazier, kettle, hanging scroll, and flower container.

The first step in a beginner's instruction is to learn how to use and care for these utensils. The instructor begins by demonstrating each. One must learn to fold the linen cloth so it does not lose its shape when the bowl is wiped. Careful instructions are given in the arrangement of the preparation room, the safest way to hold a tea bowl, filling the caddy, and placing the utensils on the mats. This takes about a month. One of the most difficult aspects of learning as a beginner—especially if one has never lived in a Japanese-style house—is how to approach, enter, and move in the tearoom as a guest. Part of the etiquette of the tearoom is learning how to wear a kimono and when to don formal *hakama* (loosely fitted pants for men). However, most students outside the headquarters of the major schools do not wear kimono to the weekly classes. Most young male students do not have them, and girls reserve them for festive occasions.

After a period of study and performance the student arrives at a point where he begins to be acutely aware of his shortcomings. To himself, his movements seem angular, his gestures sloppy. Nothing seems to go well. This is the first difficult stage of tea study. It is at this point, after all the newness has begun to wear off, that one is forced to decide between making tea a serious study or a simple pastime. Most choose the latter; the women go on to marriage, the men to their careers. Most learn a few basic ceremonies and continue to practice them, never attempting to delve into the techniques of advanced study.

Rikyu was once asked just what was entailed in serving tea well. He replied that all one had to do was "scoop out the tea into a bowl, add hot water, whip, and serve." The questioner, already a long-time student, answered that if *that* was all there was to it, he already knew. To this Rikyu countered: "If there is anyone who truly knows that, I will go immediately to him and study his Way."

From the point of view of the student there is as much danger in underestimating what he does as in overestimating. General Eisenhower, on the occasion of the opening of an exhibition of his paintings, said: "Let's not mistake this for art." The general did not make his comments in derogation, he merely meant that his nonprofessional work should not be thought of as serious. There is a feeling in the Western world that anything one doesn't do for money can't be much more than a hobby.

Tea does not have to be a mere hobby. One may not achieve an accumulation of knowledge on the subject equal to that of a professional, but still the service of tea can be the equal of that of anyone.

The Spirit of the Host

Of paramount importance to being a good host at tea is learning how to anticipate the guests' needs and to serve them well. This involves far more than etiquette, but courtesy is important in the tearoom. The teacher attempts to help the student arrive at a point where his service is smooth and accurate, where hesitation and awkwardness are overcome. Then the host can directly attend to his guests.

Tea is not a cult, for it does not distinguish between externals and some "inner" truth. The truth in tea is found in the externals. "The medium is the message." One needn't be a grand master to realize that.

Before starting lessons in tea it is good to attend a number of tea ceremonies as a guest. It is important to learn how to receive before learning how to give. And once lessons have begun it is important to have them in the company of at least one other student. In tea more than in most other traditional art forms one learns much by just watching. Rarely does a teacher give private lessons in the home of a student. In the first place, the student would have to have a full complement of utensils, and a tearoom. In the second the student would miss learning from other students.

The cost of lessons in Japan is not prohibitive, but a large collection of utensils such as is required for lessons entails more money than most of us could afford. This is a serious problem for young teachers who have graduated from intensive courses at the headquarters of the large schools.

It is good for students to purchase inexpensive utensils for practice. A teacher expects a student to work on his service at home. They can be purchased at any department store in Japan. Usually small tea shops where tea is sold for home consumption have a small selection of bowls, spoons, and basic ware. The pottery and antique shops are filled with utensils.

Aside from the simplest tray tea, the basic ceremony is the thin-tea service, *usucha*. The teacher introduces the student step by step, but the student always performs the entire ceremony in one sitting.

The Procedure

Preparations for the service are as important as the actual ceremony. The first step is the cleaning of the mats; tatami, for all their apparent cleanliness, are dusty and need constant attention. Dust sinks into the mats and accumulates. And if mats are new they are covered with a whitish powder that grinds into the kimono of the guests. New or not, mats must be swept before the arrival of guests. Brooms for this purpose may be of almost any kind, but traditionally they are made of bound rush or twigs. It is always advisable to go over the swept mats with a damp cloth.

The garden, too, is swept and watered. Most of the fallen leaves and twigs are removed from the mossy areas and the paths are cleaned and sprinkled. The stone water basin is cleared of leaves and filled with fresh water. Cobwebs bordering the entry path are removed if they intrude on places where guests will walk, but Rikyu warns against too much cleaning. The host should leave things in a state of naturalness.

A scroll should be selected and hung in the *machi-ai,* waiting arbor. This scroll should contrast with that to be hung inside the tearoom. The outside scrolls are usually pictorial.

When arrangements for the exterior have been completed, the host enters the preparation room, *mizuya*. Here he selects all the utensils to be used. He fills the caddy with the right amount of tea, selects and arranges sweets in a bowl or on individual plates, unpacks the water jar, kettle, tea bowl, tea scoop, calligraphy, flower container, chasen, and other necessities. He washes and places them in proper order beside the door which leads into the tearoom. When all this is done the host should have about an hour before the arrival of the guests.

The host picks up the hand-cut and washed charcoal, together with the tools needed for charcoal and ash preparation, and enters the tearoom. He arranges the ashes in a prescribed manner. The different ash arrangements are set according to the brazier to be used in his tea. Some pieces of glowing charcoal are brought in from the preparation room and set in the raked ashes. This small fire serves to kindle the larger fire which is laid after the guests have assembled. This charcoal arrangement is called the *shitabi*. The charcoal, usually three pieces, should be brightly glowing as the guests arrive.

The host has selected his scroll and hung it in the tokonoma for a few hours, making sure it flattens out before the guests arrive. The host, after checking this and making sure that the charcoal is burning well, goes into the garden for the second sprinkling of water. This is done lightly and should be just beginning to dry as the guests arrive. Small round mats are placed in the machi-ai, one for each guest, and a tobacco tray that contains a lighted piece of charcoal, in case guests want to smoke while waiting to be received. If it has been raining and the stepping-stones of the tea path are very wet, the host dries these with a cloth or mop.

Guests know that when the entrance gate is sprinkled with water the host is ready to receive them. If the host has a *yoritsuki,* preparation room for guests, the room has been prepared with various things for their relaxation before the service begins. The guests will not announce their presence to the host but proceed directly to the yoritsuki. When they are assembled the man designated as principal guest makes his way to the machi-ai, followed by the other guests. The host checks all arrangements and sweeps the mats once more. He then goes into the garden and greets the guests. After the greetings the host reenters the tearoom, leaving the small door slightly ajar. He goes into the preparation room and the guests wash their hands and rinse their mouths at the basin and enter the tearoom. The last guest to enter closes the entrance with a slight click. This is a signal to the host that all guests are present and seated. In some cases the host will reenter the roji to refill the water basin at this point, but most roji have water pipes that fill the basin automatically, making this unnecesary.

The host enters the tearoom and bows to the guests. He then brings the charcoal scuttle and utensils from the preparation room and prepares the second fire. He adds incense to the fire and the guests have a chance to ask about the kettle and to see the incense container.

All of the foregoing is, strictly speaking, necessary in preparing for tea ceremony. In the course of instruction students are exposed to the details of each of these, but for purposes of weekly lessons it is not often true that all such matters are attended to. If the lesson were to cover a complete, formal tea then everything would be done under the guidance of a teacher. But most often the student will only be required to prepare his utensils, arrange the second charcoal fire, and serve one kind of tea.

In the case of the most formal tea, a meal, *kaiseki,* is served. As now practiced, the service of kaiseki is a complicated and difficult affair, certainly not something one would do with any frequency as the student of a local teacher. If it were it would take about two hours and involve a lot of preparatory work. When kaiseki is presented only a scroll is shown in the tearoom. Following the meal, thick tea, *koicha,* is served after a brief intermission in the garden. During the intermission the host takes down the scroll and arranges flowers for the tokonoma. The flowers remain through the service of thick and thin teas, which may or may not be served in immediate succession. The whole ceremony would probably take about four hours if a student were to serve the meal and both teas. To perform this ceremony requires years of training, a little assistance from family or friends, and considerable courage. For those who cannot perform it with assuredness—and we are legion—it can be a most trying experience. To attend such a ceremony with a master is unforgettable.

What usually happens in a tea ceremony is that the host or student host makes one kind of tea, thin tea, and serves the guests in the course of some forty-five minutes. The host will have placed both a scroll and an arrangement by his own hand in the tokonoma and proceed directly to the rekindling of the fire after the guests have had a chance to admire the scroll, flower, and kettle. Following the guests' examination of the incense container, the host starts the service.

In a typical thin-tea service there are seventeen steps:

1. Host brings in sweets and places them before the first guest.
2. Host brings the water jar from the preparation room, places it beside himself from a kneeling position on the mats, and bows.
3. The water jar is carried to the kettle and placed on the utensil mat.
4. The tea bowl, on which the spoon and linen cloth are resting, and the caddy are brought in and placed in front of the water jar.
5. The host carries in the waste-water container, on which rests the water ladle, and inside which is the lid rest.
6. If the season is cold, the host closes the door leading to the preparation room.
7. The waste-water container and other utensils are carried the length of the service mat and arranged by the host as he kneels in the position from which he will serve tea.
8. The tea scoop and caddy are cleaned with the silk fukusa. Hot water is ladled into the tea bowl. The whisk is placed in the water and examined. The water is poured into the waste-water container, and the bowl is dried with the linen cloth.
9. The host lifts the tea scoop with his right hand, takes up the caddy with his left, and scoops tea into the bowl, while the guest takes a sweet from the bowl or plate.
10. Hot water is ladled into the already warm bowl.
11. The whisk is taken up and the tea is whipped until frothy. This procedure is repeated for each guest. The host may elect to use only one bowl, but if three or more guests are present he will probably make tea by alternating service with two bowls.
12. While the last guest is drinking, the host takes the alternate bowl, adds water from the kettle, empties the bowl, and wipes it with the chakin. As the water is being emptied, the principal guest asks the the host to conclude the ceremony, provided the guests do not wish more tea.
13. The host ladles cold water—from the water jar—into the bowl and rinses and examines the whisk.
14. The linen is placed inside the bowl along with the whisk. The scoop is cleaned and placed on the rim of the bowl.
15. Cold water from the jar is used to replenish the kettle, and at this point the principal guest will usually ask that the scoop and caddy be examined. If this is requested the caddy is cleaned and then presented with the spoon before the guests.
16. The host takes up the ladle, lid rest, and waste-water container and removes them to the prepara-

tion room. He returns for the tea bowl and on a second return removes the water jar. While the host is in the preparation room the guests examine the remaining utensils.

17. When the utensils are returned to the host's mat the host enters and discusses the scoop and caddy with the principal guest. These utensils are taken by the host to the preparation room door, where he turns to the guests, kneels, and bows. The guests return the bow and the ceremony concludes.

In most cases the host will see his guests again in the garden, after they have had a few moments to look again at the flowers and scroll hung in their honor. If the tea is conducted as part of a lesson the student cleans all the utensils he has used, goes into the tearoom to thank his teacher, and takes his place as a guest for the ceremony of the next student.

A school of tea in New York happens to be located in an office building. The school has no tea garden for instructional purposes. Students learn through lectures, books, and photographs. Many students in Japan are but rarely exposed to the complete tea ceremony with garden, arbors, and waiting room. Space limitations in Tokyo are as severe as in New York, and many teachers cannot afford to build and maintain tea huts and gardens separate from their residences. The trend is to limit the actual study of tea ceremony to the service of tea in rooms of private houses. These may or may not be specially designed for tea.

In New York and throughout Japan the lessons in the handling of utensils and the serving of tea are supplemented by regular lectures. These sometimes cover the practical aspects of serving tea, a history of techniques, but more often they are directed at the history of chado, its aesthetics and implications for daily life.

The most maddening aspect of tea for most Western students is the number and completeness of the rules. It is important to know what to do next. The beginner would quickly become frustrated were he to attempt to serve without the guidance of rules laid down by masters. Rikyu's rules are carefully thought-out standards of behavior in the tearoom, a kind of average of all our abilities. Nothing is required that a man of reasonable mind and body could not perform. Most experienced tea men do not blindly follow the rules. They improvise according to the occasion, but few who have studied Rikyu's Way would call for a wholesale dismissal of it. Rikyu's service is too smooth, too logical, too comfortable to be much improved upon.

12. The Professional's Study

The Life of the *Kenshusei*

Each tea school maintains its own training program for professionals. The requirements of the larger schools are similar, but the Urasenke institution maintains what is generally conceded to be the most difficult course of study. The institution requires a student to enroll in a three-year, full-time program. For this purpose a large and extremely well-equipped center has been constructed across from the residence of the grand master. The classes are made up of young men and women who expect to become certified instructors of the Urasenke school of tea. Graduates are thought to be the best-prepared tea professionals in Japan.

In obtaining permission to be admitted to the center a student submits complete records of his academic career. He is examined and closely interviewed. Once admitted he joins some seventy-five students from all over Japan. He is expected—with rare exceptions—to board at the school in facilities supplied by the center, leaving only for the usual holidays.

Most of the students, called *kenshusei,* remain in the course once they have been enrolled and are graduated with full certification. As kenshusei they are considered to be scholars engaged in research into every aspect of tea.

The teaching staff is made up of past graduates and a number of older, distinguished Kyoto tea teachers who are members of the Urasenke "inner family." The director is the grand master, but day-to-day operations are handled by an assistant who is himself a distinguished chajin and teacher. In addition are a number of *gyotei,* professionals who live, work, and study in the headquarters as they assist the grand master.

The students, averaging in age about twenty, bear

a very heavy load of classes and duties. Students rise at 7:30, select kimono and personal equipment they will need for the day. Breakfast is held in a common dining room, after which most students review notes on the ceremonies they will perform. (A clean-up detail, rotated among all students, rises at 6 to lay fires, arrange charcoal, and clean the many preparation rooms.)

At about 8:30, all the students enter the main house to meditate before the Sen family altar, in the Rikyu-do. Then they file across the street to the center and examine the five main tearooms, now arranged with flowers, scrolls, and kettles. These arrangements are studied by all. Every room has a preparation room adjacent to it, and an auditorium on the second floor holds as many as three classes simultaneously, with a teacher assigned to each.

A general assembly in a large tearoom is held at 9. Attendance is taken and cuts are never allowed for any class. Everyone bows as the head teacher enters. He lectures for from fifteen to thirty minutes, most likely on the calligraphy of the scroll hanging in the tokonoma. A half-hour meditation period usually precedes the lecture, but on Mondays the meditation is formal, attended by a Zen priest, and it lasts for an indeterminate length.

The students, dismissed at about 9:50, form groups of eight or nine and are assigned specific rooms. The rooms they meet in are changed daily but the students remain in the same group for about half a year. Until noon the students rotate in various ceremonies. One, two, or three students serve as guests for each host, their roles being paid as much attention to as that of the host. The teacher, who sits near the host, corrects or praises the service while lecturing to the small group. The instructors are extremely demanding, and each performance of each student receives a daily grade. Each performs an average of two services a day, one in the morning and one in the afternoon. He may proceed to another service only after having been approved by many teachers. Students are permitted to work at their own pace, with some quickly piling up records of many kinds of services while others stick to a single type for weeks or months.

After a one-hour lunch break, classes are in session until 5, after which the rooms are cleaned, flowers removed, scrolls rolled, and utensils put away in the preparation rooms.

The routine for kenshusei varies from the above in two respects: lectures are given two or three times per month by visiting chajin or scholars. If the grand master is in residence on the first of the month he will personally lecture the kenshusei, or if special Urasenke affairs are being held at temples and shrines the kenshusei are encouraged to attend as part of their instruction. When the grand master is present all the male kenshusei wear hakama. The grand master's remarks are often witty, but always forceful. He is informed of the progress of each student, knows everyone by name and sight, and will single out individuals for praise or reprimand. His word is law in the school. To be singled out by the grand master is an exceptional experience. The students are fiercely loyal to him, and to the school.

Students spend a considerable amount of free time reading in the vast tea literature and in individual practice. Television is provided in every dormitory house. The students are not removed from the world any more than are Japanese university students. They go to movies, attend rock concerts, and play an inordinate amount of baseball.

Requirements of the *Gyotei*

The professionals who are gyotei are different. Their services are on a seven-day-a-week basis. They are not free during holidays. Their principal task is to serve in the headquarters house, commonly called the Konnichi-an. They rise early and meet in a tearoom with the grand master who personally supervises their instruction. They attend every function of the household and are responsible for the condition of the tearooms and gardens which skirt every side.

At present there are about a dozen gyotei at Urasenke. The average age is around forty, all men. They serve as chief instructors for the institution, the teachers of the teachers. One becomes a gyotei only by invitation and this position is the highest to which a member of the Urasenke institution can aspire. Most gyotei are admitted for a trial period, during which they are rigidly examined by men who have spent as many as forty-five years in tea studies, not the least of whom is the grand master, who—now in his forties—has spent over thirty-five years in cha-no-yu.

The tuition for kenshusei is nominal. The cost for gyotei is nothing. These men are wholly supported by the head of Urasenke for all their lives in his service.

Gyotei have more available to them as chajin than others, for not only does Urasenke possess a magnificent treasury of utensils, but the gyotei are exposed to every kind and quality of tea and tea service to be found. The grand master's house is one place where standards are maintained in the fullest tradition. The tearooms and gardens of the headquarters are beyond compare in number and quality anywhere in Japan. They are maintained to perfection. What is more, the gyotei use them regularly for their own study.

As a group they are courteous and considerate, their service perfect without appearing so, and their way of life is disciplined and productive. Some people have compared the gyotei to the *osukiya-gashira,* tea chiefs, of the Tokugawa palaces. These men cared for all the Tokugawa tea "palaces" and utensils. There were over one hundred and twenty of these attendants at any given time. The comparison is not accurate, though there is overlapping in kinds of service performed by both groups.

The Grand Master

Today's tea masters enjoy considerable popularity. The current master of Urasenke often appears on television, is interviewed for newspaper articles and magazine stories, and is a man of affluence and influence. He travels widely, and when he travels his lectures and demonstrations are noted in the press.

In the tradition of Zen priests of old, Mr. Sen manages a considerable empire. His position is something like that of a university president who must attend to fund raising as well as to the educational and philosophical aspects of a large institution.

Mr. Sen was the first of contemporary tea masters to recognize the necessity of establishing schools abroad. In doing this he has been careful not to ignore the home front. The expansion of Urasenke in Japan has been tremendous under his leadership.

The son of the present master is being prepared for the role he will play as the next grand master, just as his father was before him. His father and a number of the most highly placed teachers at the headquarters are giving him regular instruction in matters of tea. He knows the institution he will inherit.

In the good weather of spring and summer, Urasenke holds a number of large outdoor teas, called *nodate*. The grand master presides, assisted by members of his family and the assembly of kenshusei and the gyotei. On these occasions large numbers of the Urasenke membership come to pay tribute. As a style it probably descends from Hideyoshi's and Rikyu's famous Kitano open-air ceremony. But other antecedents might be an open-air tea given by Hideyoshi in 1585, or another such occasion at Matsubara in northern Kyushu.

Nodate is always a brilliant occasion, with large red umbrellas in the sun, flowers, and beautiful kimonos in abundance. Great banners enclose a grassy area and tea is served either from *chabako,* boxed utensils, or the *tabi-dansu,* a table specially built to contain a kettle and platform for utensils. The host using a tabi-dansu sits on a small bench. An assistant carries tea to guests. Sometimes scrolls are hung from branches of trees. The openness of the service makes the occasion pleasant and informal.

Nodate need not be a service for many guests. Any individual can take his guests to a pleasant spot in the mountains and serve from a chabako. When this is done a site is selected near a clear stream. The guests use the stream as a water basin, and the stream provides water for the kettle as well.

The chabako service is taught at the Urasenke center. Rules differ slightly from those for indoor tea. The small box, usually lacquered, contains all the utensils except the kettle. It can easily be wrapped in a *furoshiki,* a square of cloth that serves as a carry-all. But chabako need not be served out of doors; it is also popular as an indoor service.

At Urasenke headquarters the *ryurei* style of tea ceremony is increasingly popular. Ryurei tea is served by a host seated in a chair or on a bench, to guests seated Western fashion. It is a kind of service developed for foreign guests by the eleventh-generation master of Urasenke. The probable date of development is 1874, and the likely occasion was an international exposition.

The ryurei room at Urasenke does not have a tatami floor. The host's table is similar to the tabi-dansu used in nodate, but here the guests are seated before tables. The use of tables and benches make this tea service comfortable for foreign guests and it is commonly used to receive Urasenke's international visitors.

All gyotei and kenshusei learn the use of ryurei equipment. In the ryurei-style rooms of the headquarters and the center the scale of the architecture has been appropriately adjusted. The rooms are hung with paintings that are conventionally framed. When more attention is paid to the design of tables and benches, this style of tea will perhaps become more popular. Throughout Japan Western furniture and Western-style rooms are found in private homes. Many Japanese themselves have come to be as comfortable, as much at home in rooms furnished with rugs, chairs, and tables as in those with tatami, kotatsu, and tokonoma. In fact, most young marrieds prefer Western- to Japanese-style living.

Ritual Tea: *Okencha* and *Okucha*

The one kind of tea ceremony carefully studied by all kenshusei and gyotei but never practiced by them is that performed by the grand master at shrines and temples. *Okencha* is a ritualistic offering of tea in a Shinto shrine. *Okucha* is the same kind of offering in a Buddhist temple. Whenever possible the gyotei and kenshusei attend these services, but only the grand master and perhaps one or two of his relatives are ever hosts for this service.

The timing for okencha and okucha is fall or spring, when the weather is good and people can gather outdoors. Okencha was first performed by either Hideyoshi or Rikyu in autumn, 1585, when Emperor Ogimachi received the two in the innermost court of the imperial palace in Kyoto. On this occasion Rikyu was given a court title. The style, therefore, developed as a highly formal act in the presence of an important official. It is always performed today in the presence of distinguished priests and temple or shrine patrons. In the case of shrine offerings, the traditional Japanese court music can be heard in accompaniment.

The grandest occasion for the presentation of okencha occurs when the new head of the tea school assumes his title and office. The present Urasenke master was elevated in ceremonies at the Heian Shrine in Kyoto, a service attended by thousands of people.

From the formality of okencha and okucha, the daisu, a large lacquered stand, developed. Use of the daisu requires extensive preparation, special utensils, and a large tearoom. The use of the stand for the display of utensils is beautiful to witness. As a formal tribute to kenshusei as they are about to be graduated, the master presents tea from the stand for the entire class. The slow-paced, highly formal service, performed in an inner room of the old house, is truly the commencement of the careers of many professional chajin.

13. Notes on Special Professional Studies

Flower Arrangement: *Chabana*

In the course of a professional's teaching it often happens that he settles on one area of special concern. Aside from gardening, architecture, ceramics, bamboo, and lacquer, a teacher may decide to study as his specialty one or more of the following: tea flower arrangement, tea food service, charcoal and ashes, or the production of tea leaves. This chapter is concerned briefly with each of these subjects.

Chabana, tea flower arrangement, is the simplest, least time-consuming act of preparation for a tea ceremony. Yet chabana is considered by many masters to be the supreme challenge of tea technique.

The few rules governing the arrangement of flowers for tea can be simply stated as follows: the flower in the tearoom should not be different from the flower in the field; nothing should be hidden; the fleeting quality of life should be conveyed.

Some masters of this art have said that nothing can or should be written as a rule for others to follow. Those here indicate that an arrangement should be simple and natural.

Japanese flower arrangement began with the priests of Buddhist temples during the reign of Prince Shotoku. The priests prepared flowers for the great temples in Nara. From these arrangements, which can be seen in slightly altered form today, many schools of flower arrangement, *ikebana,* descend. However, formal schools of specific attitudes did not emerge in Japan until the seventeenth century.

Tea-ceremony flower arrangements had already begun to be developed during the Muromachi period. Soami, Shuko, and the associates of the Ashikaga shogun are recorded to have paid special attention to the decoration of the tokonoma in their tearooms. A definite relationship was established between a given painting or calligraphy and the flowers beside it.

Arrangements of flowers for tea ceremony soon came to be the first formal element of a tea ceremony which could be used independently. One could have a tea arrangement of flowers and still not serve a tea ceremony. Within tea ceremony, the arrangements represent the season, even the very day. For the Buddhist chajin, the flowers served to remind them of their heritage and of the evanescence of life.

From the beginning, wild flowers and mountain grasses have been thought to convey perfectly the spirit of Buddhism and tea. Flowers that have large blossoms or are especially fragrant are not often found in chabana. Nor are rare flowers from hothouses or flowers out of season. A single bud with a bit of green is what one sees most often in a tearoom.

The flower is the most inevitable part of tea. Tea would be unimaginable without it. Inside the tearoom, even when there is no breeze, the petals fall just the same. Even when wild grasses are used the same feeling exists. The grasses are cut the day before, and by the time of the ceremony they are a little withered. This is natural and effective.

The first depiction in Japanese art of a host inviting guests to see a flower arrangement appears in *Ise Monogatari*. The arrangement is of willow, long and pliant. Even in this painting the arrangement looks natural.

Rikyu felt that one should use but a single bud and a twig or two. He did not advocate spectacular effects in chabana. His arrangements were of one mood, stressing a single color.

In working with a chabana master one learns that the whole arrangement is determined by the selection of the flower. The twig or twigs are chosen for the flower. The container follows suit. When these are done the flower is cut under water, placed in one hand with the twig or green. The master holds the arrangement in his hand and it is placed in the container as is. Nothing more is done to it.

As a rule, the bud or flower does not project above the rim of the container by more than a third. The emphasis is on the horizontal; twigs seem to move out from the container rather than up and above.

The whole process is so deceptively simple that it is frustrating when students cannot achieve the naturalness and spontaneity of experienced masters. It is an aspect of tea on which students and professionals work hardest.

Selections from the tearooms of the Urasenke school include these: January, peony; February, plum and aspen; March, peach; April, cherry; May, iris, wisteria, and thistle; June, bellflower, evening primrose, and summer chrysanthemum; July, rose of Sharon and bush clover; August, rose mallow; September and October, chrysanthemum; November, hazel; December, narcissus. There are about three hundred commonly used plants—including camellia, pampas grass, and willow. Willow is most often used at New Year.

Food Service: *Kaiseki*

Kaiseki, tea food service, was originally the simplest of meals. The name comes from the practice of samurai placing small heated stones next to their stomachs in the folds of their kimonos. The heated stones caused gastric juices to flow, with the result that they did not feel hungry. Kaiseki, therefore, was thought to be a token meal, not elaborate.

Early records of these show that kaiseki consisted of rice, soup, fish, and perhaps a vegetable and garnish. Judging from these records, the quantities must have been small.

Since that time kaiseki has grown to an elaborate affair, requiring a complicated menu, a large selection of service ware, and the assistance of at least one other person. The space required for preparing kaiseki is more than is provided in the traditional preparation room. It is not unusual to discover that two or three extra hibachi have been employed. As the preparation room is small these are sometimes placed outside, in the back of the tea hut. It looks as if things have gotten out of hand.

Kaiseki has come to be such a particular part of tea service that it, too, can be studied as an independent practice separate from tea ceremony. The kaiseki served by the best Japanese restaurants represents the very height of their cuisine. It is the standard against which one judges all Japanese food.

Wet sweets which are served in today's tea ceremony were originally part of kaiseki. Today they are substitutes for kaiseki. The *omogashi* and *hoshigashi,* once served with thick and thin tea respectively, are now offered according to the host's taste. The once commonly used lacquer container for sweets, *fuchidaka,* is being replaced by the more informal individual plates, *meimei kashiki,* or large bowl, *kashibashi.* Sweets are also rarely served in the *shikiro,* a large bowl with a lid. *Higashi,* thin, dry sweets, are served in the course of a full tea ceremony with meal. These are either pressed sugar forms, *oshimono,* or caramel-like, *arihei.* These are always served on a single plate for all guests.

Tea professionals are trained to write menus, select ingredients, prepare food, choose service ware, and arrange and serve the kaiseki. Each step is important. The specialists deserve respect for their accomplishment. Timing the preparation of the foods and ordering the flow of utensils from preparation room to tearoom require considerable practice. Perhaps the best way to demonstrate this is to describe briefly what is involved.

In a full, formal ceremony the guests proceed from the garden to the tearoom and have their meal before being served thick and thin tea. If the season is cold, all utensils used in the meal have been warmed beforehand. As the guests assemble in the tearoom the host wipes the rice bowls and puts a scoop of rice in each. This is placed on a portable table, *oshiki*. This table also holds covered soup bowls of lacquer. Rice bowls are also of lacquer but are slightly larger than those for soup. To complete the arrangement, a side dish is added. The three containers form a triangle, *mitsuboshi*, or "three stars." Chopsticks made from cedar, moistened, rest on the right edge of the tray, which is presented to the guests, who uncover the rice and soup bowls, left and right on the tables, and begin the meal with soup. After a while the sakè container, *choshi*, and cups are brought in, stacked on a small stand. Each guest removes the bottom one for himself. The host serves sakè to each guest. Following this the guests eat from the side dish which is an accompaniment for the wine. To enjoy kaiseki the guests must know what to eat when, the succession of tastes being arranged by the host for best effect.

The host brings in a container of rice and offers it to the guests. He also offers another helping of soup to each. If the guests accept the second helping, the soup bowls are placed on a tray, carried to the preparation room, cleaned, refilled, and returned individually. While the host is attending to the soup the guests refill their rice bowls. When the soup is served the host retires to the preparation room with the now empty rice container.

The host next brings some kind of cooked food for each guest. This requires a new plate for each. When this is served, more wine is offered. The next item is broiled fish, served in traditional stacked lacquer boxes, *jubako*, or the more convenient large dish. This is usually served with Japanese pickles. A special set of chopsticks is provided with the jubako. Both ends are used in taking portions of the fish and pickles; one for the fish, the other for pickles. These chopsticks are of fresh green bamboo. The broiled fish is placed on the side dish.

In some services of kaiseki still another dish is presented, the *shiizakana*, a specially prepared fish. Following this, wine is served for the third time. Accompanying the shiizakana the host will probably offer a small amount of seasoned green, *hitashimono*, and something boiled, *ni-awase*.

While the guests are finishing, the host has retired to the preparation room to begin serving a very light soup, *kosuimono*. This is served and bowls and plates are removed. When this is done the host enters with a container called *hassun*, in which he has prepared sea

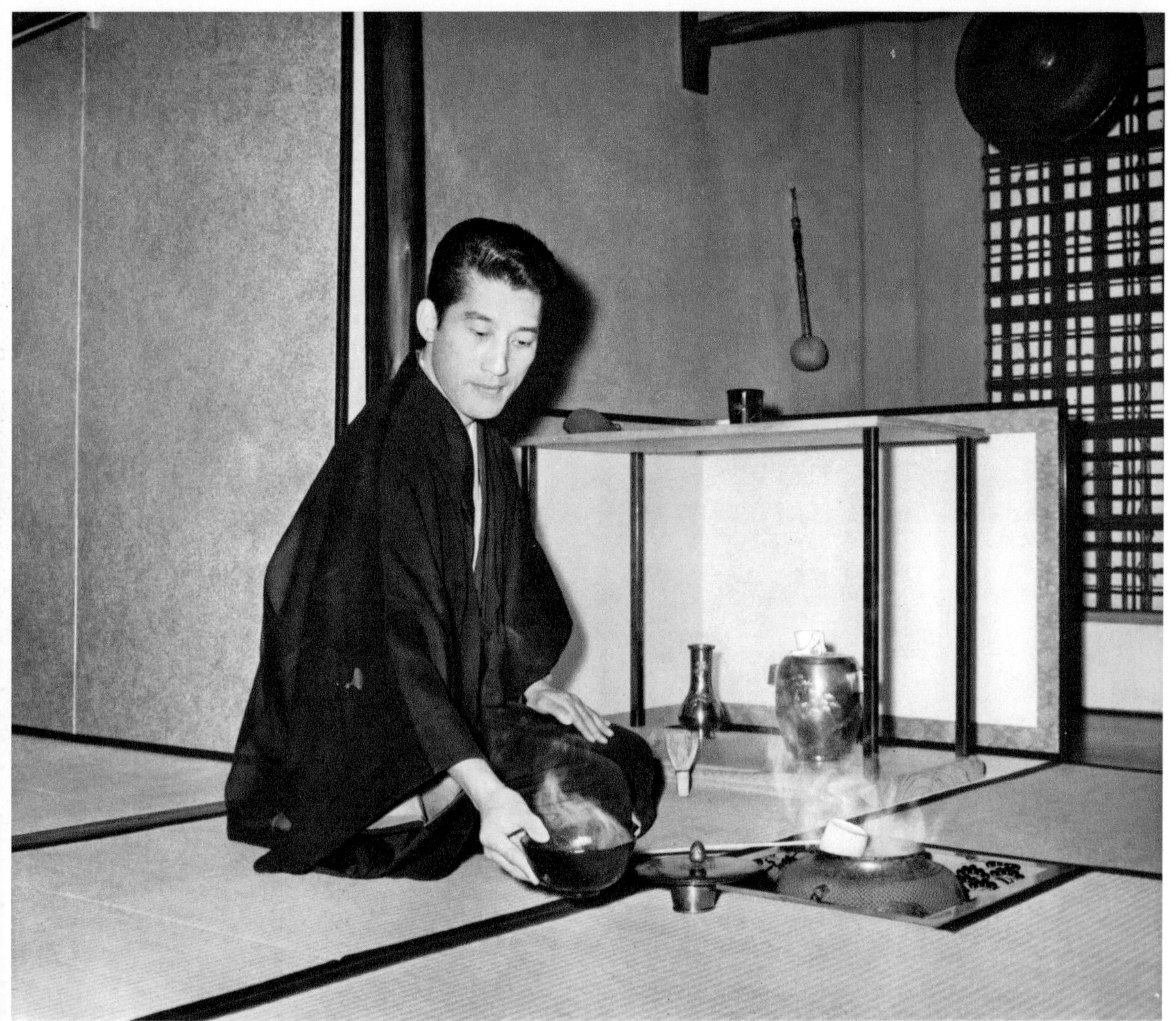

Soshitsu Sen, Grand Master of Urasenke, serving tea in the Totsutotsu-sai room at the school in Kyoto.

A tea ceremony in a large room at Urasenke. The guests are seated directly across from the host (upper left). The first guest bows as he receives the tray of sweets (upper right) and comes to the host for a bowl of tea (lower left). He thanks the host while the second guest drinks (lower right).

A tobacco tray with utensils and pipe.

A tobacco container made by Chonyu, seventh-generation Raku.

A ceramic hand-warmer in Oribe style.

▲ A Ki-zeto (yellow Seto) ware bowl for sweets. Placed on it is a pair of bamboo chopsticks.

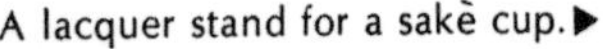

A lacquer stand for a sakè cup. ▶

Sweets for tea. (Photo by S. Fujima.) ▶

A black lacquer tray for sweets.

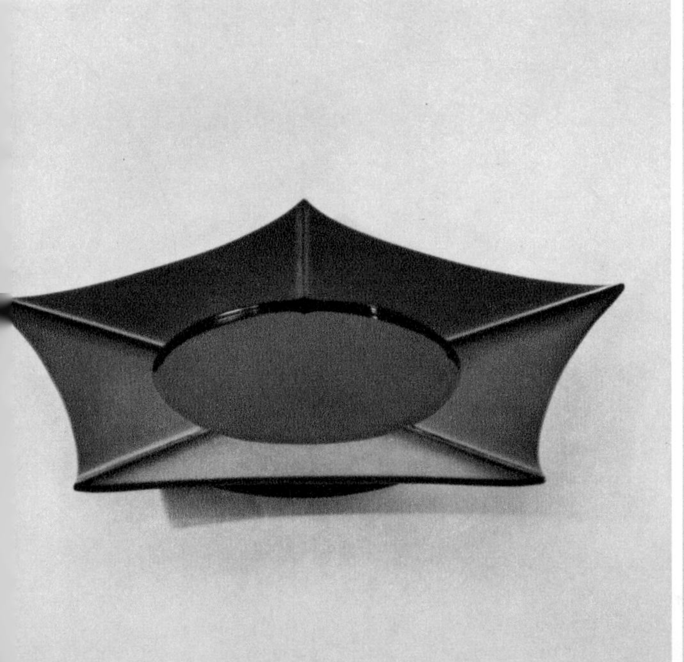

A Murasaki-gochi (purple Kochi) ware cake bowl.

Raked ashes and charcoal in a bowl used for lighting a pipe. (Courtesy of Urasenke.)

A charcoal basket made of bamboo skin.

Sumi-demae (preparation of the charcoal for the ro) at Urasenke. Note the feather duster and iron tongs.

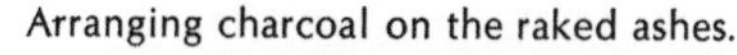

Arranging charcoal on the raked ashes.

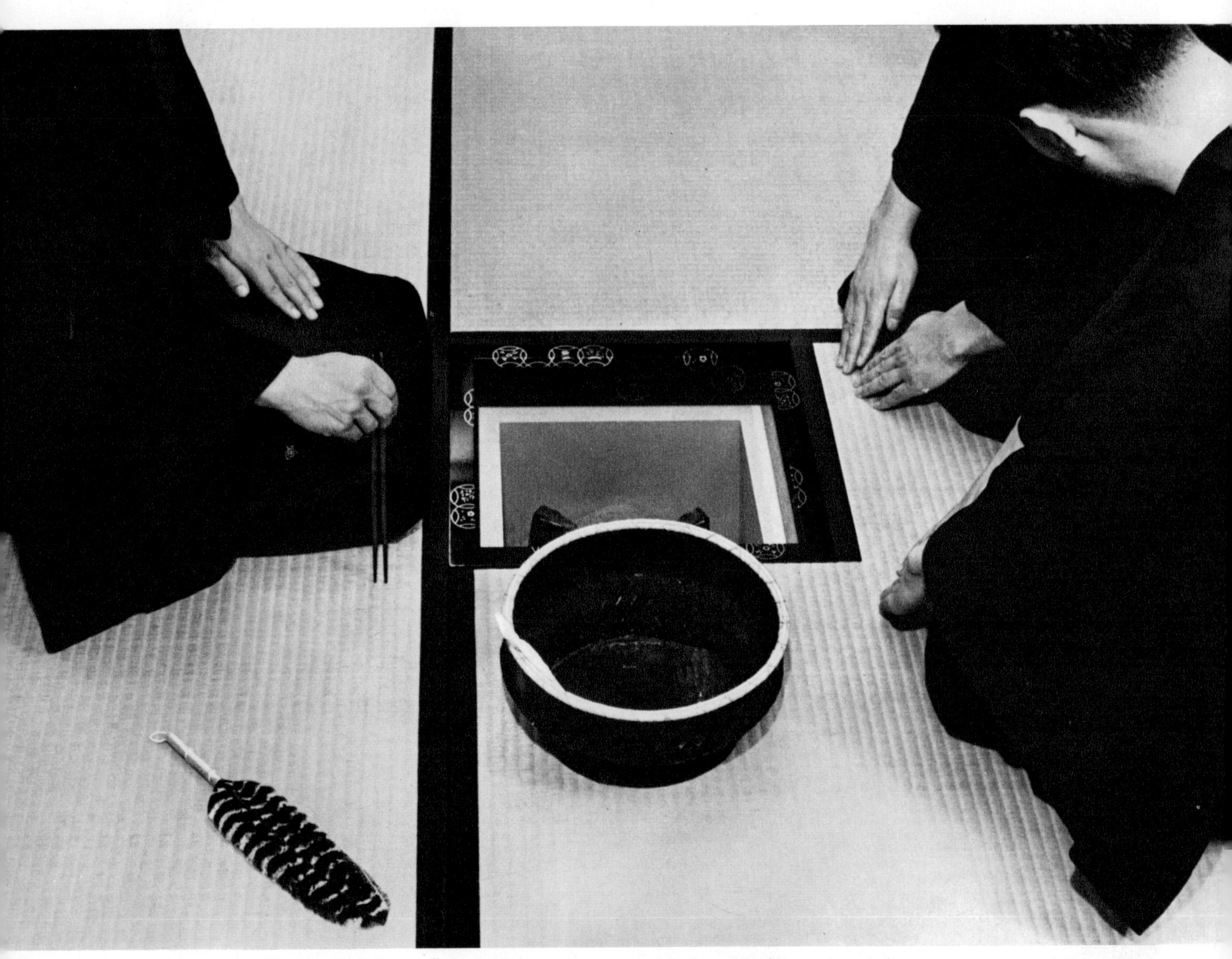

The charcoal arrangement completed, the guests bow to inspect it.

伸ばしさて前のひだを伸ばし右手に持てる緒を茶入の上にわがためて左掌にのせ緒の輪になれる所を左手の小指に挾みひだを右左と押へさて茶入を袋より出し前に置き袋の緒を下圖の如くになし袋の中へ輪を入れ打ち返して下圖の如くにし袋の定座に置くべし

所は前に準ず

一茶杓は筒に入れ帛紗を敷きて莊る也

一茶杓莊したる時は後座は必ず茶筅莊なり

一茶杓を客に出す時古帛紗を用ふ此古帛紗の使用法は師に就きて學ぶべし

●長緒茶入

一長緒茶入は下圖の如く結びて中立の間に先づ常例の通り水指を莊り其前に長緒茶

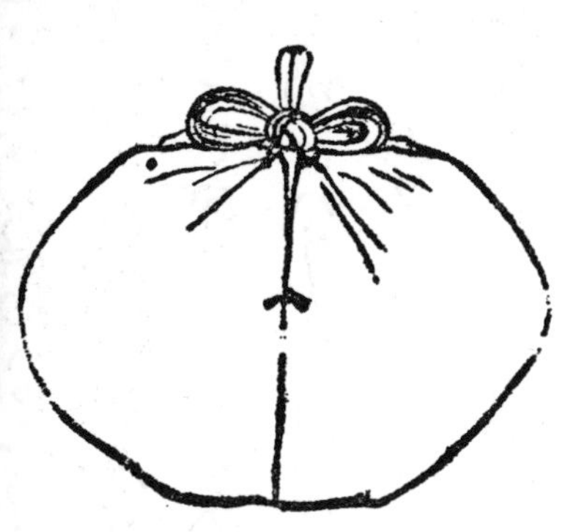

Illustrations of bags for tea caddies and how to use them, from *Konarai Juroku Kojo Denki* (Notes on Sixteen Special Items), by Tantansai, published in 1908.

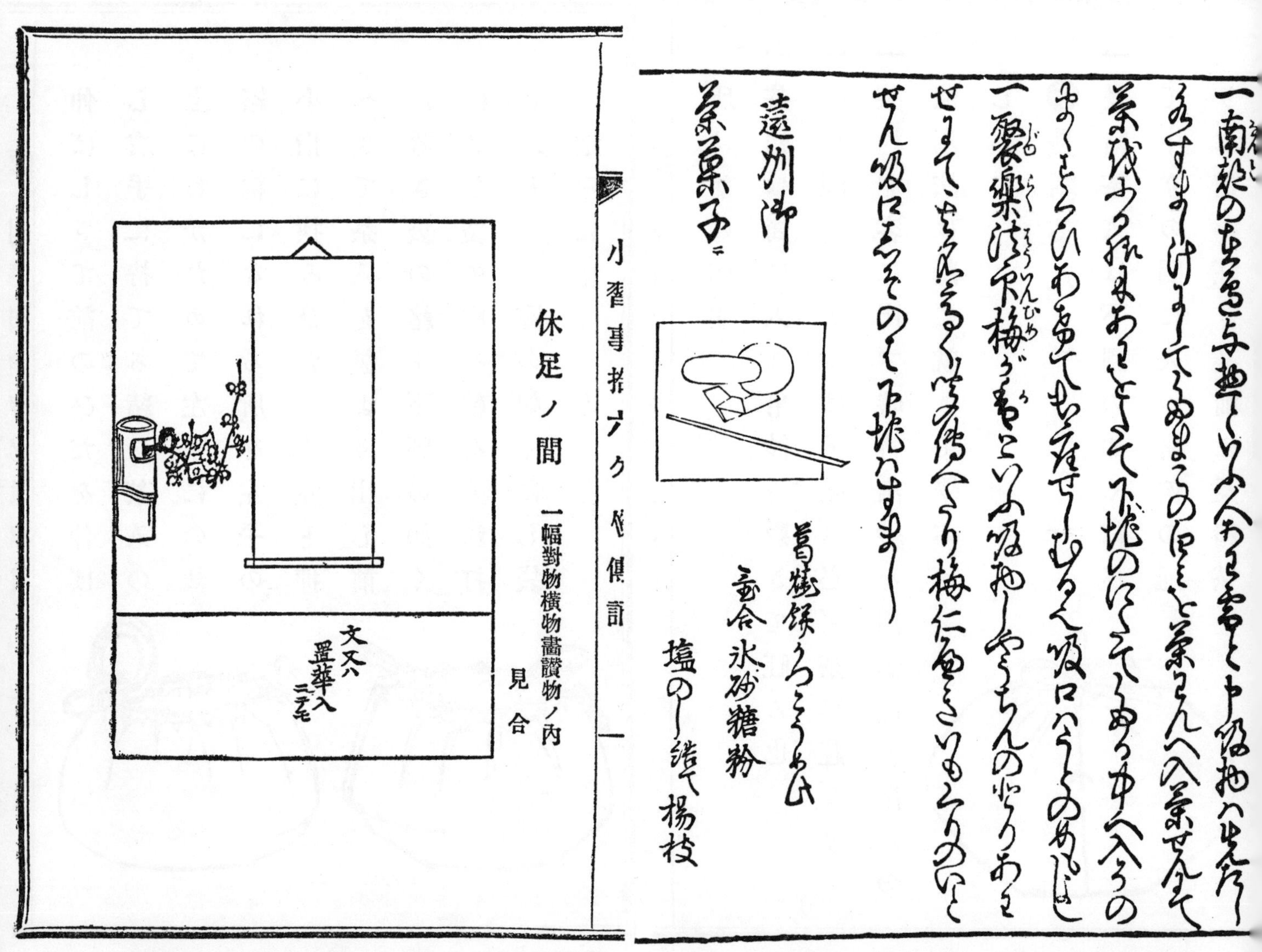

Indications for the arrangement of kakemono and *chabana* (tea flower arrangement) in the tokonoma, from *Konarai Juroku Kojo Denki.*

This and the following two illustrations show the sweets served at the Great Kitano Tea Meeting, from *Kissa Iho,* a book on tea published in 1910.

利休小野にて
御茶菓子

栗餅
香合 氷砂糖粉
ぶだうかん

此外茶菓子四季に應じて温冷の仕立第一なれハ宜
てん形窈之南都のかこあるに黒砂糖せし菓子数寄
者の納川三斎利休偶之趣御同道云菓多名に押掛
ら来て内の茶菓子なより太豆よお塩けをしてさ
よしとらふこと加ゑらけよ入てゐてうゐめ今中に浸入
たらん面に伝茶湯さら上まて此宗よる亭主の
抱数寄一様よ定めてし出宗匠茶菓子一通記

古田織部
御茶菓子

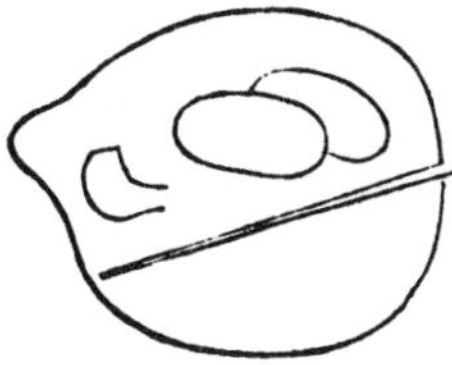

鶉焼餅かうこうし
香合
たいらきなかけ

利休御
茶菓子
大徳寺にて

草餅かうこうし
香合
朝鮮山菜生にて

三斎御
茶菓子
但馬の御会

水餅かうこうし
香合氷砂糖粉
水菓

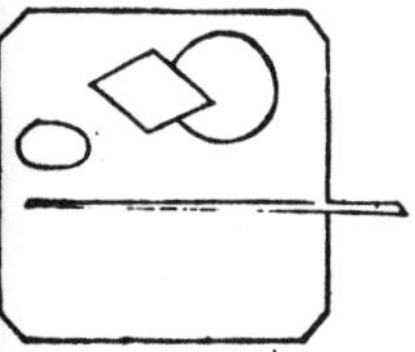

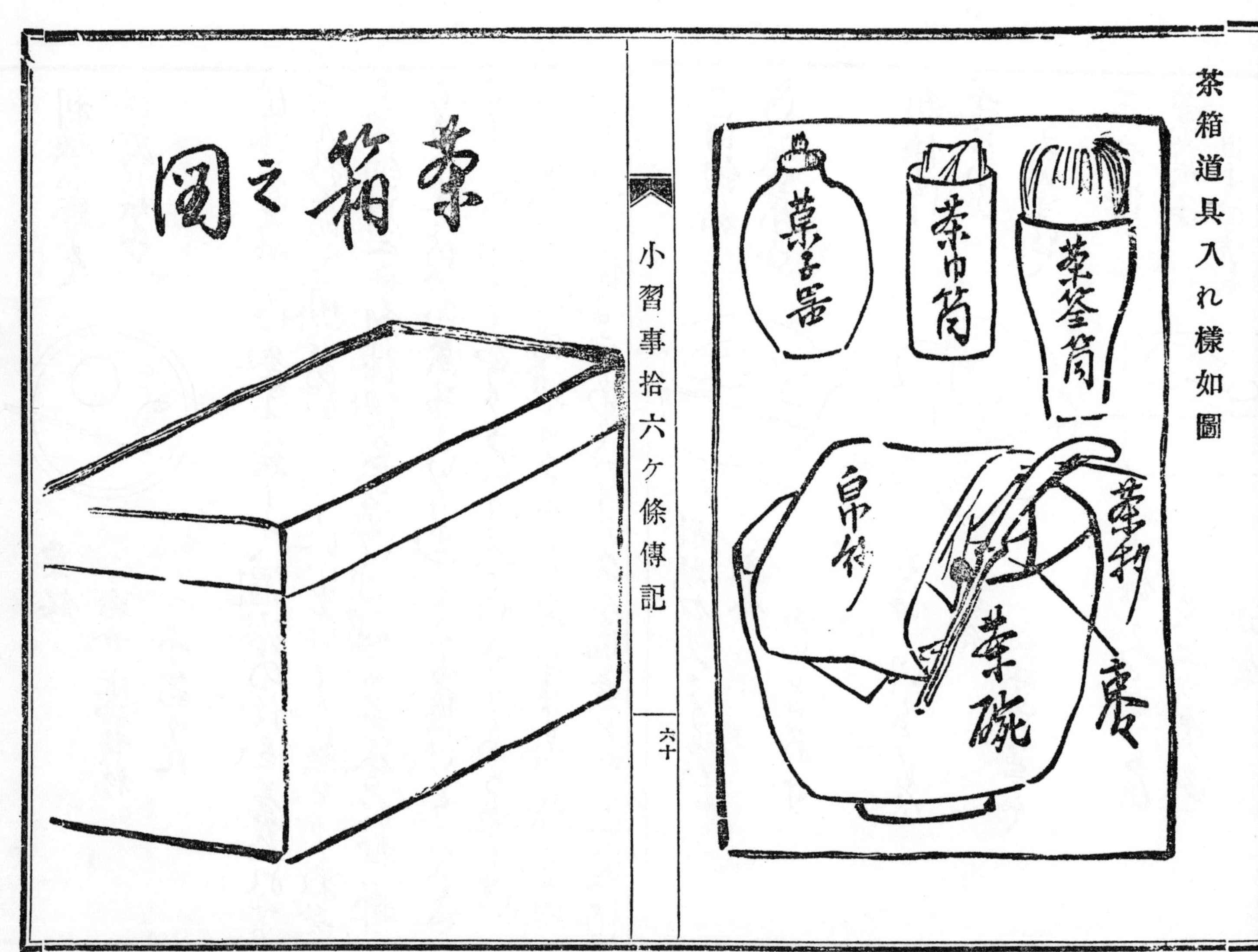

A drawing in false perspective of a *chabako,* a box for outdoor tea (left), and the utensils that are put into it (right). From *Konarai Juroku Kojo Denki.*

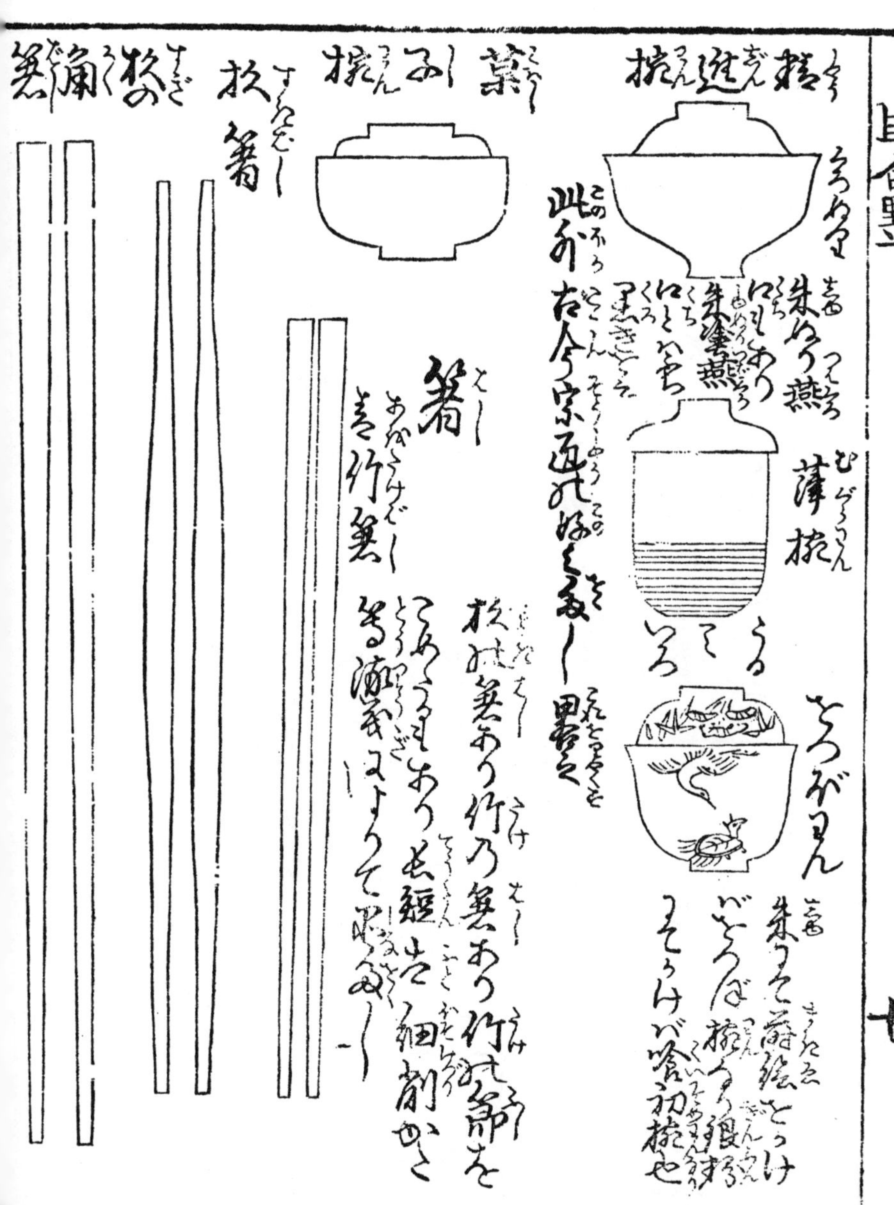

Chopsticks and lacquer soup bowls for *kaiseki* (meal-service tea). This and the following eight illustrations are from *Chado Hayagaten,* vol. 2.

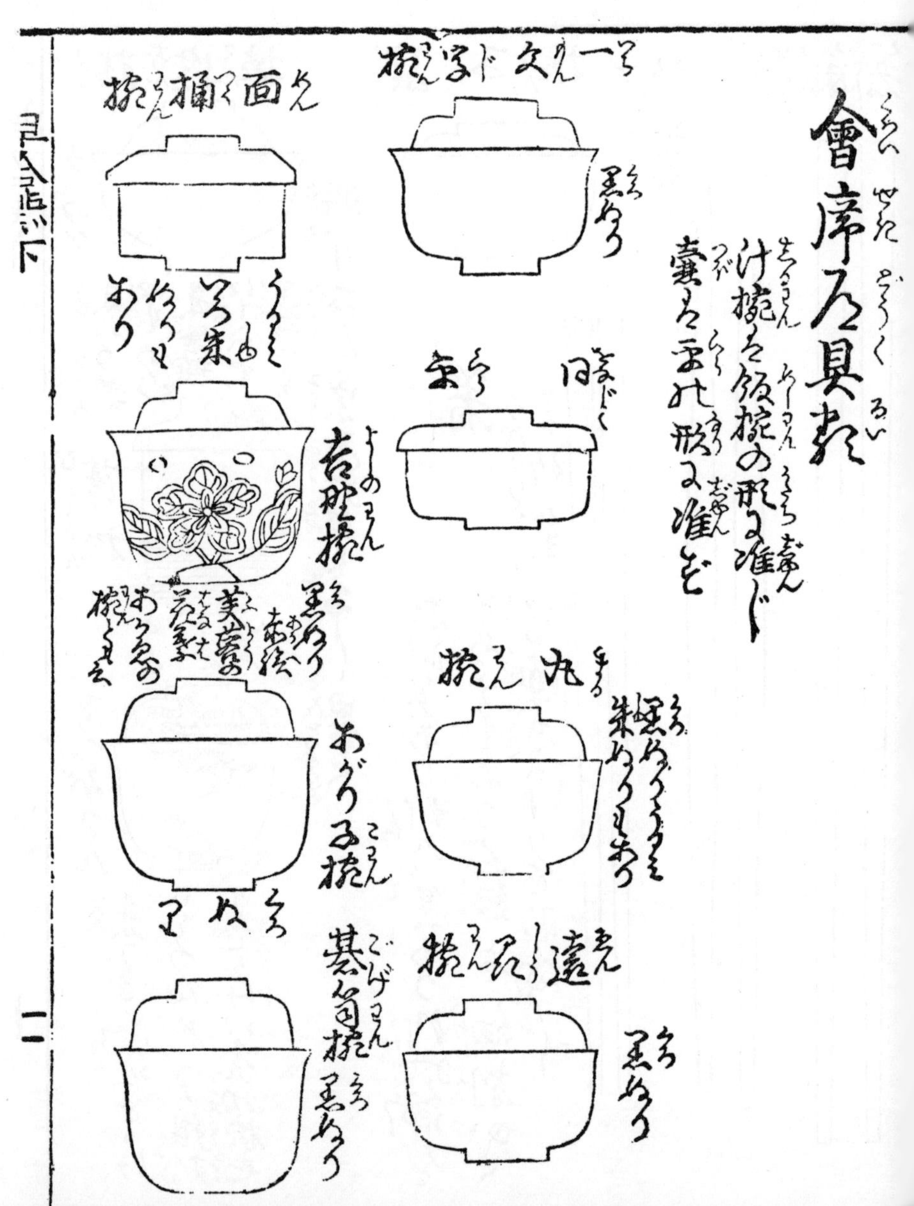

Various shapes and sizes of lacquer soup bowls for kaiseki.

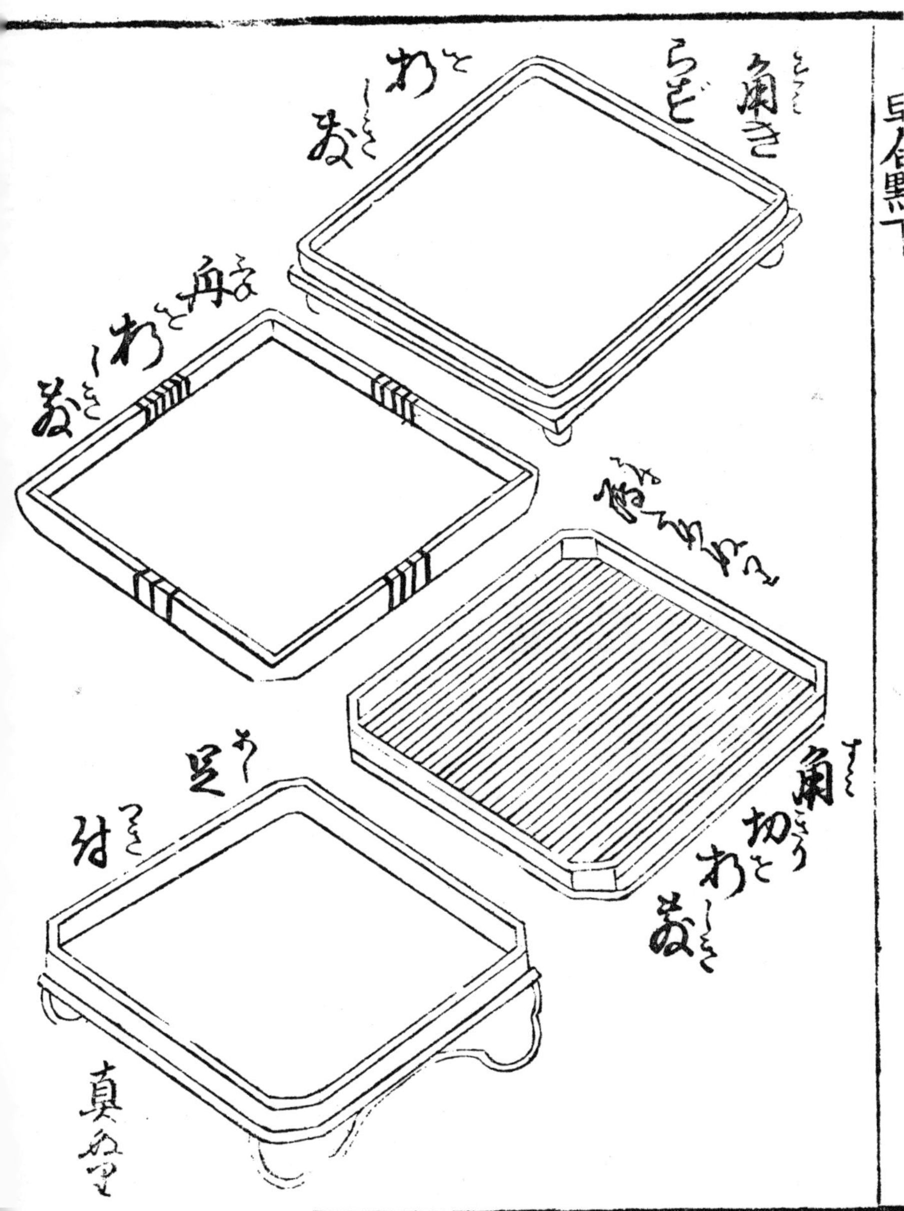

Four types of trays for use in kaiseki.

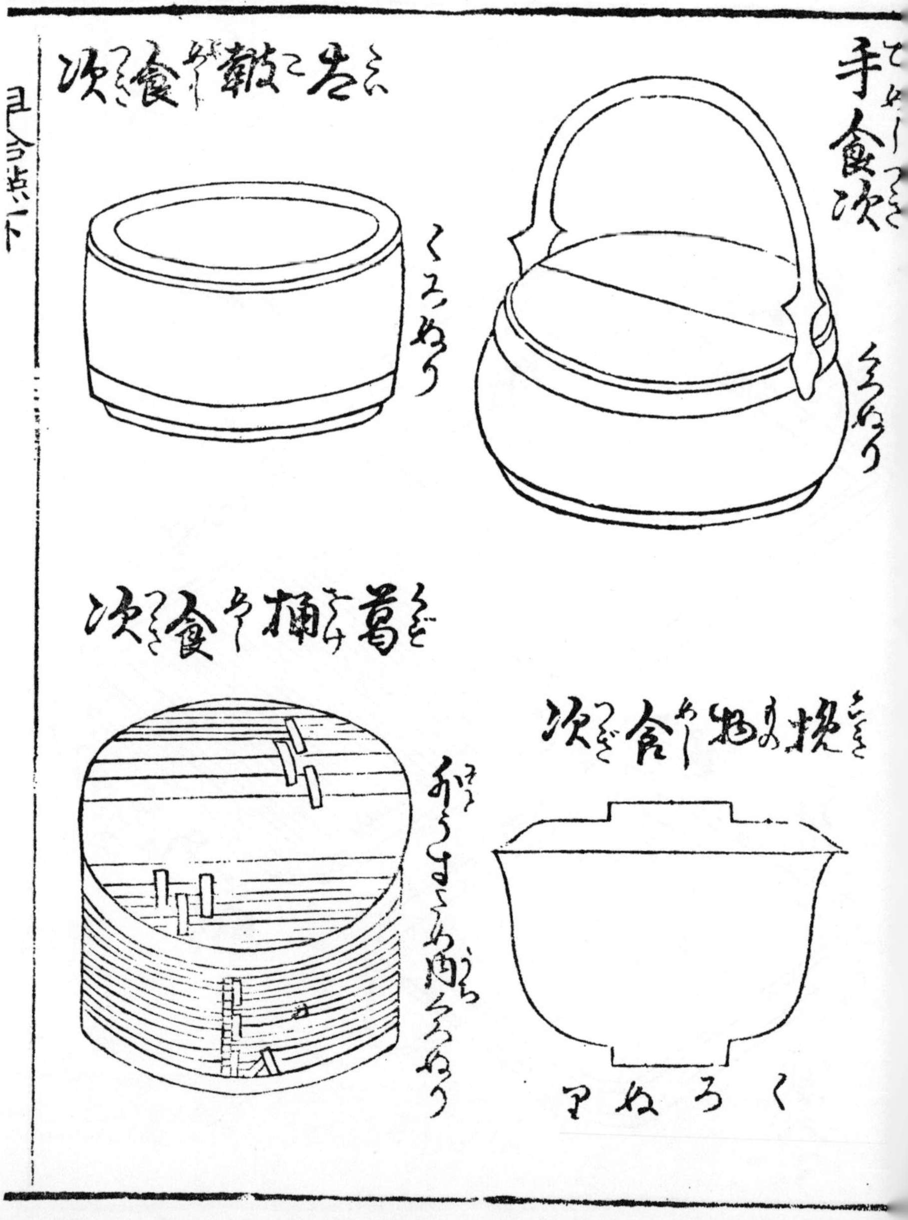

Four kinds of rice containers used in kaiseki.

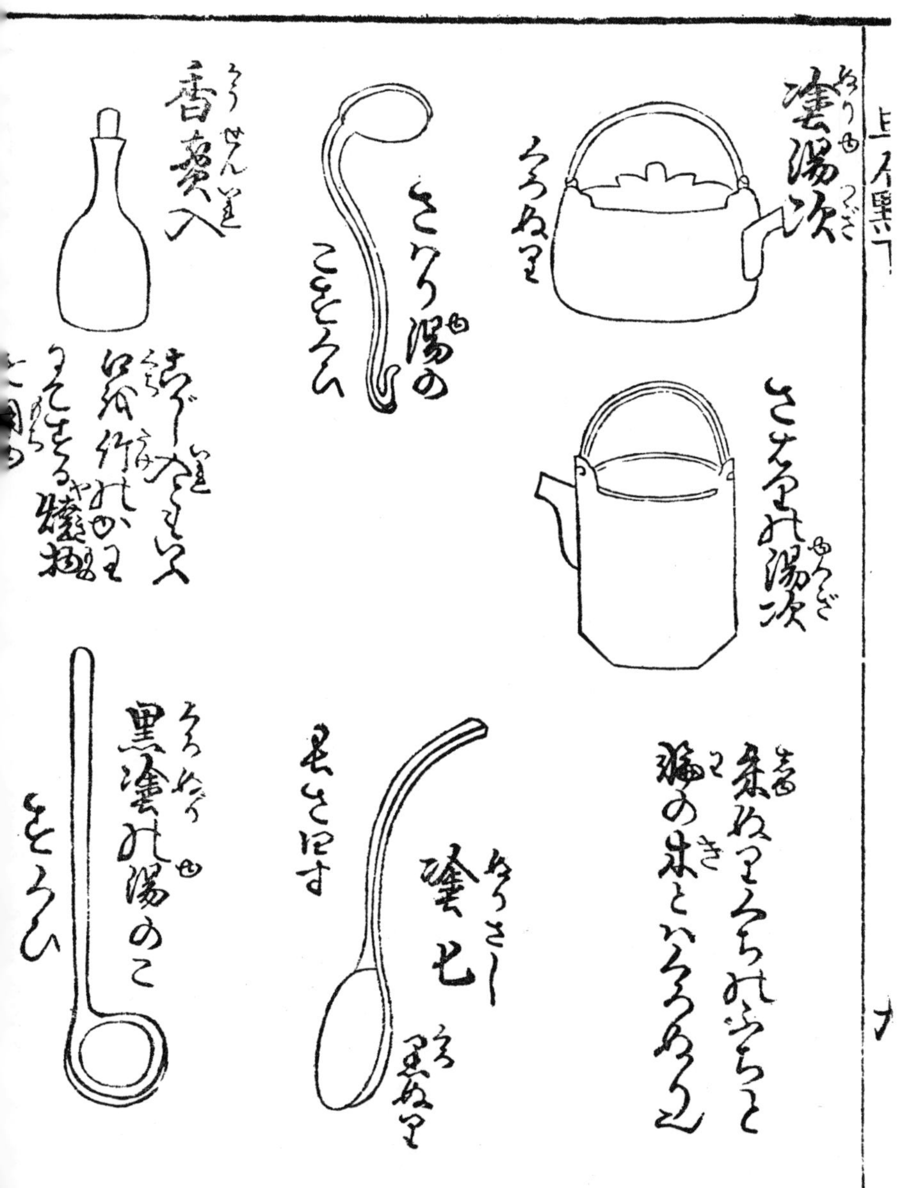

Ladles, pitchers, and a bottle for use in kaiseki.

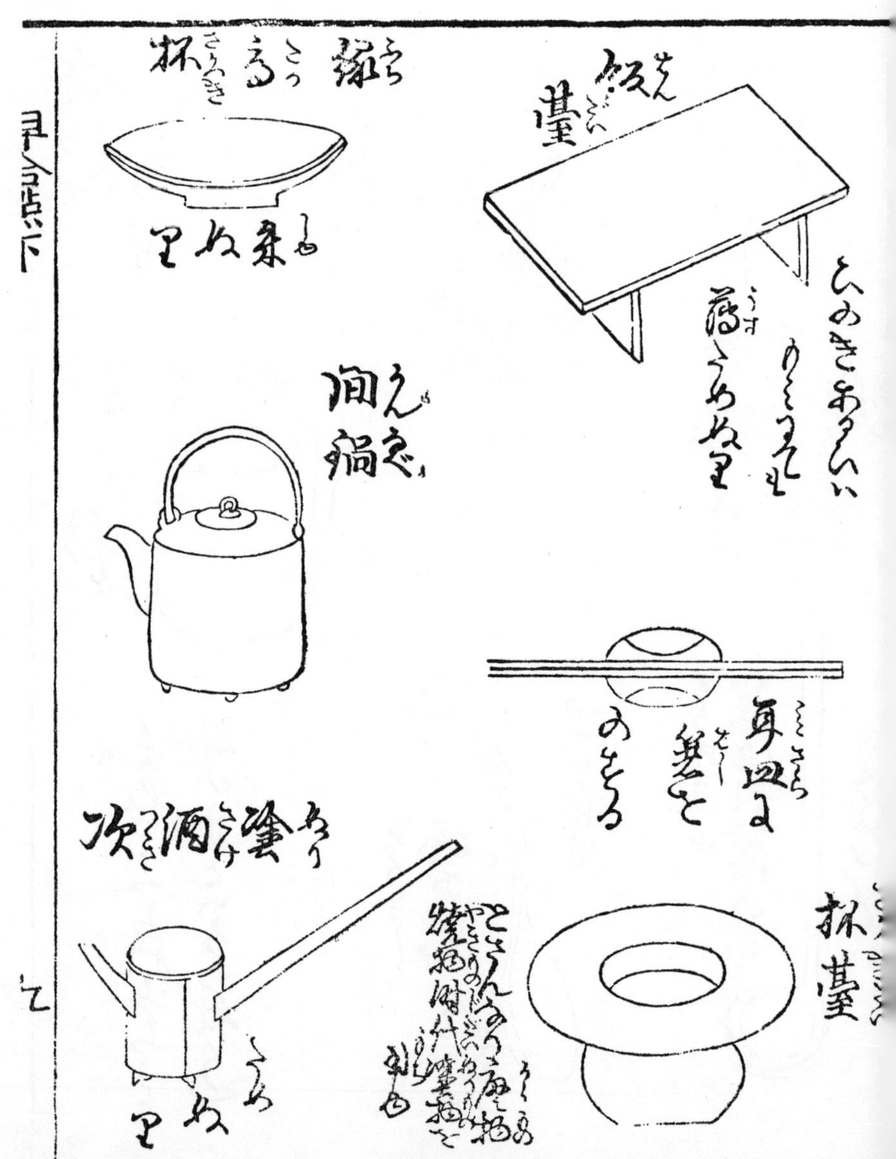

Various implements used for serving sakè with kaiseki.

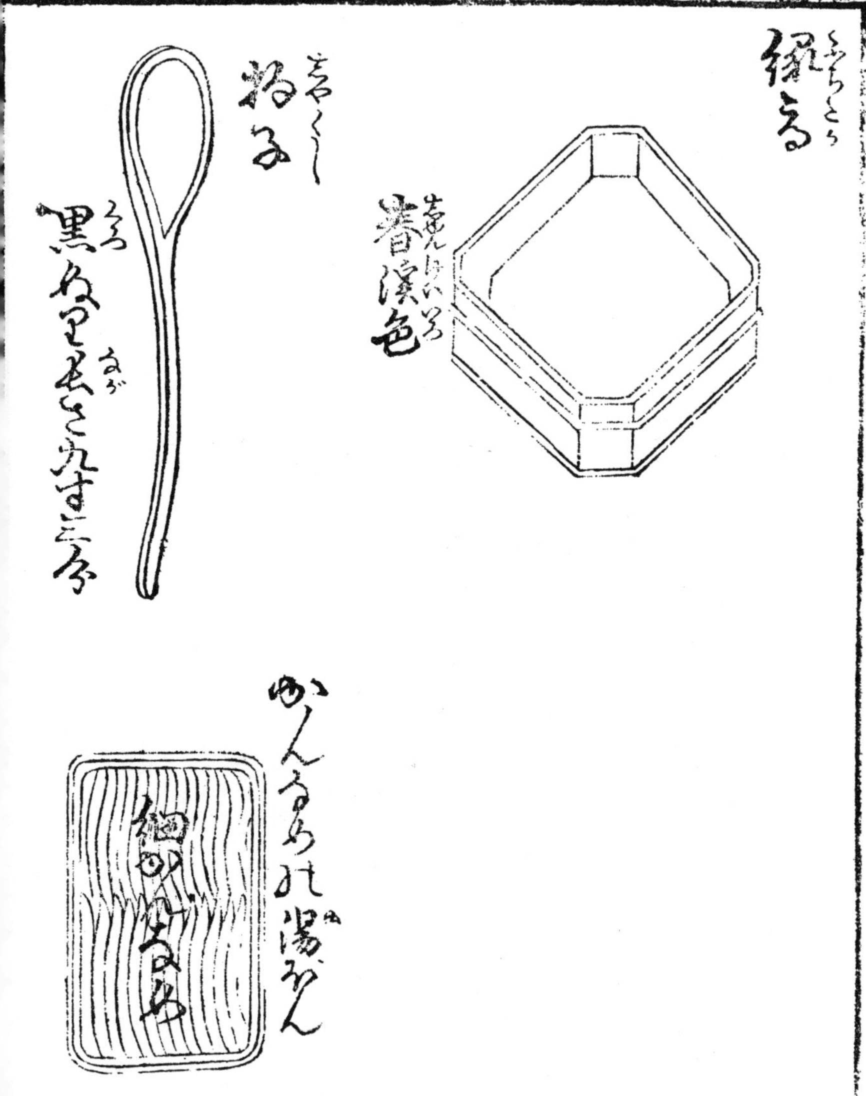

Trays and a spoon for use in kaiseki.

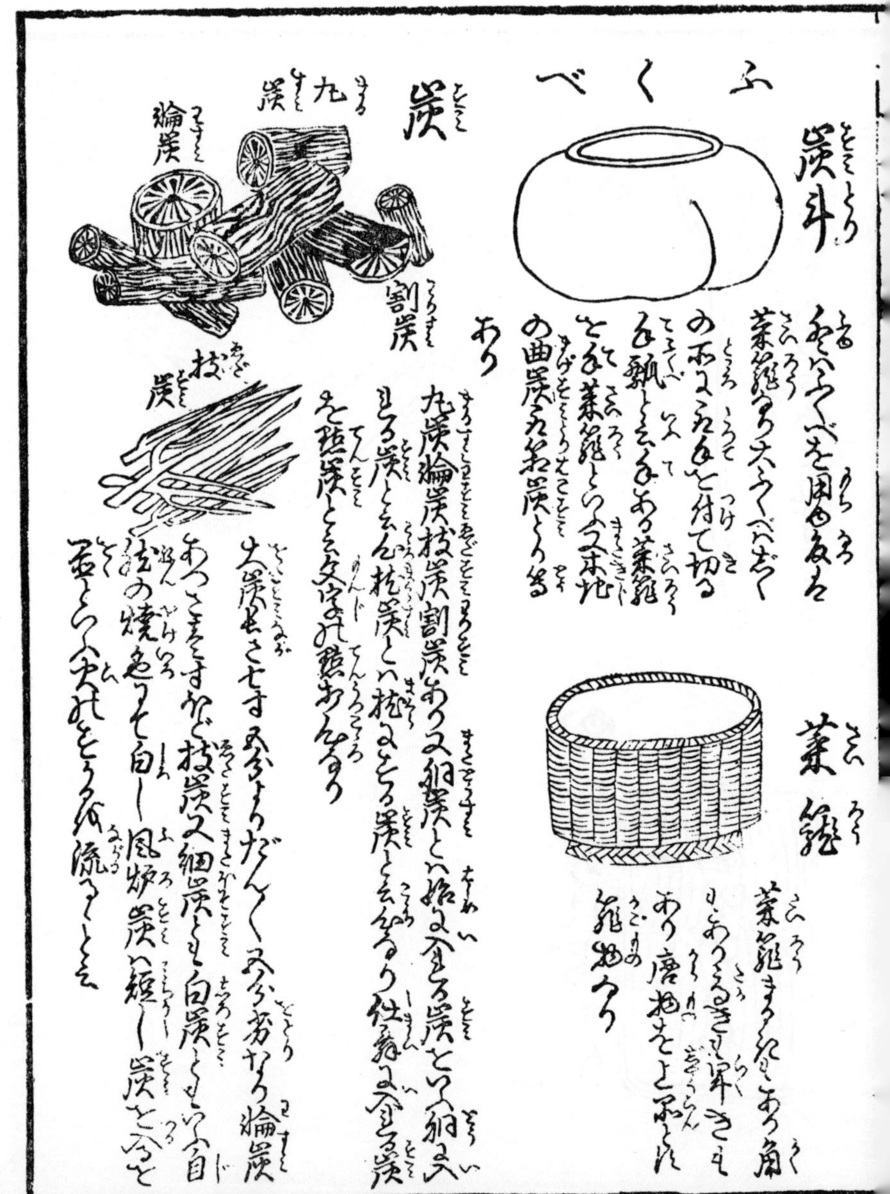

Illustrations and directions for the preparation of charcoal.

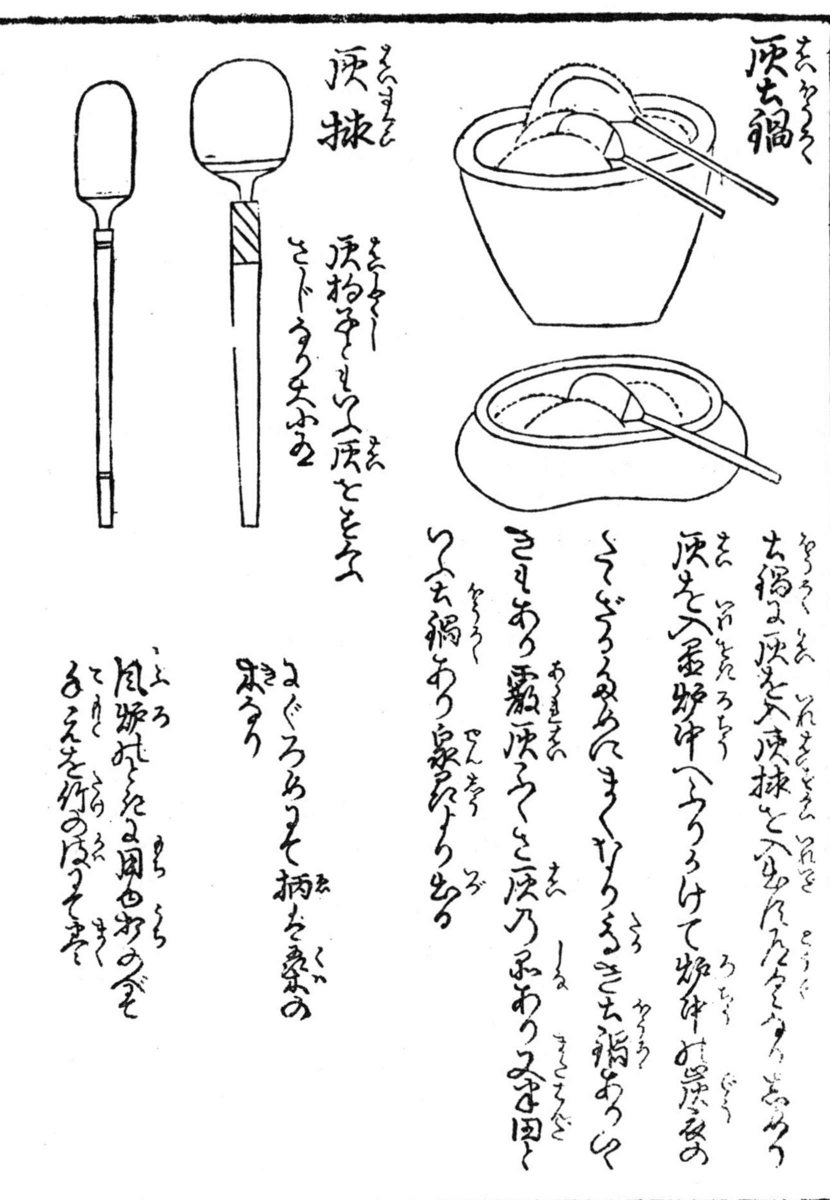

Charcoal scoops and containers.

and mountain products in small quantities. Again, wine is served; if the shiizakana has not been served, this will be the third serving of sakè. The food in the hassun is a side dish for sakè and is placed on the lid of the kosuimono bowl.

Tadachika Kuwata, remarking on the growing consumption of wine at full-scale kaiseki, believes some reassessment of the role of sakè is now in order if tea meals are not to become as they were once. With three or four servings of wine included in the regular course of kaiseki, and with the common practice now of exchanging cups with one's host, Mr. Kuwata's concern seems understandable.

A small quantity of pickles is served with the clear soup which follows. This soup consists merely of hot water poured into the soup bowl and rice bowl left on a guest's table. This cleans the lacquer bowls. The soup is drunk and the bowls are covered and placed again in their original positions on the table.

Meanwhile, the host is in the preparation room arranging the sweets which conclude the kaiseki. These are presented and the meal is completed. The guests leave the tearoom to sit for a while in the garden while the host removes the small tables and rearranges the tearoom for the two services of tea which follow.

Few beyond professionals and restaurateurs master the techniques of serving this kind of meal in the course of a tea ceremony. It is virtually impossible to serve kaiseki well without well-trained assistants.

Charcoal Preparation

Sumi, charcoal used in laying the fire for tea ceremony, is carefully attended to by students and teachers. Charcoal is specially selected, cut, and arranged for each service. Charcoal pieces for use in the fire pit number about six to a fire. These are from two-and-one-half to six inches in length. Pieces for the portable brazier, also six in number, have a length of from two to about five inches. They are in all cases cut by hand, washed, and set aside to dry.

The charcoal is washed because this prevents its staining hands as it is handled and also cleans away small particles that might spark out from the fire.

The importance of *sumi-demae,* the preparation of the charcoal fire, is that unless it is properly laid the charcoal will not ignite or burn evenly. If the charcoal does not burn well it will take a long time for the water to boil, an embarrassment to the host and a discomfort for his guests.

Ashes play a vital role in the preparation of the fire. The ash, *hai*, is carefully prepared. Raw ash is sifted through a medium sieve. A little water is added and the mixture stirred. Small particles that rise to the surface are lifted off, and the remainder is sifted again. This is then dried and sifted through an extra-fine silk sieve. The fine ash is then stored in a tight container in a damp, dark place. This is used for portable braziers.

Furo ash, made from wisteria, is almost pure white. Sometimes fallen cedar needles are burned and prepared in the same way, but are called *fujibai*, wisteria ash.

Ashes are prepared only in the summer. Ashes for the fire pit are taken several steps beyond those for the brazier; a little tea is added to the ashes as they are sifted through sieves. Sometimes fine ashes are made by burning small straws that have been soaked in salt water.

A set of tools used only for the preparation of the ash trough in which the charcoal fire is laid is a necessity for every tea student. These consist of several spoons and rakes which are used to build up the sides of the trough. The finished product resembles a valley with very smooth slopes. It is the slopes that give ventilation to the charcoal fire. Constructing one of these takes an experienced student between fifteen and thirty minutes. A novice can consume two hours or more in the process. For every shape of portable brazier there is a different style for ashes, and students must know how to lay ashes for the two major kinds of fire pits.

Growing and Grinding Tea

Fastidious tea men are said to grow their own tea. Aside from plantation owners and one private tea man of whom I have heard, this does not seem to be the case today.

Matcha, tea used only for tea ceremony, is usually associated with the village of Uji, south of Kyoto. It is produced in other places but chajin think of Uji when matcha is mentioned. The consumption of matcha is nowhere equal to the pound of regular tea drunk per month, per person in Japan.

Once Enshu and/or Kambayashi Shigeshiha discovered the technique of covering tea trees to protect their leaves from sunlight, the taste of tea, especially ground matcha, was much improved. But even before Enshu, Jo-o and others were concerned with improving ground tea for cha-no-yu. Better techniques in grinding, too, have steadily contributed to a better-tasting tea. Of special note in this is the work of such outstanding men as Ichizo Onishi and other members of the staff of the Tea Institute in Uji. It is a fact that today's matcha is a vast improvement over the tea drunk by Rikyu and tea men of the past.

Uji produces an average of one hundred twenty tons of tea a year. Nagoya, another major producer of matcha, adds another two hundred tons to this. This is little compared to the seventy-seven thousand tons of tea produced in regular, household varieties.

The Uji and Nagoya tea leaf that is ground for matcha is called *tencha*. There are about one hundred plantations in Uji for this kind of tea leaf. The distinction between thick and thin tea is very slight. Contrary to numerous tea-ceremony manuals and texts, the Tea Institute states that the primary distinction between tencha leaves selected for one or the other is color. If the leaves are a brilliant bluish green they are ground as thin tea. If the leaves are dark, purplish green they become thick tea. This coloration is an effect of the amount of sun allowed on the trees. The control over sunlight is by means of material hung over the trees for various periods of time. Fertilization too affects color, as does the method of handling some kinds of leaves. Dark green leaves are produced by shutting out more sunlight and by elaborate fertilization. Koicha leaves require careful tending. Some owners put aside special trees just to grow koicha. As a rule, when production is mixed, the upper leaves of the trees are used for thick tea and the lower for thin. The upper leaves are younger, smaller, and more delicately flavored. Tea from these small leaves costs more.

There is no real difference between the mechanical processes of preparing leaves for thick or thin tea, except in grinding. Younger leaves seem to steam and dry better than older leaves. This is perhaps why the young leaves of koicha are less bitter than the older leaves of usucha. Some people tend to use koicha even in thin-tea service because of the subtle qualities of its taste. This thick tea will cost about eighteen dollars on the average for one pound, or about twice the cost of thin tea. Grinders with extra-fine grooving are used for koicha, while slightly coarser grinders make usucha.

After grinding, usucha is slightly whitish, koicha is greener. Every year Uji produces ten times as much thin tea as thick. The Tea Institute, the government, and many individuals are working to improve the quality of the leaf and the quality of the grinding. Work is under way that promises to produce a matcha that will not lose much of its taste and color quickly; original taste and color are seriously altered now in only a week after opening a matcha container. Outstanding producers of matcha such as Nobuo Nakano have the tencha picked and quickly stored in air-conditioned chambers until grinding takes place. There are presently only one thousand grinders, *usu,* in Uji. These grind about three ounces an hour.

Too little research has been done on the grinder for matcha. Iron grinders were once introduced to replace the old—but still used—stone kind. The iron grinders failed by adversely affecting the taste and consistency of the matcha. Aside from the introduction of electricity to turn the grinders, the situation pretty much remains as it was several hundred years ago.

Very old grinders, those of about a thousand years ago, were about one half the circumference of present grinders. Their grooves were cruder than now, too, but essentially the grinder and its operation remain the same. Ichizo Onishi has spent much of the last ten years in work on the grinder. He says that the granite, *ryokusen,* grinder preserved at Butsuryu-ji, Nara, can be seen as a prototype for most Japanese usu. The

Butsuryu-ji grinder is believed to have been brought to Japan about a thousand years ago from China.

A surprising number of today's tea men grind tencha on their own usu. It is fun to do once, like making your own ice cream, but the consistency leaves much to be desired. Better to have leaves ground by the local shop.

One of the pleasures of living in Kyoto is being near Uji. You can watch tea for matcha being picked in May. If you work it right you can see the tea leaves picked, watch them being processed, have them ground to your liking, and serve the resulting matcha to your friends—all within twenty-four hours. The freshness of this tea is incomparable.

Appendix: Selected Tea Huts and Rooms

I. OUTSTANDING

Kyoto

TAI-AN: This is the only hut that is known to be definitely by Rikyu's hand. A national treasure, superbly preserved since its construction in 1582. A two-mat room, with an added one-mat area. Stepping-stones of special interest. Rikyu and Hideyoshi served tea here. If you can only see one, this is it. Seen by appointment through Myoki-an, Oyamazaki. A few minutes by train from central Kyoto. Contribution.

SHOKIN-TEI: Located in the grounds of Katsura Detached Palace, this is the tea hut perhaps most often seen in photographs. Brilliantly designed, reflecting the taste of Katsura's designer Prince Tomohito, it is probably by Enshu's hand. Seventeenth century; impressive in location and details. Seen by appointment through the Imperial Household Agency.

DOJINSAI: The first four-and-one-half-mat tearoom. In the grounds of Ginkaku-ji, in the Togu-do. Ashikaga Yoshimasa had tea in this room in about 1485. A beautiful shoin, superbly restored. By appointment.

FUSHIN-AN: An important tearoom in the grounds of Omotesenke. Rikyu's most elegant style of architecture. Reconstructed after removal from Hideyoshi's palace and again following a fire. Original design of 1587. By appointment.

MITTAN: A superb example of Enshu's early style. Constructed ca. 1606–8. Fine shelves, two tokonoma, painted fusuma, and other details of interest and importance. Carefully maintained. In the shoin building of Ryoko-in, Daitoku-ji. Very difficult to see.

YU-IN: The standard for four-and-one-half-mat rooms of simple style. Designed by Sotan, influenced by Rikyu.

Reconstructed to precise measurements following a fire. Thatched roof, exterior details, and garden should be seen. In the grounds of Urasenke. By appointment.

TEIGYOKU-KEN: Seen often in reproductions, this is an especially attractive tea hut in the well-kept grounds of Shinju-an, Daitoku-ji. After a design by Kanamori Sowa. The design dates from about 1638 and features an unusual enclosed tsukubai. By appointment.

KARAKASA-TEI: Its umbrella-like ceiling gives this hut its name. Experimental, not representative, but important to see. In the grounds of Kodai-ji. By appointment.

NARA

NOKAI-AN: In the extensive grounds of Jiko-in. Superb Katagiri Sekishu design; two and three-quarter mats. Built ca. 1661–72. Easily seen on a visit to the temple.

HASSO-AN: An eight-window hut with thatched roof. Representative of Oribe's finest work, though perhaps not by his hand. Its most recent reconstruction was in 1892. Removed from its original site to the grounds of the Nara Museum. Interior seen by appointment.

TOKYO

JO-AN: An important work by Uraku. Two and one-half mats. Unusual wall covering, distinctive design elements, and bamboo windows. National treasure. Moved to its present site in 1938. By appointment.

KAMAKURA

EIKANSAN-SO: Reflecting Sowa's taste, this hut was recently removed from its original site to Kamakura by Sutemi Horiguchi, noted architect and authority on tea. Expertly situated; important tsukubai in garden. On strictly private grounds; very difficult to see except for exterior (but that is worth seeing).

II. REPRESENTATIVE AND IMPORTANT

KYOTO

KAN-IN: Excellent tearoom in Rikyu style. In the grounds of the temple where Rikyu is buried, Juko-in, Daitoku-ji. By appointment.

KONNICHI-AN: A one-and-one-half-mat room of distinction. No tokonoma. The finest of the smallest rooms. At Urasenke. By appointment.

OKUJAKU-TEI: Part of the complex building known as Hiun-kaku. Used by Hideyoshi. In the grounds of Nishi Hongan-ji. By appointment.

SHOKO-KEN: Sansai's masterpiece, dating from about 1628. Though often repaired, it retains its original character. At Koto-in, Daitoku-ji. Open to the public.

GEPPA-RO: An excellent hut in the grounds of Katsura Detached Palace, showing the transition from so-an to shoin style. By appointment through the Imperial Household Agency.

BOSEN: An Enshu design, reconstructed in the late eighteenth century from a 1636 design. Fine proportions; unusual shoji. Difficult to see.

HASSO NO SEKI: Recent construction from Enshu's original 1624–43 design. In the grounds of Konchi-in, Nanzen-ji. By appointment.

KIHAKU-KEN: A good tearoom in a temple that publicly disclaimed tea. Quiet, good to see. In the grounds of Keishun-in, Myoshin-ji. Open to the public.

KANUN-TEI: A superb formal room of eight mats. The Kano Tanyu fusuma are justly famous. At Urasenke. By appointment.

KANKYU-AN: Rebuilt in 1925 from the original by Soshu, ca. 1672. An excellent room in a fine setting. Mushanokojisenke. By appointment.

IHO-AN: Noted for round window designed by Yoshino (1601–31). In the grounds of Kodai-ji.

SHIGURE-TEI: Attached to Karakasa-tei by an interesting covered walk. In the grounds of Kodai-ji.

SHONAN-TEI: Shoan's design. Includes three rooms and entrance. At Saiho-ji. Easily seen but not entered.

ENNAN: Said to have originally been in Oribe's garden; of his taste. Reconstructed in 1865 in the grounds of the Yabunouchi estate. Distinctive features.

TENSETSU-DO: The Rikyu shrine of Omotesenke. A Doan design. Reconstructed after a fire. Excellent features.

SA-AN: Representative of the mid-eighteenth-century popular style. Designed by Roei, it reflects Nyoshinsai's taste. At Gyokurin-in, Daitoku-ji.

TOYOBO: Said to have been built for the Great Kitano Tea Meeting. Often repaired, and removed several times. In the grounds of Kennin-ji.

HANKEI NO SEKI: A wabi structure in the grounds of the Horiuchi family estate.

RYOKAKU-TEI: Said to be by Ogata Korin. Removed to its present site at Ninna-ji.

SAKAI

HASSO NO SEKI: In the style of Sho-o. In the grounds of Kaiko-jinja.

NAGOYA

SARUMEN: The original, one of the "three great tea huts," was destroyed in 1945. Oribe-Uraku style. Recently reconstructed. In the grounds of Nagoya Castle.

Matsuė

Meimei-an: An important design by Matsudaira Fumai. Excellent setting.

Tokyo

Renge-an: Considered representative of Edosenke.

Rokuso-an: Sowa style; removed from its original site to the grounds of Tokyo National Museum.

Bijikyo: An important contemporary design by Sutemi Horiguchi, 1951.

Idemitsu Gallery Demonstration Room: A superb design by the contemporary architect Yoshiro Taniguchi. Easily seen, together with the gallery's famous art collection.

Selected Bibliography

BOOKS IN ENGLISH

Alcock, Arthur. *Art and Art Industry in Japan*. London, 1878

Austin, Robert; Ueda, Koichiro; and Levy, Dana. *Bamboo*. Tokyo, 1970

Blaser, Werner. *Japanese Temples and Teahouses*. New York, 1956

Boger, H. Batterson. *The Traditional Arts of Japan*. London, 1964

Bowes, Janus E. *Japanese Pottery*. Liverpool, 1890

Brinkley, F. *History of the Japanese People*. New York, 1915

Brooks, Van Wyck. *Fenollosa and His Circle*. New York, 1962

Conder, Josiah. *Landscape Gardening in Japan*. New York, 1912

Cram, Ralph Adams. *Impressions of Japanese Architecture and the Allied Arts*. Boston, 1930

De Bary, William Theodore, ed. *Sources of Japanese Tradition*. New York, 1958

Dening, M. Esler. *The Life of Toyotomi Hideyoshi*. Kobe, 1930

Dening, Walter. *A New Life of Toyotomi Hideyoshi*. Tokyo, 1904

Dick, Stewart. *Arts and Crafts of Old Japan*. London, 1923

Dickson, W. *Japan*. New York, 1901

Engel, David. *Japanese Gardens for Today*. Tokyo, 1959

Fujikawa, Asako. *Chanoyu and Hideyoshi*. Tokyo, 1957

Fukukita, Yasunosuke. *Tea Cult of Japan*. Tokyo, 1965

Gluck, Jay. *Zen Combat*. New York, 1962

Griffis, William Elliot. *The Mikado's Empire*. New York, 1877

Grousset, René. *Chinese Art and Culture*. Trans. by Haakon Chevalier. New York, 1959

Harada, Jiro. *A Glimpse of Japanese Ideals*. Tokyo, 1937

———. *Japanese Gardens*. Boston, 1956

———. *The Lesson of Japanese Architecture*. Rev. ed. Boston, 1954

Heldreth, Richard. *Japan As It Was and Is*. Tokyo, 1905

Horiguchi, Sutemi, and Kojiro, Yuichiro. *Tradition of Japanese Garden*. Trans. by Kokusai Bunka Shinko-kai. Tokyo, 1962

Itoh, Teiji, and Futagawa, Yukio. *The Elegant Japanese House*. Tokyo, 1969

Jenyns, Soames. *Japanese Porcelain*. New York, 1965

Kawabata, Yasunari. *Thousand Cranes*. Trans. by Edward Seidensticker. New York, 1958

Keene, Donald. *Living Japan*. New York, 1959

Kinoshita, Masao. *Japanese Architecture: Sukiya*. Tokyo, 1964

Kirby, John B., Jr. *From Castle to Teahouse: Japanese Architecture of the Momoyama Period*. Tokyo, 1962

Kishida, Hideto. *Japanese Architecture*. Tokyo, 1965

Kojiro, Yuichiro. *Forms of Japan*. Honolulu, 1964

Kuck, Loraine. *The World of the Japanese Garden*. Tokyo, 1968

Lee, Sherman. *Tea Taste in Japanese Art*. New York, 1963

Maeda, Taiji. *Japanese Decorative Design*. Tokyo, 1960

Mayuyama, Jukichi. *Japanese Art in the West*. Tokyo, 1966

McClure, Floyd A. *The Bamboos: A Fresh Perspective*. Cambridge, Mass., 1966

Miller, Roy Andrew. *Japanese Ceramics*. After the Japanese text by Eiichi Okuda, Fujio Koyama, et al. Tokyo, 1960

Mitsuoka, Tadanari. *Ceramic Art of Japan*. Tokyo, 1964

Morse, Edward S. *Catalogue of the Morse Collection of Japanese Pottery*. Cambridge, 1901

Mosher, Gouverneur. *Kyoto: A Contemplative Guide*. Tokyo, 1964

Mossmank, Samuel. *New Japan*. London, 1873

Munsterberg, Hugo. *The Arts of Japan: An Illustrated History*. Tokyo, 1957

———. *The Ceramic Art of Japan; A Handbook for Collectors*. Tokyo, 1967

———. *The Folk Arts of Japan*. Tokyo, 1958

———. *Mingei: Folk Arts of Old Japan*. New York, 1965

Nakane, Kinsaku. *Kyoto Gardens*. Trans. by Money Hickman. Osaka, 1966

Okakura, Kakuzo. *The Book of Tea*. Tokyo, 1958

Okamoto, Toyo, and Takakuwa, Gisei. *The Zen Gardens*. Vols. 1 and 2. Tokyo, 1962

Oliphant, Lawrence. *Narrative of L. Elgin's Mission to China and Japan*. 2 vols. London, 1860

Paine, Robert F., and Soper, Alexander. *The Art and Architecture of Japan*. Baltimore, 1955

Reischauer, Edwin O. *Ennin's Travels in T'ang China*. New York, 1955

———. *Japan Past and Present*. Tokyo, 1964

———, and Fairbank, John. *East Asia: The Great Tradition*. New York, 1958

Reps, Paul. *Zen Flesh, Zen Bones*. New York, 1961

Richie, Donald, and Weatherby, Meredith. *The Masters' Book of Ikebana*. Tokyo, 1966

Roberts, Laurance P. *The Connoisseur's Guide to Japanese Museums*. Tokyo, 1967

Sadler, Arthur L. *Cha-no-yu: The Japanese Tea Ceremony*. Tokyo, 1962 (first published London, 1933)

———. *The Maker of Modern Japan: The Life of Tokugawa Ieyasu (1542–1616)*. London, 1937

Sansom, George B. *Japan: A Short Cultural History*. Rev. ed. New York, 1962

———. *Japan in World History*. Vancouver, 1967

Sen, Soshitsu. *The Art of Taking Tea*. Kyoto, 1967

Senzaki, Nyogen, and McCandless, R. S. *The Iron Flute: 100 Zen Koan*. Tokyo, 1961

Shaw, R. D. M., trans. and ed. *The Blue Cliff Records: The Hekigan Roku*. London, 1961

Smith, Bradley. *Japan: A History in Art*. Tokyo, 1964

Sugimoto, Etsu. *A Daughter of the Samurai*. New York, 1926

Suzuki, Daisetz T. *Training of the Zen Buddhist Monk*. Kyoto, 1934

———. *Zen and Japanese Culture*. New York, 1960

———. *Zen Buddhism*. Ed. by William Barrett. New York, 1949

Swann, Peter C. *Chinese Painting*. Paris, 1958

———. *An Introduction to the Arts of Japan*. New York, 1958

Takakuwa, Gisei. *Gardens of Japan*. Trans. by Hirokuni Kobatake. Tokyo, 1967

Tatsui, Matsunosuke. *Japanese Gardens*. Tokyo, 1964

Ueda, Makoto. *Literary and Art Theories in Japan*. Cleveland, 1967

Ushikubo, K. J. R. *Life of Koetsu*. Kyoto, 1926

Waley, Arthur. *No Plays of Japan*. New York, 1921

Warner, Langdon. *The Enduring Art of Japan*. Cambridge, 1952

Yashiro, Yukio. *Two Thousand Years of Japanese Art*. New York, 1958

Yoshino, Tomio. *Japanese Lacquer Ware*. Tokyo, 1963

BOOKS IN JAPANESE

Chado Hayagaten (A Short Way to Understanding Chado). 2 vols. 1771

Emori, Nahiko. *Ocha no Hanashi* (Talks on Tea). Tokyo, 1967

Endo, Takeshi. *Nihon no Mingu* (Japanese Folk Art and Design). 3 vols. Tokyo, 1964

Fujioka, Ryoichi. *Nippon no Bujutsu, Cha Dogu* (Japanese Art: Tea Utensils). Tokyo, 1968

Hayashiya, Haruzo. *Cha Dogu no Nagare* (A History of Tea Utensils). Tokyo, 1966

Hayashiya, Tatsusaburo. *Zuroku Chado Shi* (Illustrated History of Chado). 2 vols. Kyoto, 1962

Honjo, Sosen. *Sekishu Sambyaku Kajo Kikigaki* (Sekishu's Three Hundred Notes on Tea). Osaka, 1966

Horiguchi, Sutemi. *Rikyu no Chashitsu* (Rikyu's Tea Huts). Tokyo, 1949

———. *Sotei, Tatemono to Chanoyu no Kenkyu* (Grass Gardens: A Study of the Buildings and Cha-no-yu). Tokyo, 1962

———; Inagaki, Ezo; and Kuwata, Tadachika. *Zusetsu Chado Taikei* (An Illustrated Outline of Chado). 7 vols. Tokyo, 1962

Iguchi, Kaisen. *Chado Yogoshu* (Chado: A Glossary). Kyoto, 1964

Isono, Fusenji. *Raku Daidai* (Raku Generations). Tokyo, 1967

Izawa, Sotatsu. *Chado Keibutsu Sho, Sekishu Konomi* (A Selection of Tea Utensils: Forms Favored by Sekishu). Osaka, 1960

Karaki, Junzo. *Sen no Rikyu*. Tokyo, 1963

Kinoshita, Keifu. *Kama, Rekishi to Kansho* (Kettles: History and Appreciation). Tokyo, 1953

Kitao, Harumichi. *Sukiya Shosaizu Fu* (Cha-no-yu Houses: Detailed Illustrations). Tokyo, 1953

———. *Take no Zokei* (Forms of Bamboo). Tokyo, 1958

———. *Tsukubai Hyaku Shu* (One Hundred Examples of Tsukubai). Kyoto, 1963

Kojiro, Yuichiro. *Gendai Kenchiku Haiken* (An Examination of Modern Architecture). Tokyo, 1967

———. *Nihon Kenchiku no Bi, Dento to Sozo* (The Beauty of Japanese Architecture: Tradition and Creation). Tokyo, 1967

Koyama, Fujio, et al. *Nippon no Yakimono, Mino* (Japanese Ceramics: Mino). Tokyo, 1963

Kuroda, Munemitsu. *Take* (Bamboo). Kyoto, 1966

Kuwata, Tadachika. *Chado Jiten* (A Dictionary of Chado). Tokyo, 1967

———. *Chado no Itsuwa* (Chado Anecdotes). Tokyo, 1967

———. *Cha no Kokoro, Chado Meigen Shu* (The Heart of Tea: Famous Remarks on Chado). Tokyo, 1966

———. *Chado no Rekishi* (History of Chado). Tokyo, 1967

———. *Sen no Rikyu*. Tokyo, 1944

Matsuyama, Yonetaro, annotator. *Hyochu Tsuda Sokyu Chanoyu Nikki* (The Annotated Cha-no-yu Diary of Tsuda Sokyu). 2 vols. Tokyo, 1937

Minamoto, Toyomune. *Daitoku-ji*. Tokyo, 1956

Nagano, Tesshi. *Chanoyu no Kama* (Cha-no-yu Kettles). Atami, 1966

Nagashima, Fukutaro. *Hyakunin no Shoseki* (Selected Works by One Hundred Calligraphers). Kyoto, 1960

Nogami, Yaeko. *Sen no Rikyu*. Tokyo, 1966

Saito, Yoshi. *Chanoyu no Shiori* (Guide to Cha-no-yu). Tokyo, 1964

Sen, Soshitsu. *Chado, Ura no Tomaya*. 4 vols. Kyoto, 1930

———. *Chanoyu, Urasenke* (Cha-no-yu: The Urasenke School). Kyoto, 1966

———. *Chashitsu Sekkei-shozu to sono Jissai* (Original Drawings and Photographs of Typical Japanese Tea Architecture and Gardens). Kyoto, 1959

———. *Urasenke Chado, Furo* (The Urasenke School of Chado: Furo). Kyoto, 1966

———. *Urasenke Chado Kyohon, Kama to Ro, Furo* (Chado Texts of the Urasenke School: Kettles, Ro, and Furo). Kyoto, 1966

———. *Urasenke Chado, Ro* (The Urasenke School of Chado: Ro). Kyoto, 1966

———. *Urasenke Chanoyu Zensho* (The Complete Book of Urasenke Cha-no-yu). Tokyo, 1966

Sen, Tantansai. *Konnichi-an*. Kyoto, 1935

Shibayama, Zenke. *Zenrin Kushu* (Zen Epigrams). Kyoto, 1962

Sugawara, Tsusai, et al. *Nippon no Kogei, Kinko* (Japanese Crafts: Metalwork). Kyoto, 1960

Tanigawa, Tetsuzo, et al. *Nippon no Kogei, Urushi* (Japanese Crafts: Lacquer). Kyoto, 1966

Yanagi, Soetsu. *Cha no Kaikaku* (Reformation of Tea). Tokyo, 1958

Series

Cha no Izumi (Sources of Tea). 26 vols. Kyoto, 1964

Chado Zenshu (Complete Writings on Chado). Ed. by Tadachika Kuwata, et al. 9 vols. Tokyo, 1955

Private Collection of a Chajin, Written in His Own Hand. Kyoto, 1906

Sekai Toji Zenshu (Ceramics of the World). 16 vols. Tokyo, 1955–58

Glossary-Index

90, 254–55; different kinds of, 253–54; boxes for, 254; appraising of, 255
chashitsu (tearoom or hut), 52, 63, 127, 132, 134–37; sizes of, 144
chawan (tea bowl): basic requirements of, 189; types of, 189–90; shapes of, 191; types of base of, 191; in Kamakura and Muromachi periods, 191; parts of, 192; Chinese-style, 192–94; Korean-style, 194–98; Japanese-style, 198–200; Raku, 200–205
chigai-dana (staggered ornamental shelves), 136, 177
Chinese tea utensils, 39, 50, 52
Chinese-style bowls, 190, 192–94
Choandoki (collection of tea anecdotes), 76–77
Chojiro, first-generation Raku potter, 201–2
chonin cha (commoners' tea), 89, 91
Chonyu, seventh-generation Raku potter, 203–4
Chuko Meibutsu (catalogue of tea utensils by Enshu), 185
collectors of tea utensils, 183–84; during Meiji period, 186–87
commoners' tea, see *chonin cha*
Conder, Josiah (*Landscape Gardening in Japan*), 128–29
cupboards, 179

daime (three-quarter mat), 141, 172
daimyo cha (lords' tea), 84
daisu (stand for tea utensils), 44, 265, 284
Dening, Walter (*A New Life of Toyotomi Hideyoshi*), 66
Doan, tea master and son of Rikyu, 81, 82
Doan *kakoi*, 142; see also *kakoi*
dobuki (building in which guests could change clothes), 126
Dochin, tea master, 51
Dogen, Zen master, 30, 39, 256
Donyu, third-generation Raku potter, 202–3
doors, *see* entrances

Edo period, *see* Tokugawa period
Eisai, Zen priest (*Kissa Yojoki*), 22–23, 38, 39, 256
Eison, Zen priest, 39–40
Enduring Arts of Japan, The (Warner), 20
Engel, David (*Japanese Gardens for Today*), 129
Ennin's Travels in T'ang China (Reischauer), 207
entrances, 53, 96, 121, 122–23, 140, 178–79, 275

fans, see *sensu*
fences, 126
Fenollosa, Ernest, 25
Fenollosa and His Circle (Brooks), 25
fire pit, see *ro*
flower arrangement for tearooms, see *chabana*
flower containers, see *hana-ire*
Freer Gallery, Washington, 185
fudoki (ancient Japanese historical and geographical records), 37
Fujikawa, Asako (*Chanoyu and Hideyoshi*), 81
Fujiwara Ietaka, Kamakura-period poet, 72
Fujiwara Sogen, disciple of Sekishu, 88
Fujiwara Teika, Kamakura-period poet, 71, 72
Fujiwara Yoken, tea master, 89
fukusa (silk napkin for wiping tea utensils), 263
fumikomi tatami (entrance mat for the host), 172
furo (portable brazier), 212–13
Furuta Oribe, tea master, 81–83, 126, 127–28, 141, 183, 187, 191, 197, 258, 261
fusuma (paper-covered sliding panels), 133, 174, 176
futa-oki (lid rest), 266

ganro (round fire pit in a tea kitchen), 179–80
gardens: dry-landscape, 95–96; for tea ceremony, 96, 121–31; plants in, 123; scope of, 123–25; care of, 128; Westerners' view of, 128–29; unplanned element in, 130; preparation for tea ceremony, 275
Gardner, Mrs. Jack, 25
gates, *see* entrances
Gengensai, eleventh Urasenke grand master, 91
grand master of tea, see *sado*
grand master of Urasenke, *see* Sen no Soshitsu
Grant, Ulysses S., in Japan, 25
Great Kitano Tea Meeting, 64–66
guests, 26–28, 275–78
gyotei (professionals assisting the Urasenke grand master), 279, 281–82

Hagi ware, 194, 259

Munsterberg, Hugo, 196
Murata Shuko, 252; *see also* Shuko
Muromachi period: tea tournaments in, 40–41, 43; flowering of art and architecture in, 41–43; tea ceremony in, 49–50; tea bowls of, 191; tea flower arrangement in, 285–86
Mushanokojisenke, 89
Muso Kokushi, Zen priest and garden designer, 124, 125
Myoe, priest, 22

naga-hibachi (rectangular brazier), 213
Nagano, Tesshi, kettle maker and scholar (*Chanoyu no Kama*), 208–9, 210–11
nail covers, 176
naka-bashira (central post of a house), 141–42
Nambo Sokei (*Namboroku*), 70
Namboroku (a compilation by Sokei of Rikyu's teachings), 70–71
Naya-shu (barn or warehouse school of tea), 47
natsume (lacquered tea caddy), 216, 250–51; see also *cha-ire*
New Life of Toyotomi Hideyoshi, A (Dening), 66
Nezu Art Museum, 199, 216
nijiri-guchi (guests' small entrance to tearoom), 53, 178–79
No drama, 42–43, 86–87
Noami, Muromachi-period artist and teacher (*Kundaikan Sochoki*), 45, 49–50
Nobunaga, *see* Oda Nobunaga
nodate (outdoor tea ceremony), 282

Oda Nobunaga, military dictator: rise to power, 55; early connections with tea, 55–56; and Rikyu, 56–57; conflict with Sakai merchants, 57; death of, 58
Ogata Kenzan, potter and painter, 199
Ogata Korin, artist, 199
Okakura, Kakuzo (*The Book of Tea*), 25
okencha (ritualistic offering of tea in a Shinto shrine), 283–84
okoshi-ezu (architectural standup designs of paper), 137–38
okucha (ritualistic offering of tea in a Buddhist temple), 283–84
Omotesenke, 89
Oribe, *see* Furuta Oribe
Oribe ware, 197
outdoor tea ceremony, see *nodate*

Pai-chang Ch'ing Kuei (Monastery Regulations of Pai-chang), 49
posts, see *hashira, naka-bashira, toko-bashira*
powdered green tea, see *matcha*
principal guest, choice of, 123

Raku Daidai (Raku Generations; catalogue of a Raku exhibition), 203
Raku ware, 200–206, 266; and Rikyu, 92, 201; bowls, 190; composition of glaze, 201
Ranjo, priest (*Shu Charon*), 61
Reece, Gerow, 257
Reischauer, Edwin: *Japan Past and Present,* 36; *Ennin's Travels in T'ang China,* 207
Rikyu, *see* Sen no Rikyu
Rikyu no Chashitsu (Rikyu's Tea Huts, by Horiguchi), 29, 125, 126
ro (winter fire pit), 96, 121, 180, 214
robuchi (wooden frame of fire pit), 213
roji (tea garden), 96, 121–31
roofs: tiles for, 138; thatch for, 138–39; bark shingles for, 139; eaves of, 139
Ryonyu, *see* Sojiro
Ryounshu (anthology of poems), 37
ryurei tea ceremony using tables and chairs, 283

sabi, 67–69
sado (grand master of tea; title), 56
sado-guchi (host's entrance to tearoom), 179
Sakamoto, Koso, calligrapher, 256
sakè, 288, 310
samurai, importance of tea to, 48
Sansom, George (*Japan: A Short Cultural History*), 85, 86–87
Sasaki Doyo, 43
sashaku, see *chashaku*
schools of tea, 87, 271–72; *see also* Senke schools of tea, Urasenke school of tea
screens, see *byobu*
scrolls, see *kakemono*
Seinyu, thirteenth-generation Raku potter, 205
Sekishu, see Katagiri Sekishu
Sen no Rikyu, tea master: and Hideyoshi, 20, 62–67, 71; four concepts of tea of, 24; and Jo-o, 47; and emphasis on simplicity, 47; and the warrior class, 48; formative years of, 50–52; innovations by, 52–53; and Nobunaga, 55–57; and the Great Kitano Tea Meeting, 64–65; income of, 66–67; criticism of, 66–67, 69–70; and Zeami, 67–69; approach to flower arrangement of, 71, 286; instructions to gardeners and car-

penters, 72; tea philosophy of, 72–73, 77; death of, 74–78; descendants of, 74, 89; last tea ceremony by, 78; poems by, 78; monthly commemorative services for, 78; and Oribe, 81–83; tea gardens of, 126, 127
Sen no Rikyu (Karaki), 67
Sen no Soeki, *see* Sen no Rikyu
Sen no Soshitsu, present grand master of Urasenke, 280–81, 282, 283, 284
Sen no Sotan, tea master: descendants of, 89; and wabi tea, 89–90; and Koetsu, 90; and Tanyu, 90; later years of, 91
Senke schools of tea: establishment of, 89; flourishing of, 91; *see also* Urasenke school of tea
sensu (fan), 263–64
seppuku (ritual suicide by disembowelment), 71, 74, 78
Sesshu, painter, 96, 255, *et passim*
setchin (toilet in tea garden), 53, 121
Seto ware, 197; tea caddies, 216
shakkei ("borrowed scenery" in a garden), 130, 175
shelves: beside the alcove, 177–78; outside the tearoom, 178; in the kitchen, 179
shifuku (brocade bags for ceramic tea caddies), 216
Shigaraki ware, 200; vases 259
shikishi mado (low window near the host's place), 175
Shino ware: bowls, 197–98; vases, 259
shoin (reception room) tea architecture, 52, 134–37
shoji (papered wooden sliding windows or doors), 135, 174, 175, 176
Shoso-in, imperial treasure repository in Nara, 56, 261
Shu Charon (essay on tea and sakè by Ranjo), 61
Shuko, tea master and Zen priest: and Ikkyu, 44; his use of tea utensils, 44; his importance to development of tea, 44; and wabi, 45; his introduction of the three basic styles of tea, 45
skylight, see *tsuki-age mado*
so-an (grass hut) tea architecture, 52, 134–37
sode kabe (wall attached to the central post of a house), 142
Sojiro (Ryonyu), ninth-generation Raku potter, 204
Sonyu, fifth-generation Raku potter, 203
Sotan Nikki (Sotan), 80–81
stepping-stones, see *tobi ishi*
stones, in a tea garden, 122, 129
Sukido Taii (mid-Edo-period book on tea ceremony, architecture, landscaping, and tea attitudes), 126–27
sukiya, see *sukiya-zukuri*
sukiya-zukuri (style of tea architecture), 127, 134
sumi (charcoal), 275, 276, 310–11
susu-dake (old, smoke-stained bamboo), 252
Suzuki, Daisetz (*Zen and Japanese Culture*), 48, 256

Tai-an tea hut, 64, 127, 135
Takayama Sosetsu, craftsman of tea whisks, 251–52
Takeno Jo-o, tea master, 46–47, 71–72; tea gardens of, 127
Tamba ware, 199, 266
Tanabe, Chikuunsai, bamboo artist, 252
Tanaka Sokei, early Raku potter, 202
T'ang China: documents mentioning tea, 35; Japanese missions to, 36–37
Taniguchi, Yoshiro, architect, 29, 195
Tannyu, tenth-generation Raku potter, 204–5
tatami (floor mats): as basic architectural module, 132, 142; sizes of, 142–43; cost of, 143, 144; cleaning of, 143–44, 274, 275; arrangement of, 144; kinds of, 144, 172
tea: in Britain, 20, 21; as medicine, 22, 38; and Christianity, 23; and Zen, 23–24, 38–40; influence on everyday life, 29–30; arrival in Japan, 35; *see also* brick tea, *matcha*
tea architecture: different styles of, 52, 134–37; space in, 132–34; paper standup models of, 137–38; modern building materials for, 138
tea bowl, see *chawan*
tea caddy, see *cha-ire, natsume*
tea ceremony, see *cha-no-yu*
tea flower arrangement, see *chabana*
tea garden, see *roji*
tea hut, see *chashitsu*
tea lessons: at tea schools, 271; from a private teacher, 271–72; tuition fees for, 272; basic utensils used in, 272–73; initial instruction in, 273; purchase of utensils for, 274
tea master, see *chajin*
tea meetings; see *cha yori-ai*
tea scoop, see *chashaku*
tea utensils: earliest, 39; signing of, 91–92; prices of, 183–84, 186, 187–88;

old catalogues of, 185; boxed for outdoor tea ceremony, 282–83
tea whisk, see *chasen*
Temmoku bowls, 191, 192–93
Tennojiya Cha Kaiki, 201
tetsubin (small hand-held kettles), 212
thick powdered tea, see *koicha*
thin powdered tea, see *usucha*
tobi ishi (stepping-stones), 122, 129
toko-bashira (post by the alcove), 177
tokonoma (alcove for art), 81, 144, 177–78
Tokugawa Ieyasu, 85
Tokugawa period, 84–86; arts and crafts in, 87; tea utensils in, 87, 186, 262; schools of tea in, 87; tea masters' pay during, 88
Toyotomi Hideyoshi, military dictator: under Nobunaga, 58–59; background and personality, 59, 60, 62, 64, 65; castles built by, 59–60, 85; influence on tea, 60–62; as tea master, 60, 62–63, 80–81; and Rikyu, 62–67; and his golden tearoom, 63; and the Great Kitano Tea Meeting, 64–66; and his heir, 77; after Rikyu's death, 80; and tea flower arrangement, 80; and his Korean campaign, 195
tray tea, 213
trivets, 212
tsuki-age mado (skylight), 176
tsukubai (stone wash basin), 53, 121–22
Tsurezuregusa (written ca. 1313), 142

Urasenke school of tea: founding of, 89; gardens at, 124; New York branch, 214, 278; full-time students of, 279–81; teaching staff of, 279; curriculum at, 279–80; tuition fees at, 281; grand master of, 280–81, 282–83, 284
usucha (thin powdered tea), 274, 311–12

wabi, 44, 45, 67–69
waiting arbor, see *machi-ai*
waiting bench, see *koshikake*
Wakan Sansai Zu-e (an eighteenth-century encyclopedia), 207
walls, 140, 173–75, 177, 178
Warner, Langdon (*The Enduring Arts of Japan*), 20
waste-water container, see *kensui*
water jar, see *mizusashi*
water ladle, see *hishaku*
Watts, Alan, 30, 271
Way of Tea, see *chado*
wells in tea gardens, 129–30
windows, 140, 175–77; to the side of the alcove, 177; in the kitchen, 179
wood, as structural material, 140
Wright, Frank Lloyd, 26

Yamada Sohen, tea master, 89
yamazato no niwa (mountain-village garden), 124–25
Yanagi, Soetsu, 70, 82–83; his *Cha no Kaikaku,* 194–95
yoji, see *kuromoji*
Yoshimasa, *see* Ashikaga Yoshimasa
Yoshimura, Junzo, architect, 29
yoshino mado (large, circular window), 176

Zeami, No actor and dramatist, 42, 43, 67, 68, 69
Zen and Japanese Culture (Suzuki), 48

THE "WEATHERMARK" IDENTIFIES THIS BOOK AS HAVING BEEN PLANNED, DESIGNED, AND PRODUCED AT THE TOKYO OFFICES OF JOHN WEATHERHILL, INC. BOOK DESIGN AND TYPOGRAPHY BY MEREDITH WEATHERBY. LAYOUT OF ILLUSTRATIONS BY NAOTO KONDO. LETTERPRESS COMPOSITION, PLATEMAKING, AND PRINTING BY GENERAL PRINTING COMPANY, YOKOHAMA. GRAVURE PLATEMAKING AND PRINTING BY NISSHA PRINTING COMPANY, KYOTO. BOUND AT THE MAKOTO BINDERIES, TOKYO. THE MAIN TEXT IS SET IN TWELVE-POINT MONOTYPE PERPETUA, WITH HAND-SET OPTIMA FOR DISPLAY.